Knitting Technology

Other Titles in the Pergamon International Library

BARBOUR	Glass Blowing for Laboratory Technicians, 2nd Edition
COLLIER	A Handbook of Textiles, 2nd Edition
HENLEY	Anodic Oxidation of Aluminium & its Alloys
HINDMARSH	Electrical Machines and their Applications, 3rd Edition
HINDMARSH	Worked Examples in Electrical Machines and Drives
LANSDOWN	Lubrication
MILLER	Practical Wiring, 2nd Edition, 2 volumes
MURPHY & JORGENSEN	Wood as an Industrial Arts Material
PARKIN & FLOOD	Welding Craft Practice, 2nd Edition, 2 volumes
UPTON	Pressure Diecasting Part 1
YORKE	Electric Circuit Theory

Pergamon Related Journals

(Free specimen copy gladly sent on request)

International Journal of Engineering Science

International Journal of Machine Tool Design & Research

International Journal of Mechanical Sciences

Mechanism & Machine Theory

DAVID J. SPENCER ATI, ACI

School of Textile and Knitwear Technology
Leicester Polytechnic, UK

PERGAMON PRESS

OXFORD · NEW YORK · TORONTO · SYDNEY · PARIS · FRANKFURT

U.K.	Pergamon Press Ltd., Headington Hill Hall, Oxford OX3 0BW, England
U.S.A.	Pergamon Press Inc., Maxwell House, Fairview Park, Elmsford, New York 10523, U.S.A.
CANADA	Pergamon Press Canada Ltd., Suite 104, 150 Consumers Road, Willowdale, Ontario M2J 1P9, Canada
AUSTRALIA	Pergamon Press (Aust.) Pty. Ltd., P.O. Box 544, Potts Point, N.S.W. 2011, Australia
FRANCE	Pergamon Press SARL, 24 rue des Ecoles, 75240 Paris, Cedex 05, France
FEDERAL REPUBLIC OF GERMANY	Pergamon Press GmbH, Hammerweg 6, D-6242 Kronberg-Taunus, Federal Republic of Germany

First edition 1983

Library of Congress Cataloging in Publication Data

Spencer, David J.
Knitting technology
Includes bibliography and index.
1. Knitting, Machine. 2. Knitting-machines.
I. Title.
TT680.S63 1983 677'.028242 82-12266

British Library Cataloguing in Publication Data

Spencer, David J.
Knitting technology.
1. Knitting, Machine
I. Title
677'.661 TT685

ISBN 0-08-024762-8 (Hardcover)
ISBN 0-08-024763-6 (Flexicover)

Printed in Great Britain by A. Wheaton & Co. Ltd., Exeter

To my wife,
SHIRLEY ANN

Preface

The aim of this book is to combine in a single volume the fundamental principles of weft and warp knitting in such a manner that its contents are useful to readers in education, industry or commerce. It thus fulfils the long felt need for a comprehensive up-to-date textbook explaining this important sector of textile technology. Aspects covered include flat, circular, full fashioned, hosiery, Raschel, tricot and crochet production. The inclusion of the historical development of the types of machines, their actions and mechanisms as well as the construction, properties and end uses of the products which they manufacture, make the book acceptable as a set text for Textile courses from technician to degree and Textile Institute examination level. It will also prove particularly suitable for professionals wishing to up-date or broaden their understanding of knitting.

The contents have been arranged for the convenient use of different levels of readership with the text gradually progressing from an explanation of basic terminology and principles to eventually encompass the most advanced aspects of the technology including the application of microprocessor controls and developments in knitting science. Care has been taken where possible to emphasize fundamental rules and principles which are less likely to be drastically altered by developments in later technology.

The indexed and referenced format of the text is supplemented by labelled diagrams and photographs so that the book may also serve as a handy reference work for study and business purposes. Terminology is defined either according to Textile Institute terms and definitions or current usage in the industry and is supplemented as necessary by American or continental terminology. Internationally accepted methods of notation help to clarify explanations of fabric structures. Although SI units and the tex yarn count system have been explained and used in the text, other systems of measurement and yarn count systems have also been employed wherever it has been considered that their usage is still of importance. A number of worked calculations have been included in certain chapters to further clarify explanations and assist students.

It is hoped that the inclusion of a number of fashion photographs will encourage design and sales personnel to come to terms with technology whilst emphasizing the importance of end-product design to technologists.

Finally I apologize in advance for any major errors and omissions in the text and hope that at a later date an opportunity may occur to remedy them.

Knossington
Leicestershire
July 1982.

David J. Spencer

Acknowledgements

I wish to express my sincere appreciation to all those individuals and organizations who have directly or indirectly contributed towards the publication of this book. Although a full list of names would be too long for publication, I would particularly like to express my gratitude to the following:

Mr. Ralph Innes who first contacted Pergamon Press on the subject of this book and then magnanimously handed over the project to me;

Mr. J. B. Lancashire who meticulously read through much of the earlier draft of the script and made many helpful comments regarding it;

Mr. Eric Keates who originally produced many technical diagrams of structures and mechanisms which are recognized throughout the knitting world by his initials E.A.K.;

Mr. Walter Bullwer who has kindly supplied many of the technical photographs;

My colleagues and other members of staff at Leicester Polytechnic particularly the library and clerical staff who have assisted me over the years in obtaining the research material and in collating my notes;

Mr. Arthur Martin who first encouraged me to study Textiles at Leicester Polytechnic;

Corahs of Leicester who sponsored my education in knitting technology and with whom I gained invaluable technical experience;

My wife Shirley Ann and my parents who have assisted with typing and amending the script with an apology to my family for the disruption which the evening and early morning routine of script writing has tended to produce.

Although it has not always been possible to utilize all the material provided for the book I would also particularly like to thank the following for their generous assistance in this matter:

Mr. John T. Millington and Mr. John Gibbon of Knitting International; Mr. Eric Hertz of Knitting Times; Mr. Lehner and Mr. Jeff Caunt of Karl Mayer; Mr. R. Bracegirdle of Leicester Museum of Technology; Dr. Georg Syamken of Hamburger Kunsthalle Museum; Mr. W. M. Whittaker of Camber International; Mr. Peter Ford, East Midlands Chairman Information Technology 82; Mr. R. Beardall of Foster Textile Sales Ltd; Mr. Lewis P. Miles of the International Institute for Cotton; Carole May of the International Wool Secretariat; Mr. Bryan Atkins of Marks and Spencer; NASA Press Information Centre; Joan Broughton of the British Knitting Export Council; Mr. Roger Munsey of Dubied; Dupont Ltd; Jacob Muller Ltd; Iropa Ltd; Maria Potemski of Corahs; Bentley Engineering Co Ltd; Smitex Ltd; Mr. B. Bliss-Hill of William Cotton Ltd; Mr. I. Brunton of Monarch and various Divisions of Courtauld's.

The author, David J. Spencer, C Text, ATI, ACFI, is a Senior Lecturer in the School of Textile and Knitwear Technology at Leicester Polytechnic. He has been an examiner and moderator in the Manufacture of Hosiery and Knitted Goods for the City and Guilds of London Institute and has written articles on knitting technology for British, American and German technical publications. He is involved in industrial liaison work through Leicester Polytechnic and is the textile adviser in a team of research technologists funded to investigate the potential of computer aided pattern recognition of faults in knitted fabrics. His early industrial experience was obtained through technical service in many different departments of Corahs the large Leicester based knitting company.

Contents

1

An Introduction to Textile Technology

Evolution of Textiles 1.1

Although man's first articles of clothing and furnishing were probably animal skin wraps sometimes stitched together using bone needles and animal sinews, he soon attempted to manipulate fibrous materials into textile fabrics, encouraged by experience gained from interlacing branches, leaves and grasses in the production of primitive shelters.

The word '*textile*' originates from the latin verb '*texere*', to weave, but as the Textile Institute's Terms and Definitions Glossary explains, it is now "*a general term applied to any manufacture from fibres, filaments or yarns characterized by flexibility, fineness and high ratio of length to thickness*".

Textile Fabrics 1.2

Textile fabrics can be produced directly from webs of fibres by bonding, fusing or interlocking to make non-woven fabrics and felts, but their physical properties tend to restrict their potential end-usage. The mechanical manipulation of yarn into fabric is the most versatile method of manufacturing textile fabrics for a wide range of end-uses.

There are three principal methods of mechanically manipulating yarn into textile fabrics: interweaving, intertwining and interlooping. All three methods have evolved from hand-manipulated techniques through their application on primitive frames into sophisticated manufacturing operations on automated machinery.

1. Interweaving (Fig. 1.1) is the intersection of two sets of straight threads, warp and weft, which cross and interweave at right angles to each other. Weaving is by far the oldest and most common method of producing continuous lengths of straight edged fabric.

Fig. 1.1.

Fig. 1.2.

2. Intertwining and twisting (Fig. 1.2) includes a number of techniques such as braiding, twisting and knotting where threads are caused to intertwine with each other at right angles or some other angle. These techniques tend to produce special constructions whose use is limited to a very specific purpose.

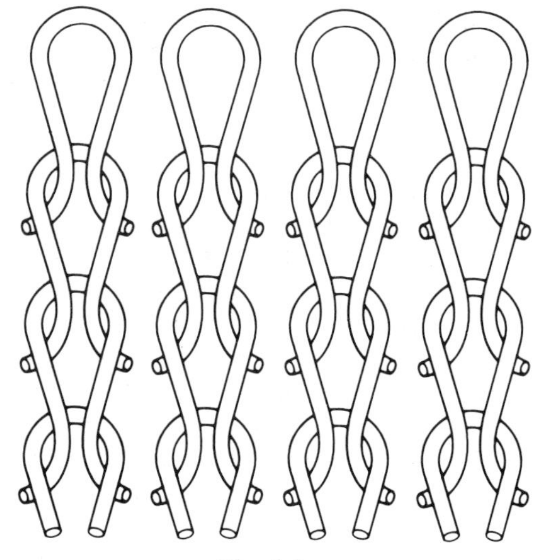

Fig. 1.3.

3. Interlooping (Fig. 1.3) consists of forming yarn(s) into loops each of which is typically only released after a succeeding loop has been formed and intermeshed with it so that a secure ground loop structure is achieved. The loops are also held together by the yarn passing from one to the next (in the simplified illustration this effect is not illustrated).

Knitting is the most common method of interlooping and is second only to weaving as a method of manufacturing textile structures. It is estimated that over 7 million tons of knitted goods are produced annually throughout the world. Although the unique capability of knitting to manufacture shaped and form-fitting articles has been utilized for centuries, modern technology has enabled knitted constructions in shaped and unshaped fabric form to expand into a wide range of apparel, domestic and industrial end-uses.

1.3 Textile Yarns and Fibres

Yarns are the raw materials manipulated during knitting, a *yarn* is defined as "*an assembly of substantial length and relatively small cross-section of fibres or filaments with or without twist*". The term thread is loosely used in place of yarn and does not imply that it is as smooth, highly twisted and compact as a sewing thread.

Textile fibres are the raw materials of the yarns into which they are spun. There are two configurations of fibres: staple fibres and filament fibres. *Staple fibres are of a comparatively short length,* for example, cotton and wool fibres which require spinning and twisting together in order to produce a satisfactory length of yarn of suitable strength. *A filament is a fibre of indefinite length,* for example, silk, which requires combining with other filaments with some twist in order to produce a yarn of sufficient bulk.

Originally all textile fibres occurred naturally, for example, animal fibres such as wool and silk and vegetable fibres such as cotton and flax. The first artificially-produced fibres were the rayons developed by the regeneration of long chain cellulose polymers which occur naturally in wood pulp and cotton linters. Derivates such as cellulose acetate and triacetate were later produced by the acetylation of cellulose polymers. *Nylon, the first truly synthetic fibre,* was invented by Wallace H. Carothers in 1938, *based on a synthetically built long chain polyamide polymer which previously did not occur naturally.* A wide range of synthetic fibre polymers including polyesters and polyacrylics have since been developed. Many of the synthetic polymers may be converted into yarns in the continuous filament form in which they were extruded during manufacturing but they may also be cut or broken into the staple fibre form to be later spun on systems originally developed for natural fibres such as wool or cotton.

The properties of more than one type of fibre may be incorporated into a fabric as the result of blending the fibres during spinning or by knitting two or more types of yarn.

Knitting requires a relatively fine, smooth, strong yarn with good elastic recovery properties, the worsted system has proved particularly suitable for spinning yarns used for knitwear, outerwear and socks and the combed cotton system for underwear, sportswear and socks.

The introduction of synthetic fibres which can be heat set in a permanent configuration has led to the development of texturing processes which directly convert these filaments into bulked yarns thus by-passing the staple fibre spinning process. During texturing, the filaments are disturbed from their parallel formation and are permanently set in configurations such as crimps or coils which help to entrap pockets of air and confer properties such as bulkiness, soft handle, porosity, drape, cover, opacity and if necessary elasticity, to the resultant yarn. Examples of yarns of this type include false twist nylon and Crimplene which is a registered trade name for a technique whereby the properties of the textured polyester yarn are modified during a second heat-setting operation so that the stitch clarity, handle and stability of the fabric is improved.

The development of synthetic fibres and their texturing processes have proved particularly beneficial to the knitting industry and have resulted in a close association between the two industries. Thus the period from the mid-1960s until 1973 is often regarded by knitters as a golden age because fashionable demand for textiles composed of synthetic fibres reached a peak during that period.[1,2]

1.4 Yarn Count Numbering Systems

A yarn count number indicates the linear density (yarn diameter or fineness) to which that particular yarn has been spun. The choice of yarn count is restricted by the type of knitting machine employed and the knitting construction, the count in turn influences the cost, weight, opacity, handle and drapability of the resultant structure. In general staple spun yarns tend to be comparatively more expensive the finer their count, because finer fibres and a more exacting spinning process are necessary in order to prevent the yarn from showing an irregular appearance.

Unfortunately, a number of differently based count numbering systems are still currently in use. Historically, most systems are associated with particular yarn-spinning systems, thus a yarn spun on the worsted system from acrylic fibres may be given a worsted count number. *The worsted system is of the indirect type based on length per fixed unit mass, i.e. the higher the count number, the finer the yarn.* The weight is fixed (1 lb) and the length unit (number of 560-yard hanks) varies. 1/24's worsted (24 × 560-yard hanks weighing 1 lb) will be twice the cross-sectional area of 1/48's worsted (48 × 560 yard hanks weighing 1 lb). 2/24's worsted indicates that the yarn contains two ends of 1/24's so that the resultant count is twice the cross-sectional area (24 ÷ 2 = 12's).

The denier system is used in continuous filament silk spinning and when the silk throwsters began to process textured synthetic continuous filament yarns, these nylon and polyester yarns were given denier count numbers. *The denier system is of the direct type based on mass per unit length, i.e. the higher the number, the finer the yarn.* The length unit is fixed (9000 metres) and the weight unit (in grams) is variable. 70-denier yarn (9000 metres weigh 70 grams) will be twice as fine as 140 denier (9000 metres weigh 140 grams). 2/70 denier will give a resultant count of 140 denier.

The tex system was introduced as a universal system to replace all the existing systems. As tex sometimes produces a count number having a decimal point, it has been found more satisfactory to multiply the count number by 10 to give a deci-tex number. The tex system has not been universally accepted, particularly for spun yarns and on the continent of Europe the metric system is used for these yarns.

The main count systems with their continental abbreviations are as follows:

Indirect Systems

Bradford Worsted System	(NeK)	– the number of 560-yard hanks which weigh 1 lb (453.6 gms).
English Woollen System (Yorkshire Skeins)	(NeW)	– the number of 256-yard hanks which weigh 1 lb.
English Cotton System	(NeB)	– the number of 840-yard hanks which weigh 1 lb.
Continental Metric System (Cotton System)	(Nm)	– the number of 1000-metre (1 kilometre) hanks which weigh 1000 grams (1 kilogram).

Direct Systems

Denier System	(Td)	– the weight in grams of 9000 metres.
Tex System	(Tt)	– the weight in grams of a 1000 metres.
Deci-tex system	(dtex)	– the weight in grams of 10,000 metres.

Conversion Formulae 1.5

Tex counts may be obtained from count numbers in other systems using one of the following formulae:

$$\frac{886}{NeK} \quad \frac{1938}{NeW} \quad \frac{591}{NeB} \quad \frac{1000}{Nm} \quad \frac{Td}{9}$$

Example

An interlock underwear fabric is weft knitted from 1/40's NeB at a weight of 5 ounces per square yard. Convert the yarn count to deci-tex and the fabric weight to square metrage.

(a) The conversion for Tex is 591/NeB so it is necessary to also multiply by 10 to obtain deci-tex.

$$\text{The deci-tex count therefore} = \frac{591}{40} \times 10 = 148$$

(b) 1 oz = 28.35 g and 1 sq yd = 0.836 m^2
Therefore 5 oz yd^2 = (5 × 28.35) = 142 g × 1/0.836 = 170 g m^2

1. GIBBON, J. E., Crimplene: profile of a yarn's problems and successes, *Hos. Trade Journal* (1965) Sept., 110–12.
2. LAW, I. M., Crimplene: a fibre legend, *Knit. Int.* (1981) June, 78–81.

Further Information

General Textiles

COLLIER, A. M., *A Handbook of Textiles*, (1974) Pergamon Press.
JOSEPH, M. L., *Introductory Textile Science*, (1966) Rinehart and Winston.

Weaving

GREENWOOD, K., *Weaving: Control of Fabric Structure*, Merrow.
LORD, P. R. and MOHAMED, M. H., *Weaving: Conversion of Yarn to Fabric*, (1976) Merrow.

Fibres

COOKE, J. G., *Handbook of Textile Fibres*, (1968) Merrow, I, II.
MORTON, W. E. and HEARLE, J. W. S., *Physical Properties of Textile Fibres*, (1975) Textile Inst. and Heinemann.

Yarns

HARRISON, P. W., *Bulk, Stretch and Texture*, (1966) Textile Institute.
RAY, G. R., *Modern Yarn Production from Manmade Fibres*, (1962) Columbine Press.
WILKINSON, G. D. A., Knitter's guide to texturising processes, *Knit. Outwr Times*, (1970) 22nd June, 57–65.
CHARNOCK, I. L. A., Yarn quality for knitting, *Text. Inst. and Ind.*, (1977) 15, (5), 175–7.
HALL, J. D., The contribution of synthetic fibres and plastics to the textile industry, *Text. Inst. and Ind.*, (1965) 3, (10), 265–7.

2

The Evolution of Knitting Technology

The term 'knitting' which is used to describe the technique of constructing textile structures by forming continuous lengths of yarn into vertically intermeshed loops has evolved from the Saxon word 'Cnyttan' which in turn was derived from the ancient Sanskrit word 'Nahyati'. Both words were less precise in their meaning indicating that knitting probably developed from experience gained by knotting and twisting yarns.

Crossed loop stitches were employed long before the open loops of modern hand pin knitting. In the case of Coptic knitting, loops of very short lengths of yarn were pulled through each other by means of single eyed needles. Knitting by using only the fingers may well have been practised as long ago as 1000 B.C. There is also a strong possibility that techniques employing rectilinear and circular peg frames in a similar manner to 'French' bobbin knitting were probably practised simultaneously with those of hand pin knitting.

2.1 The Spread of Knowledge of Hand Pin Knitting

Fig. 2.1. The Madonna Knitting Christ's Seamless Garment. The earliest recorded illustration of a knitted garment. Part of a church architectural painting by Maître Bertram (1345–1415) (Hamburg Kunsthalle Museum).

Leicester Museum possesses a bootee and gauntlet, part of a collection of articles of cross stitch construction excavated at the site of Dura-Europus in Egypt which probably pre-date the destruction of that city in A.D. 256. The skilled use of fashioning, closing, circular knitting and stitch patterning indicate an advanced understanding of hand pin knitting by this period.

Surprisingly, hand pin knitting appears to have taken nearly ten centuries to reach Italy and then spread across Europe. Maître Bertram's illustration of Mary knitting Christ's seamless garment (Fig. 2.1) is one of the earliest known illustrations of knitting (unfortunately Christ's garment is more likely to have been manufactured by the 'sprang' or braiding technique in a similar manner to the vestments of Saint Cuthbert).[1]

Knitting later became an established technique in Britain with Parliament controlling the price of knitted caps by 1488 and Henry VIII (1509–1547) becoming the first British monarch to wear knitted stockings. The first hand-knitted silk stockings appeared in England in 1550 and by 1561 Queen Elizabeth I was so impressed by their elasticity and fineness that she never again wore cut and sewn woven hose.

Principles of Hand Knitting Using Two Pins 2.2

In Fig. 2.2a the left hand pin A is retaining the previously formed row of loops (course) whilst the right hand pin B is being used to form, draw through and retain the next row of loops (course) one at a time. In Fig. 2.2b pin B has drawn the newly formed loop 2 through loop 1 which pin A now releases, allowing it to hang through the new loop. At the start of the next row, the pins may be changed hands and the action continued. If this happens, the fabric will have been turned around and the next row will mesh through from the opposite side of the fabric. As the pins are straight and pointed, skill is required to ensure the loops do not slip off the end and cause drop stitches.

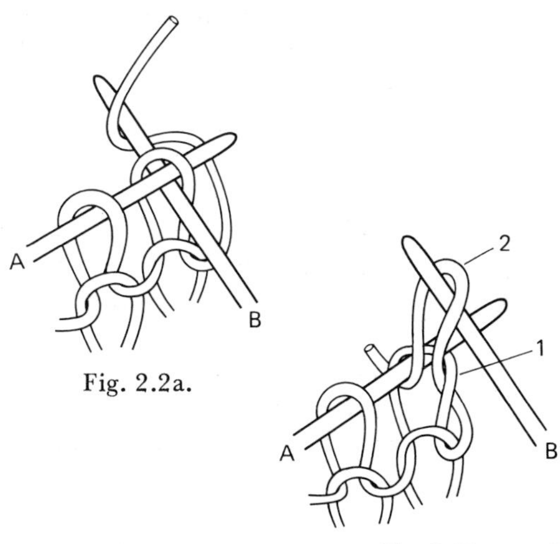

Fig. 2.2a.

Fig. 2.2b.

Invention of the Stocking Frame 2.3

The Reverend William Lee of Calverton in Nottinghamshire is generally credited with inventing the stocking frame in 1589. It offered the potential of knitting courses of loops at more than ten times the speed of hand-held pins. The concept of operation was so brilliant that, through an evolutionary process of technical refinement, modification and innovation by many inventors throughout the world over the succeeding centuries, it laid the foundation for modern weft and warp knitting and machine lace technology.

Unfortunately, little documentary information concerning Lee's early efforts and achievements has so far been traced and imaginative descriptions and paintings of a later period provide a confusing backcloth to the event. The first extant illustrations of a frame were, drawn for Colbert by the French spy Hindret in 1656 and the earliest existing frames appear to date from about 1750.

Lee's original frame was crude and knitted poor quality woollen stocking fabric with a gauge of 8 needles per inch (25 mm) – 24 per three-inch span of the needle bar. Encouraged to improve the frame in order to knit silk, he is believed to have achieved a gauge of 20 needles per inch in 1596/7 and by 1600 could sign a partnership agreement containing a penalty clause of £10 per day. Frustrated in his attempts to obtain a patent from either Elizabeth I or James I, by the fear of unemployment amongst hand knitters, Lee and his brother took their nine machines and several knitters to France at the invitation of Henry IV in 1609. He set up a workshop at Rouen, signed a partnership agreement with Pierre de Caux in 1611 and a further agreement in 1614.

The assassination of Henry IV in 1610 ended the protection of Protestant workers in France and it is believed that William's brother James brought all or most of the frames and knitters back to London and that William died in poverty in Paris whilst hiding from persecution. England then prohibited the export of stocking frames but Hindret's accurate drawings and knowledge enabled them to be built in Paris from 1656 onwards and thus the knowledge of their operation spread across Europe.

Gradually London declined as the centre of frame-work knitting and by 1750 the areas could be broadly classified as Derby for silk, Nottingham for cotton and Leicester for wool knitting. The industry then expanded rapidly until 1810 when over-production produced stagnation, unemployment and the Luddite riots. It was not until conditions improved in the second half of the nineteenth century that new innovations and inventions in knitting technology again received encouragement and practical application.

2.4 The Bearded Needle

Lee's brilliance lay in his adaptation of the peg frame and the employment of a hooked loop holder — *the bearded needle whose beard is capable of enclosing the newly formed loop* in order to draw it through the previously formed loop as the latter was released. He set the needles in a row across the width of a frame whose arrangements of moving parts was more intricate than that of the existing hand-weaving loom. By skilful hand knitting, up to 100 loops could be formed per minute whereas on Lee's first frame, 500–600 loops were made and on his later silk hose frame 1000–1500 loops per minute could be formed.

2.5 Principles of Frame Knitting

Figure 2.3 shows a side view of the knitting elements. After the weft yarn has been laid across the horizontally-mounted needle bed by hand, thin metal sinkers descend (in direction A) individually between each pair of adjacent needles to kink or sink it into a loop shape around each needle stem. Each sinker is caused to descend because it is hinged to a pivoted

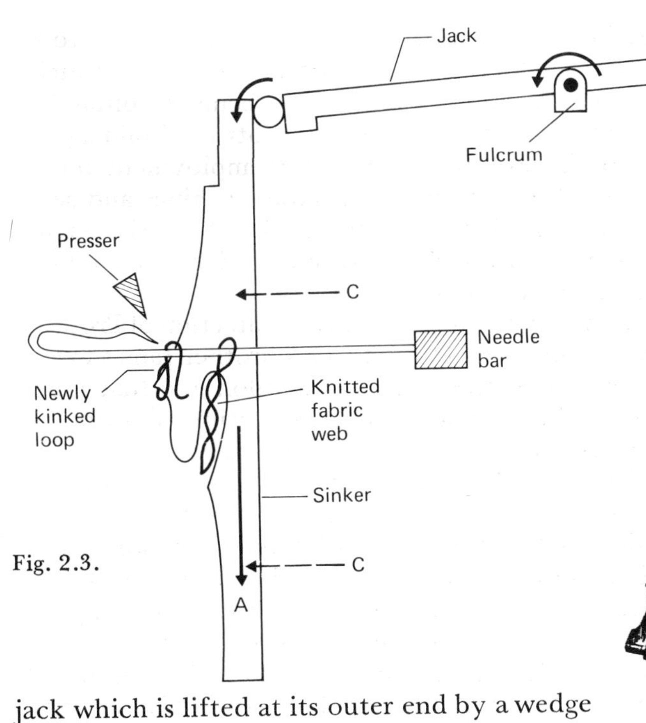

Fig. 2.3.

jack which is lifted at its outer end by a wedge shaped piece of iron termed a slurcock. The slurcock is traversed backwards and forwards (direction B) across the needle bar width by a rope. The new loop is taken under the hook of the beard by a forward advance (in direction C) of the sinkers, the beard is then closed by the presser bar so that the new loop can be drawn through the old loop.

Figure 2.4 shows a general view of the hand frame. In front of the workman's bench are the three pedals. After the weft yarn has been laid across, the right pedal is pressed down causing the rope attached to it to turn the wheel clockwise and draw the slurcock from left to right. For the next row of loops, the slurcock is traversed across from right to left by pressing down the left pedal after the yarn has been laid across. This turns the wheel in the opposite direction. The middle pedal causes the presser bar to be lowered to press and close the needle beards.

Fig. 2.4. Hand Frame (c. 1820).

(Copyright: Leicestershire Museums, Art Galleries and Record Service).

2.6 Evolution of Other Weft Knitting Machines

Although the frame was successfully adapted to rotary drive in 1769 (see section 17.1) it was not until the second half of the nineteenth century that vertical needle bars began to be employed or circular frames became commercially viable (8.6). The full potential of loop-transfer shaping was developed with the introduction of the straight bar frame (chapter 17) whilst the commercial application of the latch needle (3.16) paved the way for the flat machine (chapter 18) and also for exploiting the potential of circular knitting (8.7) and more generally, of plain, rib or purl knitting (chapter 7) and needle selection (10.5).

2.7 Development of Warp Knitting

Warp knitting, the second and smaller sector of machine knitting, was first developed by Crane and Porter in 1769 as a method of embroidery patterning on the hand frame by means of multiple warp thread guides. As the technique improved, purely warp intermeshed structures without the weft knitted ground fabric began to be knitted and Crane patented his warp loom in 1775. Tarrat is credited with developing the first efficient treadle operated warp knitting frame in 1785. Two important later developments were Dawson's wheels for shogging the guide bars and Brown's use of two separately-controlled warp-supplied guide bars. In 1807, another Nottingham framesmith, S. Orgill, introduced the rotary shaft-driven warp knitting frame, having a knitting width up to 72 inches and cam-controlled knitting motions capable of knitting up to thirty rows of loops per minute.

During the Napoleonic wars, 500 hand warp looms were producing woollen uniform fabric for the British forces. However, the power-driven weaving loom was soon to out-produce the warp loom in plain fabric and by the 1840s the fancy lace market was lost to the patterning capabilities of the Leavers lace machine. The combination of modern engineering technology and the advent of new yarns and finishing processes have at last enabled warp knitting to begin to realize the potential it first demonstrated in its early years of development.

Knitting machines can now manufacture most traditional hand-knitted designs and structures as well as being able to knit many constructions which are too fine or complex to attempt with hand-held pins. The manufacture of textile products is a highly competitive industry requiring the harnessing of modern technology to meet the rapidly-changing demands of fashion and usage. Fortunately, its unique involvement in garment as well as fabric production has provided the knitting industry with an appreciation of the need to rapidly respond to changes in consumer demand whilst knitting technology continues to provide a wide range of facilities in order to achieve this aim (Fig. 2.5).[2]

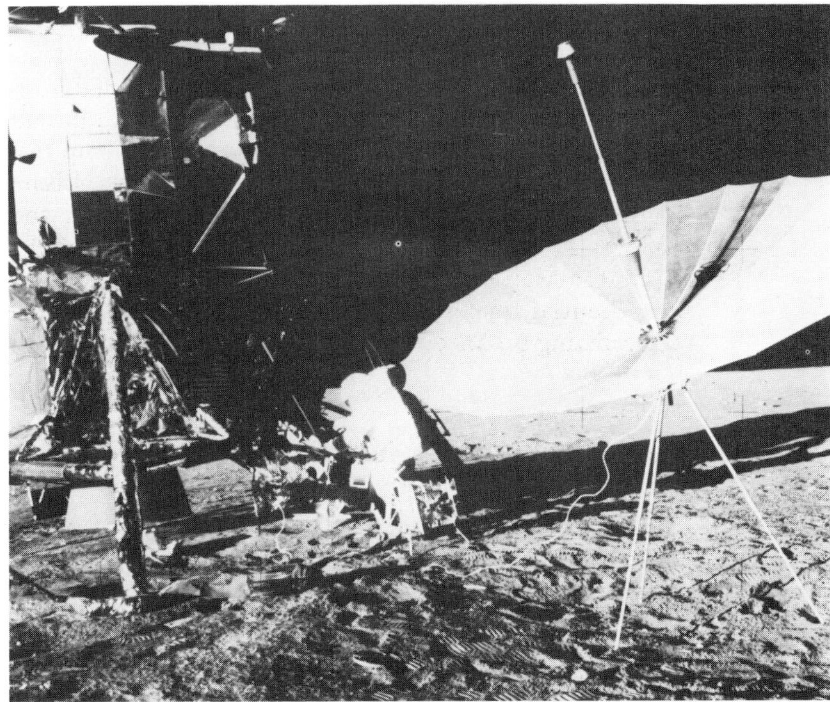

Fig. 2.5. Knitting – a space age technology, (Photo Credit NASA). The photograph taken during the Apollo 12 mission, shows the warp knitted antenna which transmitted the television pictures of the lunar landing back to Earth. The two-bar mesh fabric, weighing less than one ounce per square yard, was warp knitted from gold plated metallic yarn. (Tricot Cloth Vital to Lunar Mission, *Knit O'wr Times*, July 7, (1969), 34–7.)

1. HARTLEY, M. and INGILBY, J., The old hand knitters of the Dales, *The Dalesman*, Lancaster, Yorkshire, (1951) 2.
2. LOMBARDI, V. J., Knitting Technology – A look back, *Knit. Times Yr. Bk.*, (1981) 151–5.

Further Information

The History of Hand Pin and Framework Knitting

HARVEY, M., 2,000 years of Hand Knitting, *Knit and Haberdashery Review*, (Oct 1968) 10–11.

KIEWE, H. E., *The Sacred History of Knitting*, (1967) Art Needlework Industries.

THOMAS, M., *Mary Thomas's Book of Knitting*, (reprint 1968) Hodder.

Articles in Textile History

BRACEGIRDLE, R., *William Lee and the Stocking Frame*, (1979) Leicester Museums Information Sheet 18.

BURNHAM, D. K., Coptic Knitting, *An ancient technique*, (Dec 1972) 3, 116–24.

CHAPMAN, S. D., *The genesis of the British Hosiery Industry 1600–1750*, (Dec 1972) 3, 7–50.

CHAPMAN, S. D., *Enterprise and innovation in the British Hosiery Industry*, (Oct 1974) **5**, 14–37.

FELKIN, W., *A History of Machine Wrought Hosiery and Lace Manufactures*, (1967) David and Charles Reprints.

GRASS, M. N., *Stockings for a Queen*, (1967) Heinemann.

HENSON, G., *History of the Framework Knitters*, (1970) David and Charles Reprints.

LEVEY, S. M., *Illustrations of the History of Knitting*, (1968–70) **1**, 183–205.

PASOLD, E. W., *In search of William Lee*, (1975) **6**, 7–17.

PASOLD, E. W., *Ladybird, Ladybird*, (1977) Manchester University Press.

PONTING, K. G., *In search of William Lee*, (1978) **9**, 174–5.

RUDDINGTON, Making the Past come alive, *Knit. Int.*, (Jan 1982) 28–30.

TURNAU, I. and PONTING, K. G., *Knitted Masterpieces*, (1976) **7**, 7–23.

TURNER, J. D., The Origins and Development of the Weft Knitting Industry, *Text. Inst. and Ind.*, (1966) **4**, (9), 265–8.

VARLEY, D. E., *John Heathcoat (1783–1861) founder of the Machine Lace Industry*, (1968–70) **1**, 2–45.

The History of Knitting (a series of illustrated advertisements produced by Groz-Beckert) *Knit. Times*, (15 Sept. 1975).

Old Textbooks

QUILTER, J. H. and CHAMBERLAIN, J., Framework Knitting and Hosiery, *Hosiery Trade Journal*, (1911–1914) **1, 2, 3**.

SHINN, W. E., *Principles of Knitting*, Metuchen, (1949) **1, 2**.

WILLKOMM, G., *Technology of Framework Knitting*, translated from German by W. T. Rowlett, (1885) Leicester Technical School, **Parts I, II**.

3

General Terms and Principles of Knitting Technology

Machine Knitting 3.1

Knitted structures are progressively built up by converting newly fed yarn into new loops in the needle hooks, *the needles then draw these 'new loops' head first through the 'old loops'* which they have retained from the previous knitting cycle. The needles at the same time release, *cast off* or '*knock-over*' old loops so that they hang suspended by their heads from the feet of the 'new loops' whose heads are still held in the hooks of the needles. A cohesive structure is thus produced by a combination of the intermeshed loops and the yarn joining those loops together through which it passes.

Knitted Loop Structure 3.2

The knitted loop structure may not always be noticeable because of the effect of structural fineness, fabric distortion, additional pattern threads, or the masking effect of finishing processes. Unless however, the intermeshing of the loops is securely achieved by the needles receiving new loops before their old loops are cast off and the ground structure is not fractured during finishing or wear, a breakdown or separation of the structure will result. The properties of a knitted structure are largely determined by the interdependence of each stitch with its neighbours on either side and above and below it. Knitted loops are arranged in rows and columns roughly equivalent to the warp and weft of woven structures termed 'courses' and 'wales' respectively.

A Course 3.3

A course is a predominantly horizontal row of loops (in an upright fabric) produced by adjacent needles *during the same knitting cycle.* (The last five words reduce confusion when describing complex weft knitted fabrics.)

In weft knitted fabrics (with the exception of intarsia and wrap insertion) a course is composed of yarn from a single supply termed a course length. *A pattern row is a horizontal row of cleared loops produced by one bed of adjacent needles*. In a plain weft knitted fabric this is identical to a course but in more complex fabrics a pattern row may be composed of two or more course lengths. In warp knitting each loop in a course is normally composed of a separate yarn.

3.4 A Wale

A wale is a predominantly vertical column of needle loops produced by the *same needle knitting at successive knitting cycles* and thus intermeshing each new loop through the previous loop. In warp knitting a wale can be produced from the same yarn if a warp guide laps around the same needle at successive knitting cycles thus making a pillar or chain stitch lapping movement. Wales are joined to each other by the sinker loops or underlaps.

3.5 Stitch Density

The term *stitch density* is frequently used in knitting instead of a linear measurement of courses or wales, it *is the total number of needle loops in a square area measurement* such as a square inch or three square centimetres. It is obtained by multiplying, for example, the number of courses and wales, per inch together. Stitch density tends to be a more accurate measurement because tension acting in one direction in the fabric may, for example, produce a low reading for the courses and a high reading for the wales, which when multiplied together cancel the effect out. Usually pattern rows and courses are, for convenience, considered to be synonymous when counting courses per unit of linear measurement.

3.6 Technically Upright

A knitted fabric is technically upright when its courses run horizontally and its wales run vertically with the heads of the needle loops facing towards the top and the course knitted first at the bottom of the fabric.

3.7 Design Appearance Requirements

The terms face, back and upright are purely technical descriptive terms and do not indicate the manner in which the structure is used by the designer, for example socks are usually worn upside down compared with their knitted courses, the technical back of structures are often used for pile effects, curtains may be hung sideways, and diagonal stripes can be achieved in dresswear by cutting fabric at an angle.

The Knitting Machine 3.8

Originally the term machine referred to a mechanism on a bearded needle frame such as the fashioning mechanism on the straight bar frame. Today it refers to the complete assembly.

A knitting machine is thus an apparatus for applying mechanical movement, either hand or power derived, to primary knitting elements in order to produce knitted structures from yarn. The machine incorporates and coordinates the action of a number of mechanisms and devices each performing specific functions which contribute towards the efficiency of the knitting action.

The main features of a knitting machine (see Fig. 13.1) are listed below:

1. The frame or carcass, normally free-standing and either circular or rectilinear according to needle bed shape, provides the support for the majority of the machine's mechanisms.
2. The machine control and drive system coordinates the power for the drive of the devices and mechanisms.
3. The yarn supply consists of the yarn package or beam accommodation, tensioning devices, yarn feed control and yarn feed carriers or guides.
4. The knitting system includes the knitting elements, their housing, drive and control as well as associated pattern and selection and garment length control devices (if equipped).
5. The fabric take-away mechanism includes fabric tensioning, wind-up and accommodation devices.
6. The quality control system includes stop motions, fault detectors, automatic oilers and lint removal systems.

Machines may range from high-production, limited-capability models to versatile multipurpose models having extensive patterning capabilities. The more complex the structure, the lower the knitting speed and the higher the potential fault rate. The simplest of the knitting machines may be hand powered and manipulated, whereas power-driven machines may be fully automatically controlled.

The Needle 3.9

The hooked metal needle is the principal element of machine knitting. During yarn feeding the hook is opened to release the retained old loop and to receive the new loop which is then enclosed in the hook. The new loop is then drawn by the hook through the old loop which slides on the outside of the bridge of the closed hook. *All needles* must therefore *have some method of closing the needle hook* to retain the new loop and exclude the old loop.

3.10 Fabric Draw-off

Fabric is always drawn from the needles on the side remote from their hooks. When two sets of needles are employed, either arranged vertically or at some other angle to each other, each set of hooks will face away from the other set and the fabric will be produced and drawn away in the gap between the two sets.

3.11 The Front of Rectilinear Needle Bar Machines

All rectilinear needle bar machines have a front and a back. *The front of the machine is the side to which the fabric is drawn away*, removed and inspected during knitting. If the machine has a single vertical needle bar its hooks will face towards the back. If the machine has two vertical needle bars the fabric will be drawn down between them and will then pass underneath one needle bar and will be removed from that side of the machine. Therefore, in this type of machine, the front needle bar will be that whose hooks face in the direction of fabric removal, whilst the hooks of the back needle bar will face towards the back of the machine. On warp knitting machines, the guide bars and their corresponding warp beams are numbered and described according to their position in relation to the front and back of the machine. On circular weft knitting machines, there is no front or back as the fabric is drawn towards the centre usually below the needle circle.

3.12 Basic Knitting Action of a Needle

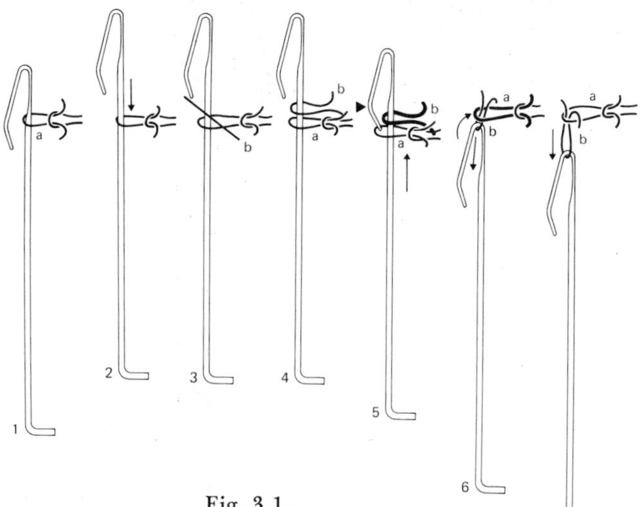

Fig. 3.1.

Figure 3.1 (1–7) illustrates the basic action of a needle. Except for the manner in which the hook is closed (in this case by pressing the beard) the knitting action is similar for all needles. The arrows indicate the relative movement of the loops along the needles (whether the needle moves through the loops or the loops are moved over the needle by some other elements depends upon the machine design).

The Bearded Needle 3.13

As mentioned above (2.4) the bearded or spring needle was the first to be produced. *It is the cheapest and simplest type to manufacture* being made from a single piece of metal in machine gauges as fine as 60 needles per inch, with the needles being pliered to ensure accurate needle spacing. When bearded needles are reciprocated in their bed the action is a collective one because of the problems of individual pressing and needle movement. The seriatim action of weft knitting is thus achieved by other loop-controlling elements which move the loops along the needle stems. A knitting section occupies considerable space on revolving cylinder machines limiting productivity. Selective pressing facilities are available on some weft and warp knitting machines. Bearded needle machines are unable to compete in the production of plain types of fabric and are now restricted to speciality structures.

In weft knitting, accurate control of the loops throughout the knitting sequence makes the bearded needle sinker wheel and loop wheel frames particularly suitable for the production of plush and inlay, whilst the ease of flexing and deflection of the bearded needle makes the sinker wheel and straight bar frame useful for loop transfer effects.

Main Parts of the Bearded Needle 3.14

There are five main parts of the bearded needle (Fig. 3.2):

1. *The stem* around which the needle loop is formed.
2. *The head* where the stem is turned into a hook to draw the new loop through the old loop.
3. *The beard* which is the curved downwards continuation of the hook that is used to separate the trapped new loop inside from the old loop as it slides off the needle beard.
4. *The eye* or groove cut in the stem to receive the pointed tip of the beard when it is pressed, thus enclosing the new loop.
5. *The shank* which may be bent for individual location in the machine or cast with others in a metal 'lead'.

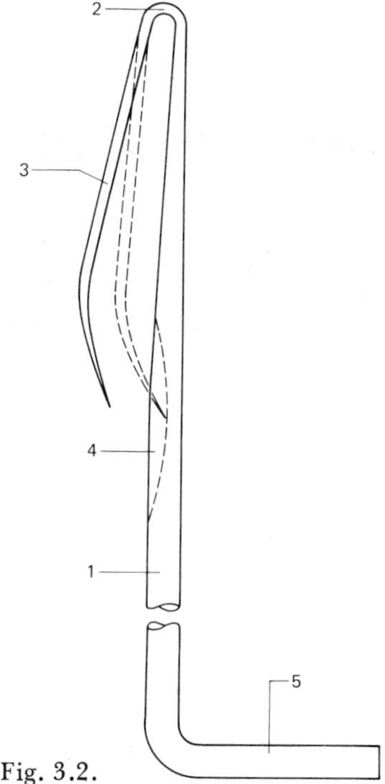

Fig. 3.2.

3.15 Knitting Action of the Bearded Needle

The knitting action of a bearded needle has been described and illustrated previously (Fig. 3.1). Depending upon the machine the needles are usually set either vertically or horizontally. When pressing occurs, the beard tip enters the eye to close the beard and enclose the new loop, the presser may be in the form of a bar, blade, verge or wheel with either the presser or the needle remaining stationary whilst the other element moves towards it.

3.16 The Latch Needle

Pierre Jeandeau patented the first latch needle in 1806 but it was Matthew Townsend's practical patents in 1849, which began the challenge to the 260-year reign of the bearded needle. It is a more expensive needle to manufacture than the bearded needle and is more prone to making needle lines. It has the advantage of being self acting or loop controlled, so that individual movement and control of the needles enables stitch selection to be achieved. For this reason, *it is the most widely used needle in weft knitting* and is sometimes termed the 'automatic needle'. Precisely manufactured latch needles are now knitting very high quality fabric.

The old loop is cleared from the hook automatically when the needle is lifted because the loop slides down inside the hook and contacts the latch or tumbler causing it to pivot open and allowing the loop to slide off the latch down on to the stem. The hook is closed automatically after yarn feeding by lowering the needle, because the old loop which was on the stem slides upwards contacting and pivoting the latch tightly closed and drawing and enclosing the newly fed loop inside the hook. Latch needles thus knit automatically as they are reciprocated. Except in Raschel warp knitting machines they are arranged to move independently in their tricks or grooves. They can operate at any angle but often require latch-guard or latch-opening facilities as there is a tendency for catches to spring closed as the old loops are cleared from the open latches.

Individually moving latch needles can draw and form their own needle loops, unlike bearded needles and needles in warp knitting machines which move as a unit and thus require sinkers or guides to form the loops around their stems. The Germans classify the first method as 'Strickerie' or loop drawing and the second method as 'Wirkerie' or loop forming.

Variation of the height of reciprocation of a latch needle at a feeder can produce missing, tucking or knitting and depth of descent may determine loop length. Specially designed latch needles are capable of facilitating rib loop transference by selective lifting. Double-ended purl needles can slide through the old loop in order to knit from an opposing bed and thus draw a loop from the opposite direction.

Features of the Latch Needle 3.17

The latch needle has nine main features (Fig. 3.3):

1. *The hook* which draws and retains the new loop.
2. *The slot* or *saw-cut* which receives the latch-blade (not illustrated).
3. *The cheeks* or *slot walls* which are either punched or riveted to fulcrum the latch-blade (not illustrated).
4. *The rivet* which may be plain or threaded. This has been dispensed with on most plate metal needles by pinching in the slot walls to retain the latch blade.
5. *The latch-blade* which locates the latch in the needle.
6. *The latch spoon* which is an extension of the blade and bridges the gap between the hook and the stem covering the hook when closed as shown in broken lines.
7. *The stem* which carries the loop in the clearing or rest position.
8. *The butt* which enables the needle to be reciprocated when contacted by cam profiles on either side of it forming a track. Double-ended purl type needles have a hook at each end, whilst one hook knits, the inactive hook is controlled as a butt by a cam reciprocated element called a slider.
9. *The tail* which is an extension below the butt giving additional support to the needle and keeping the needle in its trick.

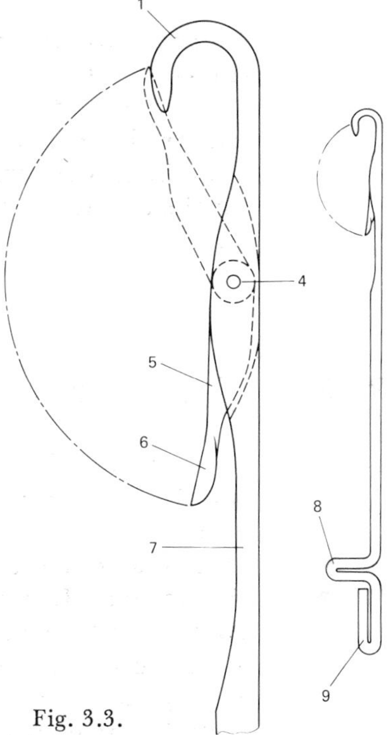

Fig. 3.3.

Knitting Action of the Latch Needle 3.18

Figure 3.4 shows the position of a latch needle as it passes through the cam system completing one knitting cycle or course as it moves up and down in its trick or slot.

1. The head of the needle hook is level with the top of the verge of the trick, the loop formed at the previous feeder is in the closed hook. It is prevented from rising as the needle rises by holding-down sinkers or web holders which move forward between the needles and hold down the sinker loops.
2. *Latch opening.* As the needle butt passes up the incline of the clearing cam, the old loop which is held down by the sinker, slides inside the hook and contacts the latch, turning and opening it.
3. *Clearing height.* When the needle reaches the top of the cam the old loop is cleared from the hook and latch spoon on to the stem. At this point the feeder guide plate acts as a guard to prevent the latch from closing the empty hook.
4. *Yarn feeding and latch closing.* The needle starts to descend the stitch cam so that its latch is below the verge with the old loop moving under it. At this time the new yarn is fed through a hole in the feeder guide to the descending needle hook as there is now no danger of the yarn being fed below the latch. The old loop contacts the underside of the latch causing it to close on to the hook.

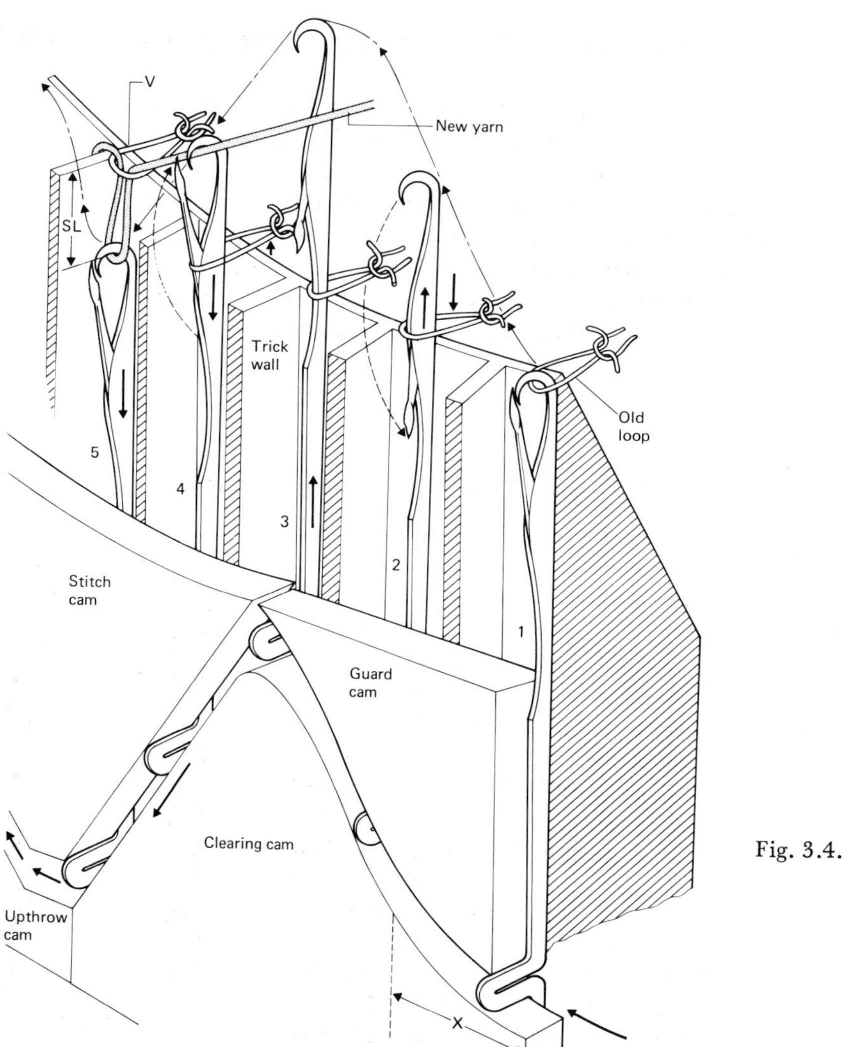

Fig. 3.4.

5. *Knocking-over and loop length formation.* As the head of the needle descends below the top of the trick the old loop slides off the needle and the new loop is drawn through it. *The continued descent of the needle draws the loop length, which is approximately twice the distance the head of the needle descends* below the surface of the sinker or trick-plate supporting the sinker loop. The distance is determined by the depth setting of the stitch cam which can be adjusted.

The rest position occurs between positions 1 and 2 when the open needle hook just protrudes above the needle trick verge. In this position a feeder would be passed without the needle receiving a new loop and the old loop would not be cast off so that a float stitch would be produced. The tucking in the hook position occurs between positions 2 and 3 when the needle can receive the new yarn but the old loop has not been cleared from the open latch.

Friction and Frictionless Needles 3.19

There are two types of latch needle, friction and frictionless. Friction needles have a slight flex, cramp or bend in the tails so that they contact the side-walls of the tricks in which they are housed. They are used in open cam systems where cams may be introduced or taken out of action to divert the needle path. Frictionless needles are employed in closed cam-tracks which have guard or safety cams on the opposite side to the knitting cams, to produce a completely enclosed track through which the needles run, otherwise the freely moving needles would be thrown out of their tricks at high speed.

The Bi-partite Compound Needle 3.20

Jeacock of Leicester patented a compound needle (of the sliding latch type) as long ago as 1856, but no type has found much use in weft knitting, whereas in warp knitting it is re-emerging as a major challenger to the other two needles. Its two separately-controlled parts, the hook and tongue members, are precisely designed. They rise and fall together but as the hook moves at a faster rate, the hook is open at the top of the rise and closed at the bottom of the fall.

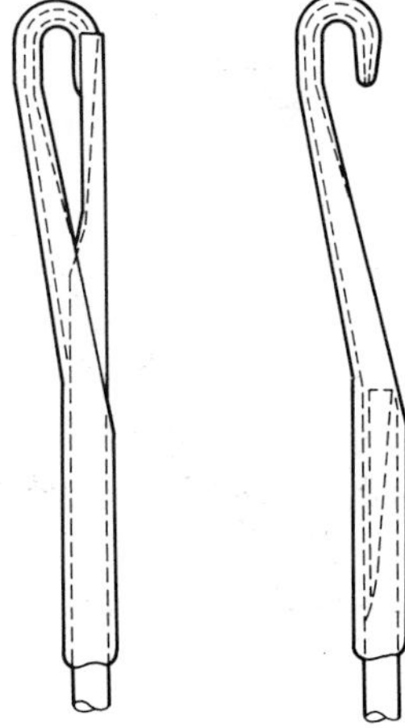

Fig. 3.5.

There are two types of compound needle in current use, the tubular pipe needle (Fig. 3.5) where the tongue slides inside the tube of the hook and the open stem pusher type (Fig. 3.6) where the tongue of closing wire slides externally along a groove on the edge of the flat hook member. The pusher type is cheaper and simpler to manufacture and its two parts are capable of separate replacement, whilst its dimensions are narrower allowing tighter stitches to be produced. During the late 1940s and 1950s, the pipe needle was employed in James Morton's high speed FNF Tricot warp knitting machine, first introduced in 1938, whereas today it is the open stem needle which is finding most widespread use in warp knitting.

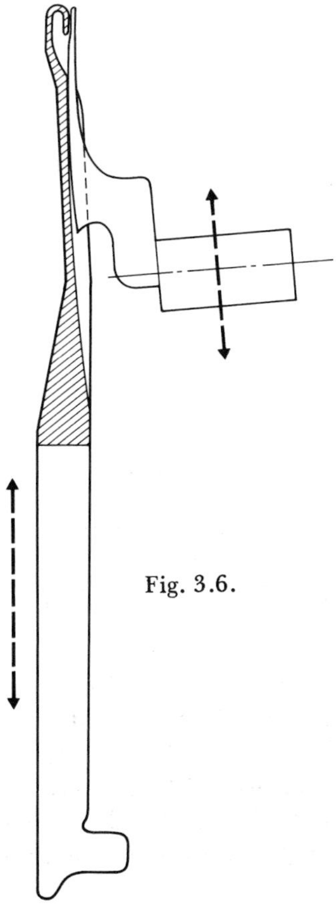

Fig. 3.6.

The compound needle is expensive to manufacture and each part requires separate and precise control from a drive shaft or cam system. In warp knitting where needles operate *en masse* this is not too difficult but for individual needle operation in weft knitting it would require two separate cam-tracks with problems of cam adjustment or alteration. There is no compound needle which draws its own loops and the yarn feeding area of the hook is more critical than for the bearded or latch needle because the yarn cannot be fed on to the tongue, whereas it can be fed on to the beard or open latch and will still be taken into the needle hook.

The compound needle has a short, smooth and simple action, without latch or beard inertia problems. The slim construction and short hook makes it particularly suitable for the production of plain, fine warp knitted structures at high speed. It can knit chain stitches continuously without the loops rising with the needles and its sturdy construction gives it an ability to resist the effect of deflection normally generated by elastic yarns or thick and thin places in spun yarns passing through the needles.

3.21 Machine Gauge

Normally all primary elements (those directly involved in the knitting action) in the same machine are set to the same gauge. Except for the sinker wheel machine, where the needles radiate outwards from their dial location, the gauge measured at the point of needle location is the same as that at the point of loop formation. The pitch or distance between one needle and another is proportional to the needle gauge or thickness and therefore to the space available for the yarn. As the diameter of a yarn is proportional to its count, a relationship exists between the range of optimum counts of yarn which may be knitted on a particular machine and its machine gauge. Machine gauge thus influences choice of yarn and count, and affects fabric properties such as appearance and weight. For a given machine diameter or width, finer gauge machines tend to knit a wider fabric as more wales are involved. For example a 30-inch diameter circular machine might have 1716 cylinder needles in 18 G and 1872 cylinder needles in 20 G. Coarse gauge machines have latch needles with larger dimensions requiring greater movements. During knitting the size of the knitting cams are correspondingly large so less cam systems can be accommodated around a given machine diameter (for example 30 inches) so therefore coarser gauge machines often have fewer feeders.

Originally, needles were cast in small metal blocks termed leads which were then fitted into the needle bar. In the bearded needle straight bar frame, the needles were cast two to a lead and gauged in the number of leads per 3 inches of the needle bar which is equivalent to a gauge of the number of needles in 1½ inches. In bearded needle warp knitting machines the needles were cast three to a lead giving a gauge directly in needles per inch. In the Raschel warp knitting machine the needles were cast in 2-inch leads giving a Raschel gauge of needles per 2 inches. In latch needle weft knitting machines the gauge is normally expressed in needles per inch which in the U.S.A. is referred to as 'cut', being short for the phrase 'tricks per cut per inch'.

Further Information

HURD, J. C. H. and MILLINGTON, J. T., The latch needle. Where do we go from here? (IFKT Paper), *Knit. Int.*, (June 1979) 50–4.

LANCASHIRE, J. B., Counts and gauges. *Hos. Trade Journal,* (Dec. 1958) 77–9.

LANCASHIRE, J. B. and KEATES, E. A., Knitting needles survey, *Hos. Trade Journal*, (Aug. 1961) 98–100.

ROXBURGH, J., The compound needle: a developing element, *Knit. Times*, (12 May 1980) 64–71.

SPEETJENS, J. T., The impact of needle design on knitted fabric quality (ASKT Paper), *Knit. Times*, (4 April 1977) 18–20.

The compound needle: its background, *Knit. O'wr Times Yr bk*, (1970) 110–12.

4

Basic Mechanical Principles of Knitting Technology

4.1 The Sinker

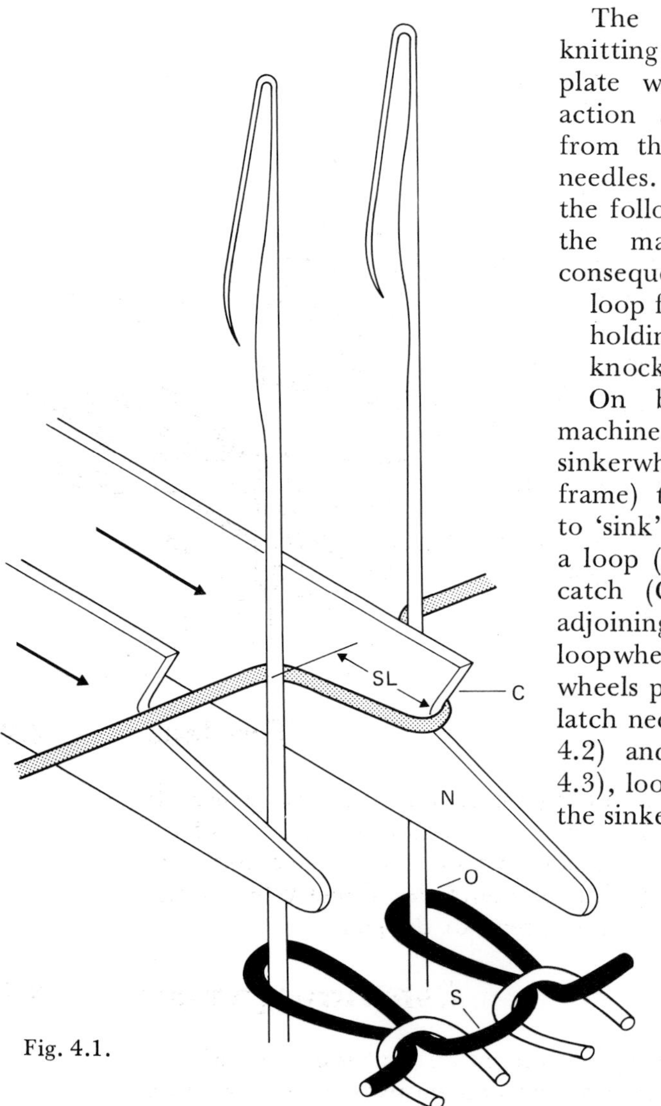

Fig. 4.1.

The sinker is the second primary knitting element. It is a thin metal plate with an individual or collective action approximately at right angles from the hook side between adjoining needles. It may perform one or more of the following functions dependent upon the machine's knitting action and consequent sinker shape and movement:

loop formation,
holding-down,
knocking-over.

On bearded needle weft knitting machines of the straight bar frame and sinkerwheel type (as on Lee's hand frame) the main purpose of a sinker is to 'sink' or kink the newly laid yarn into a loop (Fig. 4.1) as its forward edge or catch (C) advances between the two adjoining needles. On the bearded needle loopwheel frame, the blades of burr wheels perform this function whereas on latch needle weft knitting machines (Fig. 4.2) and warp knitting machines (Fig. 4.3), loop formation is not a function of the sinkers.

A second and more common function of sinkers on modern machines is to hold down the old loops at a lower level on the needle stems than the new loops which are being formed and prevent the old loops from being lifted as the needles rise to clear them from their hooks. In Fig. 4.1 the protruding nib or nose of the sinker (N) is positioned over the sinker loops of the old loops (O) preventing them from rising with the needles. On tricot warp knitting machines and single bed weft knitting machines, a slot or throat (T in Fig. 4.2) is cut to hold and control the old loop. The sole function of the sinker may be as a web holder or stitch comb as on the Raschel warp knitting machine in which case only the underside of the nose performs the function. On latch needle weft knitting machines, the holding-down sinkers have a rectangular gap cut on their upper surface remote from the nose into which the sinker cam race fits to positively control the sinker's movement.

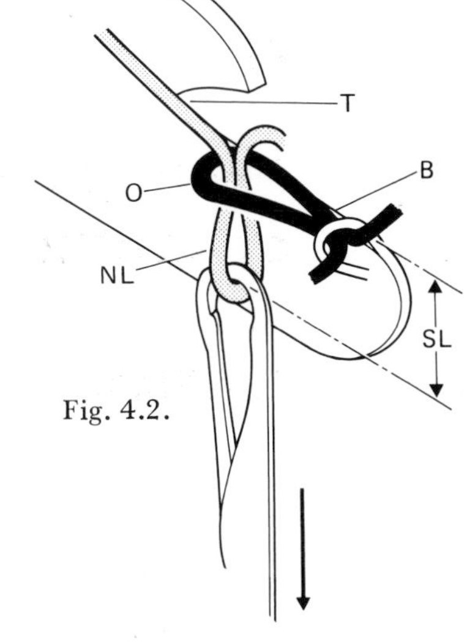

Fig. 4.2.

Holding-down sinkers enable tighter structures with improved appearance to be obtained, the minimum draw-off tension is reduced, higher knitting speeds are possible and knitting can be commenced on empty needles. Holding-down sinkers may be unnecessary when knitting with two needle beds as the second bed restrains the fabric loops whilst the other set of needles move.

The third function of the sinker – as a knock-over surface – is illustrated in Fig. 4.2 where its upper surface or belly (B) supports the old loop (O) as the new loop (NL) is drawn through it. On tricot warp knitting machines the sinker belly is specially shaped to assist with landing as well as knock-over. On latch needle machines, the verge or upper surface of the trick-plate (V in Fig. 3.4) serves as the knock-over surface.

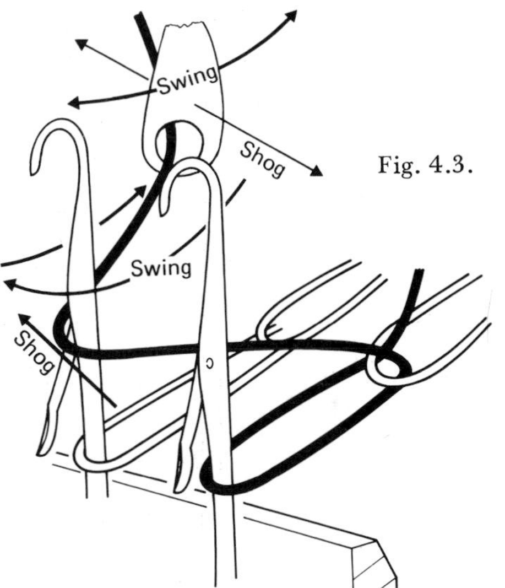

Fig. 4.3.

The Jack 4.2

The Jack is a secondary weft knitting element which may be used to provide flexibility of latch needle selection and movement. It is placed below and in the same trick as the needle and has its own operating butt and cam system. The needle may thus be controlled directly by its butt and cam system or indirectly by the movement of the jack.

Cam Arrangement 4.3

All needles have a reciprocating action either *en masse* or seriatim, except on the bearded needle sinkerwheel and loopwheel frames where the fixed needle circle merely revolves. Cams are the devices which convert the rotary machine drive into a suitable reciprocating action for the needles or other elements. The cams are carefully profiled to produce precisely-timed movement and dwell periods and are of two types, engineering cams and knitting cams. The movements may be represented in the form of a time displacement graph.

Circular engineering cams or high speed eccentrics indirectly control the motion of bars of elements which move *en masse* as single units in Cottons Patent and warp knitting machines. They are attached to a rotary drive shaft situated parallel to and below the needle bar. A number of identical cams are positioned along the shaft to ensure correctly aligned movement. The drive is transmitted and adapted via cam-followers, levers, pivots and rocker shafts. One complete 360-degree revolution of the drive shaft is equivalent to one knitting cycle and it produces all the required movements of the elements once only in their correct timing relationship.

In warp knitting machines, four types of cam drive have been employed: single acting cams, cam and counter cam, box cams and contour cams. The first type requires a powerful spring to negatively retain the cam truck or follower in contact with the cam surface, bounce and excessive wear occurs at speed. The cam and counter cam arrangement provides a cam and its follower in each direction of movement but is obviously more expensive to manufacture. The box or enclosed cam employs a single cam follower which is guided by the two cam races of a groove on the face of the cam. However, change of contact from one face to the other causes the follower to turn in the opposite direction producing wear which cannot be compensated. The contour, ring or pot cam is the reverse of the box cam as the cam profile projects out from one face of the cam in the form of lip with a cam-follower placed on either side of it. This is a popular and easily adaptable arrangement. Although cams are comparatively cheap, simple and accurate, at speeds above 800 courses per minute they are subject to excessive vibration. For this reason, at speeds in excess of that, eccentric drive is now employed.

The eccentric is a form of crank which provides a simple harmonic movement with smooth acceleration and deceleration. Its widespread use is the result of adapting this simple motion and modifying it to the requirements of the warp knitting machine so that even dwell (stationary periods) in the element cycle can be achieved. On the FNF compound needle machine, the movements of two eccentric drive shafts, one turning twice as fast as the other, were superimposed on each other. Now, however, the simpler single eccentric drive is successfully driving element bars at speeds of 2000 courses per minute or more.

The other type of cam, *the angular knitting cam* (see Fig. 3.4) acts directly onto the butts of needles or other elements to produce individual or seriatim movement in the tricks of latch needle weft knitting machines as the butts pass through the stationary cam system (revolving cylinder machines) or the cams pass across the stationary tricks (reciprocating cam-box flat machines or rotating cam-box circular machines).

On weft knitting machines, yarn feeds must move if the cams move, in order to supply yarn at the knitting point, and if the cam-boxes rotate the yarn packages and tackle must rotate with them. If, however, the yarn carriers reciprocate as on flat machines their yarn supply packages may be situated in a suitable stationary position.

Generally garment-length producing machines have revolving or reciprocating cam-boxes because movement changes required during the garment sequence can be initiated from a single control position as the cam-boxes pass by for the start of the next revolution or traverse, also the garment lengths are stationary and may be inspected or removed during knitting. Large-diameter fabric-producing machines tend to be of the revolving cylinder type because the weight of revolving multi-feeder yarn packages and tackle creates inertia problems which reduces efficiency and knitting speeds whereas the revolving fabric roll and take-up mechanism is less of a problem.

Knitting cams are attached either individually or in unit form to a cam-plate and, depending upon machine design, are fixed, exchangeable or adjustable. In the latter case, this might occur whilst the machine is in operation on garment-length machines. Elements, such as holding-down sinkers and pelerine points are controlled by their own arrangement of cams attached to a separate cam-plate. At each yarn feed position there is a set of cams consisting of at least a raising cam, a stitch cam and an upthrow cam whose combined effect is to cause a needle to carry out a knitting cycle if required. On circular machines there is a removable cam section or door so that knitting elements can be replaced.

The raising cam causes the needles to be lifted to either tuck, clearing loop transfer or needle transfer height depending upon machine design. A swing cam is fulcrummed so that the butts will be unaffected when it is out of the track and may also be swung into the track to raise the butts. A bolt cam can be caused to descend into the cam track and towards the element tricks to control the butts or be withdrawn out of action so that the butts pass undisturbed across its face, it is mostly used on garment-length machines to produce changes of rib.

The stitch cam controls the depth to which the needle descends thus controlling the amount of yarn drawn into the needle loop, it also functions simultaneously as a knock-over cam.

The upthrow or counter cam takes the needles back to the rest position and allows the newly-formed loops to relax. The stitch cam is normally adjustable for different loop lengths and it may be attached to a slide together with the upthrow cam so that the two are adjusted in unison. In Fig. 3.4 there is no separate upthrow cam, section X of the raising cam is acting as an upthrow cam.

Guard cams are often placed on the opposite side of the cam-race to limit the movement of the butts and to prevent needles from falling out of track.

Separate cam-boxes are required for each needle or associated element bed and they must be linked together to ensure coordination. If the cam-box itself is moving from right to left the needle butts will pass through in a left-to-right direction. On circular fabric machines the cams are designed to act in only one direction but on flat and circular leg-wear machines, the cams are symmetrically arranged to act in both directions of cam-box traverse with only the leading edges of certain cams in action.

All cam systems are a compromise between speed, variety, needle control and selection systems.[1]

4.4 The Two Methods of Yarn Feeding

As mentioned in the knitting action (Fig. 2.1(3)), yarn feeding involves either (i) moving the yarn past the needles or (ii) moving the needles past a stationary yarn feed position. When the yarn moves past the needles, the fabric will be stationary because the loops hang from the needles. This arrangement exists on all warp knitting machines and on weft knitting machines with straight beds or circular machines with stationary cylinder and dials. On straight machines of both weft and warp type the yarn carrier or guide has a reciprocating traversing movement which takes it towards and away from a suitably-placed yarn supply. On stationary cylinder and dial machines, however, the yarn supply packages must rotate in order to keep with the continuously revolving yarn feeds. Because the

Fig. 4.4. Simple Hand-turned Griswold Type Machine (Walter Bullwer, Leicester Polytechnic). T = Stationary Needle Tricks; C = Revolving Cam-box; F = Revolving Feeder; D = Replaceable Dial and Needles; B = Technical Back of Plain Fabric.

latch needle beds of these flat and circular weft knitting machines are stationary, it is necessary to reciprocate the cam-carriages and revolve the cam-boxes so that the needle butts of the stationary tricks pass through and the needles are thus reciprocated into a knitting action at the exact moment when the traversing feed supplies a new yarn (Fig. 4.4).

Most circular weft knitting machines have revolving needle cylinders and stationary cams, feeders and yarn packages. In this case, the fabric tube must revolve with the needles as must the fabric rollers and take-up mechanism.

4.5 The Three Methods of Forming Yarn into Needle Loops

There are three methods of forming the newly-fed yarn into the shape of a needle loop:

1. Fig. 4.1. *By sinking the yarn into the space between adjacent needles using loop forming sinkers* or other elements which approach from the beard side. The action of a straight bar frame is illustrated but a similar action occurs on other bearded needle weft knitting machines. The distance SL which the catch of the sinker moves past the hook side of the needle is approximately half the stitch length.
2. Fig. 4.2. *By causing latch needles to draw their own needle loops down through the old loops* as they descend one at a time down the stitch cam. This method is employed on all latch needle weft knitting machines. The distance SL which the head of the latch needle descends below the knock-over surface (in this case, the belly of the knock-over sinker), is approximately half the stitch length.
3. Fig. 4.3. *By causing a warp yarn guide to wrap the yarn loop around the needle.* The lapping movement of the guide is produced from the combination of two separate motions, a swinging motion which occurs between the needles from the front of the machine to the hook side and return and a lateral shogging (or racking) of the guide parallel with the needle bar on the hook side and also the front of the machine. The swinging motion is fixed but the direction and extent of the shogging motion may or may not be varied from a pattern mechanism. This method is employed on all warp knitting machines and for wrap patterning on weft knitting machines. The length of yarn per stitch unit is generally determined by the rate of warp yarn feed.

1. FINDLAY, P. M., Machine capabilities in relation to quality standards, *Text. Inst. and Ind.*, (1977) **15**, (5), 177–8.

Further Information

WHEATLEY, B., The principles of cam and eccentric drive systems for warp knitting machines, *Knit. Times*, (26 June 1972) 46–50.

The Potential of Knitting

BRUNNSCHWEILER, D. Present and future prospects for knitting and weaving, *Journal Text. Inst.*, (1962) 610–627.

COOKE, W. D., Knitted fabrics from textured yarns, *Text. Inst. and Ind.*, (1977) **15**, (3), 92–5.

CZELNY, K. T. J., The use of knitted fabrics in the automotive industry, *Text. Inst. and Ind.*, (1975) **13**, (4), 103, 6, 7.

FORSYTH, J. C., The influence of weaving on other fabric forming techniques, *Text. Inst. and Ind.*, (1965) **3**, (1), 8–11.

GOADBY, D. R., New developments using existing knitting machinery, *Knit. Int.*, (June 1976) 61–3.

GOTTLIEB, N., Warp knitting on the move, *Text. Inst. and Ind.*, (1968) **6**, (6), 150–2.

HURD, J. C. H., The increasing scope for knitted fabrics in apparel, *Text. Inst. and Ind.*, (1965) **3**, (11), 1–3.

REISFELD, A., Classification of textile fabrics. *Knit. O'wr Times*, (26 Feb. 1968) 47–58.

SMITH, J. M., Continuing diversity of warp knit fabrics and applications, *Knit. Int.*, (Oct. 1977) 40–3.

THOMAS, D. G. B., Knitted industrial fabrics, *Text. Inst. and Ind.*, (1973) **11**, (8), 213–15.

5

Elements of Knitted Loop Structure

The Needle Loop 5.1

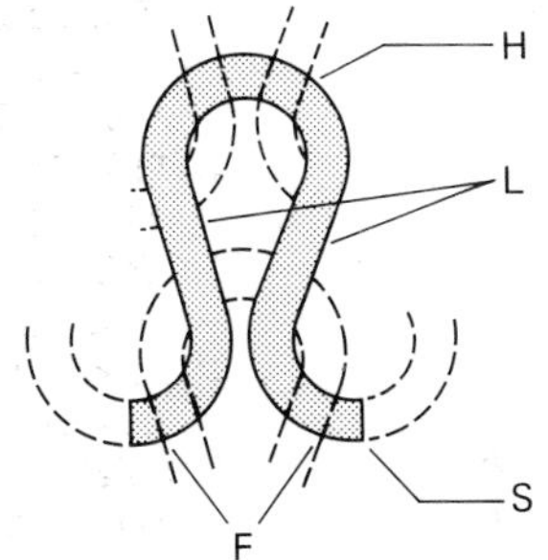

Fig. 5.1.

The needle loop (Fig. 5.1) is the simplest unit of knitted structure. When the tension in the fabric is balanced and there is sufficient take-away tension during knitting it is an upright noose which was originally formed in the needle hook. It consists of a *head and two side limbs* or legs. At the base of each leg is a foot which meshes through the head of the loop formed at the previous knitting cycle of that needle. The yarn passes from the foot of one loop formed by it into the foot and leg of the next loop formed by it. In warp knitting the feet may be open or closed (in the latter case the guide passes across the back of the needle around whose hook it formed a loop). In weft knitting the feet are normally open because the yarn supply usually continues in the same direction across the hooks and does not return across the backs of the needles. Closed loops may be produced on bearded needle weft knitting machines by twisting a loop over as it is transferred to another needle or by using a twizzle beard which closes onto the back of the needle so that the loop twists over as it is cast off – the former is occasionally still employed on sinkerwheel machines.

The Sinker Loop 5.2

The sinker loop (shown at S in Fig. 5.1) *is the piece of yarn which joins one weft knitted needle loop to the next.* It is so termed because on bearded needle frames it is the loop-forming sinker which forms the needle loop and as a consequence also produces a sinker loop. Sinker loops are, however, automatically produced by the action of the latch needle as it draws its own needle loop. A sinker loop will show on the opposite side of the fabric to the sides of the loop because the needle loop is drawn onto the opposite side from which the yarn was originally fed. The terms sinker loop and needle loop are convenient descriptive terms but their precise limits within the same loop length are impossible to define exactly.

5.3 Warp Knitted Laps

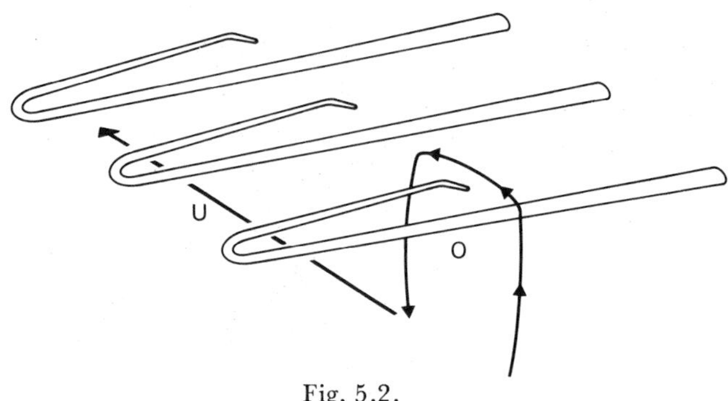

Fig. 5.2.

Loops are termed laps in warp knitting because the guides lap the warp yarn around the needles in order to form the loops, the laps may be either open or closed. On the original warp frame (as on many present-day crochet machines) the needle bar was in a horizontal and not a vertical position with its beards facing upwards (Fig. 5.2). To produce a needle loop it was thus necessary to swing the guide upwards and shog it over the top of the needle hence *the term 'overlap'* which *refers both to the movement and to the loop which it forms*. Similarly, the guides were shogged under the needles to new starting positions for the next overlap and *this movement and the lapped thread it produces is still termed an 'underlap'*. In the warp knitting cycle it is always understood that the overlap precedes the underlap.

5.4 The Overlap

The *overlap (Fig. 4.3) is a shog usually across one needle hook by a warp guide which forms the warp yarn into the head of the loop*. The swinging movement of the guide to the hook side and the return swing after the overlap produce the two side limbs of the loop which has a very similar appearance on the face side of the fabric to a needle loop produced by weft knitting. Only exceptionally rarely are overlaps taken across two needles as this produces severe tension on the warp yarn and the knitting elements because the needles knock-over in unison. Double needle bar overlaps generally also have a poor appearance and physical characteristics because the second overlap will have a different configuration of underlaps to the first overlap. In the former, the underlap will be passing along the course to the next overlap in the same manner as a sinker loop whereas in the latter, the underlap will lap up to the next course in the normal manner of an underlap.

5.5 The Underlap

The underlap shog occurs across the side of the needles remote from the hooks, on the front of single bar and in the centre of double bar needle machines, it supplies the yarn between one overlap and the next (Fig. 5.3).

Generally ranging from nothing up to three needles; in extent it can be 14 needle spaces or more, depending upon design of machine and structure, although efficiency and speed tend to be reduced. Underlaps as well as overlaps are essential in all warp knitted structures in order to join the wales of loops together, but they may be contributed by a different guide bar to those for the overlaps.

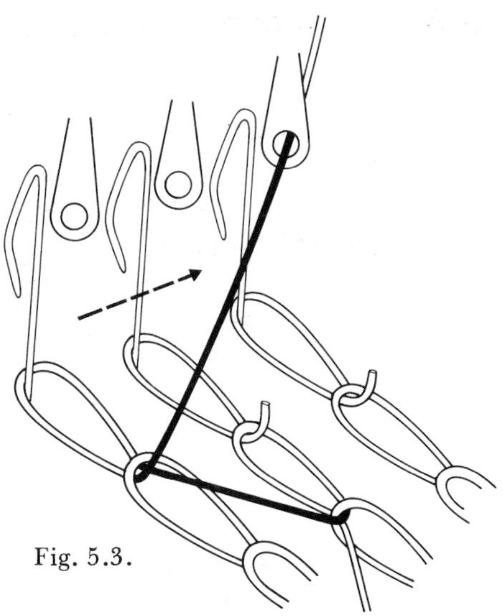

Fig. 5.3.

Closed Lap 5.6

A closed lap is produced when an underlap follows in the opposite direction to the overlap and thus laps the thread around both sides of the needles (Fig. 5.4).

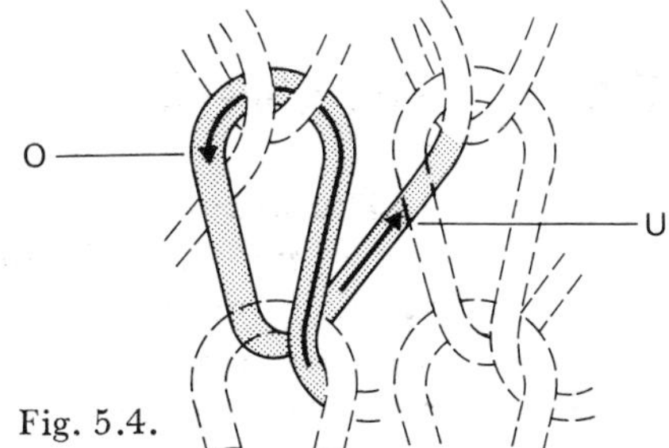

Fig. 5.4.

Open Lap 5.7

An open lap is produced either when the underlap is in the same direction as the overlap, or it is omitted so that the next overlap commences from the space where the previous overlap finished (Fig. 5.5). Closed laps are heavier, more compact, opaque and less extensible than open laps produced from the same yarn and at a comparable knitting quality.

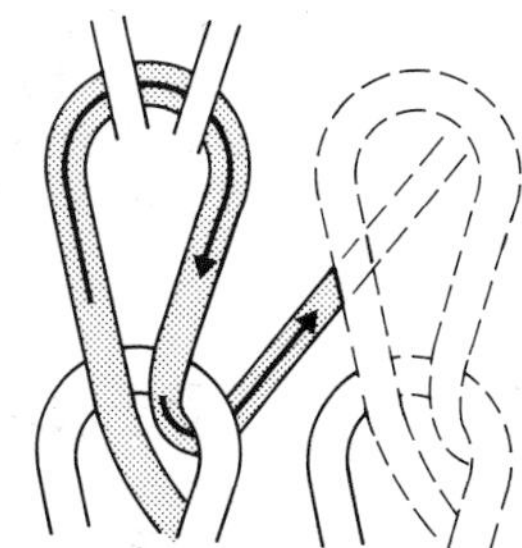

Fig. 5.5.

5.8 Wrapping

Wrapping is a method of patterning with warp threads on a single jersey weft knitted base structure using specially-controlled thread guides which make unidirectional warp knitted laps around selected needle hooks which are empty ('warp insertion') or already have a new weft knitted loop ('embroidery plating' or 'wrap striping'). The technique is used on some half-hose and circular single-jersey machines.

5.9 The Knitted Stitch

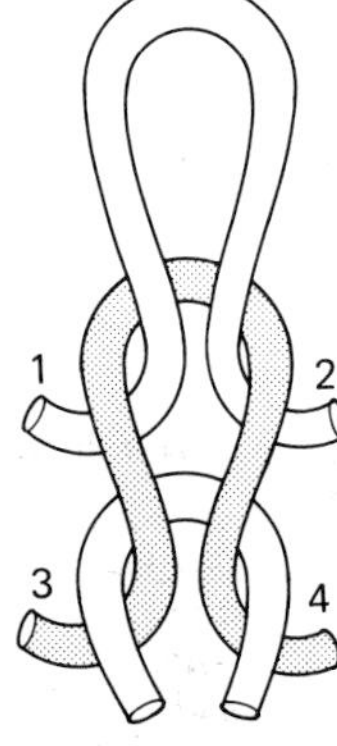

Fig. 5.6.

The knitted stitch is the basic unit of intermeshing and usually consists of three or more intermeshed loops, the centre loop having been drawn through the head of the lower loop which had in turn been intermeshed through its head by the loop which appears above it (Fig. 5.6). A repeat unit of a stitch is a minimum repeat of intermeshed loops which can be placed adjoining other repeat units to build an unbroken sequence in width and depth. *Whenever a new loop is intermeshed as a single loop through an old loop, its side limbs will be restricted at the base of the loop by the head of the old loop.*

The term stitch is also unfortunately, frequently used in knitting terminology to refer to the configuration of yarn associated with a single needle as in the case of stitch length. *Stitch length is theoretically a single length of yarn which includes one needle loop and half the length of yarn (half a sinker loop) between that needle loop and the adjacent needle loops on either side of it.* Generally, the larger the stitch length the more elastic and lighter the fabric, and the poorer its cover opacity and bursting strength.

5.10 The Intermeshing Points of a Needle Loop

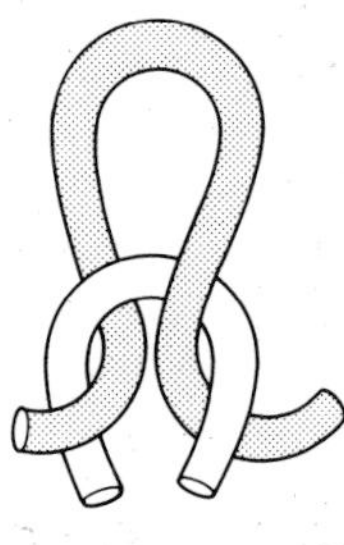
Fig. 5.7.

All needle loops or overlaps have four possible intermeshing points, 1 and 2 at the head, where the next new loop will be drawn through by that needle and 3 and 4 at the base where the loop has intermeshed with the head of the previously formed loop (Fig. 5.6). The intermeshings at 1 and 2 are always identical with each other as are intermeshings 3 and 4 with each other. It is impossible to draw a new loop through the old loop so that its two feet are alternately intermeshed (Fig. 5.7). It could only be achieved by taking the yarn package through the old loop. Although this would produce a locked loop, the package would not be large enough to provide a continuous supply.

A new loop can thus only be intermeshed through the head of the old loop in a manner which will show a face loop stitch on one side and a reverse loop stitch on the other side, because the needle hook is uni-directional and can only draw a new loop down through an old loop.

The Face Loop Stitch 5.11

This side of the stitch *shows the new loop coming through towards the viewer as it passes over and covers the head of the old loop* (Fig. 5.8). Face loop stitches tend to show the side limbs of the needle loops or overlaps as a series of interfitting 'V's. The face loop-side is the underside of the stitch on the needle.

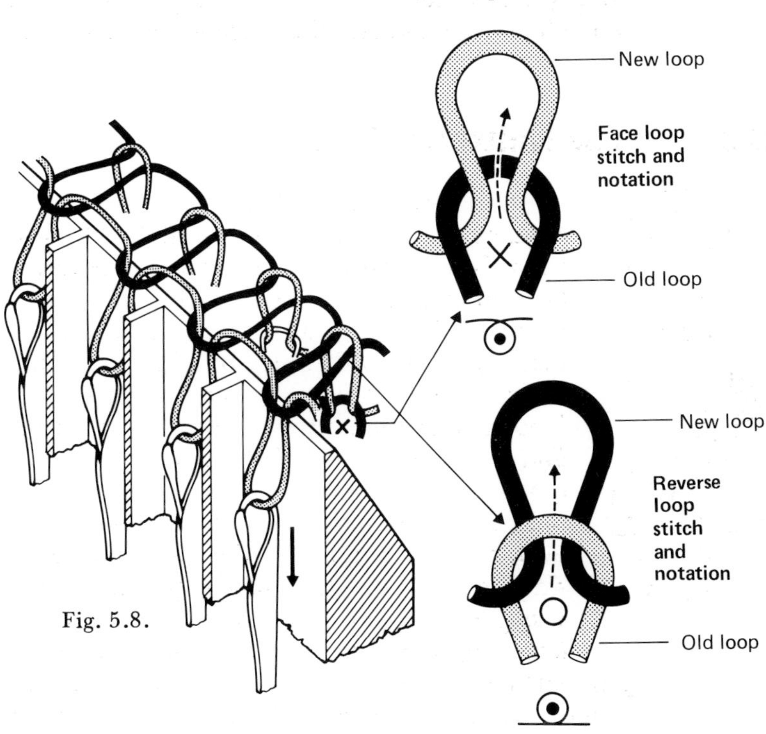

Fig. 5.8.

The Reverse Loop Stitch 5.12

This is the opposite side of the stitch to the face loop-side and *shows the new loop meshing away from the viewer as it passes under the head of the old loop*. Reverse stitches show the sinker loops in weft knitting and the underlaps in warp knitting most prominently on the surface. The reverse loop-side is the nearest to the head of the needle because the needle draws the new loops downwards through the old loops (cf. Fig. 4.4).

Single-faced Structures 5.13

Single-faced structures are produced in warp and weft knitting by the needles (arranged either in a straight line or in a circle) *operating as a single set*. Adjacent needles will thus have their hooks facing towards the same direction and the heads of the needles will always draw the new loops downwards through the old loops in the same direction so that intermeshing points 1 and 2 will be identical with intermeshing points 3 and 4.

The under surface of the fabric on the needles (termed the 'technical face' or 'right side') will thus only show the face stitches in the form of the side limbs of the loops or overlaps as a series of interfitting 'V's. The upper surface of the fabric on the needles (termed the 'technical back' or left side) will only show reverse stitches in the form of sinker loops or underlaps and the heads of the loops.

5.14 Double-faced Structures

Double-faced structures are produced in weft and warp knitting *when two sets of independently-controlled needles are employed with the hooks of one set knitting or facing in the opposite direction to the other set*. The two sets of needles thus draw their loops from the same yarn in opposite directions, so that the fabric, formed in the gap between the two sets, shows the face loops of one set on one side and the face loops of the other set on the opposite side. The two faces of the fabric are held together by the sinker loops or underlaps which are inside the fabric so that the reverse stitches tend to be hidden. Sometimes the two faces are cohesively produced and are far enough apart for the connecting sinker loops or underlaps to be severed in order to produce two single-faced fabrics.

5.15 A Balanced Structure

This is a double-faced structure which has an identical number of each type of stitch produced on each needle bed and therefore showing on each fabric surface usually in the same sequence. These structures do not normally show curling at their edges. Balanced structures need not, however, have the same design in coloured yarns on either surface.

5.16 Face and Reverse Stitches on the Same Surface

These are normally produced on purl weft knitting machines which have double-headed needles capable of drawing a face stitch with one hook and a reverse stitch on the other, so that intermeshing points 1 and 2 will not always be identical with intermeshing points 3 and 4.

Selvedged Fabric 5.17

A selvedged fabric is one having a 'self-edge' to it and can only be produced on machines whose yarn reciprocates backwards and forwards across the needle bed so that a selvedge is formed as the yarn rises up to the next course at the edge of the fabric.

Cut Edge Fabric 5.18

Cut edge fabric is usually produced by slitting open a tube of fabric produced on a circular machine. A slit tube of fabric from a 30-inch (76 cm) diameter machine will have an open width of 94 inches (2.38 m) (πd) at knitting and before relaxation.

Tubular Fabric 5.19

This may be produced in double-faced or single-faced structures on circular machines, or in a single-faced form on straight machines with two sets of needles provided each needle set only knits at alternate cycles and that the yarn only passes across from one needle bed to the other at the two selvedge needles at each end, thus closing the edges of the tube by joining the two single-faced fabrics produced on each needle set together.

Upright Loop Structures 5.20

Structures with upright loops in straight wales are only produced if the tension of the yarn on either side of the needle loop head is balanced. This condition often exists in weft knitted structures becaused balanced sinker loops enter from either side of the needle head but it may be disturbed by racking, by knitting twist lively yarn or by traversing pressing-down elements.

Warp knitted structures, however, seldom have perfectly upright overlaps because the underlaps, even if they enter from either side of the overlap head, rarely balance each other. When closed laps are produced, both underlaps will be on one side of the previous overlap head, causing it to incline towards that direction. Even a progressive open lap will not produce a balanced loop structure because the underlap entering the overlap head from below will not balance the effect of the underlap on the opposite side as it leaves for the course above. Single guide bar fabrics are thus very unstable structures and it is one of the reasons why most warp knitted structures are produced from two or more sets of warp threads often with guide bars supplying yarn to each needle, but lapping in opposition so that the tension of their underlaps tend to balance each other.

5.21 Knitting Notations

A knitting notation is a simple, easily-understood symbolic representation of a knitting repeat sequence and its resultant fabric structure which eliminates the need for time consuming and possibly confusing sketches and written descriptions (Fig. 5.8). A method universally recognized for warp knitting lapping diagrams and also popular for weft knitting running thread path notations involves the use of point paper. *Each point represents a needle* in plan view from above and after the thread path has been drawn, *it also represents its stitch.* Each horizontal row of points thus represents adjacent needles during the same knitting cycle and the course produced by them. The lowest row of points represents the commencing course in knitting and it must be understood that when analysing structures, the courses are normally unroved in a reverse order to the knitting sequence.

When knitting with a single set of needles, each vertical column point represents the same needle at successive knitting cycles or a wale in the resultant structure. For double needle bar knitting, every second row represents the back needle bar and its wales with all needle books facing towards the top of the paper to facilitate the drawing of a continuous lapping movement. For weft knitting with two sets of needles it is assumed that the lower row of points represent needles whose hooks face towards the bottom of the paper and the upper row, needles whose hooks face towards the top of the paper.

The second notational method is that developed by the Leicester School of Textiles for weft knitting only. In this method, squared paper instead of point paper is employed with each square representing a needle or stitch. An 'X' symbol is placed in a square where a face stitch occurs and an 'O' where there is a reverse stitch. When notating each stitch it is necessary to examine the intermeshing direction at the base of the loop because the intermeshing at its head determines the direction of the intermeshing of new loops formed above it.

6

Comparison of Weft and Warp Knitting

Yarn Feeding and Loop Formation 6.1

Even when the needles are fixed or act collectively in a weft knitting machine, *yarn feeding and loop formation will occur at each needle in succession* across the needle bed during the same knitting cycle (Fig. 6.1). All or a number of the needles (A,B,C,D) are supplied in turn with the same weft yarn during the same knitting cycle so that the yarn path (in the form of a course length) will follow a course of the fabric passing through each needle loop knitted from it (E,F,G,H).

In a warp knitting machine there will be a simultaneous yarn-feeding and loop-forming action occurring at every needle in the needle bar during the same knitting cycle (Fig. 6.2). All needles (A,B,C,D) in the needle bar are simultaneously lapped by separate warp guides (E,F,G,H). As all needles receive their overlaps simultaneously, a guide underlapping from one needle to another will be passing from one knitting cycle or course to the next so that the warp yarn passes from an overlap produced in one course to an overlap produced in a succeeding course (for example, guide F underlapping from needle B to needle A).

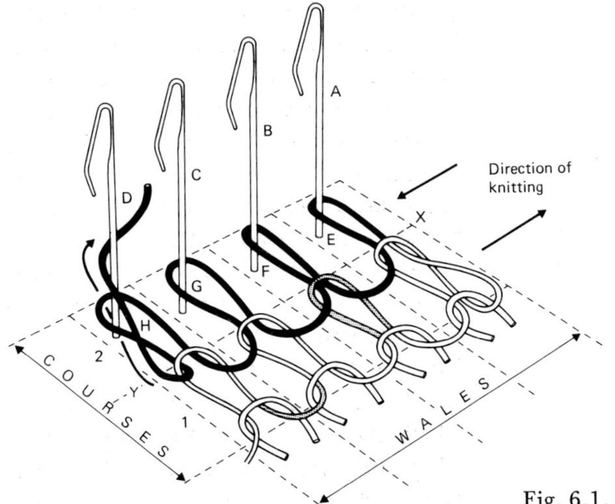

Fig. 6.1.

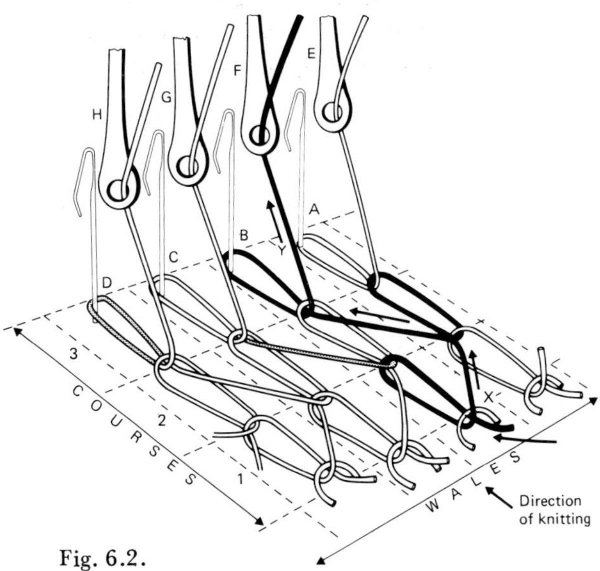

Fig. 6.2.

6.2 The Two Industries

Occasionally both knitting techniques are combined in a single machine, generally, however, the techniques have tended to diverge to produce entirely separated industries each having its own specialist technology, machine builders, fabric characteristics and end-uses.

Weft knitting is the more widely spread and larger of the two sectors and accounts for approximately one quarter of the total yardage of apparel fabric compared with about one sixth for warp knitting. Weft knitting machines, particularly of the garment length type, are attractive to small manufacturers because of their versatility, relatively low total capital costs, small floor space requirements, quick pattern and machine changing facilities and possibility of short production runs and low stock holding requirements of yarn and fabric.

A major part of the weft knitting industry is directly involved in the assembly of garments using operations such as overlocking (Fig. 6.3), cup-seaming (Fig. 6.4) and linking which have been specifically developed to produce seams with compatible properties to those of weft knitted structures.

There are, however, production units which concentrate on the knitting of continuous lengths of weft knitted fabric for apparel, upholstery and furnishings and certain industrial end-uses.

Warp knitted fabric is knitted at a constant continuous width although it is possible to knit a large number of narrow width fabrics within a needle bed width usually separating them after finishing. There is considerable potential for changing fabric properties during the finishing process as well as during knitting.

It is also possible to produce length sequences such as scarves with fringed ends, articles produced on double needle bar Raschels based on the tubular knitting principle, and scalloped shaping of net designs by cutting around the outline after finishing.

British Celanese set the trend for the establishment of large vertically-organized warp knitting plants self-sufficient in beaming and dyeing and finishing operations, when during the 1930s they

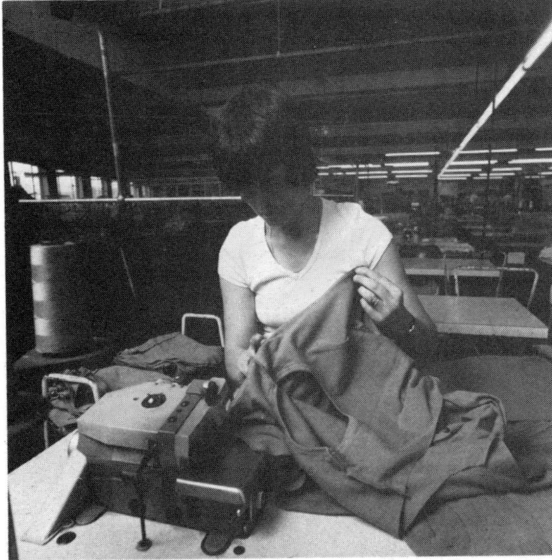

Fig. 6.3. Overlock Seaming (Corah).

Fig. 6.4.

installed large plants with a total of 600 two-guide bar locknit machines in order to convert their acetate and viscose rayon yarn into lingerie, shirting, blouse and dress fabrics. The much later introduction of continuous filament nylon and polyester yarn proved an ideal raw material for high-speed conversion into fine gauge warp knitted fabrics. From the mid 1950s, the patterning potential of multi-guide bar Raschels has been progressively improved based particularly on the conversion of nylon and polyester filament yarns. Thus the lace and curtain net trade taken from warp knitting during the 1820s by twist, bobbinet and Leaver's lace machines has been extensively regained.[1] Warp knitting suffered in the swing of fashion away from continuous filament synthetic yarns towards blended spun yarns in solid fabrics so there has been a tendency for the industry to seek new markets in household furnishings, car upholstery (Fig. 6.5) and industrial cloths.

Fig. 6.5. Warp Knitted Car Upholstery (Karl Mayer).

Staple fibre spun yarns and textured continuous filament yarns create major difficulties for warp knitters. The precise setting of the elements, their fine gauging, the frequent plating of two yarns in a needle hook, and the supply of parallel ends of yarn, necessitate the use of fine and therefore expensive yarns. Problems can be caused by lint accumulation or filamentation and the increased cross-sectional area of these yarns seriously reduces the total length of warp yarn which can be accommodated for a specific warp beam flange diameter, thus increasing handling costs and machine down-time. For example, increasing the warp beam diameter from 21 to 40 inches (53–100 cm) enables the total length of accommodated warp to be quadrupled, but changing the yarn from 30 denier flat nylon to 150 denier textured polyester decreases the total length of accommodated warp ten-fold.

6.3 Productivity

Productivity (P) is expressed in pattern rows per minute. In warp knitting this is the same as courses but in weft knitting more than one course (and therefore feeder) may be required to produce one complete pattern row, i.e. a complete row of needle loops adjacent to each other.

Warp knitting $P = R \times E$, where R is the number of cam-shaft revolutions per minute and E is the machine efficiency.

Weft knitting $P = F \times R$ or $T \times E \div C$, where F is the number of active yarn feed points, R or T the number of machine revolutions or cam-carriage traverses per minute and C the number of courses or colours which comprise one pattern row.

6.4 Machine Design

In warp knitting machines all elements of the same type (needles or sinkers or guides of one guide bar) act as a single unit and are therefore fitted into, and controlled from an element bar. Each guide in the same (conventional) guide bar requires the same warp-yarn feed rate and tension and this is most conveniently achieved by supplying a large number of parallel ends of warp yarn to the guide bar from a warp beam. The shogging movement of the guide bars is most conveniently controlled from one end of the machine. *All these factors tend to restrict warp knitting machines to rectilinear frames and straight needle bars* (Fig. 23.1).

In weft knitting machines there are only a limited number of yarn feed positions often requiring different rates of yarn feed so these are supplied from yarn packages such as cones. As the needles knit in serial formation, the weft knitting machine frame may be arranged with either a circular or a straight needle bed depending upon end-use requirements.

Individual element movement (particularly of latch needles) enables weft knitting machines to produce designs and structures based upon needle selection for loop intermeshing and transfer and this also facilitates the production of garment parts shaped on the knitting machine. Weft knitted loops tend to distort easily under tension and yarn can freely flow from one loop to another under greater tension, a characteristic which aids form fitting and elastic recovery properties (Figs 6.6, 6.7, 6.8). Change of yarn by horizontal striping is another major weft knitting patterning technique.

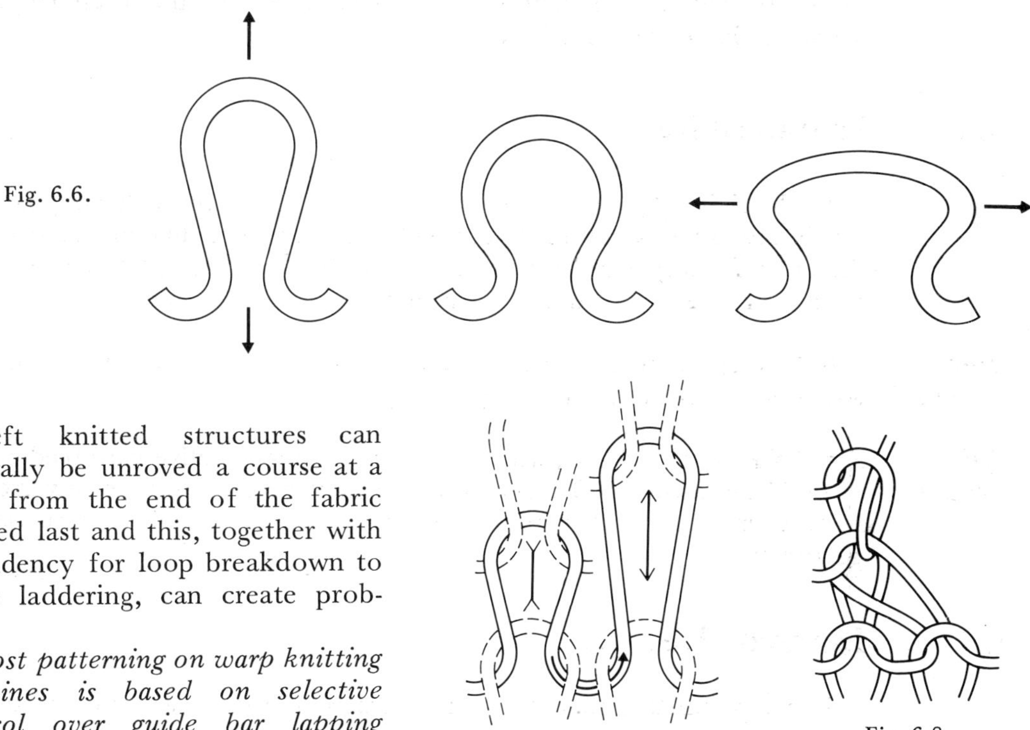

Fig. 6.6.

Fig. 6.7.

Fig. 6.8.

Weft knitted structures can generally be unroved a course at a time from the end of the fabric knitted last and this, together with a tendency for loop breakdown to cause laddering, can create problems.

Most patterning on warp knitting machines is based on selective control over guide bar lapping movements (i.e. the direction and extent of the overlap and underlap movements) *and on the threading* of the individual guides of each guide bar (i.e. with or without warp threads or with different types or colours of yarn). Yarn change by striping is not available on warp threads.

Warp knitted threads tend to have an approximately vertical path through the structure which makes the warp threads less likely to fray or unrove and in the absence of weft threads allows almost any width up to the full knitting width to be achieved. Effects in open work and colour can be obtained without the use of special mechanisms and lapping movements can be arranged to produce fabrics ranging from dimensionally-stable to highly-elastic without necessarily changing the type of yarn.

6.6 Course Length and Run-in Per Rack

In weft knitting, *the term 'course length' refers to the measurement of a straight length of yarn knitted by all or a fraction of the needles in the production of a particular course.* It consists of the stitch length X the number of needles knitting that stitch length. It may be measured at a yarn feed during knitting or after unroving the yarn from a knitted fabric either as a complete course length or from the wales between two vertical cuts in the fabric. In Fig. 6.1, the length of black yarn between X and Y would be the course length.

In warp knitting, run-in per rack is equivalent to course length in weft knitting, and is measured in inches or millimetres. All threads from the same warp are supplied from the same beam-shaft under identical conditions of yarn feed and tension so it is only necessary to measure the length of one representative runner from each warp. *The 'rack' is an internationally recognized unit of 480 courses or knitting cycles.* For fabric weight calculations, the threading arrangement of each bar must also be taken in consideration.

The simplest method of measuring run-in is to divert one thread through two guide eyes so that it runs at right angles to the rest of the warp sheet at that point, it is then marked and after the machine has been run for 480 cam-shaft revolutions, the distance the mark has moved towards the needles is measured. The length of yarn in an average stitch unit can be calculated by dividing the run-in by 480.

In Fig. 6.2, the length of black warp thread between X and Y would be the run-in if the measurement was multiplied by 160, giving a total of 480 courses.

6.7 Fabric Quality

The term fabric quality is sometimes used when referring to wales and courses per inch or centimetre, either in knitted or finished relaxed state. As knitted loops tend to assume a recognizable configuration the results can give an indication of the approximate stitch length and possible machine gauge used in knitting the structure provided the state of relaxation and type of structure is taken into consideration. Generally the higher the figure for a given linear measurement, fabric structure and state of relaxation, the finer the machine gauge and the smaller the stitch length.

6.8 Structural Modifications Commonly Used in Weft and Warp Knitting

Certain techniques are possible during the knitting action which can radically change the physical appearance and properties of a knitted structure. These techniques may be broadly divided into four groups as laying-in, plating, openwork and plush/pile. Although these techniques can be achieved on most knitting machines, slight modifications are often necessary and the more sophisticated versions of these techniques may require specially-designed knitting machines.

Laying-in 6.9

An inlaid fabric consists of a ground structure of knitted (overlapped) threads which hold in position other non-knitted threads which were incorporated (laid in) into the structure during the same knitting cycle. An inlaid yarn is never formed into a knitted loop although in weft knitted single jersey it is necessary to form it into tuck stitches in order to hold it within the structure. When weft knitting with two sets of needles or when overlapping on the front guide bar of a warp knitting machine it is possible to introduce the inlaid yarn into the structure merely by supplying the yarn across the backs of the needles (remote from the hooks) in order to trap it inside the fabric. *Inlaid yarns are trapped inside double needle bed fabrics by the loops or overlaps and towards the back of single needle bed fabrics by the sinker loops or underlaps.*

Dependent upon the fabric construction and the types of yarns employed, laying-in may be used to modify one or more of the following properties of a knitted structure:

stability, elastic stretch and recovery, handle, weight, surface interest and visual appearance (Fig. 13.4).

Laying-in offers the possibility of introducing fancy, unusual, inferior or superior yarns whose physical properties such as thickness (linear density, count), weakness, irregular surface or cross-sectional area, elasticity or lack of elasticity render them difficult for knitting in the normal manner. An inlay yarn may have a yarn count which is 6–8 times heavier than the optimum count for that machine type and gauge under normal knitting conditions.

Laying-in yarn carriers or feeder guides may be of the conventional type or they may be specially designed for their function and type of yarn, the ground yarn is knitted normally as for any structure. *An inlay yarn normally assumes a relatively straight configuration* with hardly any reserve of yarn to distort or flow towards an area of the fabric under tension. It therefore requires less yarn than for knitted loops and tends to confer stability unless an elastomeric yarn is used in which case the elastic stretch and recovery properties of the fabric will be improved.

Weft insertion is a special type of laying-in where the yarn is laid onto special elements which in turn introduce it to the needles at the correct moment during the knitting cycle instead of the yarn guide laying the yarn directly into the needles.

Although the possibility exists for introducing both weft and warp threads into either weft knitted or warp knitted fabrics during knitting, many attempts at this technique have failed to produce viable alternative structures as regards cost, design or end-use properties to effectively compete against woven structures.[2–5]

In warp knitting, laying-in is achieved, even on single needle bar machines, *by omitting the overlap* movement *and* merely *underlapping on the inlay guide bar.* Provided the inlay guide bar is always BEHIND a guide bar which is knitting normally with overlaps, the front guide bar overlaps and underlaps will trap the inlay underlaps into the technical back of the structure. (Fig. 27.1).

In weft knitting on machines with a single needle bed it is not possible to lay-in a yarn by merely traversing a yarn carrier across the backs of the needles because the yarn will not be trapped by the sinker loops of the knitted loops, the inlaid yarn must occasionally pass across the hooks of the needles to form a tuck stitch and thus hold itself into the structure (Fig. 13.3).

6.10 Plating

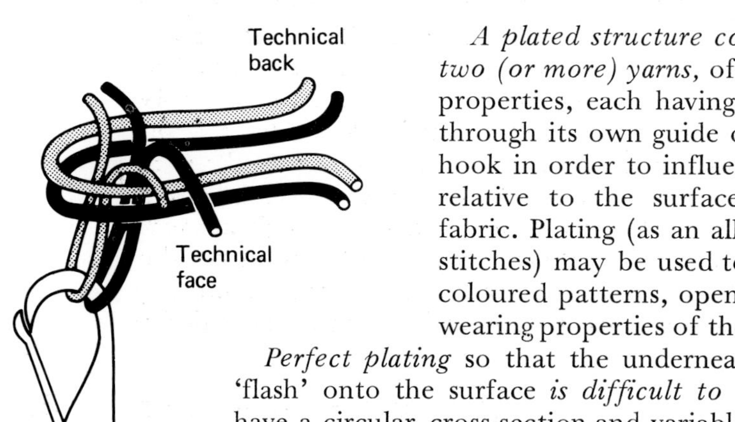

Fig. 6.9.

A plated structure contains loops composed of two (or more) yarns, often with differing physical properties, each having been separately supplied through its own guide or guide hole to the needle hook in order to influence its respective position relative to the surface (technical face) of the fabric. Plating (as an all-over effect or on selected stitches) may be used to produce surface interest, coloured patterns, openwork lace or to modify the wearing properties of the structure.

Perfect plating so that the underneath yarn does not show or 'flash' onto the surface *is difficult to achieve* with yarns which have a circular cross-section and variable properties. It is essential to control yarn tension, angle of feed and the already-formed loops throughout the whole knitting cycle. If the two yarns are of similar count they should be approximately half the normal yarn count for that gauge of machine. As the yarns slide along the underside of a normally-curved needle hook they may roll over each other and thus destroy their plating relationship, for this reason, needles with sharply curving Tansley Plating Angle hooks are often preferred.

The basic rule of plating is that the yarn positioned nearest to the needle head shows on the reverse side of the needle loop and therefore shows on the surface of reverse stitches (Fig. 6.9). The second yarn is in a lower position[6] and tends to show on the face stitches of weft and warp knitted structures (Figs 6.10, 6.11). The second yarn will be prominent on both sides of rib fabrics unless it is tucked (tuck plating) by the second set of

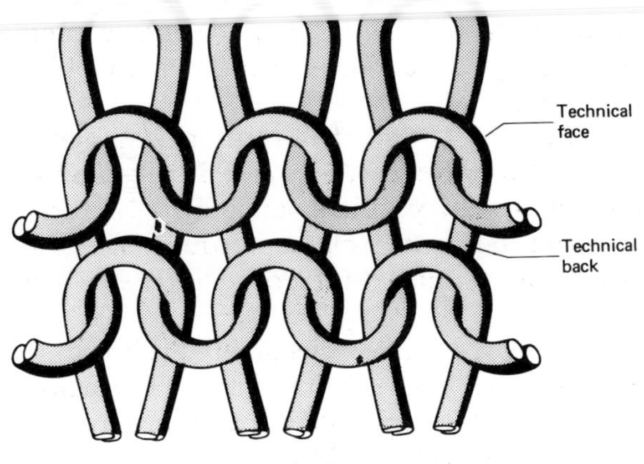

Fig. 6.10.

Fig. 6.11.

needles because the face stitches tend to dominate both sides. In purl fabrics, face stitches will show the second yarn, and reverse stitches the first yarn.

In tricot warp knitting many fabrics are produced where two guide bars simultaneously overlap the same needle in opposite directions and thus produce a plated structure. *The front guide bar threads* strike the needle stems first and at a lower level during the return swing after the overlap, so they *tend to plate on top on the technical face*. This relationship may, however, be upset if the two guide bars overlap in the same direction, as the back guide bar threads then tend to slide over the front bar threads and thus assume a lower position. *Normally the front guide bar threads also show on the technical back* as well as the front because as the underlaps emerge from out of the head of the previous loop they are laid on top of the new overlaps in turn and the front bar underlap is laid down last (Fig. 6.11).

Openwork Structures 6.11

Knitting is noted for its production of openwork as well as close knitted structures. A close structure is one where the stitches provide a uniform cover across the fabric and hold the wales securely together. *An openwork structure* has normal securely-intermeshed loops but it *contains areas where certain adjacent wales are not so tightly joined to each other* by their underlaps or sinker loops as they are to the wales on their other side so that the unbalanced tension causes them to move apart producing apertures at these points. The arrows in Fig. 6.12 indicate the movement of adjacent wales

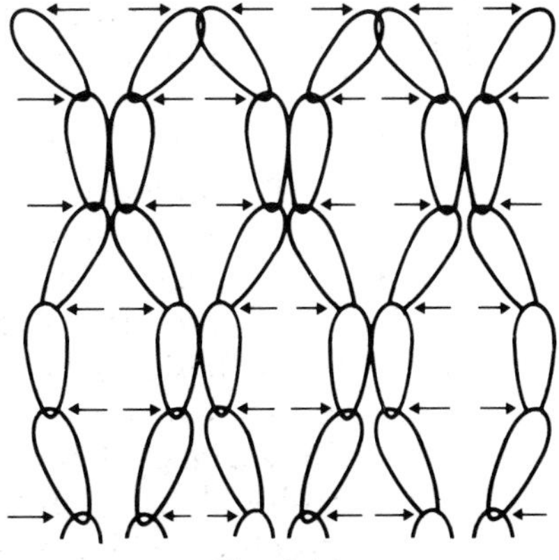

Fig. 6.12.

Fig. 6.13. Bra and Briefs made from elastic Raschel Lace Fabric. Note also the scalloped, elasticated edge trimmings (Dupont 'Lycra').

towards each other at points where they are most securely joined together thus producing an aperture on the other side of each wale.

Semi-transparent structures are produced in a similar manner but instead of having apertures, the yarn crossing between the wales is less than elsewhere and thus provides less cover at these points.

Semi-breakthrough or honeycomb structures have certain yarns which produce an open work effect whilst others produce an all-over close structure so that the aperture is closed on one side of the fabric.

Openwork apertures may be a number of courses in depth and as a result of tension distortion within the structure they may cause adjacent wales to be considerably further apart than the actual distance between two adjacent needles during knitting.

In weft knitting only, openwork structures may be produced by the introduction of empty needles and/or by using special elements to produce loop displacement.

Openwork structures are used for fancy laces and nets for dresswear, underwear (Fig. 6.13), nightwear, lingerie, sportswear, linings, blouses and shirts, drapes and curtaining and industrial fabrics.

6.12 Plush and Pile Constructions

Although the terms plush and pile originally referred to specific woven structures they are often used synonymously today in referring to a very wide range of weft and warp knitted constructions. The essential difference between a plush and pile structure is that the *pile, normally composed of a different type of yarn, should stand out almost at right angles from the knitted ground surface*. Both plush and pile surfaces may consist of either cut or uncut loops of yarn and in the case of high pile, slivers of fibres instead of yarns are used. Generally, the production of and finishing. One or more of the following techniques is normally involved in the production of the two types of fabric: special points or other elements in the knitting machine, excess feeding of the pile yarn and raising or brushing of the pile surface during finishing.

Although a certain amount of double-faced pile fabric is produced, the majority of plush and pile fabric has its surface effect on the technical back of single-faced constructions with the sinker loops or underlaps being used to produce the effect. A variation of this technique is to use a double needle bar machine, pressing off on the second set of needles to produce the pile surface. Yet another method is to employ a double needle bar Raschel machine to knit two separate ground constructions each with its own yarns, one on each needle bar and to supply the pile yarn across between the two needle bars. The pile is later cut to separate the two needle bar ground fabrics and thus produce two separate single-sided cut pile fabrics.

1. Lace making: From craft to computer, *Text. Horizons*, (1982) 2, (2) 30–32.

2. KNAPTON, J., *Making Textiles*, Shirley Institute Seventh International Seminar, (Oct. 1974) page 5 of published papers.
3. LOMBARDI, V. J., Modern variants on the weft knit theme, *Knit. Int.*, (Oct. 1976) 50–5.
4. NIEDERER, K. W., Knit weaving, *Knit. Int.*, (Dec. 1977) 49–50.
5. WHEATLEY, B., Co-We-Nit (Part 3), *Knit. O'wr Times*, (22 July 1968) 45–51.

6. In single-jersey plating, the yarn for the technical back is actually fed at a low angle across the open latches from a hole drilled vertically in the feeder guide, whilst the face yarn is fed at a sharp angle above it into the open hooks from a hole drilled horizontally into the side of the guide. As the latches close, the back yarn is lifted into the hook above the face yarn thus ensuring the correct plating relationship in the fabric.

Further Information

ENGELHARD, O., Warp versus weft knitting, *Hos. Trade Journal*, (Aug. 1967) 92–5.

7

The Four Primary Base Structures

7.1 Introduction

Four primary structures – plain, rib, interlock and purl – are the base structures from which all weft knitted fabrics are derived. Each is composed of a different combination of face and reverse meshed stitches knitted on a particular arrangement of needle beds. Each primary structure may exist alone, in a modified form, with stitches other than normal cleared loops, or in combination with another primary structure in a garment length sequence.

Plain is produced by the needles knitting as a single set, drawing the loops away from the technical back and towards the technical face side of the fabric.

Rib requires two sets of needles operating in between each other so that wales of face stitches and wales of reverse stitches are knitted on each side of the fabric.

Interlock was originally derived from rib but *requires a special arrangement of needles knitting back-to-back* in an alternate sequence of two sets so that the two courses of loops show wales of face loops on each side of the fabric exactly in line with each other thus hiding the appearance of the reverse loops.

Purl is the only structure having certain wales containing both face and reverse meshed loops. Although normally knitted on machines employing double-ended latch needles, some V-bed flat machines with rib loop transfer and racking facilities can knit structures of this type.

Single-jersey machines can only produce one type of base structure. Rib machines, particularly of the garment producing type, can often produce sequences of plain knitting. Interlock machines can sometimes be changed to rib knitting, whilst purl machines are capable of producing rib or plain knitting sequences during the production of a garment or other knitted article.

7.2 Plain

Plain (the stocking stitch of hand knitting) is the base structure of ladies' hosiery, fully fashioned knitwear and single-jersey fabrics. Its use in ladies' suitings was popularized by Lily Langtry (1852–1929) known as

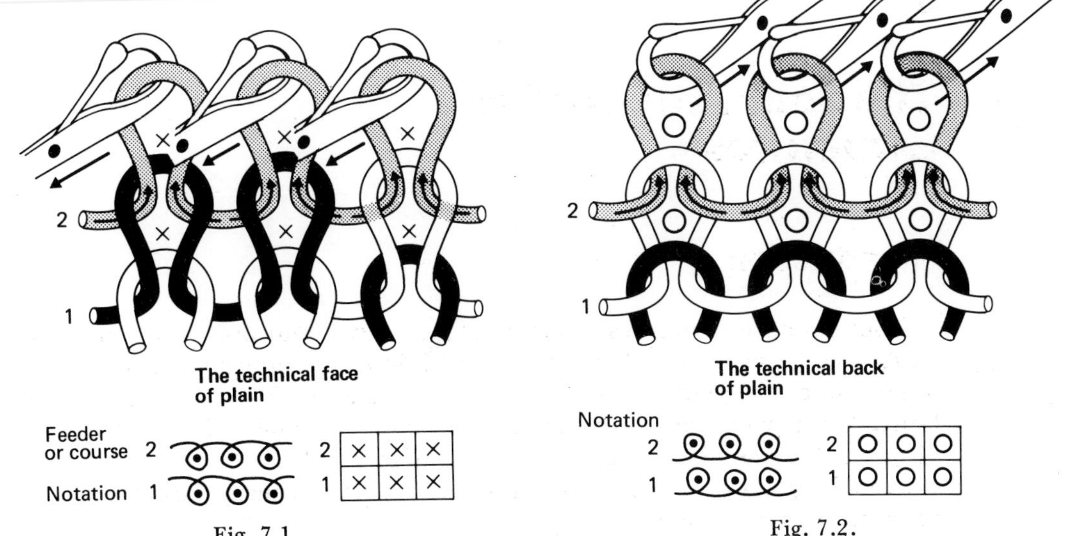

Fig. 7.1.

Fig. 7.2.

the 'Jersey Lily' after her island birthplace. Other names for plain include stockinette whilst in the U.S.A. the term 'shaker stitch' is applied to it when knitted in a coarse gauge of about 3½ needles per inch (25 mm).

Its *technical face* (Fig. 7.1) is smooth, with the side limbs of the needle loops *having the appearance of columns of Vs* in the wales, these are useful as design units when knitting with different coloured yarns. On the *technical back*, the heads of the needle loops and the bases of the sinker loops form *columns of interlocking semi-circles* (Fig. 7.2) whose appearance is sometimes emphasized by knitting alternate courses in different coloured yarns.

Plain can be unroved from the course knitted last by pulling the needle loops through from the technical back or from the course knitted first, by pulling the sinker loops through from the technical face side. Similarly, *if the yarn breaks, needle loops successively unmesh down a wale and sinker loops unmesh up a wale*, this structural breakdown is termed *laddering* after 'Jacob's Ladder!'[1] It is particularly prevalent in ladies' hosiery where loops of fine smooth filaments are in a tensioned state, to reduce this tendency certain ladder-resist structures have been devised. The tendency of the cut edges of plain fabric to unrove and fray when not in tubular or flat selvedged form can be overcome by securing them during seaming.

Knitted structures have a three-dimensional structure as shown in Fig. 7.3. At the point where the new needle loop is drawn through the old loop (I) the structure is composed of two yarn thicknesses (diameters) instead of one. The needle loop is therefore held down both at its head (H) and its feet (F) by loops in the same wale but its side limbs tend to curve upwards at (II). When the fabric is cut the loops are no longer held in this configuration so that *the fabric curls towards the face at the top*

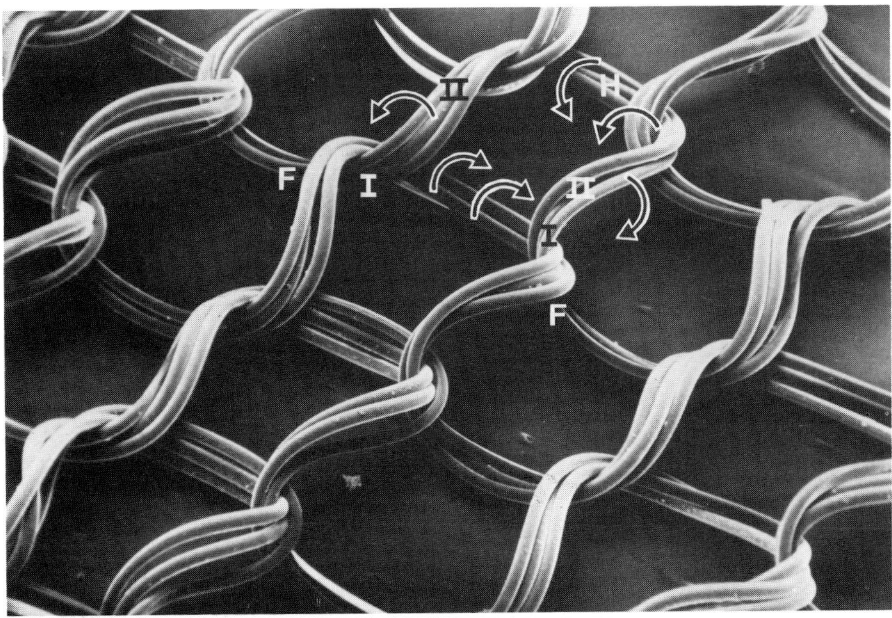

Fig. 7.3. The technical face of a plain knit hosiery fabric (Milliken AGILON) magnified X 130 by a stereoscan electron microscope. The arrows indicate the direction in which the fabric will tend to curl if it is cut. (By permission of *Knit. Times*, official publication of NKSA USA.)

and bottom and towards the back at the sides. The same configuration causes face meshed wales of loops to be prominent in rib fabrics and the heads of loops and the sinker loops to be prominent in wales of purl stitches.

Plain is the simplest and most economical weft knitted structure to produce and has the maximum covering power. It normally has a potential recovery of 40 per cent in width after stretching.

7.3 Production of Single-Jersey Fabric on a Circular Latch Needle Machine

Most single-jersey fabric is produced on circular machines whose latch needle cylinder and sinker ring revolve through the stationary knitting cam systems, which together with their yarn feeders are situated at regular intervals around the circumference of the cylinder. The yarn is supplied from cones, placed either on an integral overhead bobbin stand or on a free-standing creel, through tensioners, stop motions and guide eyes down to the yarn feeder guides. The fabric, in tube form, is drawn downwards from inside the needle cylinder by tension rollers and is wound onto the fabric batching roller of the winding down frame. The winding down mechanism revolves in unison with the cylinder and fabric tube and is rack-lever operated via cam-followers running on the underside of a circle, the centre of the cylinder is open and the machine is referred to as *an open top or sinker top machine.*

Compared with a rib machine, a plain machine is simpler and more economical with a potential of more feeders, higher running speeds and the possibility of knitting a wider range of yarn counts. The most popular diameter is 26 inches giving an approximate finished fabric width of 60–70 inches. An approximately suitable count may be obtained using the formula $Nc = G^2/18$ or $Nw = G^2/15$, where Nc = cotton spun count, Nw = worsted spun count, G = gauge in npi. For fine gauges a heavier and stronger count may be necessary.

The Knitting Head 7.4

Figure 7.4 shows a cross section of the knitting head all of whose stationary parts are shaded.

1. Yarn feeder guide which is associated with its own set of knitting cams.
2. Latch needle.
3. Holding-down sinker, one between every needle space.
4. Needle cylinder (in this example, revolving clockwise).
5. Cylinder driving wheel.
6. Cylinder driving gear.
7. Sinker-operating cams which form a raised track operating in the recess of the sinker.
8. Sinker cam-cap.
9. Sinker trick ring which is simply and directly attached to the outside top of the needle cylinder thus causing the sinkers to revolve in unison with the needles.
10. Needle retaining spring.
11. Needle-operating cams which, like the sinker cams are stationary.
12. Cam-box.
13. Cam-plate.
14. Head plate.
15. Cylinder driving pinion attached to the main drive shaft.

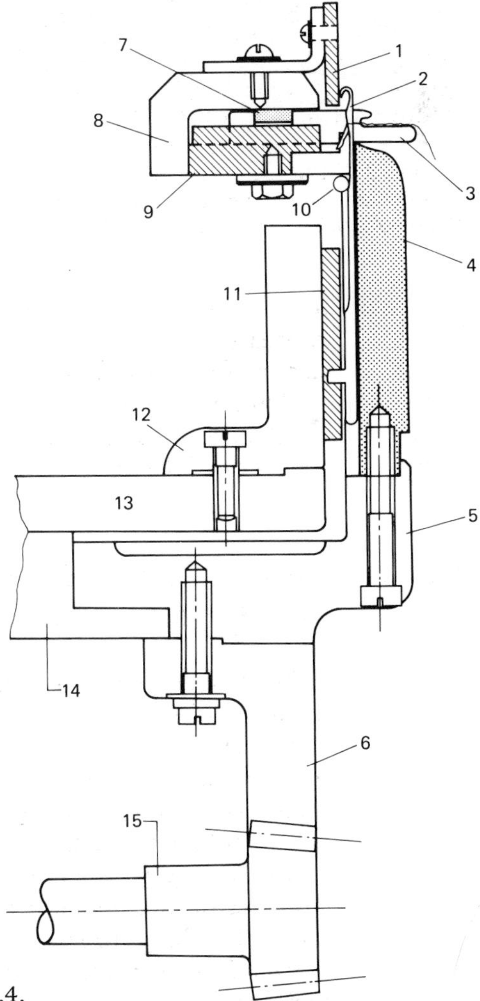

Fig. 7.4.

7.5 The Knitting Action

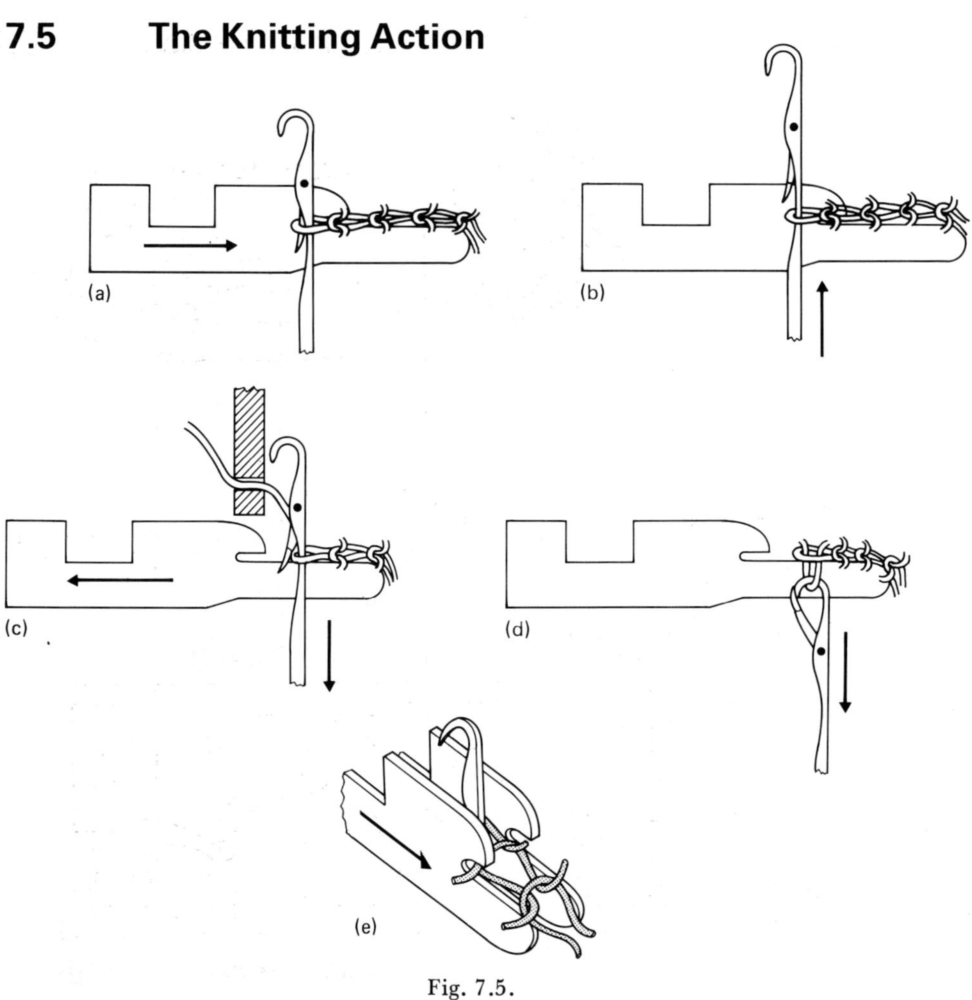

Fig. 7.5.

Figure 7.5 (A–E) shows the knitting action of a latch needle and holding-down sinker during the production of a course of plain fabric.

A. *Tucking in the hook or rest position.* The sinker is forward, holding down the old loop whilst the needle rises from the rest position.
B. *Clearing.* The needle has been raised to its highest position clearing the old loop from its latch.
C. *Yarn feeding.* The sinker is partially withdrawn allowing the feeder to present its yarn to the descending needle hook and also freeing the old loop so that it can slide up the needle stem and under the open latch spoon.
D. *Knock-over.* The sinker is fully withdrawn whilst the needle descends to knock-over its old loop on the sinker belly.
E. *Holding-down.* The sinker moves forward to hold down the new loop in its throat whilst the needle rises under the influence of the upthrow cam to the rest position where the head of the open hook just protrudes above the sinker belly.

The Cam System 7.6

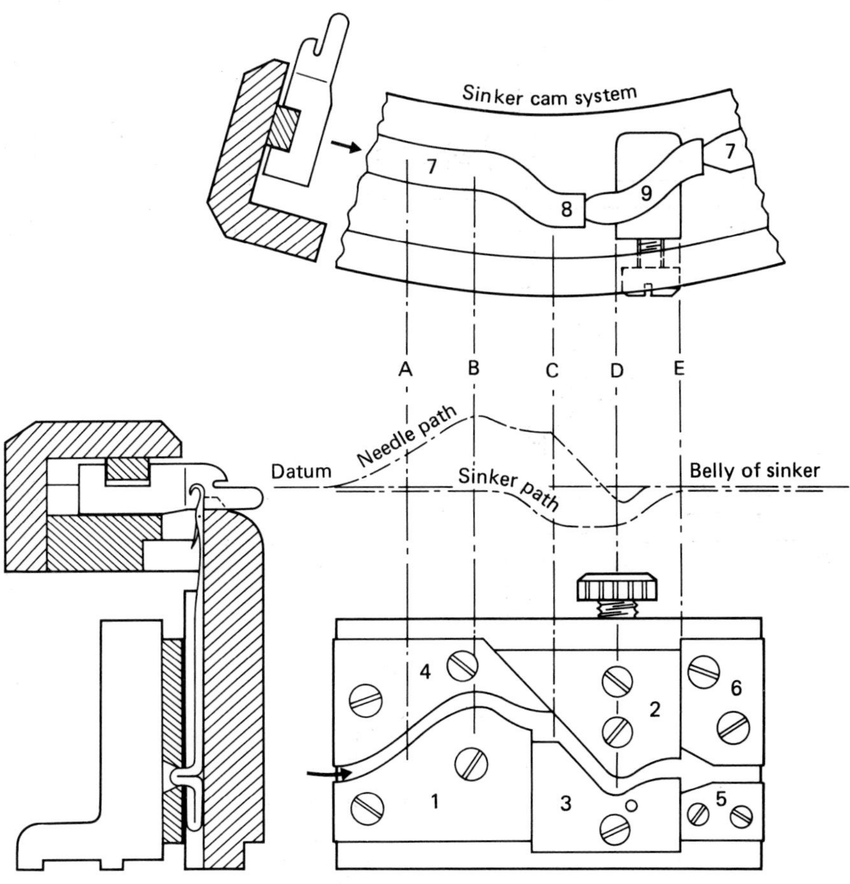

Fig. 7.6.

Figure 7.6 shows the arrangement and relationship between the needle and sinker cams as the elements pass through in a left to right direction with the letters indicating the positions of the elements at the various points in the knitting cycle. The needle cam race consists of the following, the clearing cam (1) and its guard cam (4), stitch cam (2) and upthrow cam (3) which are vertically adjustable together for alteration of stitch length, return cam (5) and its guard cam (6).

The three sections of the sinker cam race are the race cam (7), the sinker-withdrawing cam (8) and the sinker-return cam (9) which is adjustable in accordance with the stitch length.

Sinker Timing 7.7

The most forward position of the sinker during the knitting cycle is known as the push point and *its relationship to the needles is known as the sinker timing.* If the sinker cam-ring is adjusted so that the sinkers are advanced to the point where they rob yarn from the new stitches being formed, a lighter-weight fabric with oversized sinker loops and smaller needle loops is produced. If the ring is moved in the opposite direction a tighter, heavier fabric is produced having smaller sinker loops and larger needle loops. The timing is normally set between these two extremes.

7.8 Rib Fabric

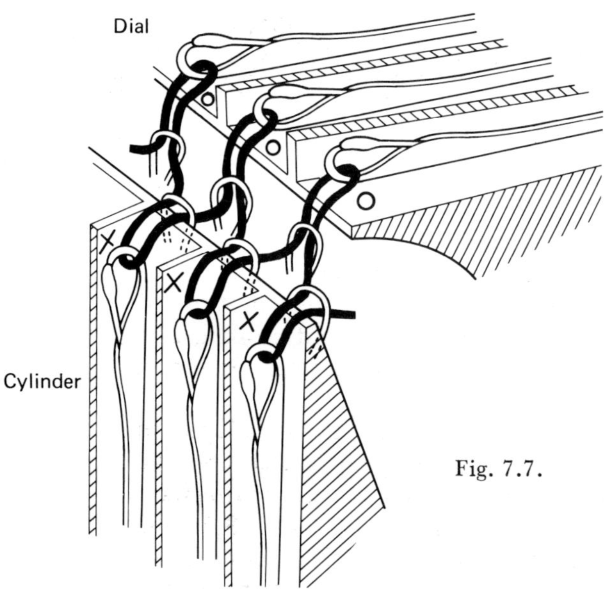

Fig. 7.7.

The simplest rib fabric is 1 X 1 rib. The first rib frame was invented by Jedediah Strutt of Derby in 1755 who used a second set of needles to pick up and knit the sinker loops of the first set. It is now normally knitted with two sets of latch needles (Figs 7.7, 7.8).

Rib has a vertical cord appearance because the face loop wales tend to move over and in front of the reverse loop wales. As the face loops show a reverse loop intermeshing on the other side, 1 X 1 rib has the appearance of the technical face of plain fabric on both sides until stretched to reveal the reverse loop wales in between.

1 X 1 rib is produced by two sets of needles being alternately set or gated between each other. *Relaxed 1 X 1 rib is theoretically twice as thick and half the width of an equivalent plain fabric, but it has twice as much width-wise recoverable stretch.* In practice 1 X 1 rib normally relaxes by approximately 30 per cent compared with its knitting width.

1 X 1 rib is balanced by alternate wales of face loops in each side, it therefore lies flat without curl when cut. It is a more expensive fabric to produce than plain and is a heavier structure, the rib machine also requires a finer yarn than a similar gauge plain machine. Like all weft-knitted fabrics it can be unroved from the end knitted last by drawing the free loop heads through to the back of each stitch and *it can be distinguished from plain by the fact that the loops of certain wales are withdrawn in one direction and those of others in the opposite direction*, whereas the loops of plain are always withdrawn in the same direction from the technical face to the technical back.

Rib cannot be unroved from the end knitted first because the sinker loops are securely anchored by the cross-meshing between face and

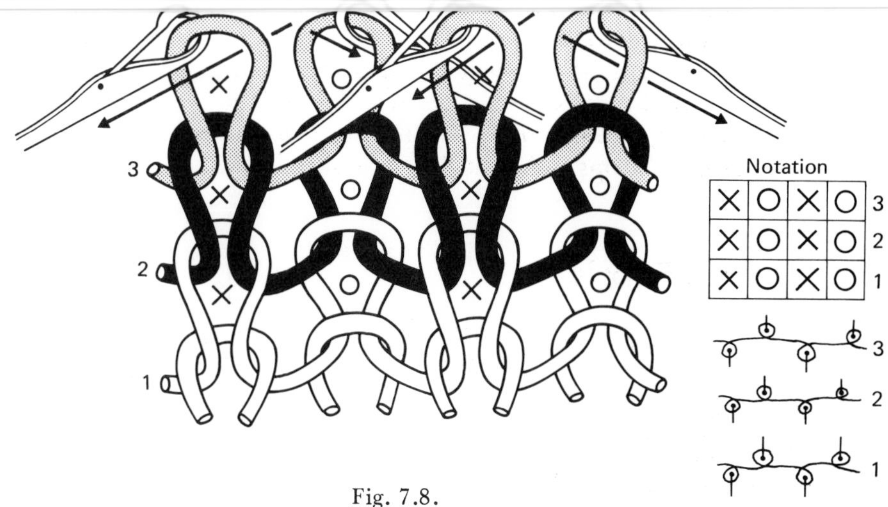

Fig. 7.8.

reverse loop wales, this characteristic, together with its elasticity, makes rib particularly suitable for the extremities of articles such as tops of socks, the cuffs of sleeves, rib borders for garments, and stolling and strapping for cardigans. Rib structures are elastic, form-fitting, and retain warmth better than plain structures.

There are a range of rib set-outs apart from 1 X 1 rib, the first figure in the designation indicates the number of adjacent plain wales and the second figure, the number of adjacent rib wales. Single or simple ribs have more than one plain wale but only one rib wale such as 2/1, 3/1, etc. Broad ribs have a number of adjacent rib as well as plain wales, for example 6/3 Derby Rib (Fig. 7.9). Adjacent wales of the same type are produced by adjacent needles in the same bed without needles from the other bed knitting in between them at that point.

The standard procedure for rib set-outs is to take out of action in one bed, one less needle than the number of adjacent needles required to be working in the other bed (Fig. 7.9). In the case of purl machines, the needles knit either in one bed or the other, so there are theoretically the same number of needles out of action in the opposite bed as are knitting in the other. In the case of 2/2 rib (Fig. 7.9), Swiss rib is produced on a rib machine by taking one needle out of action opposite the two needles knitting. English rib is produced on a purl maching (or rib machine) with two empty tricks opposite to the two needles knitting, the latter type of rib is considered to be less elastic. Swiss rib is sometimes confusingly termed 2/3 rib because 2 out of 3 needles in each bed are knitting. It is not possible to commence knitting on empty needles with the normal 2 X 2 arrangement because the two needles in each bed will not form individual loops, they will make one loop across the two hooks. One needle bed must be racked by one needle space so that the 2 X 2 needle set-out is arranged for 1 X 1 rib, this is termed 'skeleton 1 X 1', after

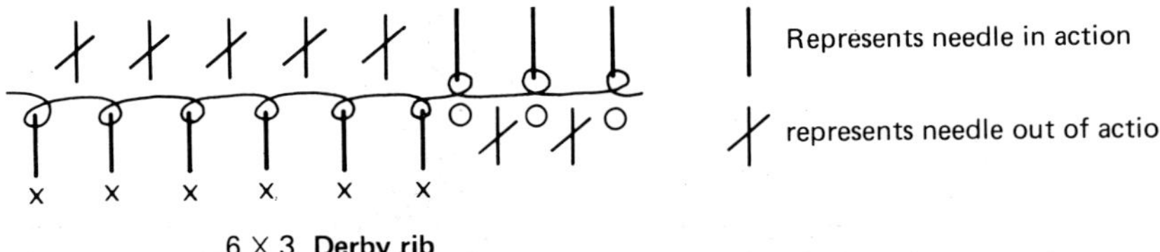

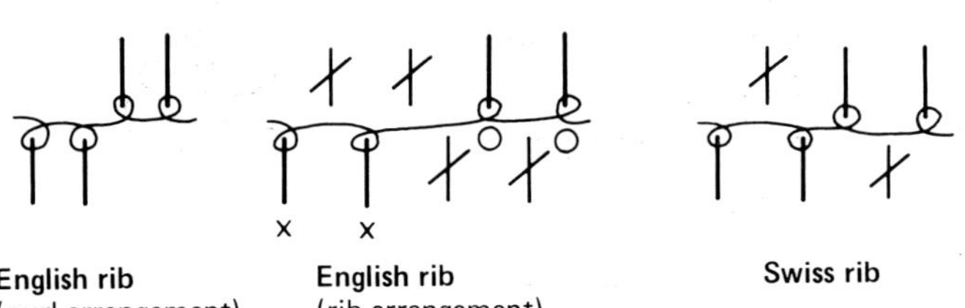

Skeleton 1×1 rib

Fig. 7.9.

knitting the set-up course, the bed is racked back so that 2 × 2 rib knitting can commence.

Tubular cover courses

A direct change of knitting from 2 × 2 to 1 × 1 rib brings every third needle into action, but at the first course the limbs of the loops produced on those needles open out producing apertures between every two wales which spoil the appearance of the structure. This problem is overcome by knitting a tubular course of single jersey on all needles in one bed then on all needles in the other bed. On each side the sinker loops draw the wales together and prevent the loops on the newly introduced needles from forcing the wales apart.

7.9 Knitting Action of a Circular Rib Machine

The knitting action of a circular rib machine is shown in Fig. 7.10.

A. *Clearing*. The cylinder and dial needles move out to clear the plain and rib loops formed in the previous cycle.
B. *Yarn Feeding*. The needles are withdrawn into their tricks so that the old loops are covered by the open latches and the new yarn is fed into the open hooks.
C. *Knocking-over*. The needles are withdrawn into their tricks so that the old loops are cast off and the new loops are drawn through them.

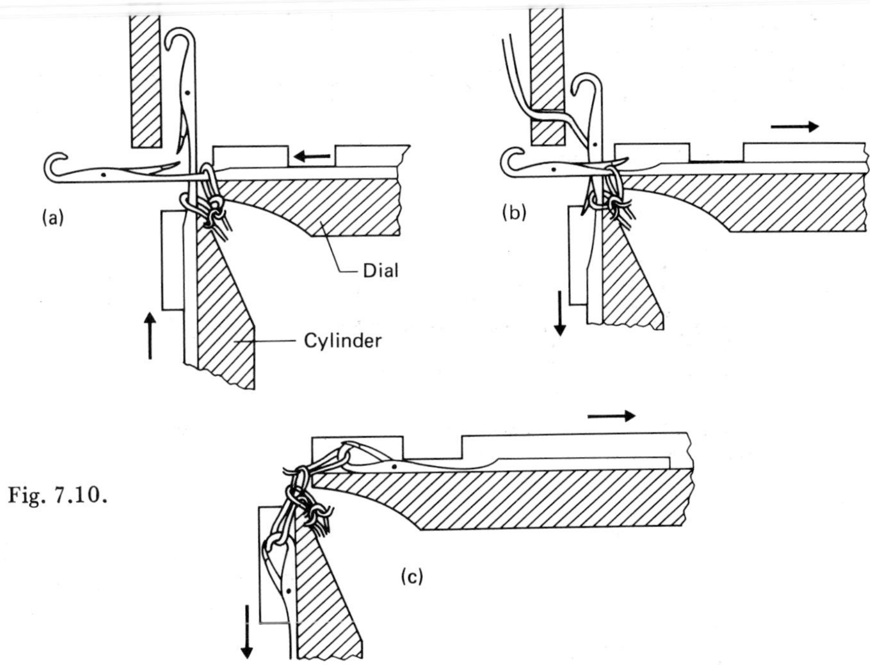

Fig. 7.10.

In a gauge range from 5 to 20 npi an approximately suitable count may be obtained using the formula $Nc = G^2/8.4$, where Nc = cotton count and G = npi. For underwear fabric a popular gauge is 14 with a count of 1/30's.

Needle Timing 7.10

Needle timing is the relationship between the loop-forming positions of the dial and cylinder needles measured as a distance in needles between the two stitch cam knock-over points. Collective timing adjustment is achieved by moving the dial cam-plate clockwise or anti-clockwise relative to the cylinder, individual adjustment at particular feeders as required is obtained by moving or exchanging the stitch cam profile (Fig. 7.11).

Synchronized timing also known as point, jacquard and 2 X 2 timing, *is* the term used *when the two positions coincide* with the yarn being pulled in an alternating manner in two directions by the needles thus creating a high tension during loop formation (Fig. 7.12).

With delayed, rib (Fig. 7.13), or interlock timing the dial knock-over occurs after about four cylinder needles have drawn loops and are rising slightly to relieve the strain. The dial loops are thus composed of the extended loops drawn over the dial needle stems during cylinder knock-over, plus a little yarn robbed from the cylinder loops. The dial loops are thus larger than the cylinder loops and the fabric is tighter and has better rigidity, it is also heavier and wider and less strain is produced on the yarn.

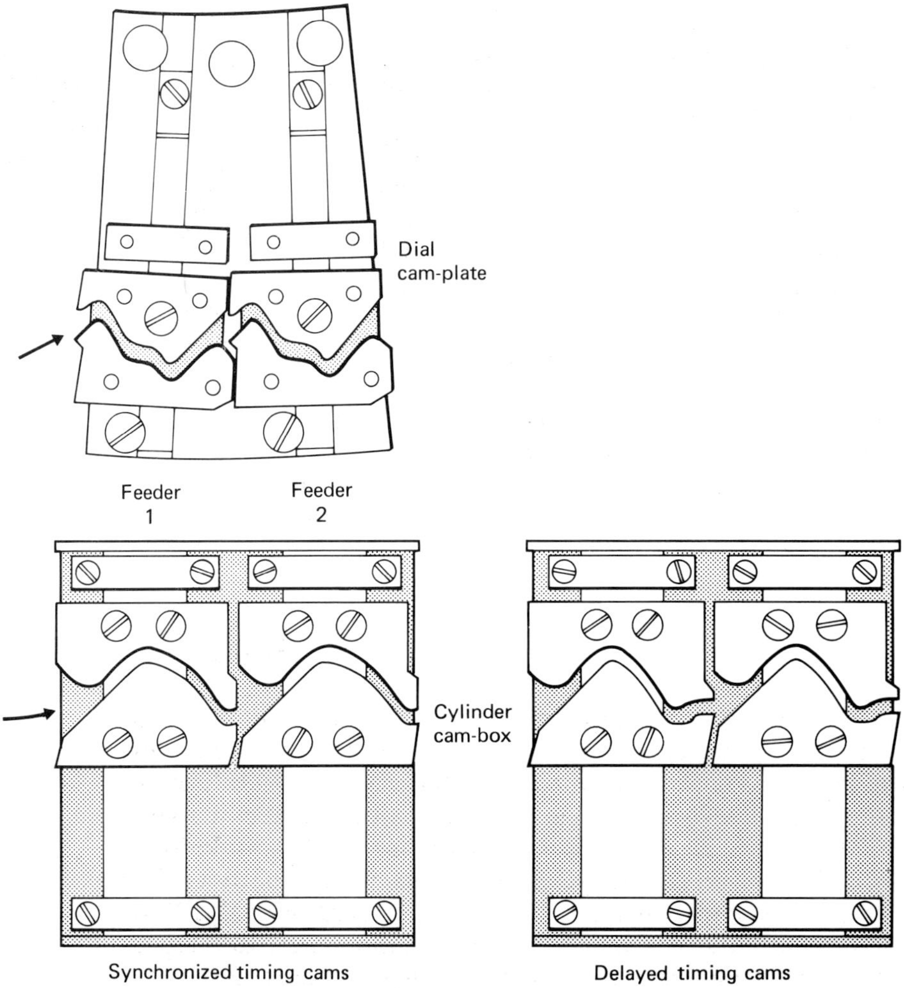

Dial cam-plate

Feeder 1

Feeder 2

Cylinder cam-box

Synchronized timing cams

Delayed timing cams

Fig. 7.11.

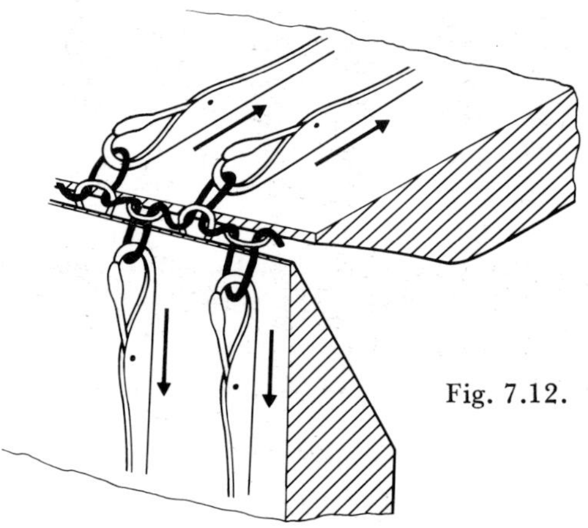

Fig. 7.12.

Rib jacquard or broad ribs cannot be produced in delayed timing because there will not always be cylinder needles knitting either side of the dial needles from which to draw yarn. Although the dial knock-over is delayed, it is actually achieved by advancing the timing of the cylinder knock-over (Fig. 7.11).

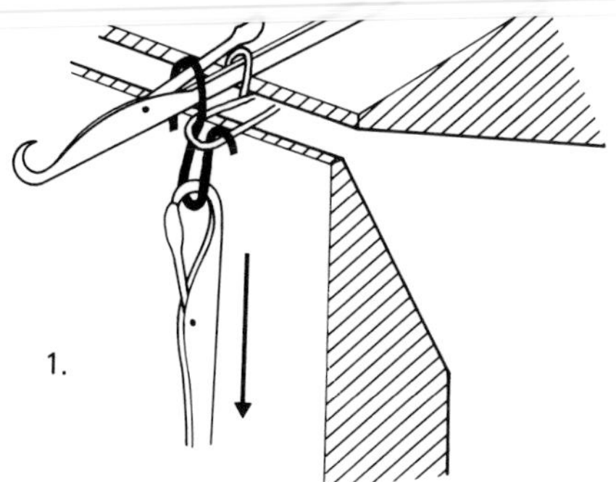

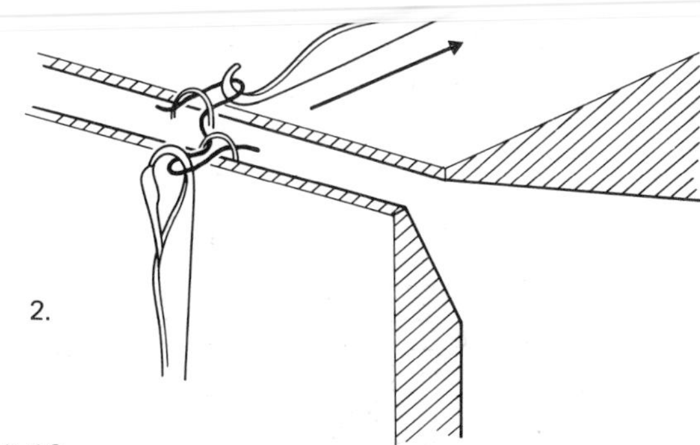

Fig. 7.13.

Advanced timing is the reverse of delayed timing in that the cylinder loops rob from the dial producing tighter dial loops, advancement can only be about one needle, this type of timing is sometimes used in the production of figured ripple double jersey fabrics where selected cylinder needles can rob from the all knitting dial needles.[2]

Interlock 7.11

Although the American Scott and Williams Patent for interlock of 1908 was extended for 20 years, underwear manufacturers found the needles expensive, especially on the larger 20 inch diameter model, suitable hosiery twist cotton yarn only became available in 1925, and the first stationary cam-box machine appeared in 1930. Originally interlock was knitted almost solely in cotton on 20 gauge (needles per inch) machines for underwear, a typical weight being 5 ozs per square yard using 1/40's S cotton, but from the 1950s onwards 18 gauge machines were developed for knitting double jersey for semi-tailored suitings because the open width fabric could be finished on existing equipment. As the machines became more versatile in their capabilities, the range of structures became greater.

Interlock has the technical face of plain fabric on both sides but its smooth surface cannot be stretched out to reveal the reverse meshed loop wales because the wales on each side are exactly opposite to each other and are locked together (Fig. 7.14). Each interlock pattern row (often termed an 'interlock course') requires two feeder courses each with a separate yarn which

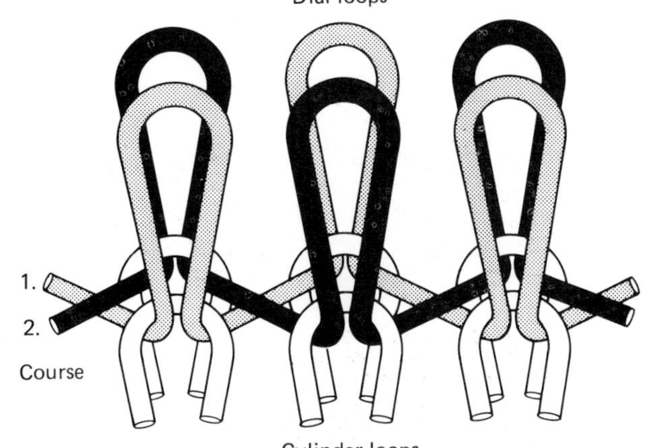

Fig. 7.14.

knits on separate alternate needles producing two half-gauge 1 × 1 rib courses whose sinker loops cross over each other, thus odd feeders will produce alternate wales of loops on each side and even feeders will produce the other wales.

Interlock relaxes by about 30–40 per cent or more compared with its knitted width so that a 30-inch diameter machine will produce a tube at 94-inch open width which finishes at 60–66 inches wide. It is a balanced, smooth stable structure, which lies flat without curl. Like 1 × 1 rib, it will not unrove from the end knitted first but it is thicker, heavier and narrower than rib of equivalent gauge, and requires a finer, better, more expensive yarn.

As only alternate needles knit at a feeder, interlock machines can be produced in finer gauges, with less danger of press-offs than rib. Interlock knitting is, however, more of a problem than rib knitting because productivity is half, less feeders can be accommodated, and there are finer tolerances. When two different-coloured yarns are used, horizontal stripes are produced if the same colour is knitted at two consecutive feeders and vertical stripes if odd feeders knit one colour and even feeders knit the other colour. The number of interlock pattern rows per inch is often double the machine gauge in needles per inch.

The interlock structure is the only weft knitted base *not normally used for individual needle selection* designs because of the problems of cylinder and dial needle collision. However, selection has in the past been achieved by using four-feeder courses for each pattern row of interlock. Long and short cylinder needles not selected at the first two-feeder courses for colour A being selected at the second two feeders for colour B.

Eightlock is a 2 × 2 version of interlock which may be produced using an arrangement of two long and two short needles, provided the tricks are fully cut through to accommodate them and knock-over bits are fitted to the verges to assist with loop formation on adjacent needles in the same bed. It was first produced on double-system V-bed flat machines having needles with two butt positions each having its own cam system, giving a total of eight locks, four for each needle bed and making one complete row per traverse, 4 × 4 and 3 × 3 arrangements can also be produced. It is a well-balanced, uniform structure with a softer, fuller, handle and greater width-wise relaxation and more elasticity than interlock. Simple geometric designs with a four wale wide repeat composed of every two loops of identical colour, can be achieved with careful arrangement of yarns.

7.12 Production of Interlock Fabric

Interlock is produced mainly on special cylinder and dial circular machines and on some double-system V-bed flat machines (Fig. 7.15). An interlock machine must fulfil the following requirements:

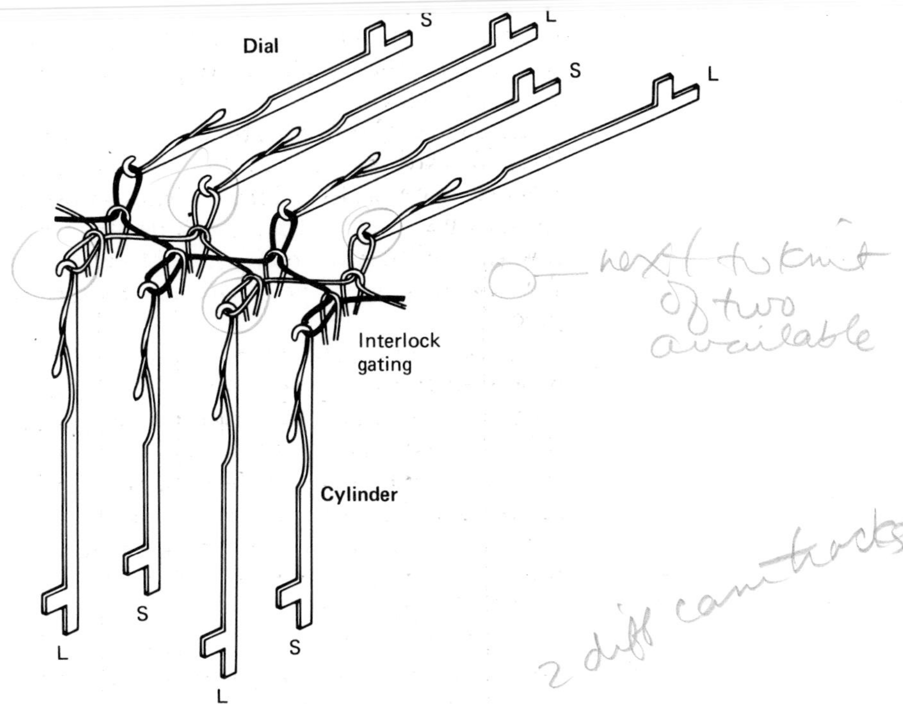

Fig. 7.15.

1. Interlock gating, the needles in two beds must be exactly opposite to each other so only one of the two can knit at any feeder.
2. Two separate cam systems in each bed, each controlling half the needles in an alternate sequence, one cam system controls knitting at one feeder and the other at the next feeder.
3. The needles are set out alternately, one controlled from one cam system the next from the other, diagonal and not opposite needles in each bed knit together.

The conventional interlock machine has needles of two different lengths, *long needles knit in one cam-track and short needles knit in a track nearer to the needle heads*. Long needle cams are arranged for knitting at the first feeder and short needle cams at the second feeder. The needles are set out alternately in each bed with long needles opposite to short needles. At the first feeder long needles in cylinder and dial knit, and at the second feeder short needles knit together, needles not knitting at a feeder follow a run-through track.

Example of Interlock Cam System 7.13

Figure 7.16 shows the necessary cylinder and dial needle camming to produce one course of ordinary interlock fabric which is actually the work of two knitting feeders. In this example the dial has a swing tuck cam

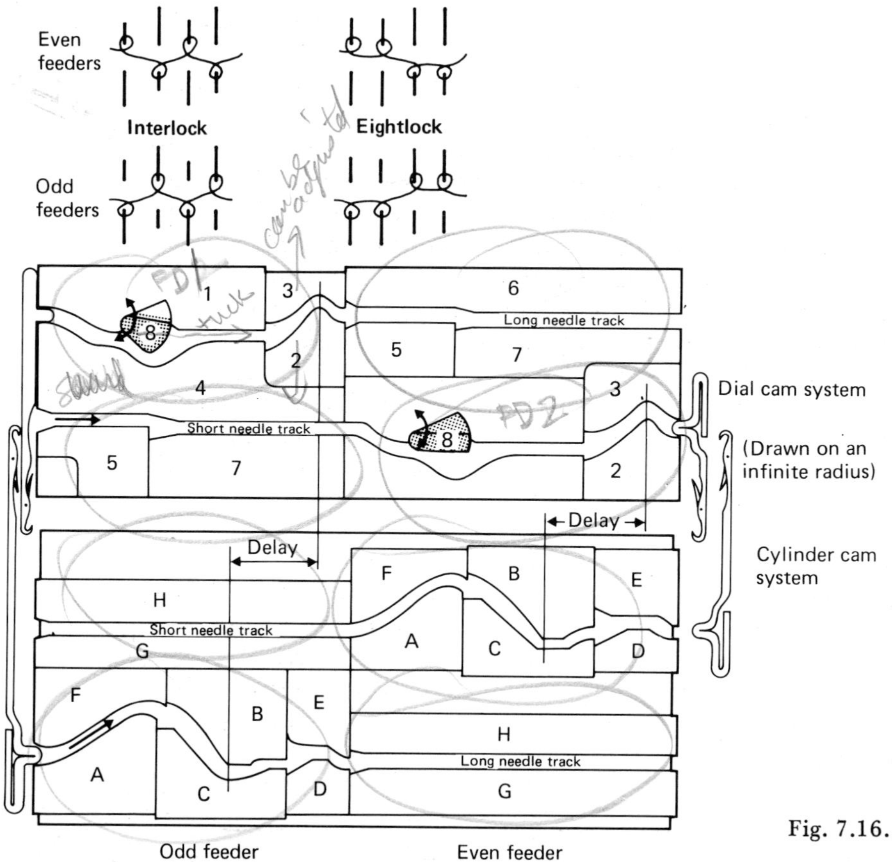

Fig. 7.16.

which will produce tucking if swung out of the cam-track and knitting if in action.

Cylinder cam system

A. Is a clearing cam which lifts the needle to clear the old loop.
B, C. Are the stitch and guard cams respectively and are vertically adjustable for varying stitch length.
D. Upthrow cam, to raise cylinder needle whilst dial needle knocks over.
E, F. Guard cams, to complete the track.
G, H. Provide the track for the idling needles.

Dial cam system

1. Raising cam to the tuck position only.
2, 3. Dial knock-over cams (adjustable).
4. Guard cam to complete the track.
5. Auxiliary knock-over cam to prevent the dial needle re-entering old loop.
6, 7. Provide the track for the idling needles.
8. Swing type clearing cam, which may occupy the knitting position as shown at feeder 1 or the tuck position as shown at feeder 2.

Interlock thus requires eight cam systems or locks in order to produce one complete course, two cam systems for each feeder in each needle bed. Basic cylinder and dial machines and flat-machines having this arrangement are often referred to as eight-lock machines.

Purl was originally spelt 'pearl' and was so named because of the similar appearance to pearl droplets.

Purl structures have one or more wales which contain both face and reverse loops which can only be achieved with double-ended latch needles or by rib loop transfer. The semi-circles of the needle and sinker loops produced by the reverse loop intermeshing tend to be prominent on both sides of the structure and this has led to the term *'links-links'* being generally applied to purl fabrics and machines. *Links* is the *German word for left* and *it indicates that there are left or reverse loops visible on both sides.*[3] In a similar manner the German term for rib is rechts-rechts.

The tricks of the two needle beds in purl machines *are exactly opposite to each other and in the same plane* so that the single set of purl needles, each of which has a hook at either end, can be transferred across to knit outwards from either bed (Fig. 7.17). Knitting outwards from one bed, the needle will produce a face meshed needle loop with the newly-fed yarn whilst the same needle knitting outwards with its other hook from the opposite bed will produce a reverse meshed needle loop (Fig. 7.18). As the needle moves across between the two needle beds, the old loop slides off the latch of the hook which produced it and moves along the needle towards the other hook which it cannot enter because it will pivot the latch closed (an action which must not occur until the new yarn has been fed to this hook).

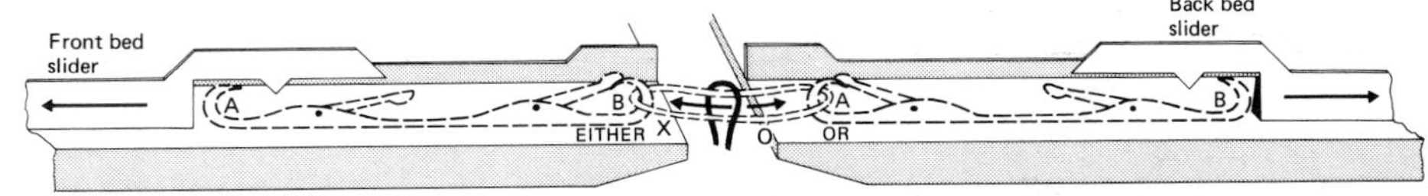

Fig. 7.17.

(NB The same needle has been drawn twice to show its two possible knitting bed positions)

The needle hook which protrudes from the bed knits with the yarn, whilst *the hook in the needle trick acts as a butt and is controlled by an element termed a slider* (Fig. 7.19). There is a complete set of sliders with their noses facing outwards from each bed. It is the sliders whose butts are controlled by the knitting and needle transfer cam systems in each bed and they in turn control the needles. For this purpose, each slider is normally provided

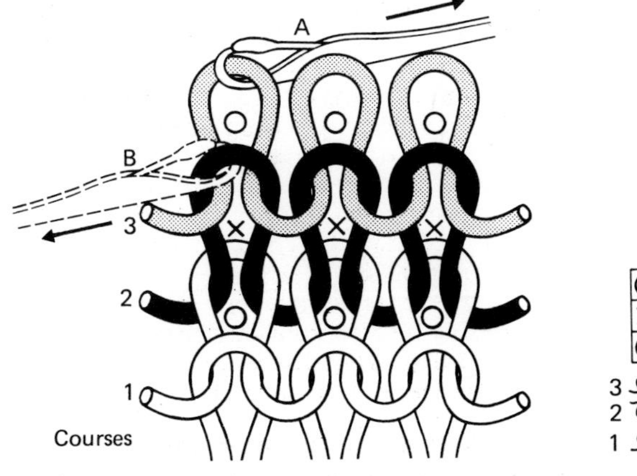

Fig. 7.18.

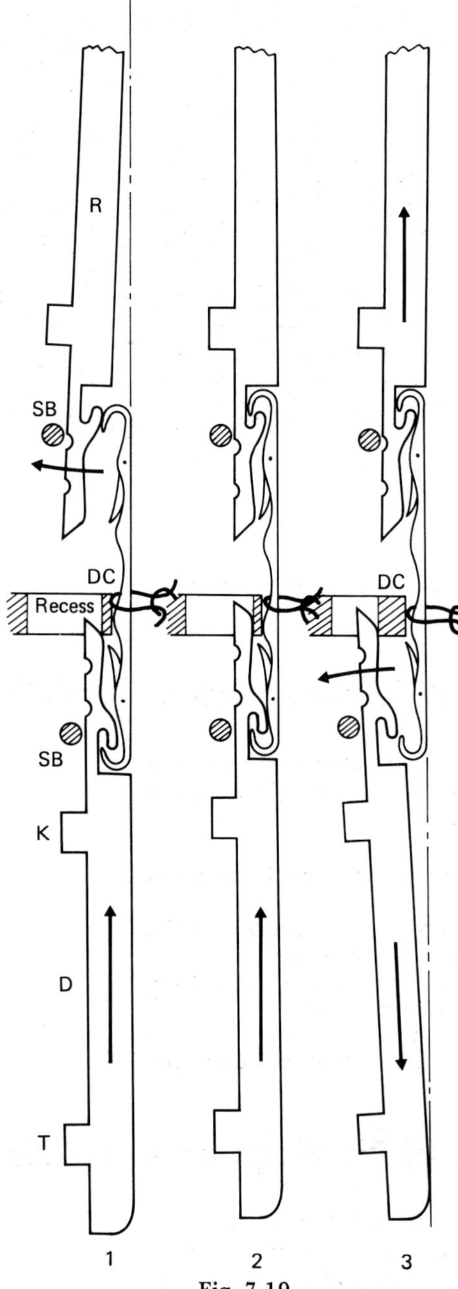

Fig. 7.19.

2	O	X
1	X	O

Fig. 7.20.

with two butts, a *knitting butt* (K) near to its head and the needles-hook, and a *transfer butt* (T) near to its tail; each has its own cam system and track.

There are two types of purl needle bed machine, flat purls, which have two horizontally-opposed needle beds and circular purls, which have two superimposed cylinders one above the other, both types of machine are capable of producing garment length or other article sequences.

V-bed rib machines will knit purl stitch designs if rib loops are transferred across to empty needles in the opposing bed which then commence to knit in the same wale.

The simplest purl is 1 × 1 *purl* which is the garter stitch of hand knitters and *consists of alternate courses of all face and all reverse loops* and is produced by the needles knitting in one bed and then transferring over to the other bed to knit the next course (Fig. 7.18). Its lateral stretch is equal to plain, but its length-wise elasticity is almost double. When relaxed the face loop courses cover the reverse loop courses making it twice as thick as plain. It can be unroved from both ends because the free sinker loops can be pulled through at the bottom of the fabric. In America 1 × 1 purl is sometimes made up at right angles to the knitting sequence and is then termed Alpaca stitch.

Another simple purl is moss stitch which consists of face and reverse loops in alternate courses and wales (Fig. 7.20). Basket purls consist of rectangular areas of all X or all O loops which alternate with each other, examples include 5 × 3 (Fig. 7.21), 7 × 3, 4 × 4 (Fig. 7.22). On some of the older machines, a collecting row with all needles knitting in one bed making a plain course is necessary before needles change over beds.[4]

The reverse stitches of purl give it the appearance of hand knitting and this is enhanced by using softly spun yarns. It is particularly suitable for baby wear, where width and length stretch is required, and also for adult knitwear. The double-cylinder half-hose machine is actually a small diameter purl machine

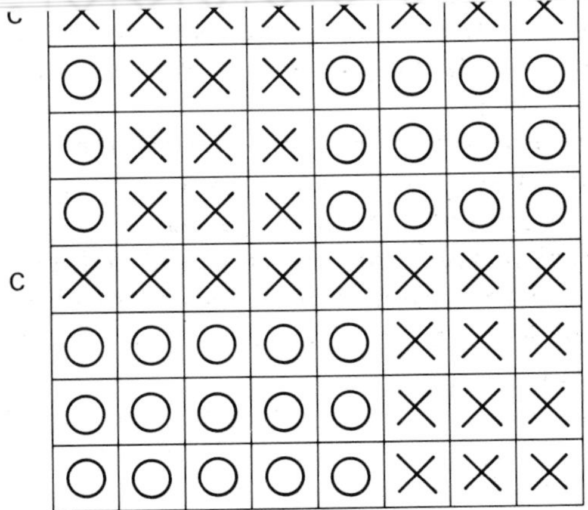

(c = collecting row)

Fig. 7.21.

O	O	O	O	X	X	X	X
O	O	O	O	X	X	X	X
O	O	O	O	X	X	X	X
O	O	O	O	X	X	X	X
X	X	X	X	O	O	O	O
X	X	X	X	O	O	O	O
X	X	X	X	O	O	O	O
X	X	X	X	O	O	O	O

Fig. 7.22.

which produces ribs by retaining needles in the same set out for a large number of successive courses.

Purl Needle Transfer Action 7.15

The following conditions are necessary in order to achieve the transference of a purl needle from the control of a slider in one bed into the control of a slider in the opposite bed (Fig. 7.19):

1. Engagement of the head of the receiving slider with the needle hook which was originally knitting from the opposing bed.
2. Cam action causing the head of the delivering slider to pivot outwards from the trick and thus to disengage itself from the other hook of the needle.
3. Sufficient free space to allow the heads of the sliders to pivot outwards from their tricks during engagement and disengagement of the needles.
4. A positive action which maintains the engagement of the head of a slider with a needle hook throughout its knitting cycle by ensuring that it is depressed down into the trick.

The Use of Dividing Cams 7.16

Figure 7.19 illustrates the transfer action, using *dividing cams* on a revolving double-cylinder machine with internal holding-down sinkers and stationary cam-boxes. The dividing cam principle for slider disengagement was, until recently, in widespread use on half-hose machines although it had already been replaced on the double-cylinder garment length purl machines which succeeded the original Spensa purl machine.

The dividing cam is an internally profiled cut-through recess in a flat plate attached horizontally and externally to the cylinders at a position half-way between them. There is a recess cam position for the top cylinder and another for the bottom cylinder in a different position in the same plate. The principle of the dividing cam operation is that it forms a wedge shape of increasing thickness between the upper surface of the needle hook and the under surface of the extended nose of the delivering slider pivoting it away from the cylinder so that it disengages from the needle hook.

1. The delivering slider (D) advances with the needle so that the nose of the slider, which is extended into a latch guard, penetrates the profiled recess of the dividing cam. The outer hook of the needle contacts the hook underneath the head of the receiving slider (R), pivoting it out of the cylinder, but it immediately returns and –
2. It engages with the needle hook under the influence of a coil spring band (SB) which surrounds each cylinder and ensures that the slider heads are depressed into contact with the needle hooks.
3. As slider D revolves with the cylinder, it passes along the wall of the dividing cam (DC) which increases in thickness, so that the slider is pivoted outwards and disengages from the needle hook. Slider D then returns to its cylinder whilst slider R retires into its cylinder taking the needle with it ready for the next knitting feed.

7.17 The Use of Spring-loaded Cams

Figure 7.23 illustrates the *spring-loaded cam method of slider disengagement* used in the SPJ type machine which is the successor of the Spensa purl, but has stationary cylinders (without internal sinkers) and revolving cam-boxes, a similar technique is being generally introduced into double-cylinder half-hose machines although these have revolving cylinders. At the moment of disengagement, the spring-loaded cam presses onto the tail of the delivering slider (D) causing its head to swing away from the cylinder and to disengage itself from the needle hook. The action is made possible by the tapering under surface of the slider tail.

This method is simpler and safer and operates well at high speeds. The latch guard nose of the slider is extended and pointed to act as a latch-opener as the receiving slider meets the approaching head of the needle, whose latch is specially shaped to facilitate the action (Fig. 7.24). This action reduces the danger of press-offs occurring through latches closing onto empty hooks (on the Spensa purl two ends of yarn were knitted so that yarn breakage and a subsequent press-off was less likely to occur).

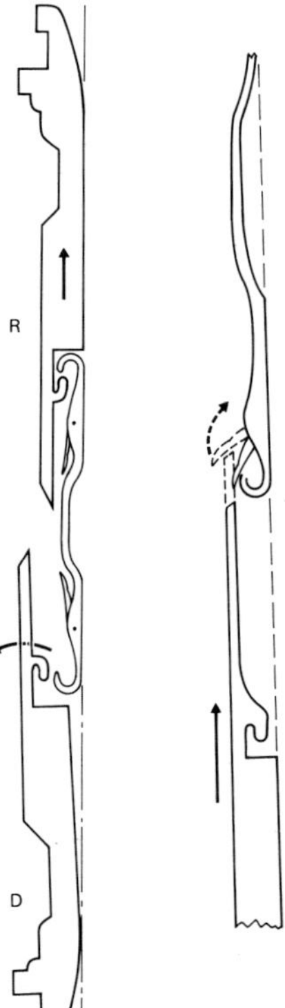

Fig. 7.23.

Further Information

1. DAVIES, W., *Hosiery Manufacture*, (1923) Pitman, 129.
2. PAEPKE, H., Fundamentals of delayed and synchronised timing, *Knit. O'wr Times*, (8 May 1967) 145–151.
3. WILLKOMM, G., *Technology of Framework Knitting*. (1885) (Eng. Trans. ROWLETT, W. T.) Hewitt, Leicester. First Part, Chapter 2, p. 78.
4. LANCASHIRE, J. B., Focus on purl knitting, *Hos. Trade Journal*, (March 1961) 84–8.

8

The Various Types of Weft Knitting Machines

8.1 Fabric Machines and Garment Length Machines

Weft knitting machines may be broadly grouped as either:

1. *Fabric machines knitting fabric in a continuous uninterrupted length of constant width*, or
2. *Garment length machines which have an additional garment-control mechanism to coordinate the knitting action* in the production of a garment length structured repeat sequence in a wale direction.

8.2 Fabric Machines

Fabric, yard-goods or piece-goods machines knit fabric at high speed which is manually cut away from the machine, usually in roll form, when a convenient length has been knitted. Most fabric is knitted on circular machines of the revolving needle cylinder type because of their productivity, it therefore requires splitting into open width unless used in tubular body width. It is finished on continuous finishing equipment and is cut and sewn into garments or it is used for household and industrial fabrics. The productivity, versatility and patterning facilities of fabric machines vary considerably.

8.3 Garment Length Machines

Garment length machines tend to be in coarser gauges than the fabric machines. They *include straight bar frames, most flats, hosiery, legwear and glove machines and circular garment machines* including sweater strip machines, producing knitwear, outerwear and underwear. On these machines, the garment sequence control and timing/counting device initiates any alterations to the other facilities on the same machine necessary in order to convert a continuous fabric into a garment length construction sequence. The control may have to initiate correctly timed changes in some or all of the following, cam-settings, needle set-outs, feeders and machine speeds. It must be able to override and cancel the effect of the patterning mechanisms in rib borders and be easily adjustable for different garment sizes, also the take down mechanism must be more sophisticated during the sequence and on some machines it is required to take away separated garment pieces.

Garments may be knitted to size either in tubular or in open width and, in the latter case more than one garment might be knitted simultaneously, whilst large-diameter circular machines may knit a garment sequence which is later split into two or more garment widths.

Garment length knitting sequences vary considerably:

The simplest circular machines produce repeat sequences of rib borders and body panels in a continuous fabric at high speed which require cutting into lengths, and a welt to be produced during seaming.

Most machines produce a firm welt at the start of each garment and either a knitted separation course between each length or press-off separation of each piece. In the latter case, the machine must be capable of commencing knitting of the next garment length on empty needles.

The amount of shape introduced into the garment also varies, some rely entirely on shaping during making up, some are stitch shaped, others are shaped by reciprocating knitting or by fashioning.

Whereas garments cut from fabric are completely assembled during seaming others require very little making-up and integrally-knitted articles are completed on the knitting machines.

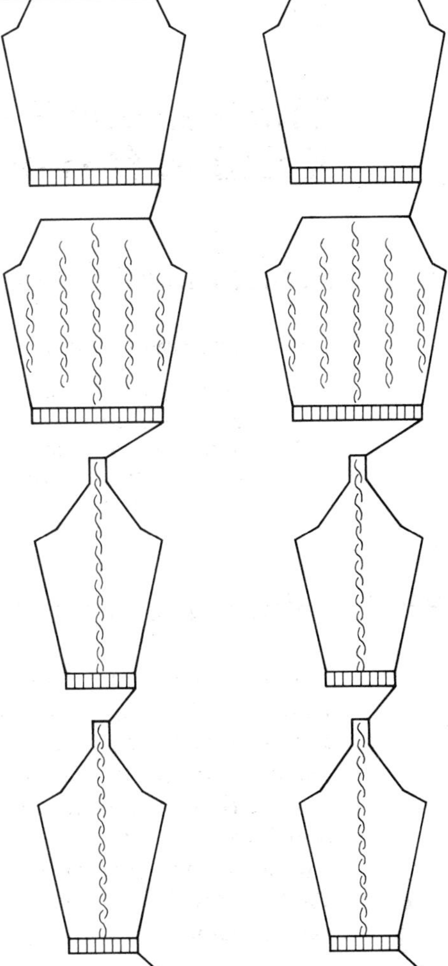

Fig. 8.1.

Certain straight bar and flat machines may be programmed to carry out a sequential cycle so that each major panel of the garment (front, back, two sleeves) is produced in turn, thus reducing matching-up problems created by variations in yarn and knitting which may occur when parts for the same garment are not knitted on the same machine (Fig. 8.1).

Underwear may be either in garment length or fabric form whereas knitwear is normally in garment lengths generally coarser than 14 npi and jerseywear is usually in fabric form often finer than 14 npi.

The three main classes of weft knitting machinery may be broadly classified as either straight bar frames, flats or circulars, according to their general design and needle bed arrangement.

8.4 Straight Bar Frames

Straight bar frames are a specific type of machine having a vertical bearded needle bar whose movement is controlled by circular engineering type cams attached to a revolving cam-shaft in the base of the machine. *The machine is usually divided into a number of sections each capable of knitting a separate but identically-dimensioned garment panel.* The needles press their beards against a fixed pressing edge, loop formation is achieved by horizontally moving sinkers, and knocking-over occurs when the needles descend between knock-over bits.

Rackably controlled points transfer loops to fashion shape the garment panels at their selvedges by widening or narrowing the knitting width. On completion of the garment length sequence, the panels are pressed-off from the needle bar. Rib frames with two needle bars have long been available, but the knitting action is cumbersome and rib has never been as popular as classic fully-fashioned plain knitwear fabric, produced with a single needle bar. The welt and border sequence at the beginning of each panel is achieved by one of the following methods:

1. Knitting a rib border fabric on a separate flat machine and *running* it *onto the empty needles* of the frame one loop after the next and then knitting the plain fabric panel onto it.
2. Using a frame of the *Rib to Plain type*, this has an ancillary needle bar which cooperates in the knitting of the rib border.
3. Employing a *welt-turning device* on the frame to produce a turned welt consisting of double thickness plain fabric. This method is more popular in the U.S.A. and is also used for producing welts on fully-fashioned stockings.

Straight bar frames are long, capitally expensive machines which because of their multi-sections and in spite of their intermittent knitting action are highly productive in a very narrow sphere of garment manufacture. The knitting width is rather restricted and fashion tends not to encourage full exploitation of the fashion-shaping and stitch-patterning potential of the machine.

The machines are noted for the production of high quality garments as a result of the gentle knitting action, low fabric tension and fashion shaping which reduces the waste of expensive yarn during cutting and is emphasized on the garments by carefully-positioned fashion marks.

8.5 Flat Machines

The typical flat machine has two stationary beds of tricks in which the latch needles and other elements slide during the knitting action and from which their butts project and are controlled as they pass through the tracks formed by the angular cams of a bi-directional cam system attached to the underside of a carriage which with its selected yarn carriers, traverses in a reciprocating manner across the machine width (Fig. 8.2).

Fig. 8.2. Examples of Flat Knitting Machines. 1 = Jacquard Power Flat; 2 = Hand Flat; J = Jacquard Selection Steels; P = Paste Board Movement Cards.

The machines range from hand propelled and manipulated models to fully-automated electronically-controlled power-driven machines. The four classes of flat machines are (i) the V-bed (Vee-bed) flat which is by far the largest class; (ii) *flat bed purl machines* which employ double ended needles; (iii) machines having a *single bed* of needles which include most domestic models and the few hand manipulated intarsia machines; and (iv) the *uni-directional multi-carriage machines* made by one manufacturer.

As with all knitting machines, there is a separate cam system for each needle bed, the two systems are linked together by a bow or bridge which passes across from one needle bed to the other. The systems for each needle bed are symmetrically arranged so that knitting and in some cases loop transfer may be achieved in either direction of carriage traverse.

The intermittent action of the carriage traverse and its low number of knitting systems (often only two and usually a maximum of four) reduces productivity but enables major cam changes to occur when the carriage is clear of the active needles. The flat machine is the most versatile of weft knitting machines, its stitch potential includes needle selection on one or both beds, racked stitches (Fig. 19.10), needle-out designs, striping, tubular knitting, changes of knitting width and loop transfer. A wide range of yarn counts may be knitted per machine gauge including a number of ends of yarn in one knitting system, the stitch length range is wide and there is the possibility of changing the machine gauge. The operation and supervision of the machines of the simpler type is relatively less arduous than for other weft knitting machines. The number of garments or panels simultaneously knitted across the machine is dependent upon its knitting width, yarn carrier arrangement, yarn path and package accommodation.

Articles knitted on flat machines range from trimmings, edgings and collars to garment panels and integrally knitted garments.

8.6 Circular Machines

The term circular covers all those weft knitting machines whose needle beds are arranged in circular cylinders and/or dials, including latch, bearded and very occasionally compound needle machinery, producing a wide range of fabric structures, garments, hosiery and other articles in a variety of diameters and machine gauges.

There are two types of circular bearded needle single-jersey fabric machines still manufactured, the sinkerwheel machine and the loop wheel frame. To reduce confusion, it is best to reserve each term only for that machine type, terms such as French or Terrot type for the sinkerwheel and English type for the loopwheel frame can be misleading. Both have the following features in common; needles fixed in a revolving circle

Fig. 8.3. Examples of Large-Diameter Circular Knitting Machines. 1 = Plain Cylinder and Dial Fabric Machine; 2 = Rib Jacquard Machine; 3 = Double Cylinder Purl Garment Length Machine.

Fig. 8.4. Examples of Small-Diameter Footwear Machines. 1 = Seamless Hose Machine; 2 = Double Cylinder Half-Hose Machine.

with the loop formation and knitting action being entirely achieved by ancillary elements moving yarn and loops along the needle stems, a fabric tube knitted with its technical back facing outwards, knitting feeds occupying a considerable amount of the needle cylinder and a comparatively low productivity compensated by an ability to produce unusual and superior-quality knitted structures.

Revolving cylinder latch needle machines produce most weft knitted fabrics. They are of two main types – open top, and cylinder and dial. Open top, sinker top or single-jersey machines have one set of needles usually arranged in the cylinder. Except in the case of certain effect fabric machines such as pelerine, cylinder and dial machines are of either the rib or interlock type. Machines of both types may or may not have patterning capabilities (Fig. 8.3).

Circular garment length machines are generally of body-width size or larger having a cylinder and dial arrangement or a double cylinder or they are of the small-diameter hosiery type with either a single cylinder, a cylinder and dial, or double cylinders (Fig. 8.4).

8.7 Development of the Circular Weft Knitting Technique

During the last 200 years numerous inventors have assisted the development of circular weft knitting technology towards its present state of sophistication and diversity. Whilst Decroix's patent of 1798 has been considered to be the first for a circular frame, Marc Brunel's 'tricoteur' of 1816 is probably the first practical working example of such a frame. Efforts were concentrated, during the subsequent 30 years, on improving the knitting action of this frame with its revolving dial of fixed needles radiating horizontally outwards and having their beards uppermost. In 1845, Fouquet applied his Stuttgarter Mailleuse wheels to the frame and their individually moving, loop-forming sinkers provided the sinkerwheel frame with the capability of knitting high quality fabric, a possibility later exploited by Terrot who improved its patterning facilities and marketed the frame throughout the world.

In 1849, Moses Mellor produced a revolving circular frame with vertically-arranged bearded needles facing outwards from the needle circle, this later developed to become the loopwheel frame. In the same year, Matthew Townsend patented uses for the latch needle and by 1855, Pepper had produced a commercial machine with a single set of movable latch needles and two feed points, this was soon followed by Aiken's circular latch needle rib machine of 1859 which also contained movable needles. Henry Griswold took latch needle knitting a stage further by moving the needles individually and directly via their bent shanks in his world famous hand-operated, revolving cam-box small diameter sock machine of 1878 (Fig. 4.4).

The first small diameter revolving cylinder machine appeared in about 1907 but there was still much strenuous effort required by machine builders before circular latch needle machines could seriously begin to challenge bearded needle straight and circular machines in the production of high quality knitted articles.

Further Information

HURD, J. C. H., Towards automation in hosiery, knitwear and knitted fabric, *Text. Inst. and Ind.*, (1974) 12, (4), 113 (4 pages).

LANCASHIRE, J. B., 75 years of weft knitting history, *Hos. Trade Journal*, (Jan. 1969) 178–186.

Knitting machinery: a guide to primary types, *Knit. O'wr Yr Bk.*, (1970) 97–9, 412.

9

Stitches Produced by Varying the Timing of the Needle Loop Intermeshing

Weft knitted stitches described so far have been composed entirely of knitted loops. A knitted loop stitch is produced when at each yarn feed, a needle receives a new loop and knocks-over the old loop which it held from the previous knitting cycle, so that the old loop now becomes a needle loop of normal configuration.

Other types of stitch may be produced on each of the four-needle arrangement base structures by varying the timing of the intermeshing sequence of the old and new loops. These stitches may be deliberately selected as part of the design of the weft knitted structure or they may be produced accidentally by a malfunction of the knitting action so that they occur as fabric faults. When these stitches are deliberately selected, a preponderance of knitted loop stitches is necessary within the structure in order to maintain its requisite physical properties. Generally, the needles produce knitted loop stitches prior to the commencement and at the termination of these selected stitches and there are usually certain needles which are knitting normally during the same cycles as these stitches are produced.

Apart from the knitted loop stitch, the two most commonly-produced stitches are the float stitch and the tuck stitch. Each is produced with a 'held loop' and shows its own particular loop most clearly on the reverse side of the stitch as the limbs of the held loop cover it from view on the face.

The Held Loop 9.1

A held loop (Fig. 9.1) is an old loop which the needle has retained and not released and knocked-over at the next yarn feed. A held loop can only be retained by a needle for a limited number of knitting cycles before it is cast-off and a new loop drawn through, otherwise the tension on the yarn in the loop becomes excessive even though there is a tendency to rob extra yarn from adjacent loops in the same course. The limbs of the held loop are often elongated as they extend from its base intermeshing in one course to where its head is finally intermeshed a number of courses higher in the structure, alongside it in adjacent wales there may be normally-knitted loops at each course.

A held loop may be incorporated into a held stitch without the production of tuck or miss stitches in either single- or double-faced structures.

In single-faced structures it can only be produced on machines whose feeds or needles have a reciprocating action so that the yarn only passes across needles which are knitting, otherwise a float stitch would be produced. Held stitches of this type are used for producing three-dimensional shaping such as heel and toe pouches for footwear, held loop shaping on flat machines and designs in solid colour intarsia. Held stitches are produced in double-faced structures by holding loops on one bed whilst continuing to knit on the other thus producing horizontal welt and cord effects.

9.2 The Drop or Press-off Stitch

A drop stitch fault will result if a needle releases its old loop without receiving a new one, sometimes this technique is used to achieve a press-off on all needles in a set between garment length sequences. A drop stitch or press-off stitch is used very occasionally in flat knitting to cause certain loops in a plain structure to be much larger than the rest. Knitting takes place on only one bed of needles and selected needles in the other bed pick up loops which are immediately pressed-off by not receiving a new yarn. The yarn from the pressed-off loops flows into the adjacent loops in the other bed making them larger, giving the impression of a much coarser gauge. Drop stitch wales are sometimes used to provide a guide for the cutting operation. A secure structure is only produced when a needle retains its old loop if it does not receive a new loop.

9.3 The Float Stitch

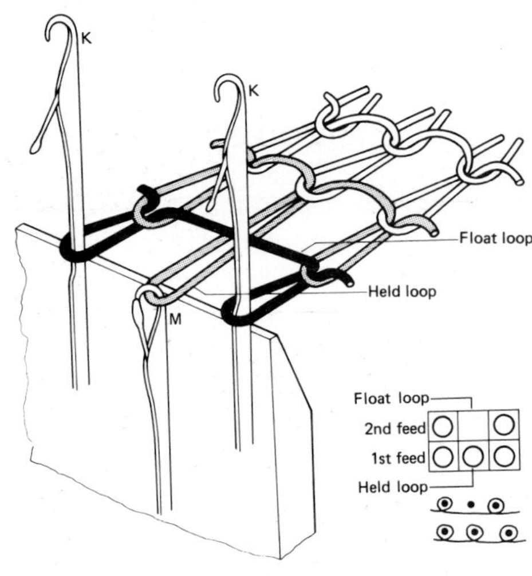

Fig. 9.1.

A float stitch (Fig. 9.1) is composed of a held loop, one or more float loops and knitted loops. It is produced when a needle (M) holding its old loop fails to receive the new yarn which passes, as a float loop, to the back of the needle and to the reverse side of the resultant stitch, joining together the two nearest needle loops knitted from it.

The float or welt stitch (Fig. 9.2) shows *the missed yarn floating freely on the reverse side of the held loop* which is the technical back of single jersey structures, but is the inside of rib and interlock structures. The float extends from the base of one knitted or tucked loop to the next and is notated either as an empty square or as a by-passed point, it is assumed that the held loop extends into the courses above until a knitted loop is indicated.

A single float stitch has the appearance of a 'U' shape on the reverse of the stitch. Structures incorporating float stitches tend to exhibit faint horizontal lines, they are narrower because the wales are drawn closer together and the held loop robs yarn from adjacent loops thus reducing width-wise elasticity and improving fabric stability.

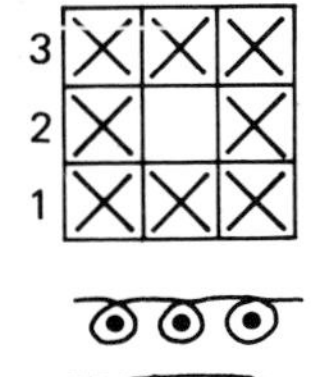

Fig. 9.2.

Under normal take-down tension and yarn elasticity the maximum number of successive floats on the same needle is four. Six adjacent needles are usually the maximum number for a continuous float because of reduced elasticity and problems of snagged threads, especially in continuous filament yarns and coarse gauges. Missing is useful for hiding an unwanted coloured yarn behind the face loop of a yarn of a selected colour when producing jacquard designs in face loops of different colours (adjacent needle floating Fig. 9.8, successive floating on same needle Fig. 9.9).

The miss stitch can occur accidentally as a fault as a result of incorrectly set yarn feeders.

Float Plating 9.4

Float plating produces an openwork mesh structure in single jersey and involves feeding two yarns in a plating relationship to needles having forward hooks (Fig. 9.3). A heavy yarn (A), for example, 30 denier, is fed at a high level and is only received by needles selected to that height whereas the fine yarn (B), possibly 15 denier, is fed at a lower level and is received and knitted by every needle. Two course

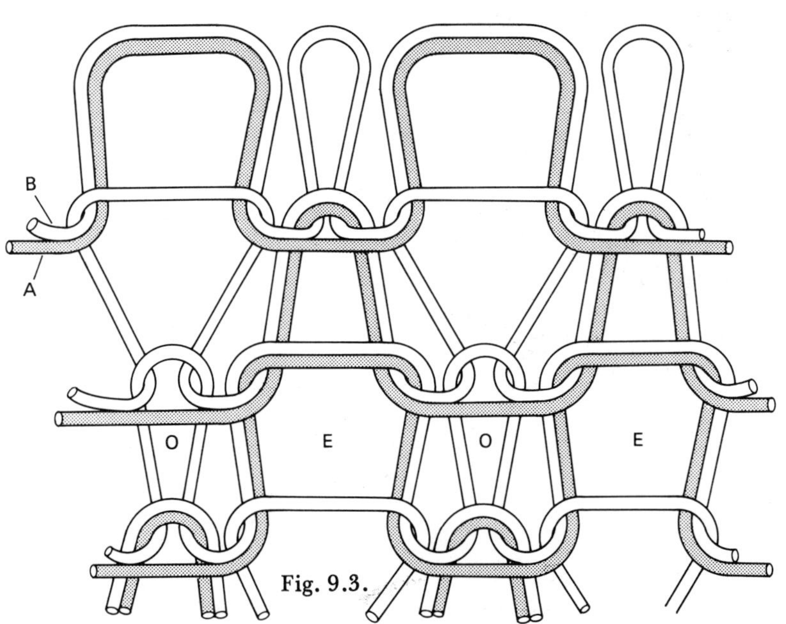

Fig. 9.3.

fishnet is the most popular structure having a repeat two wales wide and four courses deep. At the first two feeders, odd needles (O) knit only the thin yarn and even needles (E) knit plated loops, at the next two feeders the sequence is reversed. Knitting and missing of the heavy yarn causes an expansion of alternate stitches. The two-course sequence may be extended to three or four courses and it is possible to plate the heavy yarn on a needle selection basis. The structure has been used for ladder-resist shadow welts in stockings and for textured designs as well as for underwear and mesh structures on circular single-jersey machines[1] in gauges from 14 to 24 needles per inch (25 mm).

9.5 The Tuck Stitch

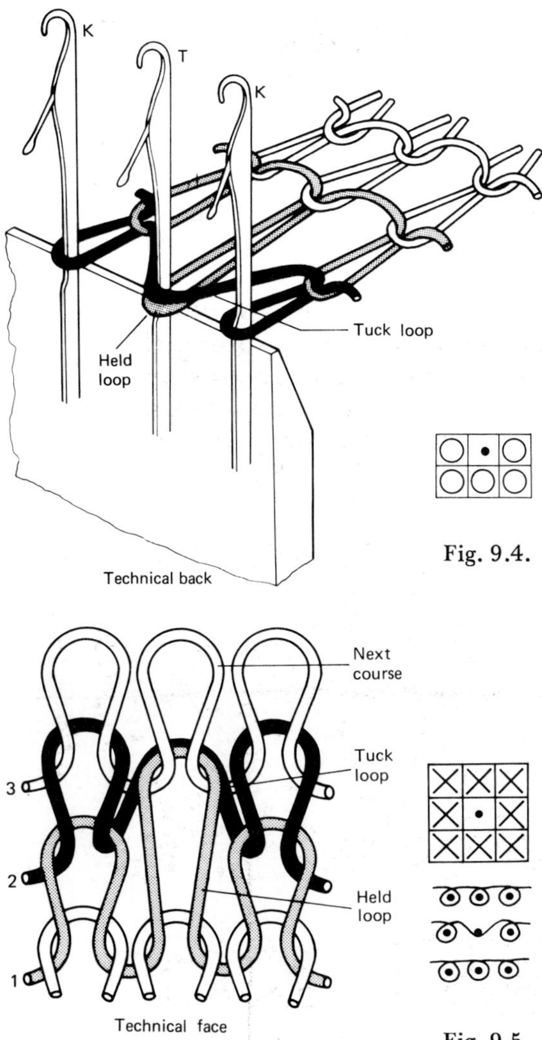

Fig. 9.4.

Fig. 9.5.

A *tuck stitch* is composed of a held loop, one or more tuck loops, and knitted loops (Fig. 9.4). It *is produced when a needle holding its loop (T) also receives the new loop which becomes a tuck loop* because it is not intermeshed through the old loop, but is tucked in behind it on the reverse side of the stitch (Fig. 9.5).

Its side limbs are therefore not restricted at their feet by the head of an old loop so that they can open outwards towards the two adjoining needle loops formed in the same course. The tuck loop thus assumes an inverted V or U-shaped configuration as the yarn passes from the sinker loops to the head which is intermeshed with the new loop of a course above it in the normal manner so that the head of the tuck is on the reverse of the stitch. The side limbs of tuck loops thus tend to show through onto the face between adjacent wales as they pass in front of sinker loops. Tuck stitch structures show a faint diagonal line effect on their surface. In analysis, a tuck stitch is identified by the fact that its head is released as a hump shape immediately the needle loop above it is withdrawn, whereas a knitted loop would require to be separately withdrawn and a miss stitch would always be floating freely on the technical back.

The tuck loop configuration can be produced by two different knitting sequences:

1. *By commencing knitting on a previously empty needle* (Fig. 9.6). As the needle was previously empty there will be no old loop in the wale to restrict the base of the first knitted loop and in fact even the second loop tends to be wider than normal. The effect is clearly visible in the starting course of a welt. By introducing rib needles on a selective basis an openwork pattern may be produced on an essentially plain knit base.

2. *By holding the old loop and then accumulating one or more new loops in the needle hook.* Each new loop becomes a tuck loop as they and the held loop are knocked-over together at a later knitting cycle and a new loop is intermeshed with them. This is the normal method of producing a tuck stitch in weft knitting (Fig. 9.4).

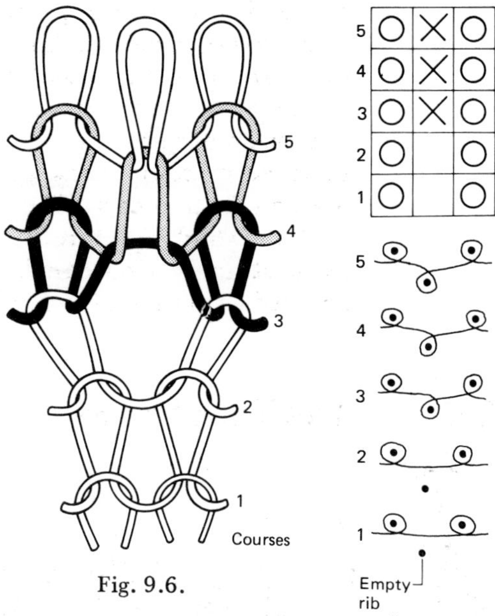

Fig. 9.6.

Successive tucks on the same needle are placed on top of each other at the back of the head of the held loop and assume a straighter and more horizontal appearance theoretically requiring less yarn. Under normal conditions, up to four successive tucks can be accumulated before tension causes yarn rupture or needle damage, the limit is affected by machine design, needle hook size, yarn count, elasticity and take-down tension (Fig. 9.9).

Each side of the head of a tuck loop is held by a sinker loop (S) from the course above (Fig. 9.7). When tucking occurs across two or more adjacent needles, the head of the tuck loop will float freely across between these two sinker loops, after which a sloping side limb will occur. Dependent upon structural fineness, tucking over six adjacent needles is usually the maximum unit before snagging becomes a problem.

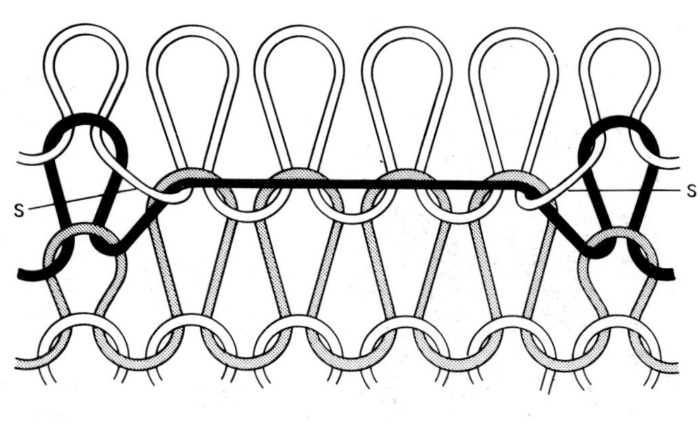

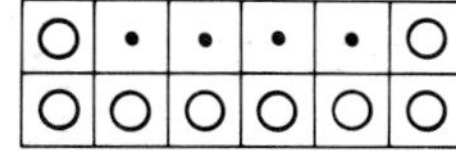

Fig. 9.7.

A tuck loop is notated either as a dot placed in a square or as a semi-circle

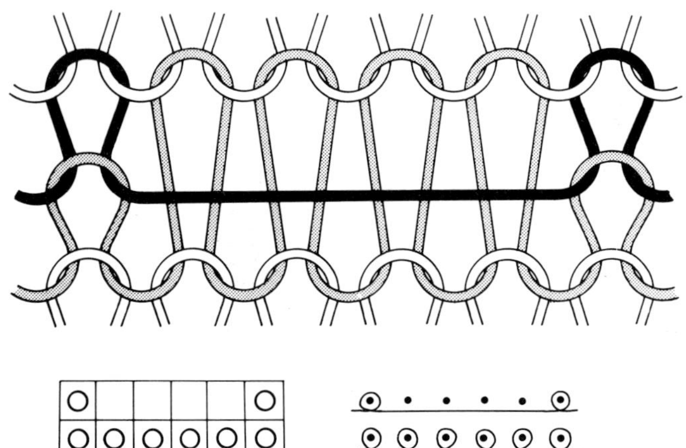

Fig. 9.8. Four adjacent floats.

onto a point, whilst the held loop is assumed to extend from the course below the tuck up to the course where the next knitted loop is notated and where it intermeshes.

Tuck stitches may occur singly, across adjacent needles (Fig 9.7), or on the same needle at successive knitting cycles (Fig. 9.9).

Selective 'tucking in the hook' (Fig. 9.10) is achieved on latch needle weft knitting machines by lifting the needle about half-way to clearing so that although the old loop slides down and opens the latch it does not slip from it, it remains as a held loop in the hook where it is joined by the new loop which becomes a tuck loop as the needle descends the stitch cam. The latch needle, because of its loop controlled knitting action, is capable of being lifted to one of three positions to produce either *a miss, a tuck or a knit loop*; this *is* sometimes *termed the 'threeway' technique* (Fig. 9.11). Cams split into tuck and clearing height cams are known as cardigan cams on V-bed flat machines, they were not fitted to older machines so that only collective 'tucking on the latch' (Fig. 9.12) of all needles in one bed is obtained by raising the stitch-cam causing needles not to descend low enough for the held loop on the outside of the latch to be cast-off so this remains with the tuck loop which is inside the hook. Apart from lack of selection, this method also is insecure in that there is a danger of the held loop slipping off and producing an intermeshed loop with the tuck, converting it to a knitted stitch.

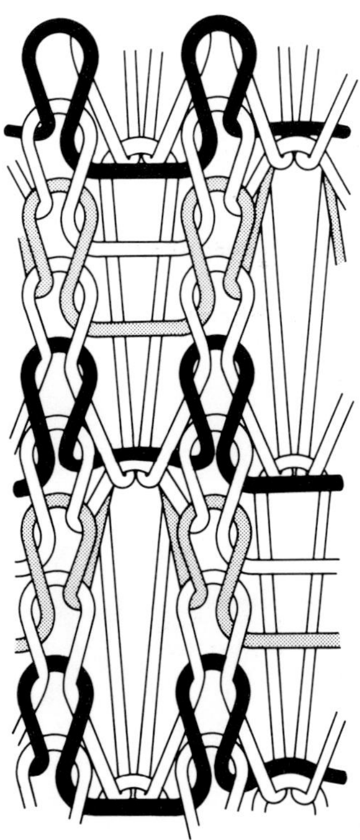

Fig. 9.9. Tuck/Float Rib.

The first tuck presser bearded needle frame was invented in Dublin in 1745. A bearded needle tucks when its beard is mis-pressed so that the old loop is not cast-off and remains as a held loop inside the beard with the newly fed tuck loop. Tucking for inlay may be achieved by deflecting certain needles during inlay feeding so that this yarn passes across the beards of the selected needles forming a tuck instead of floating across their backs. Selective tucking requires cut-away pressing edges or individually controlled presser bits.

Tucking occurs accidentally as a result of stiff latches,

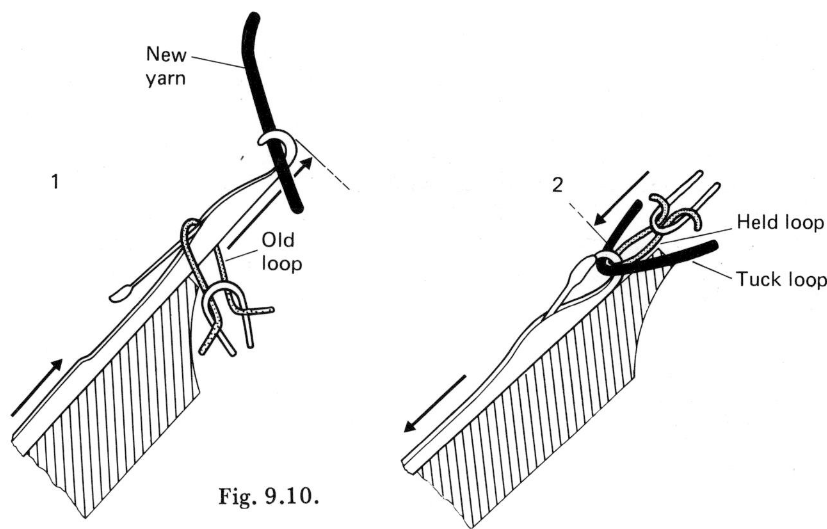

Fig. 9.10.

imperfect pressing, or imperfect knocking-over of old loops, or thick places in yarn.

Tuck loops reduce fabric length and length-wise elasticity because the higher yarn tension on the tuck and held loops causes them to rob yarn from adjacent knitted loops making them smaller and providing greater stability and shape retention. The fabric width is increased because the

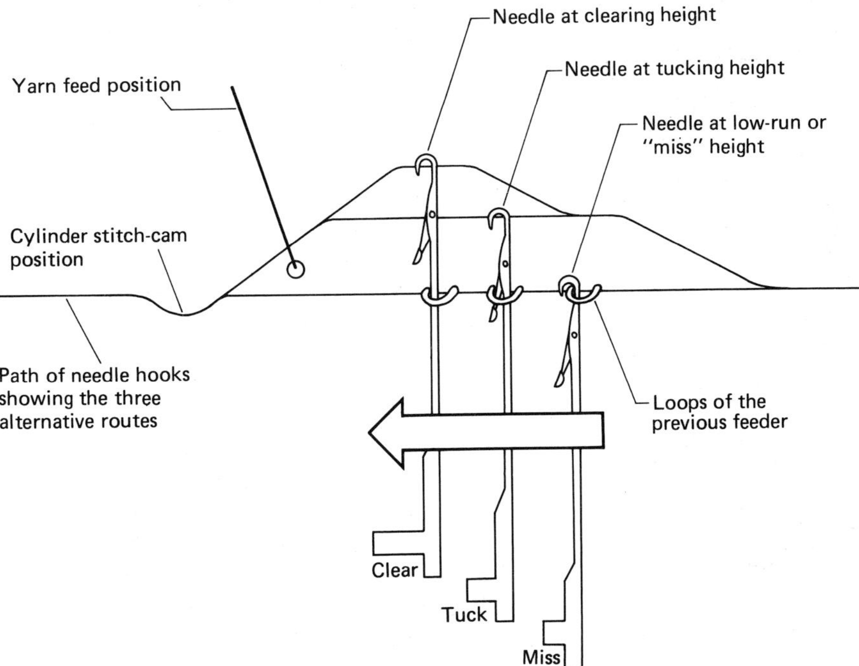

Fig. 9.11. In this illustration the needles have been turned 90° in order to show the position of the latch in relationship with the loop of the previous feeder.

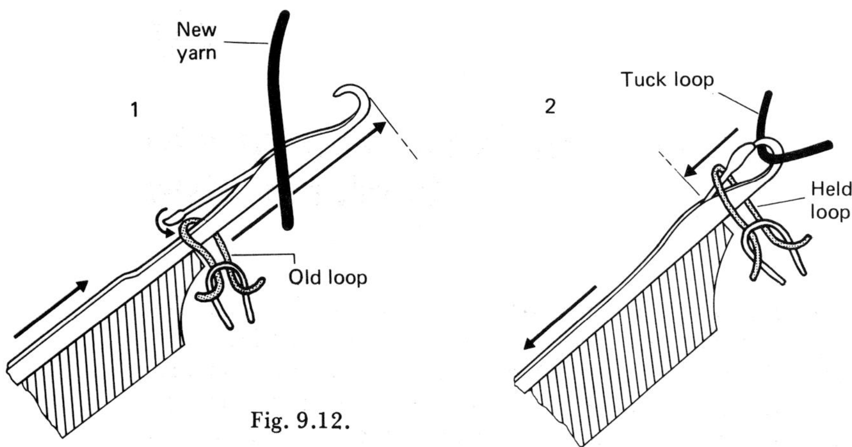

Fig. 9.12.

tuck loops pull the held loops downwards causing them to spread outwards and making extra yarn available for width-wise elasticity. Fabric distortion and three-dimensional relief is caused by tuck stitch accumulation, displacement of wales and by varying numbers of tuck and knitted stitches per wale.

Tuck stitches are employed in accordion fabrics to tie in the long floats produced on the back of single-jersey knit/miss jacquard, thus reducing the problems of snagging which occur with filament yarns. The tuck stitch may also be employed to produce openwork effects, improve the surface texture, produce stitch-shaping, reinforce, join double-face fabrics, improve ladder-resistance and to produce mock fashion marks.

Further Information

LANCASHIRE, J. B., Uses of the tuck stitch, *Hos. Trade Journal*, (June 1961) 158–161.

Tuck loops in jacquard knitting, *Hos. Trade Journal*, (April 1963) 123–8.

1. GOADBY, D. R., Camber single jersey Louvnit machine, *Knit. Int.*, (Dec. 1978) 46–7.

10

Coloured Stitch Designs in Weft Knitting

Ornamentation for design purposes may be introduced at the fibre, the yarn, or the dyeing and finishing stage as well as at the knitting stage. Apart from different colours, it may take the form of structural or surface interest. In fibre form it can include a variation of fibre diameter, length, cross-section, dye uptake, shrinkage and elastic properties. In yarn form it includes fancy twist and novelty yarns as well as the combined use of yarns produced by different spinning or texturing processes. The dyeing process which provides the possibility of differential and cross-dyeing of fabrics with more than one fibre, may occur at any point in manufacturing from fibre to finished article.[1] The finishing process can completely transform the appearance of a relatively uninteresting structure either as an all-over effect or on a selective basis; it may also introduce heat or chemically-derived shaping. Finally, printing and particularly transfer printing[2] can introduce coloured designs onto plain colour surfaces whilst embroidery stitching may produce relief design motifs in one or more colours (usually onto garment panels).

The knitting of stitch designs always involves a loss of productivity compared with the knitting of plain unpatterned structures. Machine speeds are lower, less feeds can generally be accommodated, efficiency is less and design changes are time-consuming and dependent upon technique and machine type. In many cases more than one feeder course is required to knit each pattern row.

At the knitting stage, apart from stitches for surface interest and other functional purposes, four techniques may, if required, be employed to produce designs in coloured stitches, these are: horizontal striping, intarsia, plating and individual stitch selection.

Horizontal Striping 10.1

Horizontal striping is achieved by supplying yarn of more than one colour from the feeds of a machine which is knitting a plain type of fabric structure (Fig. 10.1). By careful arrangement of the packages of coloured yarns on a large diameter multi-feeder machine, an elaborate sequence of stripes, having a depth which is repeated at each machine revolution, is obtained.

However, machines with few feeds (particularly garment length and

Fig. 10.1. An attractive use of horizontal striping for a jogging sweater (International Institute for Cotton).

hosiery machines) would have severely restricted design capabilities without the facility of yarn changing by striping finger selection which can provide a choice of one from four or five yarns at a particular feed point during each machine revolution.

On flat and straight bar frames, yarn carrier changes can take place during the pause in knitting on the completion of each traverse, but on circular machines, striping finger changes must occur whilst the needle cylinders or cam-boxes rotate so that a slight overlap of the two inter-changing yarns is essential to maintain a continuous yarn flow at the knitting point. As one yarn finger is withdrawn from the needle circle with its yarn cut free and securely trapped and held for later re-selection, the newly-selected finger in the same unit or box is simultaneously introduced into the needle line with its trapper releasing the held cut end of yarn and allowing it to flow from its package to the needles. The facility of an individual cutter and trapper for each yarn in the unit is mechanically more complex but it enables a yarn as thin as 30 denier nylon to be trapped alongside a yarn as thick as 5/1's cotton.

Although striping is useful for the introduction of a draw-thread in a full course and splicing reinforcement on a part-course basis, the mechanism is not precise enough for individual stitch patterning. Its speed of operation and versatility has, however, been improved by employing electronic control so that the 'engineered' placing of stripes in the length of a garment part is now possible.[3,4]

Intarsia 10.2

Intarsia designs or large motifs are a development of part course horizontal striping, being composed of areas of pure colour each consisting wholly of loops of one colour without floating threads and with perfect selvedged edges. As well as plain or 1 × 1 rib, other stitches such as purl or cable may be utilized. A design course may contain a large number of colours as the knitting width is divided into adjoining blocks of contiguous needles, each block knitting a separate coloured area for which it is exclusively supplied with its own particular yarn by means of reciprocation (flat or straight bar frames) or oscillation (small diameter circular machines). Unequalled colour definition is thus achieved with no adverse effect upon the physical properties of the structure such as extensibility (Fig. 10.2).

Fig. 10.2. A Dragon (original by Gountei Sadahide 1858). This cashmere sweater illustrates the possibilities for designing with coloured stitches. It was knitted on a hand-operated Dubied intarsia machine and the 14-colour motif contains 132,000 stitches. (Courtesy of Pringle and the British Knitting Export Council).

Careful positioning and control of the yarn traverses from course to course determines the design and integration of the coloured areas into a cohesively knitted structure with a slight overlap of adjoining areas, as well as the intermeshing when the loops of one area terminate and those of another commence in a particular wale. Manual thread laying enables a 'pure join' of adjoining areas by the interlocking of their selvedge yarns course by course, whereas most automatic knitting of intarsia entails some form of overlapping (encroachment) of adjoining areas into each other towards the right at one course and towards the left at the next. A slight saw-tooth effect across one, two or more wales is thus produced at the join which should be kept to minimum and the plating of knitted or tuck loops can be employed.[5]

Traditionally, intarsia is skilfully knitted by hand-laying the various yarns into the appropriate needle hooks as they are cammed upwards on hand-operated stationary needle bed machines, such as the circular

Griswold type sock machine or the flat bed Dubied model 00 machine. High quality woollen Argyle tartan socks can be knitted in this manner consisting of diamond-shaped designs crossed diagonally by one-wale wide stripes termed overchecks.[6]

Argyle socks can also be knitted automatically with plated overchecks, whilst the Scheller BSW straight bar frame knits tartan squares with vertical intarsia stripes and wrap guide plated overchecks interrupted at alternate courses by full width horizontal striping. Intarsia panels are achieved on straight bar frames by using multiple carrier rods with automatic screw spindle control of the carrier stops.[7] Intarsia patterning as an optional extra on automatic flat machines is becoming increasingly sophisticated with precise yarn positioning and needle selection and carrier traversing which may be controlled electronically.[8]

Although intarsia ensures that expensive yarns are fully utilized on the surface of the design, it is only generally suitable for geometrical type designs and not for figure designs in small areas. It is, therefore, a slow speed, expensive, specialized technique which is subject to the whims of fashion.

10.3 Plating

Plating is widely used for single jersey, plush, openwork float and interlock fleecy. However, with the exception of warp thread embroidery plating, the use of coloured yarns to produce plated designs has diminished in weft knitting. Plating requires great precision and offers limited colour choice with poor definition compared with the improved facilities offered by knit and miss needle selection of coloured stitches. In reverse plating, two yarns (usually) of contrasting colour are caused to change over positions at the needle head by controlled movement of specially-shaped sinkers or yarn feed guides. In sectional plating (straight bar frames), the ground yarn knits continuously across the full width whilst the plating carrier tubes, set lower into the needles, supply yarn in a reciprocating movement to a particular group of needles so that the colour shows on the face.

10.4 Individual Stitch Selection

Individual stitch selection is the most versatile and widely employed method of knitting designs in colour (or self-colour) (Fig. 10.3). It is based on the relative positioning of an element during a knitting cycle determining which stitch from a choice of two (or more) is produced in its corresponding wale at a particular feeder course of a machine revolution or traverse. Latch needle weft knitting machines are especially suitable because their individually tricked and butted elements offer the

Fig. 10.3. Patterning with rib needle selection. This outfit was designed by Bill Gibb for Annette Carol. It has a pattern repeat of over 6 metres and was knitted on a 7-gauge, 33-inch diameter RTR garment machine having cardomatic control. The yarn was 2/24's Bright Courtelle.

possibility of independent movement. Dependent upon machine and element design and cam arrangement, one or more of the following stitches may be produced; knit, tuck, miss, plated, plush, inlay, loop transfer and purl needle transfer.

The following rules apply to individual element selection of stitches:

1. If each set of elements has butts of identical length and position and the cam-track is fixed, each element will follow the same path and produce an identical stitch in its corresponding wale at that feeder course (Fig. 3.4).
2. If each feed in the machine has the same arrangement of fixed cams, identical stitches will be knitted in each wale at every feeder course (Fig. 7.1).
3. When the butts of adjacent elements are caused to follow different paths through the same cam system, different stitches may be knitted in adjacent wales of the same feeder course (Fig. 9.11).
4. When butts of the same element are caused to follow a different path through successive cam systems in the same machine, more than one type of stitch may be produced in the same wale (Fig. 9.4).
5. Unless the device is of the variable type which can present a different selection commencing in the first wale of each traverse or machine revolution, the design depth in feeder courses will be the number of operative feeds on the machine. If the device is variable the design depth will be increased by a multiple of the number of different selections available per device (see chapter 11).

10.5 Weft Knitted Jacquard

Weft knitted jacquard designs are built up from selected colour face loops on a base fabric of either single jersey, 1 X 1 rib, or links-links (purl). The face loop needles are individually selected, usually once per pattern row, to rise and take one yarn from a sequence of different coloured yarn feeders on a knit or miss basis. In two-colour jacquard, certain needles will be selected to knit colour A and at the next feeder there will be a negative selection with the remaining needles knitting colour B so that the face loops of two feeder courses combine to produce one complete row of face pattern loops. In three-colour jacquard, each needle will be selected to knit once and miss twice at a sequence of three feeders so that three feeder courses will produce one pattern row. The greater the number of colours in a pattern row, the lower the rate of productivity in pattern rows per machine revolution or traverse, assuming striping is not employed.

10.6 Single-Jersey Jacquard

Single-jersey jacquard (Fig. 10.4) in knit and miss stitches produces a clear stitch definition exemplified by Fair Isle designs used in woollen cardigans and pullovers. The floats to some extent reduce the lateral extensibility of the garments and when continuous filament yarns are used in gauges of 18 npi or less, the floats on the technical back can create problems of snagging. Single-cylinder sock machines may knit 1 X 1 float stitch jacquard, odd needles being selected for knit and miss whilst even needles knit at every feed, thus reducing the coloured yarn

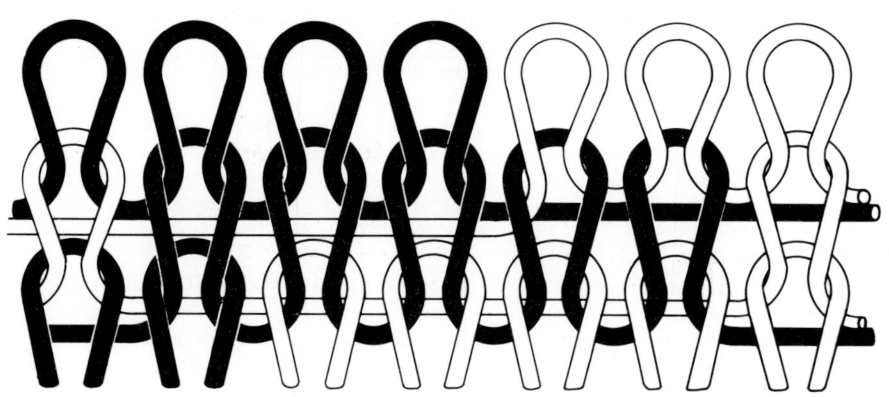

Fig. 10.4

floats to a single needle. The clarity of the coloured pattern areas is only slightly impaired.

Accordion Fabrics 10.7

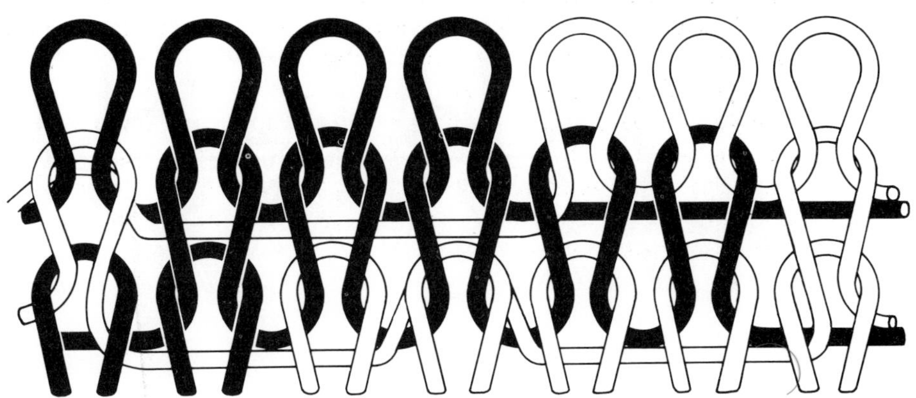

Fig. 10.5

In accordion fabrics (Fig. 10.5), the long floats are held in place on the technical back by tuck stitches. They were originally developed using knit and miss pattern wheel selection, needles required to tuck (if not selected to knit) were provided with an extra butt in line with a tuck cam placed immediately after the pattern wheel selection. In straight accordion every odd needle was of this type. Alternative accordion provides a better distribution of tuck stitches, odd needles had a tuck butt position in line with cams placed at odd feeders and even needles had another butt position for cams at even feeders. With both these types of accordion, tuck stitches can occur close together causing distortion of face loops and allowing unselected colours to 'grin' through between adjacent wales onto the face. The third type of accordion – selective accordion – is most widely used but it requires a three-step pattern wheel or other selection device which can select the tuck loops so that they are carefully distributed to create the minimum of stitch distortion on the face of the design.

Rib Jacquard 10.8

In rib jacquard (Fig. 10.6), *tuck stitches are unnecessary as the other set of needles knits the backing loops and thus overcomes the problems of floats.* On circular machines, the selection is on the cylinder needles only and the dial needles knit the backing, whereas on flat machines both needle beds may have selection facilities. With horizontally striped backing, all dial needles will knit at every feeder thus producing an unbalanced

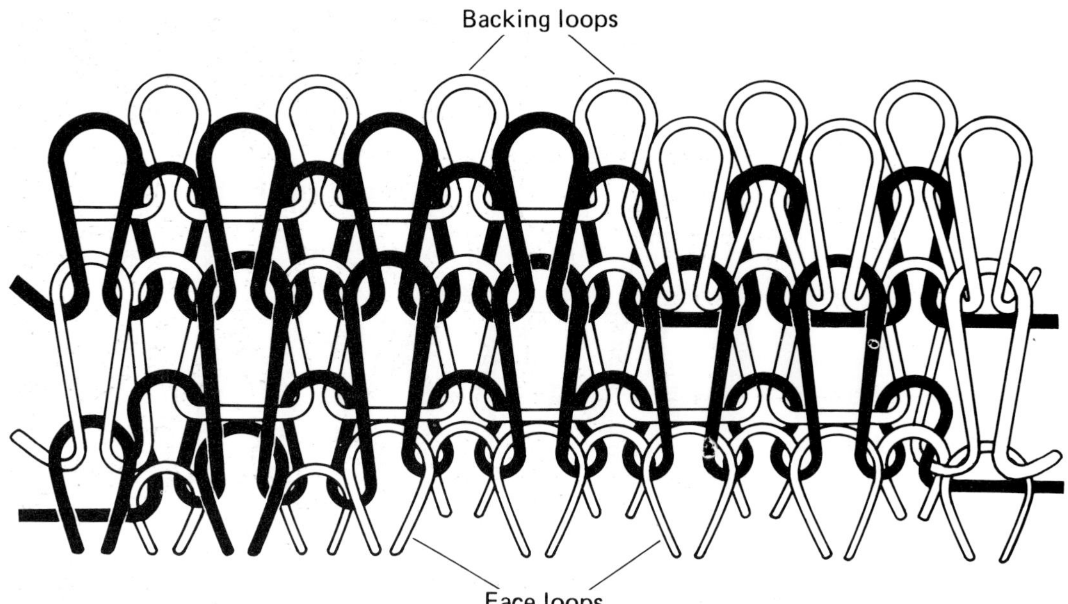

Fig. 10.6

structure with more backing rows of stitches than pattern rows. In the case of three-colour jacquard, there will be three times as many backing rows as face pattern rows. This type of backing ensures that the maximum yarn floats are only across one needle space and there is thus little loss of lateral extensibility – a pre-requisite for garment length and hosiery knitting. For double-jersey fabrics, birdseye or twill backing (see Fig. 13.9) is preferred as this is a more stable structure which is better balanced and has a pleasing scrambled colour appearance on the backing side. It is achieved by knitting the backing on alternate needles only and arranging for each colour to be knitted by odd backing needles at one feeder and even needles at the next. The optimum number of colours is usually three.

Whereas flat jacquard patterns have equal numbers of loops in each wale of the pattern repeat, blister and relief patterned fabrics do not. Links-links purl machines (particularly hosiery machines) may have facilities for knitting combined colour and stitch effects. Usually, the needles in one bed knit continuously so that the lateral extensibility of the structure is not too adversely affected. Float bolt patterning is more restricted, at the first feed needles selectively transferred to the bottom cylinder knit together with those remaining in the top cylinder, at the second feed, the latter knit alone with the miss stitches floating at the back of the held plain loops of the previous course. In combined links-links and three-colour float jacquard, needles may be selected to knit in the bottom cylinder at any one of the three feeds whilst the needles which remain in the top cylinder knit at each of the three feeds producing floats behind held plain loops (Fig. 10.7).

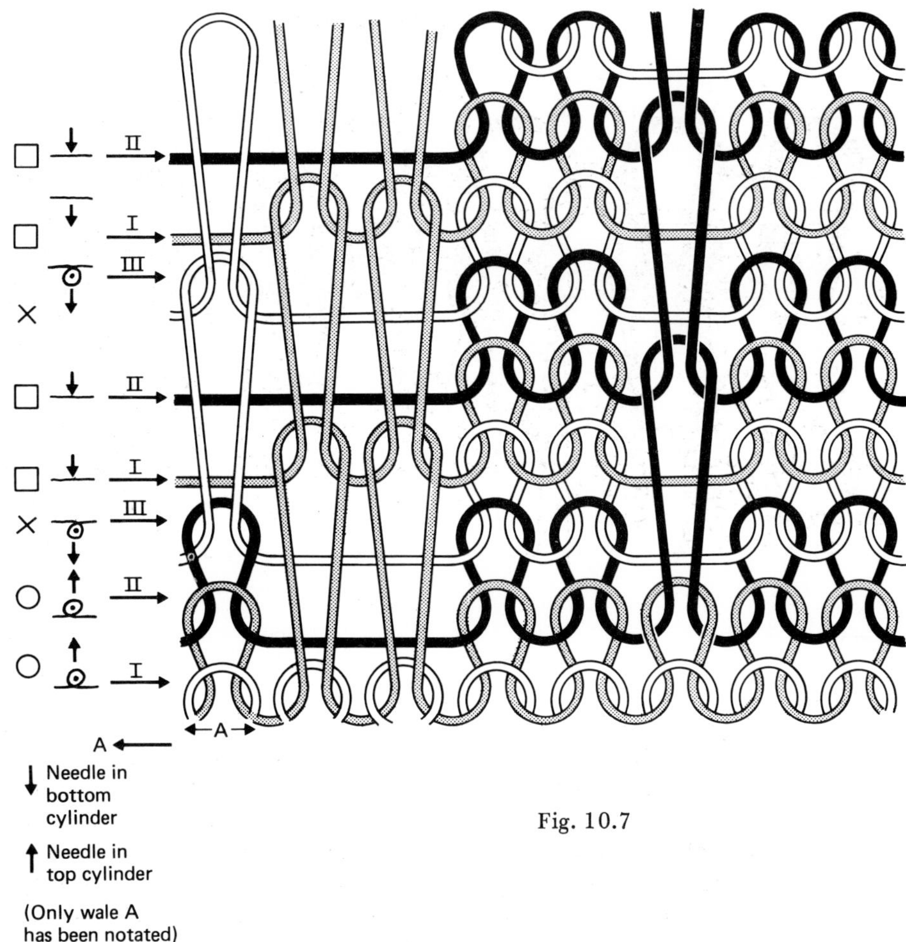

Fig. 10.7

Worked Example 10.9

The squared diagram illustrates part of a three-colour jacquard design. Each face stitch being represented by a square.

Using the running thread form of notation provide:

(a) A representation of the design for single-jersey knit/miss jacquard.

(b) A Repeat of the representation of the first two pattern rows for:

(i) straight accordion.

(ii) alternate accordion.

(iii) selected accordion.

(c) A representation of the first two pattern rows as rib jacquard with:

(i) Horizontally striped backing.

(ii) Vertically striped backing.

(iii) Birds eye backing.

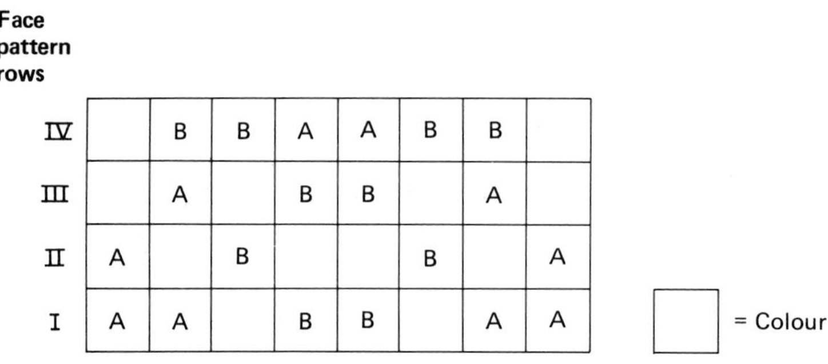

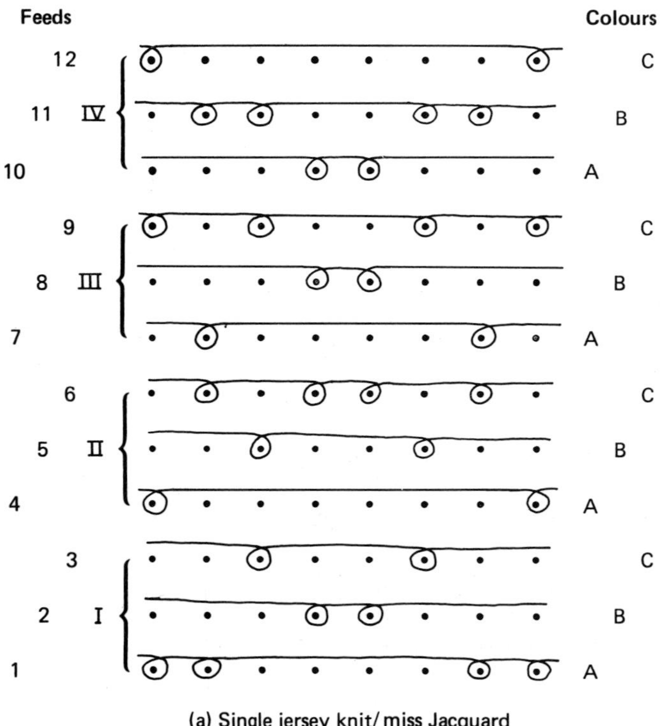

(a) Single jersey knit/miss Jacquard

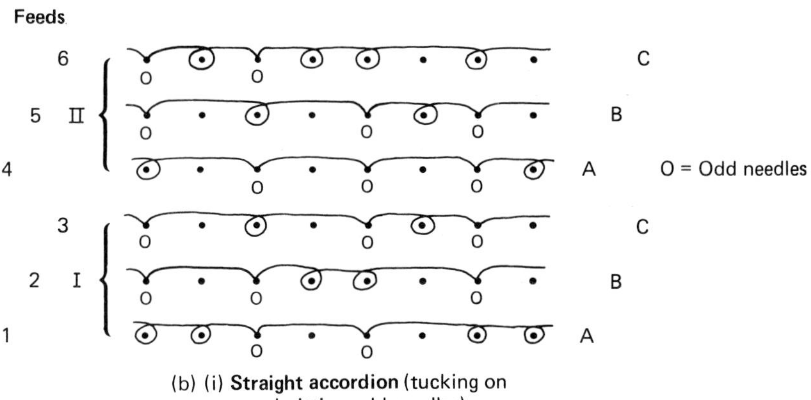

(b) (i) **Straight accordion** (tucking on non-knitting odd needles)

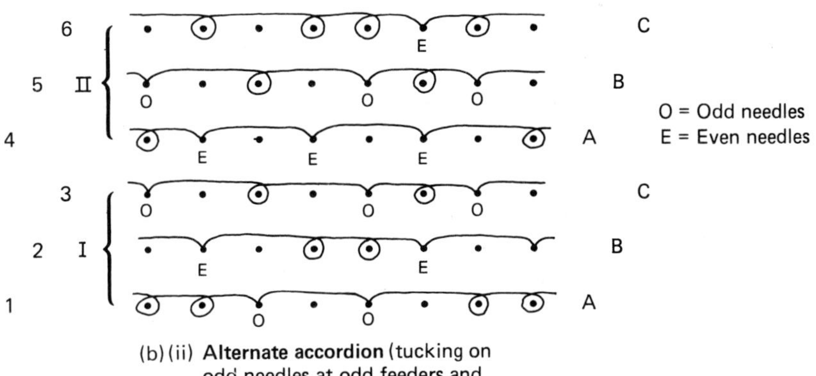

(b) (ii) **Alternate accordion** (tucking on odd needles at odd feeders and even needles at even feeders when non-knitting)

KT-H

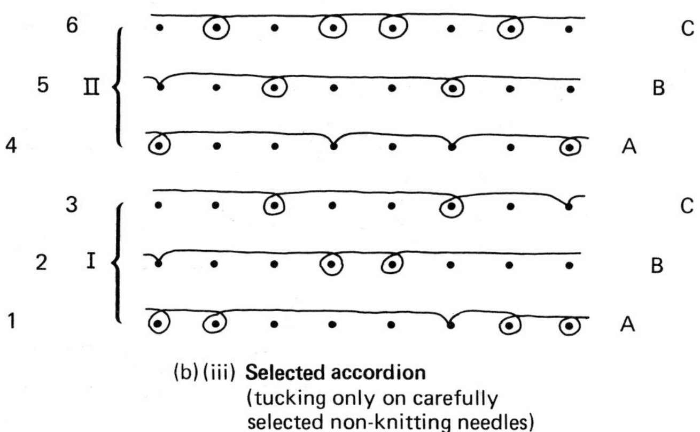

(b) (iii) **Selected accordion**
(tucking only on carefully selected non-knitting needles)

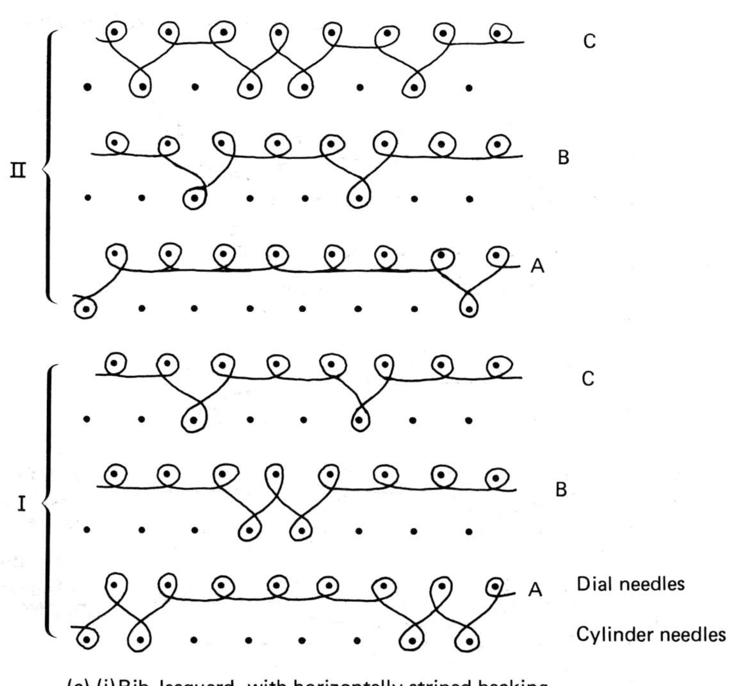

(c) (i) Rib Jacquard with horizontally striped backing

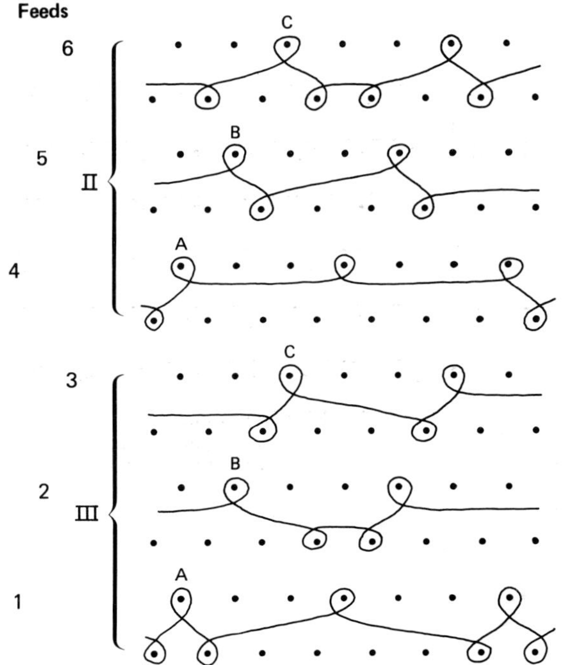

(c)(ii) Rib Jacquard with vertically striped backing

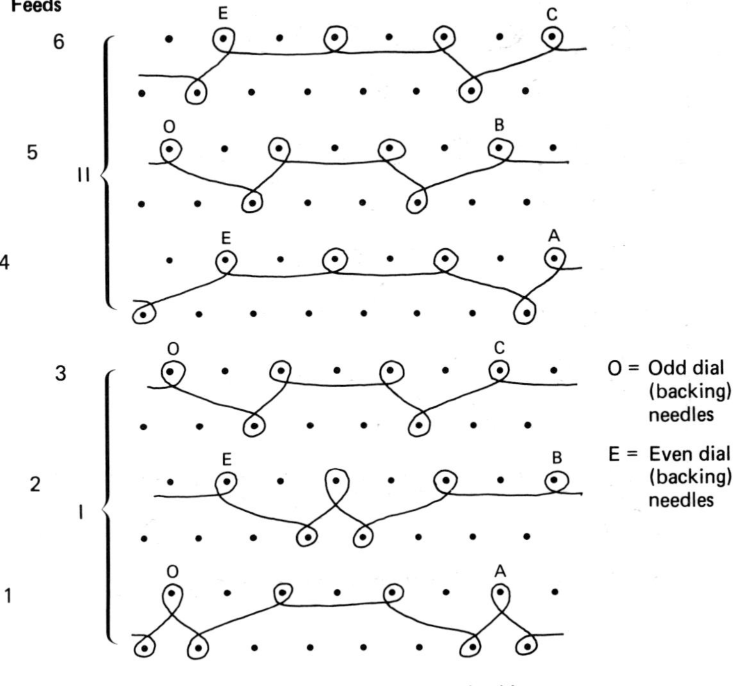

(c)(iii) Rib Jacquard with birds eye backing

1. HAIGH, D., Dyeing and finishing of knitted goods, *Hos. Trade Journal*, (1970) Leicester, 147 pp.
2. VOGEL, R., *Wirkerie-und-Strickerei Technik 29*, (1979) (first English issue), 41–44.
3. CARROTTE, F., Monarch electronic stripers, *Knit. Int.*, (July 1981) p. 40–1 and Aug. p. 88–9.
4. GOADBY, D. R., Camber micro-electronic striping system, *Knit. Int.*, (May 1981) 95–6.
5. Intarsia knitting. *Hos. Trade Journal*, (Dec. 1964) 134–141.
   LANCASHIRE, J. B., The knitting of intarsia fabrics, *Hos. Trade Journal*, (Nov. 1957) 66–70.
6. LANCASHIRE, J. B., How to knit argyle designs on half-hose machines. *Knit. O'wr Times*, (18 Sept. 1967) 22–3, 43.
7. LANCASHIRE, J. B., Intarsia patterning on spring needle full fashioned frames, *Knit. O'wr Times*, (17 April 1967) 13, 15, 89.
   INNES, R., Bentley Cotton intarsia, *Knit. Times*, (15 April 1975) 205–10 and (26 July, 1976) 29–33.
   INNES, R., Scheller intarsia, *Knit. Times*, (21 April 1980) 12–3; *Knit. Int.*, (June 1980) 101.
8. Dubied DRC 3, *Knit. Int.*, (March 1979) 61–3.
   Stoll ANVH 1, *Knit. Int.*, (May 1980) 48–9.

11

Pattern and Selection Devices

Simple patterning and quick rib changes (during garment knitting) can be achieved in a limited width repeat when element butts are at one of a range of lengths or positions associated with particular raising cam arrangements. The cam arrangement and element butt repeat set-out will determine the pattern area. Popular methods employ different butt lengths and cam thicknesses or (and) different butt positions and cam tracks.

Different Lengths of Butt 11.1

Whereas butts of normal length extend into the track formed between cams and are guided at their elements by contact with their profiled edges, a butt of shorter length may not reach into the track and will pass across the face of the cam and be unaffected by its profile (Fig. 11.1). The same principle is employed when cams are withdrawn into their cam-plate or the elements are depressed into their tricks thus reducing the effective length of their butts. *The principle of butt lengths is that the element with the longest butt is always contacted first* as a cam is brought into operation and the shortest butt is only affected when the cam is fully in action.

For example, a tuck cam might be partly in action raising long and medium butt needles but allowing short butt needles to pass across at miss height, whilst the succeeding clearing cam is set to raise only long butt needles, leaving medium butt needles at tuck height. If short, instead of long butt needles are required to be lifted, it is necessary to contact and lower the long butt needles before they reach the raising cam which is placed fully in action to lift the short butt needles remaining in line with it.

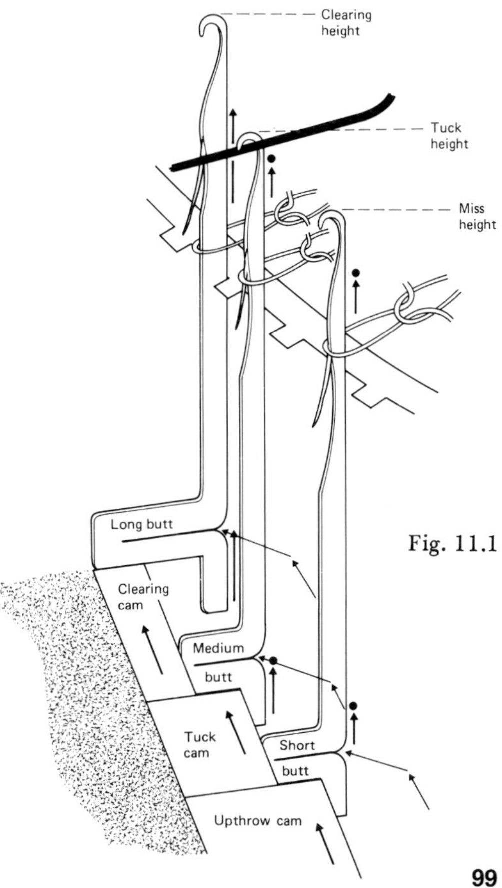

Fig. 11.1

Separately butted and cam-controlled elements known as push-jacks may be placed below the needles in their tricks. As their butt set-out need not correspond to that of the needles, a greater selection potential is available than through the needle butts alone. Long butt jacks can thus be used to positively lift short butt needles. Jack butt set-outs are particularly suitable for obtaining pre-determined rib set-outs in garment length sequences.

11.2 Different Butt Positions

This principle is employed in the interlock cam system. In single-jersey multi-cam-track (raceway) machines needle butts may be positioned in one of between two and five tracks which at every feed position have fixed but exchangeable knitting, tucking or missing cams. In some machines (as in jacquard machines) a common top butt is controlled by a stitch cam-track whereas in high speed machines the exchangeable cams also incorporate the stitch and guard cam shape and are located on a common slide for stitch length adjustment (Fig. 11.2).

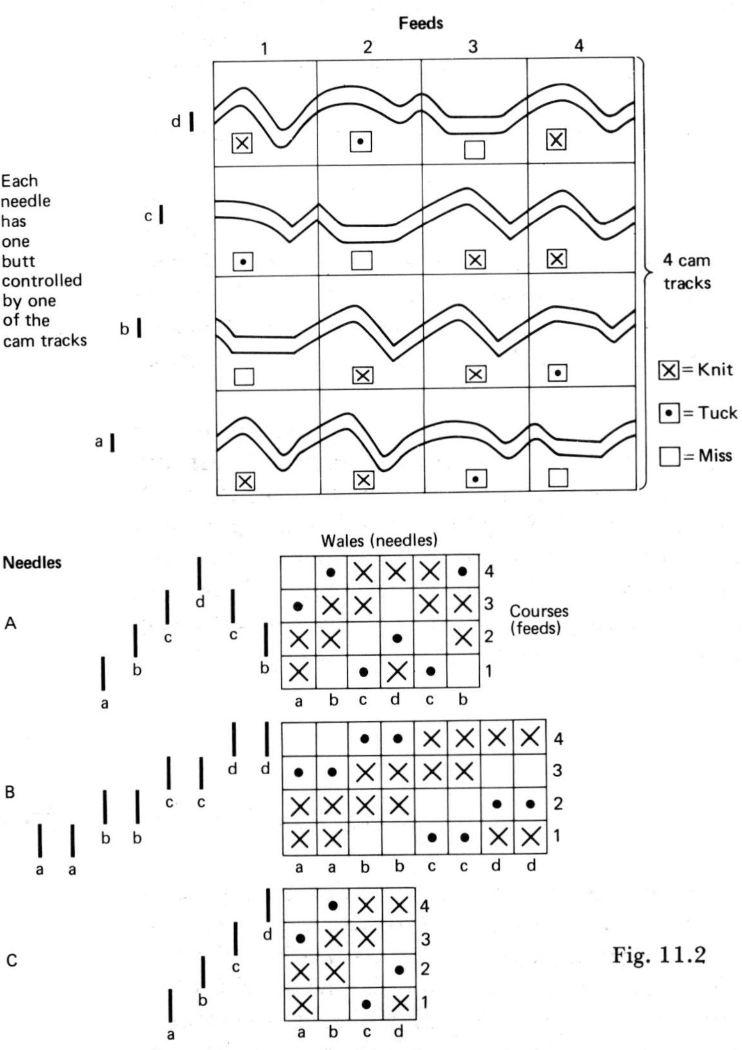

Examples of needle butt set-outs with the unchanged cam arrangement above will produce the three types of pattern illustrated.

Fig. 11.2

Multi-Step Butt Set-Outs 11.3

Although some selection devices, including pattern wheels, operate onto element butts of one height position, many patterning arrangements involve the use of a single selection butt for each element placed at one of a choice of height positions. The total number of different heights often directly influences the width repeat in wales. *It is generally most convenient to arrange and retain a butt set-out which is a factor of the needle bed* so that the pattern widths exactly repeat across it.

The two most common geometrical butt set-outs are straight and mirror repeat although combinations of the two are possible.

A *straight* (diagonal, echelon or up-and-up) *butt set-out* is arranged in an ascending order in the direction of knitting (Fig. 11.2). Each butt position is used once only in the set-out repeat so the pattern width is equal to the number of available butt positions.

A *mirror repeat* (reflex chevron, up-and-down, or geometric) *butt set-out* is a mirrored continuation of the straight set-out with the butts descending in sequence after the highest position see Fig. 11.7. The top and bottom butts are not used in the descending sequence as the former would produce two identical adjacent wales in the same repeat whereas the latter would produce two identical adjacent wales with the first wale of the next repeat. This set-out thus produces a symmetrical design width about a common centre wale with the right side identically mirroring the left side.

With geometric selection, the top butt position is only used in mirror repeats so that these are *exactly twice the width of straight set-outs* and both are a factor of the number of cylinder needles. For example, an 18 npi 30-inch diameter machine with 1728 cylinder needles using a small area fixed selection might have 24 butts positions (and pattern comb teeth) for a straight set-out repeating 72 times around the cylinder and an extra top butt and tooth used only for mirror repeat set-outs making 25 up and 23 down giving a width of 48 butts repeating 36 times around the cylinder.

Selection Devices 11.4

Selection devices vary considerably in their facilities and their pattern-changing and pattern-area capabilities. *A device is positioned to operate in advance of a raising cam system* (usually associated with a knitting feed position) to select the path which the element operating butts will follow as they pass through that system. Each possible path will cause the element to be moved in a different manner resulting in the knitting of a different type of stitch. Usually a selection decision determines the choice of two butt paths.

11.5 Element Selection

Element selection involves three aspects:

1. The *initiation* and *presentation* of the selection decision usually as a YES or NO, the presence or absence of a tooth, a peg, a punched hole or an electrical impulse. Normally there is a selection in advance of each raising cam with each feeder course being associated with a particular selection device.

2. The *transmission of the selection* decisions from the device and their reception by elements in each trick of the needle bed. One of three methods is normally employed for this task:

(a) Employing *individual raising cams* when required, for each element raising butt (pattern wheel selection).

(b) By *selectively pushing* the elements upwards in their stationary tricks to align their raising butts into action with the path of traversing or rotating cam systems (full mechanical jacquard selection).

(c) By the *selective retraction* of elements into the interior of their tricks so that their raising butts no longer project out into the path of the cams. This method is widely used for mechanically and electronically initiated selection on circular and flat machines especially when employing geometric multi-butt set-outs of selection butts. Raising butts may be selected to miss a complete raising cam or only the final upper section between tucking and clearing height.

3. *Translation of the selection decision into a knitting movement.* This is still a completely mechanical action of a raising butt following or failing to follow the profile of a raising cam and thus causing an element to be lifted or not lifted in its trick during a stitch formation cycle. The shape of the raising cam profile is usually unaffected by the technique of the selection device when not incorporated within it.

Normally all selection devices of one circular machine will hold an equal number of width selections and an equal number of depth selections so that when each device is aligned to commence selection at the same starting trick (wale). Equal widths of selection will occur at each feeder course and will be aligned into rectangular selection areas exactly framed by the courses and wales of the fabric (Fig. 11.3).

11.6 Selection Area Arrangement

Dependent upon the type of device, four arrangements of the selection areas around the fabric tube are possible:

1. *Full jacquard selection* can produce a selection area of theoretically unlimited depth and a width equal to the number of needles in the cylinder so that the design exactly surrounds the fabric tube without repeating.

2. *Pattern wheels* have a circumference selection which is not an exact factor of the number of cylinder needles so that their selection areas follow the spiral path of the feeder courses around the fabric tube. In the starting wale of each machine revolution the base of the areas will thus

have risen by the number of feeder courses knitted in one machine revolution compared with its position in the same starting wale at the previous machine revolution (X in Fig. 11.3a).

3. *Fixed geometric selection devices* (step jack devices) provide only one selection width at each device which is unchanged from one machine revolution to the next (Fig. 11.3b). Machines employing this type of device are termed small area or intermediate jacquards because, although their pattern area potential is limited, they have sufficient feeders and speed to be employed in the production of plain structures as well as jacquards. A complete design depth is thus produced at each machine revolution composed of the number of active feeders courses so that the base of the design will have risen by that number of courses each time it is recommended in the starting wale, but no displacement of design is noticeable between the adjacent finishing and starting wales of the fabric tube.

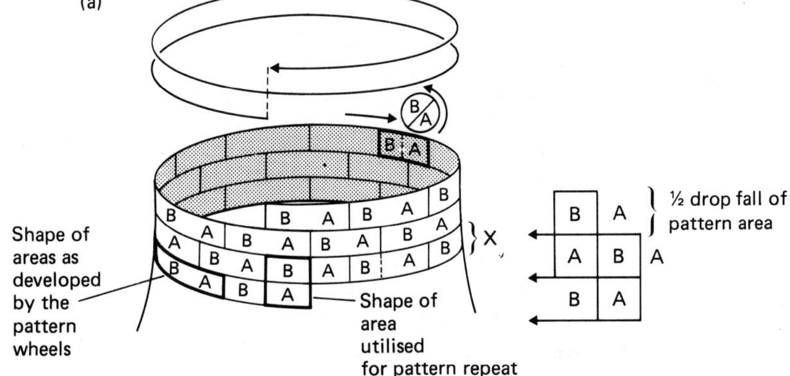

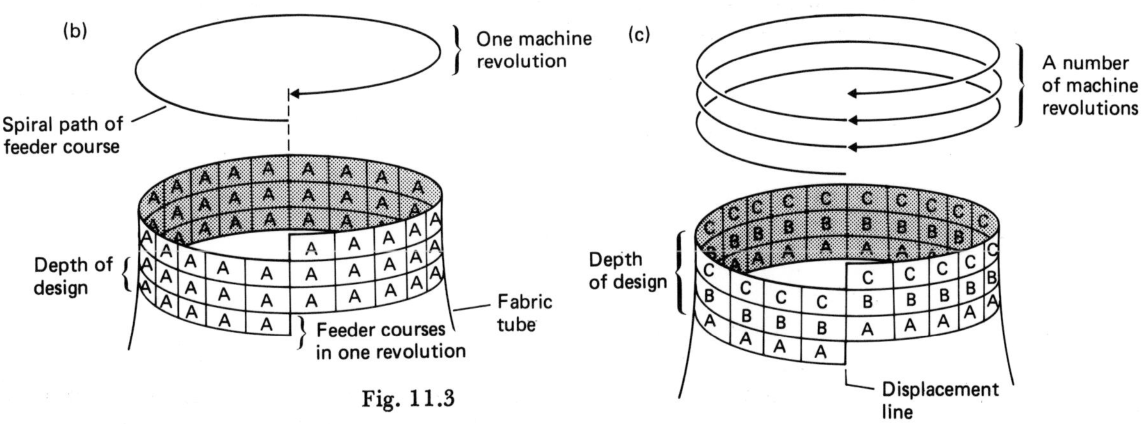

Fig. 11.3

4. *Non-fixed geometric selection devices* hold a limited number of different selection widths so that a new selection width may be presented commencing in the starting wale of each machine revolution (Fig. 11.3c). Double-jersey machines using non-fixed selection are termed large-area

jacquards.[1] A design depth is thus developed which is a multiple of the number of machine revolutions in the sequence of selection presentations. These devices produce a displacement line between the starting and finishing wales of the tube in the form of a rise by the number of feeder courses in one revolution. Usually the tube is split open along this line during finishing.

The potential depth of non-fixed selection devices is increased by the ability to dwell (retain) a selection for a number of machine revolutions, and to rack the selection sequence forwards or backwards by one or two steps.

Only in the case of full jacquard selection on machines with stationary needle bed tricks (certain flat machines and revolving cam-box circular machines) can a successive row of selection decisions be kept in permanent alignment with each trick. On other revolving cam-box machines and flat machines the selection devices pass across the tricks with their associated cam-sections or in the case of revolving cylinder machines they remain with their cam-sections as the cylinder revolves past them.

Wheels of discs turn in continuous alignment but in the opposite direction to the cylinder so that each trick in turn receives a decision from the selection sequence around the wheel periphery. The element butts being selected may be set-out at the same height. Although the selection is in a fixed set-out in a pattern wheel, the pattern depth is spirally developed over a number of machine revolutions. On machines with selector wheels, a tape may rearrange the selection set-out for the

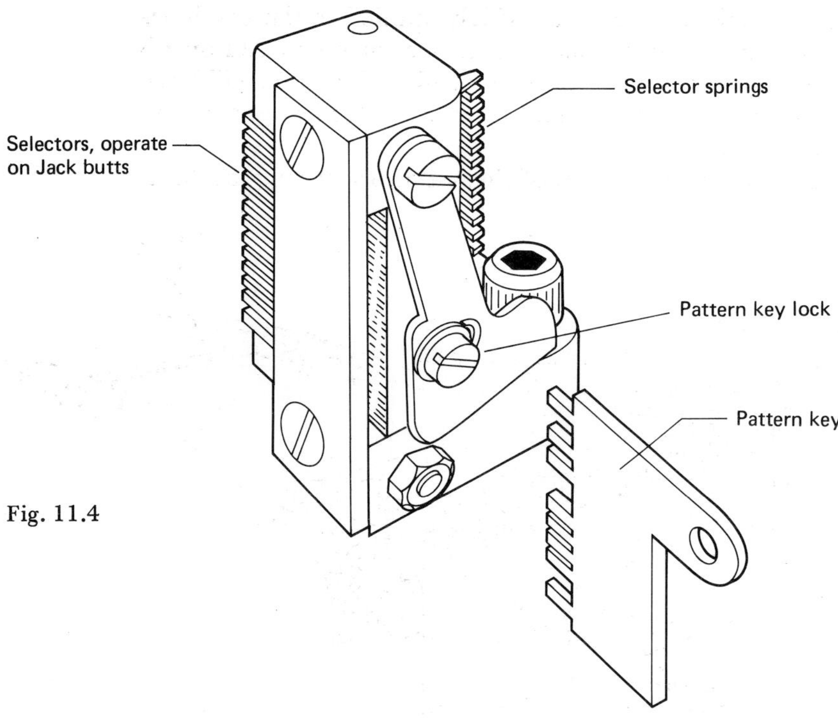

Fig. 11.4

next machine revolution or a different disc selection may be switched into operation.

With multi-butt selection, the selection butt at each trick can be placed at one of a number of different heights usually in a geometric set-out which will determine the pattern width. As either the selection device or the needle cylinder is revolving, the selection is transferred from the device by a bank of spring-loaded plates or electronically-controlled selectors which pivot across to contact any selection butts at that height as they pass (Fig. 11.4).

On mechanical selection devices a vertical row of selection teeth or pegs at each station pushes the respective height plates towards the needle bed. With non-fixed selection, a different row of selection may be aligned at the start of each machine revolution at each device in turn.

Full Jacquard Mechanical Needle Selection 11.7

This method provides the possibility of independent selection over the full width of the stationary needle bed in a simultaneous movement for all needles on flat machines or onto blocks of adjacent needles on revolving cam-box circulars, with a theoretically unlimited depth of traverses or revolutions dependent upon the number of jacquard steels or the length of the jacquard rolls. Each column of holes is allocated to a particular needle with a new selection being presented by each part turn of the prism or roller. The arrangement has been widely applied to flat machines (see section 19.2 for a description) and has also been employed on rib jacquard and garment length purl machines produced by the Wildman Jacquard company. Low speed, a limited number of feeders and coarse gauge have restricted its use.

Figure 11.5 illustrates the arrangement of elements on a circular machine.

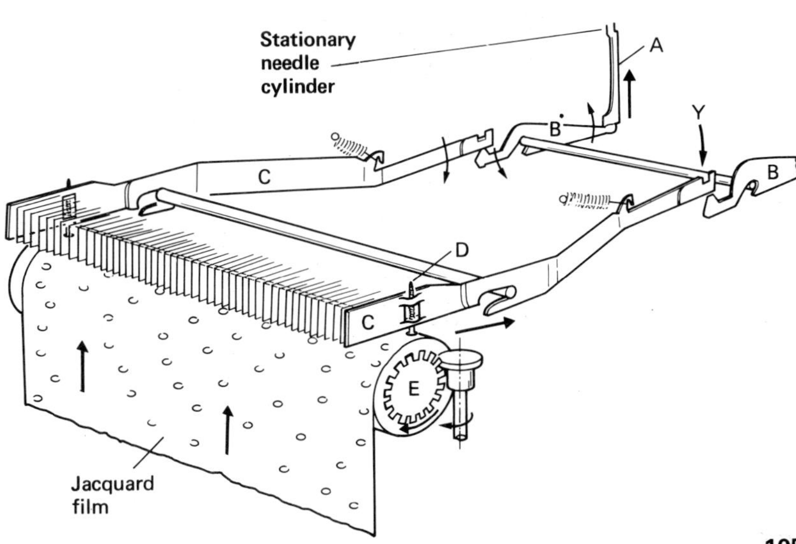

Fig. 11.5

Selectors and lifters are arranged in groups of 48 termed an automat which is controlled by a 48-track film and roller. On a 30-inch (76 cm) diameter 14-gauge machine there will be 28 automats arranged around the periphery of the needle cylinder. Beneath each cylinder needle there is a jack (A) whose tail is supported by the inner end of a pivoted lifter lever (B). Resting on the outer end of lever B is the inner end of a pivoted automat lever (C). The outer end of lever C holds a spring-loaded pin (D) which rest on top of the film roll as it passes over a grooved roller (E).

A punched hole in the film causes a needle to knit. The automat pin falls through the hole into the roller groove. As the feeder approaches, the roller is turned by 1/12 of a revolution causing all automat levers whose pins have entered its groove to be moved forwards. A cam revolving with the cam-box presses down on the inward end of all advanced automat levers at Y which in turn press down onto the outer ends of their lifter levers causing the inner end of each to be pivoted to raise their jacks into alignment with a raising cam so that the needles above them are raised to knit. The action also pivots the automat levers so that their pins are lifted out of the holes whilst the return springs withdraw them so that their pins are in line with the next row of selection holes.

When no hole is punched, the automat lever is not advanced so the effect of the depressing cam is not transmitted to the lifter and the needle remains in the miss position. Pattern preparation can be time-consuming as just one row of two-colour jacquard around the machine will require 2 × 1,344 separate punched hole positions.[2]

11.8 Multi-Step Geometric Selection

This method has developed from the Brinton trick wheel of 1926 which first employed single butted depressible selectors beneath the cylinder needles rather than in an intermediate drum. Figure 11.6 illustrates a device used on Wildt Mellor Bromley machines of the RTR range for either rib jacquard or rib loop transfer selection in circular garment lengths. The pattern drums move with their cam selections and have a circumference of 40 vertical rows of selection. As each drum passes the garment control mechanism it may be caused to single or double rack forwards or single rack backwards or be bluffed to dwell and retain the same selection for the next machine revolution. Thus within the pattern depth, forty different feeder courses are possible for each pattern drum.

Each vertical column around the drum has a height of either twenty-four or thirty-six selection positions depending upon the model. This depth corresponds to the pattern width repeat. The drums are either drilled with holes to receive push-in metal pegs or are equipped with grooved tricks for the insertion of pattern jacks whose butts are snipped off according to the pattern. The latter arrangement is generally preferred as the jacks can be prepared in a less laborious operation whilst the machine is knitting another design. A bank of spring-loaded selector plates, corresponding in height to the possible selection heights, works with each drum to transmit the selection to the cylinder.

The tail of each cylinder needle is supported by the upper ledge (A) of a spring-tailed lifting jack. A selector presser (B) is placed in front of each jack in a trick. The presser has a complement of twenty-four or thirty-six pattern butts corresponding to the width repeat, all except one butt (X) are removed so that a chevron or echelon pattern butt set-out is arranged around the needle cylinder.

The tail of the lifting jack is sprung outwards so that its raising butt (G) is in line with the raising cam (F) (F may be either a clearing cam or a rib loop transfer cam). If butt G follows the profile of cam F the jack will lift its cylinder needle to either knit or transfer its loop depending on the cam position and shape.

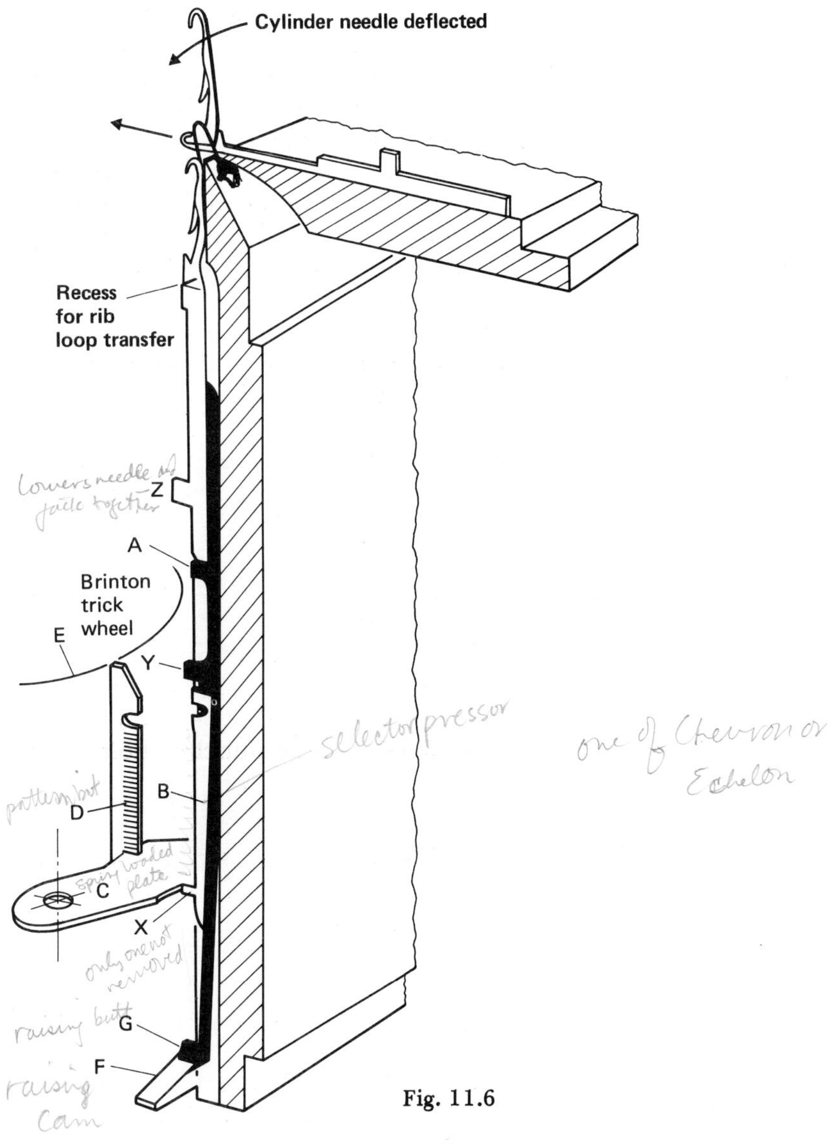

Fig. 11.6

The selection is indirect, requiring a decision for non-movement of the needle. When a pattern bit (D) is placed in the vertical row of the drum directly facing the cylinder at the same height as the pattern butt (X) of a needle jack presser, the spring-loaded plate (C) at that height will be pivoted towards the cylinder so that it presses against butt X as it passes by causing the tail of the jack to be depressed into the cylinder so that its butt (G) goes behind the raising cam (F) and the needle is not lifted.

Needle butt Z is used to lower the needle and this in turn lowers the jack ready for selection at the next section. The effect of the selection may be cancelled (for example in the rib border) by introducing a raising cam to lift all jacks by means of butts Y.

Mayer have utilized racking peg drums on revolving cylinder garment

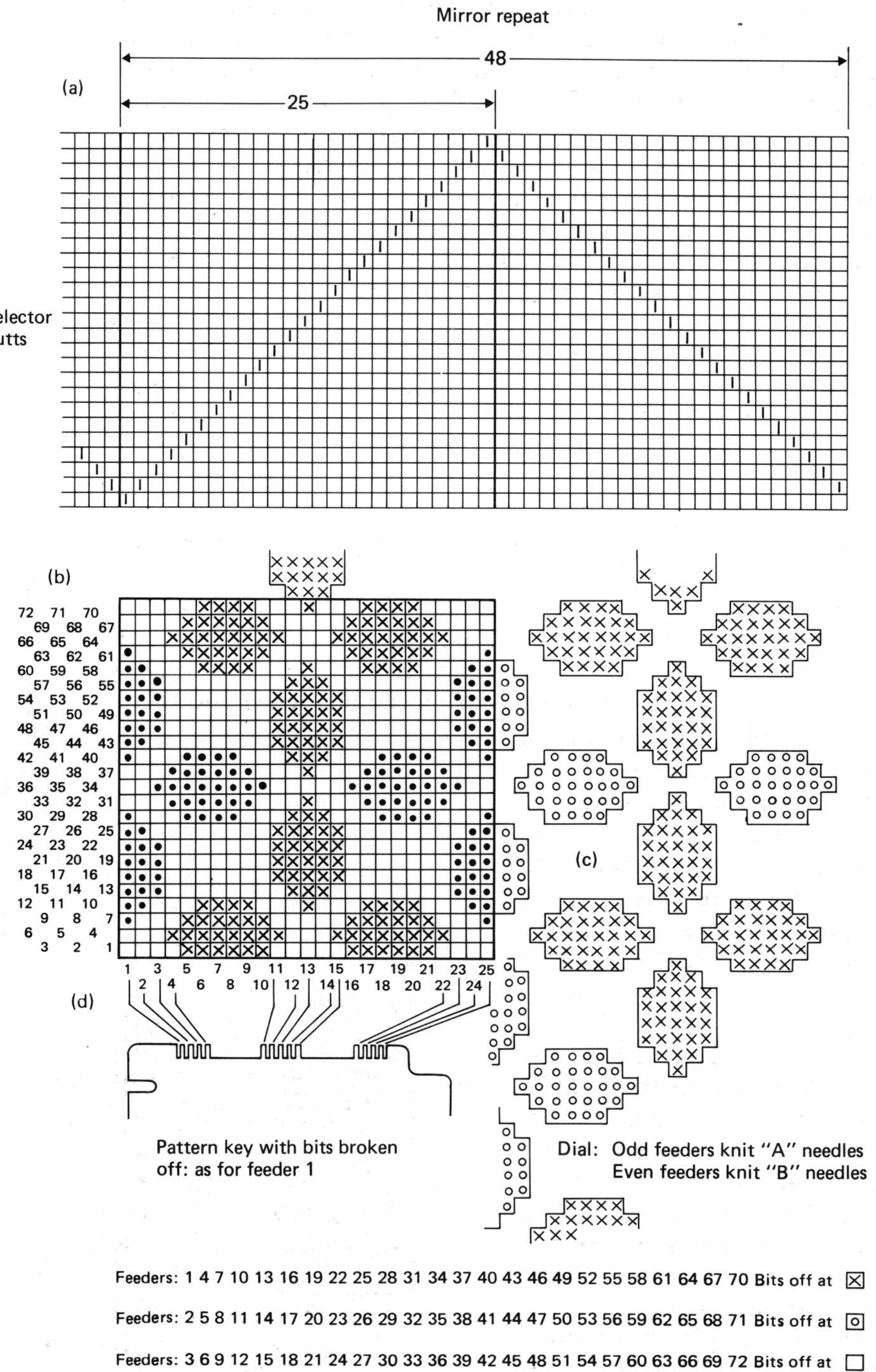

Feeders: 1 4 7 10 13 16 19 22 25 28 31 34 37 40 43 46 49 52 55 58 61 64 67 70 Bits off at ☒

Feeders: 2 5 8 11 14 17 20 23 26 29 32 35 38 41 44 47 50 53 56 59 62 65 68 71 Bits off at ⊡

Feeders: 3 6 9 12 15 18 21 24 27 30 33 36 39 42 45 48 51 54 57 60 63 66 69 72 Bits off at ☐

Fig. 11.7

length, rib jacquard and also single-jersey machines. Different height links on a control chain can be used to alter an eccentric as it passes by at each revolution of the cylinder and this in turn causes each drum to be singly or doubly racked or bluffed as it passes around the machine. On the single-jersey MJT machine, the rows of holes around the peg drums are arranged in two vertically staggered rows each thirty-two positions deep. At the first row, pegs cause needle jacks to be depressed and miss the raising cam whereas holes leave jacks unaffected to pass onto the tuck cam. A peg in the second row, acting later, will cause further jacks to be depressed leaving their needles at tuck height whereas a hole allows jacks and their needles to continue to pass over the raising cam to clearing height.

Since the mid-1960s, toothed pattern keys or combs have proved popular for fixed multi-step geometric selection (Fig. 11.7), firstly, on double-jersey machines and later, on single-jersey machines. The Wildt Mellor Bromley MSJ is an example of the former and the JSJ, an example of the latter. At each of the seventy-two feeds is a double-sided toothed key, on the latest MSJ a knit miss selection is provided for two feeders – one with each side whereas on the JSJ the left side of the key can select for miss or tuck and the right-side teeth select jacks at tuck height to either remain there or to go to clearing height.

The Camber single-jersey Cheminit machine (Fig. 11.8) employs a number of unusual features to provide multi-butt fixed indirect selection for knit, tuck and miss at feeds placed three per diametral inch for gauges as fine as 40 npi.[3] Selection occurs onto jacks placed in a wider and therefore coarser gauge cylinder (A) than the needle cylinder (B), which is set above and inside it. The jacks have an upper selection butt (C) which may be at any one of twenty-five height positions for straight or mirror repeat set-outs.

There is a module (D) at each feeder containing a bank of twenty-five pairs of spring-loaded selector slides. A small shallow raising cam (E) is attached to the inner end of each slide which can lift any jack with a selection butt at that height. The first (right) slide (F) of each pair has a tuck cam and the second (left) slide (G) has a clearing cam. Using a slide retraction device, a 25-tooth comb (H) is inserted in a vertical position into the left side of each module contacting the slides towards their outer ends.

When a tooth is completely removed from the comb (I) the corresponding pair of slides spring towards the cylinder and their cams lift any jack with a

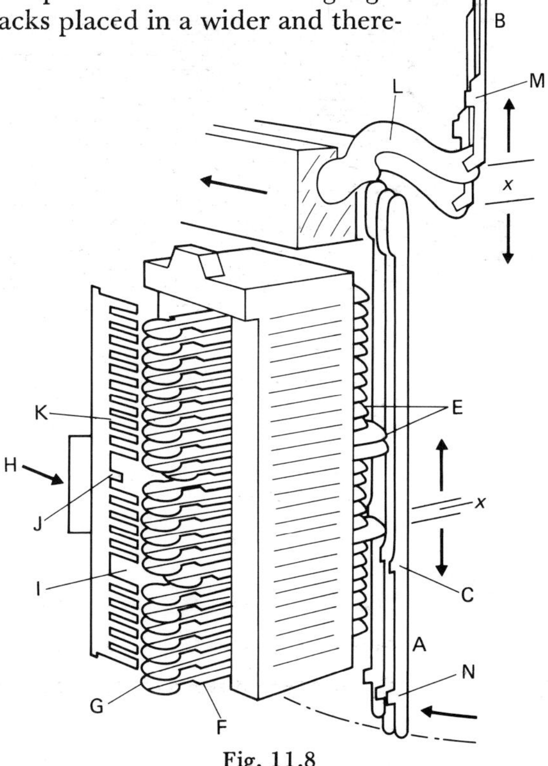

Fig. 11.8

selection butt at that height causing the needles above to knit. If a tooth is half removed (J) it only penetrates far enough into the module to restrain the left (clearing cam) slide holding it away from the cylinder whilst the right (tuck cam) slide remains in action causing needles to tuck. If a tooth is complete (K) it will be long enough to restrain the right, as well as the left slide, so that both will be inactive and corresponding jacks and needles will not be raised thus producing miss stitches.

An intermediate leverage of 4:1 between the jack-lifting movement and the cylinder needles is achieved by horizontal clavettes (L) one of which rests on top of each jack with its outer end protruding into a fixed but pivoted position whilst its inner free end supports the raising butt of the needle. The leverage effect of the clavette converts a small lifting movement of the jack by the pair of slide cams at a shallow angle to the horizontal plane, into a larger lifting movement of the cylinder needle between miss and clear position equivalent to a raising cam angle of 59 degrees.

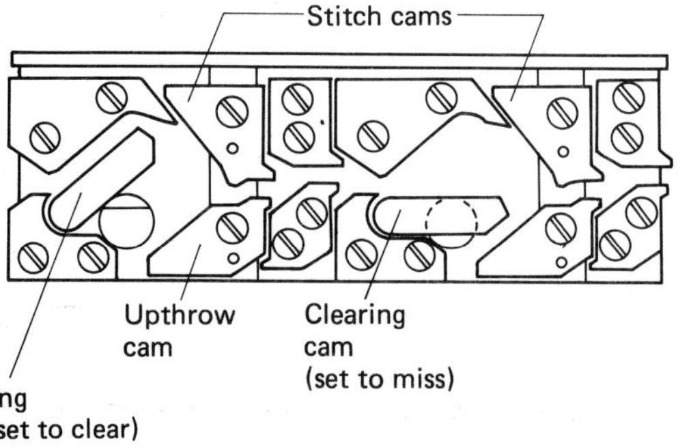

Prior to reselection the elements are automatically lowered as the stitch cam lowers the needles, by means of butt M whilst the lower butt of the jacks (N) is acted on by a levelling cam.

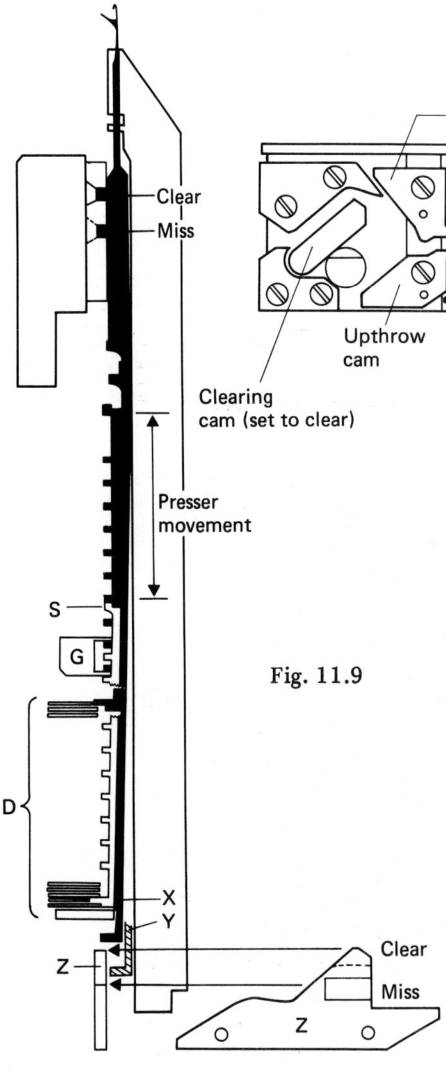

Stitch cams
Upthrow cam
Clearing cam (set to miss)
Clearing cam (set to clear)
Clear
Miss
Presser movement
S
G
D
X
Y
Z
Clear
Miss
Z

Fig. 11.9

Disc selection has proved popular on Wildt Mellor Bromley machines of the RJ rib jacquard type since 1967.[4–6] At each feed, replaceable disc stacks are rotated in unison with the machine drive. On 72-feeder machines the stacks are accommodated at two alternately staged heights. When a disc tooth contacts the bottom half-butt of a presser (X in Fig. 11.9) it causes the jack tail (Y) which supports it to be retracted into the cylinder so that its tail butt misses the raising cam (Z) and the needle which is supported by the jack is not lifted to knit.

Presser half-butts are of two types; those with an upper half-butt (X in Fig. 11.9) are placed in odd cylinder tricks and those with a lower half-butt are placed in even tricks.

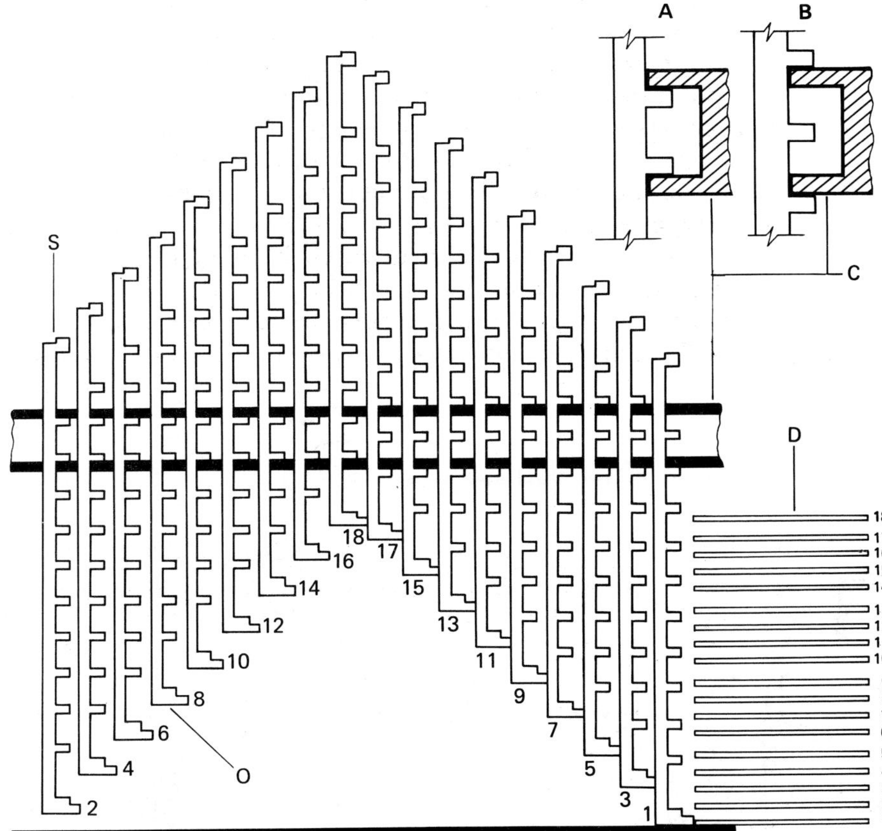

Fig. 11.10

A selection disc is actually composed of a pair of discs – the teeth of the upper one selecting odd needles by means of the upper half-butt – and the teeth of the lower one selecting even needles by means of the lower half-butt (0 in Fig. 11.10). As each only selects alternate needles their teeth are cut twice as coarse as the machine gauge and are centred for these needles. The total number of teeth in a selection disc determines the pattern width which may be 144 wales in 28 gauge.

At any cylinder revolution a disc at the same height at each stack will be selecting. After each revolution the pressers may be raised or lowered to a different height so that their half-butts are aligned with a different disc selection. In this way, as many as 18 discs, each for a selection at a different cylinder revolution may be accommodated at each stack.

The height control of the pressers is achieved through their identically-arranged and carefully-spaced guide butts of which each may have as many as 10 depending upon the height of the disc stacks. During each cylinder revolution, two of these butts are in contact with a guide channel which surrounds the cylinder so that the pressers are held at a constant height. Three bolt cams situated at a short break in the channel provide the choice of serially lifting, lowering or retaining (bluffing or dwelling) the pressers at the same height for the next cylinder revolution. Introduction or withdrawal of each cam is controlled by separate tracks on a punched hole film which racks once per cylinder revolution and thus has a major effect on the pattern depth.

Figure 11.10 illustrates the change of presser height (S) at each of eighteen cylinder revolutions so that its half-butt obtains the selection from every disc (D) in the stack. Notice that during the revolutions whilst the presser is being lifted, its guide butts occupy position 'A' in the guide channel (C) so that the half-butt is always opposite an even-numbered disc and when lowering the presser, its guide butts occupy position 'B' so that the half-butt is aligned with odd-numbered discs. The discs must therefore be stacked in this order of use during pattern preparation.

11.9 Monofilm Selection

The Dubied Wevenit large area rib jacquard machine employs design wheels whose selectors may be rearranged after each cylinder revolution by means of punched hole tracks on an endless steel ribbon monofilm. The film passes around the cylinder in the opposite direction to it being driven by the outer surfaces of the wheels and is wound in spiral form into a storage container from the centre of which it is being continuously withdrawn. The film is typically long enough for 52 complete circuits of the machine each being a complete rearrangement of the design wheel set-out for one cylinder revolution.

The number of selectors in a wheel (typically 96) determines the pattern width. When a rearrangement of the design wheels is required, the selectors are levelled so that their noses protrude onto the passing film surface. If at the exact position for that selector the film is unpunched, the selector will be pushed into the wheel and its foot will then rest on a sliding raising block inside the wheel. As the wheel turns towards the cylinder the block will slide upwards inside the wheel and the selector will be lifted. Its head is then pushed towards the cylinder so that it depresses the tail of a jack (clavette) which is fixed by a pivot to a buttless cylinder needle. The clavette butt misses the raising cam and the needle is not lifted. If a hole is not punched in the film at that position the nose of the selector will not be pushed in, it will not be lifted in the wheel so that the clavette butt will follow the raising cam and the cylinder needle will knit.

There are four sliding blocks inside each wheel, each is capable of lifting 1/4 of the selectors. Once the sliding blocks are raised they may be retained in this position thus fixing the selection for the wheel because the film will be unable to contact the noses of the raised selectors and the other selectors in the wheel cannot be lifted as the blocks are out of action. Cancellation of the selection by lowering the blocks and levelling the selectors can be achieved after each cylinder revolution by a cam which revolves with it and can thus contact each wheel in turn, the action of this cam may be centrally controlled by a multivar tape mechanism which can hold insertable clips.

The noses of the selectors are arranged at one of four levels corresponding to the four tracks of the monofilm. Half of the thirty-six wheels (feeders) are rearranged by two of the tracks and the other half by the other two tracks.

The levelling of the selectors in a wheel is carefully sequenced so that it occurs precisely in advance of their contacting a particular portion of the film. In this way, exact portions of each circuit of the film can be allocated to each wheel whilst the rest of the film in the circuit will pass over the wheel without rearranging its selectors.[7,8] There have been no comparatively recent developments with this technique.

The Pattern Wheel 11.10

The pattern wheel is a cheap, simple device occupying little space and is unique in employing separate raising cams in the form of pattern bits to select and move individual elements, if necessary to three different positions in their tricks (Fig. 11.11). It is most popular in single-jersey machines either as an inclined wheel for needle or point selection, or as a hori-

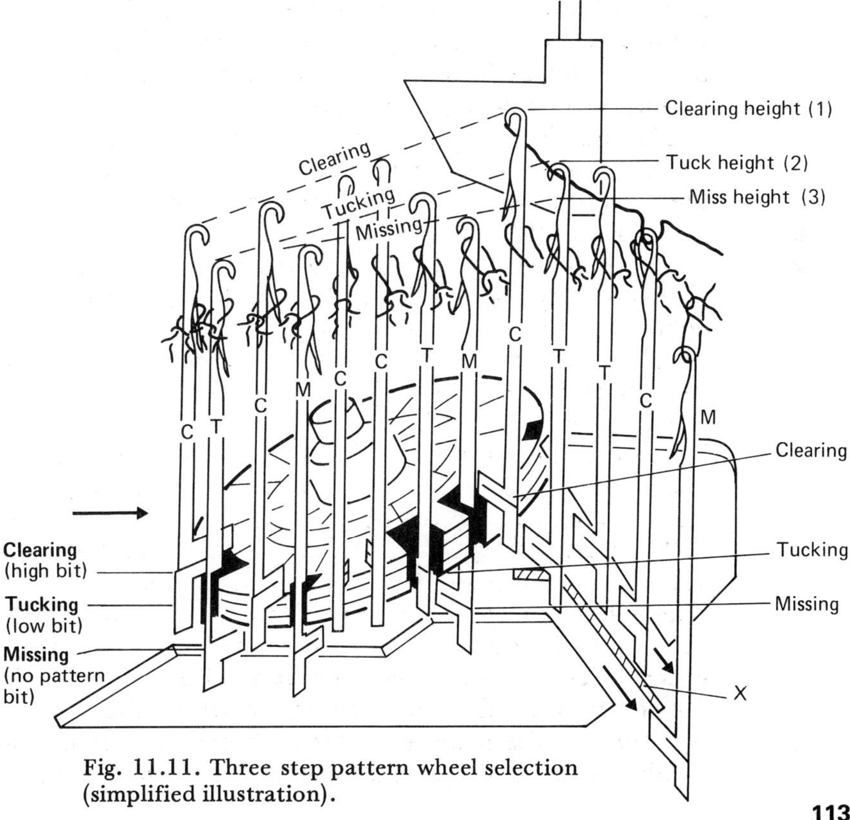

Fig. 11.11. Three step pattern wheel selection (simplified illustration).

zontal wheel for plush sinker selection. The pattern set-out which is unchanged during knitting, uses bits which are either re-usable and are inserted into the tricks or are break-off teeth on pre-prepared discs. The wheels, tricked to the same gauge as the revolving cylinder needles, are driven continuously in the opposite direction either by the needle butts meshing with their tricks or by gearing from the cylinder. The wheels are of the gain or loss type compared with the needle cylinder so they do not produce an exact number of complete turns in one machine revolution. The design areas can have a depth greater than the number of feeds, but are built up in a spiral manner, compared with the courses, around the fabric tube.

The inclined pattern wheel, like all selection devices is normally placed at each feeder. It is set at an angle of 20–40 degrees in place of the solid raising cam so that as it turns it lifts any element whose butt rests on a pattern bit. The needles will all have a butt of the same size in the same position. With a three position wheel (Fig. 11.11), a needle entering an empty trick will remain at miss height (3), a needle supported by a low bit will be a lifted tuck (2), and a needle supported by a high bit will be lifted to clear (1). Needles left at miss height are lowered by a wing cam (X) to ensure that they do not inadvertently receive yarn.

Some machines have four-finger striping selection available at each feeder wheel which considerably increases the pattern depth and scope. Another device often used in conjunction with striping is a pattern placer, tuck bar, or pattern cancellation device which is a moveable raising cam usually acting onto a butt at a level lower than the pattern wheel. When the cam is raised into action it causes all needles to be lifted to knit and thus cancels the selection for a number of courses so that alternating bands of design and plain single colour may be produced.

11.11 Pattern Design Areas

The principles governing design areas apply to all wheels, including sinkerwheels with plush and plain plating sinkers, provided that their set-out remains unchanged during knitting (Fig. 11.12). The wheels are generally of the same size and gauge on the same machine. The needle producing the starting wale of the design is marked and as the cylinder turns during the first revolution, it will align with the marked starting trick of each wheel in turn to ensure that their selections commence above each other in the same wale. As the widths will be of the same size and similarly arranged in each wheel, they will be built-up into a pattern depth each exactly aligned with the previous one, commencing with the first feeder selection. They will therefore be arranged as columns of pattern widths around the fabric tube.

A rectangular design area is developed if the chosen width (W) is the highest common factor (hcf) of the cylinder needles (wales in the fabric tube) (N) and the tricks (T) in one wheel.

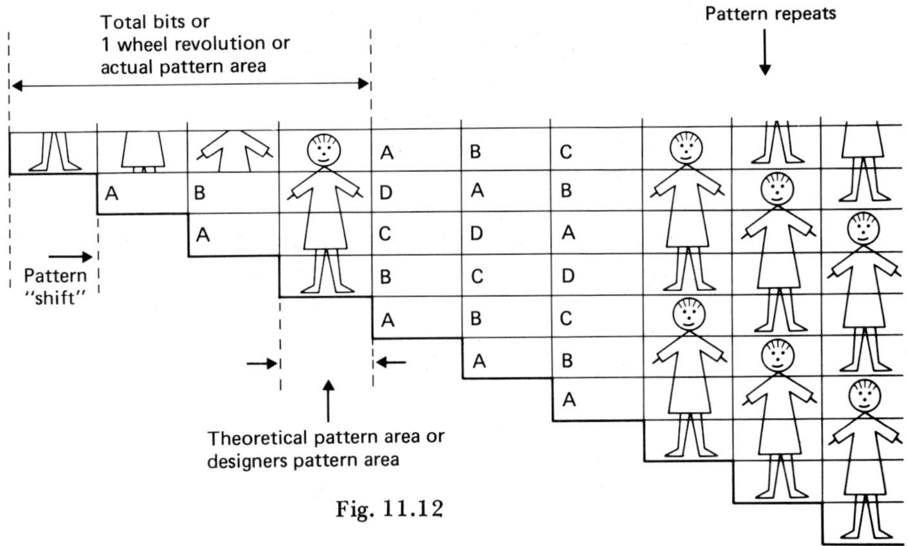

Fig. 11.12

A non-spiral design area, showing no fall (f) in courses from one pattern width to the next across the fabric, is produced when T is an exact factor of N so that $W = T$. In one machine revolution the wheels will make an exact number of turns and their starting tricks will re-align with the starting needle in the cylinder thus completing the pattern depth. The number of pattern width columns around the fabric tube (P) = $N \div W$. The pattern depth (D) in feeder courses = Feeders (F) $\times$ depth per feed or number of widths in one wheel (d). To convert the number of courses to pattern rows it is necessary to divide them by the number of colours (C) in the design.

Example: If $N = 1400, T = 140, F = 36, C = 2$.

Calculation: $W = 140$ (hcf of N and T),

$P = N \div W = 10,$

$d = T \div W = 1,$

$D = F \times d = 36 \div C = 18.$

With a design area of 140 wales by 18 pattern rows, it is too wide and too shallow for most designs.

Spirally developed designs are used because they provide a greater pattern depth but as a consequence they also produce a fall between one adjacent pattern area and the next one adjacent to it. They occur when T is not an exact factor of N (i.e. $N = nT + RT$) where n = a number of whole turns of the wheel and R is a fraction of a turn. At the second revolution the starting tricks in the wheels will not re-align with the starting needle in the cylinder and the continuous selection of the wheels will have 'shifted' or 'moved on' compared to the cylinder needles. Each wheel can be set out with more than one width ($d > 1$) and W will be a factor of R, so that a different width selection will be produced in the first column of design and in all the others in turn at the next machine revolution, as a result of the shift of the wheels.

The pattern depth will therefore be increased by a multiple of d and it will be built up during d revolutions of the machine after which the starting tricks of the wheels will again re-align with the starting needle in the cylinder because by then they, as well as the cylinder, will have completed an exact number of turns. The disadvantage of spirally developed designs is that each wheel is producing a number of different pattern width selections in adjacent columns along the same feeder course and as these are for different courses in the pattern depth, the pattern areas will appear to fall from one column to the next. The fall (f) is expressed by the difference between the two adjacent widths in courses in the direction of knitting which is towards the right in fabric produced on machines with clockwise revolving cylinders. It must be understood that each wheel has shifted sideways by the same amount so that its width selections are placed exactly above those of the first wheel's and are in the correct sequence for the depth. Therefore, although the areas show a fall or drop, the courses are always correctly placed within their depths.

Half-drop design areas occur when $N = nT + \frac{1}{2}T$ so that $W = \frac{1}{2}T$ and $d = 2$. It will take two machine revolutions to develop the pattern depth in the starting pattern column but the wheels will, as they turn, place the selection for their second width in the adjacent column and thus produce a half-drop of the pattern area. Using the previous machine data as guide, $N = 1400 + \frac{1}{2}T = 1470$; W = hcf of N and $T = 70$; $N \div T = 10\frac{1}{2}$; $P = 21$, $D = F \times 2 = 72$. The wheel of the first feeder will make course width 1 and $F + 1$, as the two widths will occur in adjacent columns the fall will be 36 courses in a total depth of 72 courses. Again, using the previous data it is possible to produce two identical design areas but with different spirally-developed falls if the needle cylinder is changed. Example: $W = 35$, d will be 4, $D = F \times 4 = 144$, $W = \frac{1}{4}T$, N can either be (a) 1400 − W or (b) 1400 + W.

(a) Assuming $N = 1365$, $N \div T = 9\frac{3}{4}$, $P = N \div W = 39$.
The first feeder will make courses $1, 1 + F, 1 + 2F, 1 + 3F$ or courses 1, 37, 73, and 109. As the wheel makes a ¾ turn at the start of the next machine revolution, each course must be placed ¾ of the way around the wheel so that course 109 will be produced in the column to the right of 1 making a drop of 108 courses. Substituting P and d in the indeterminate $dy = N/Wx - 1$, the fall may be calculated as Fx (x represents the number of cylinder revolutions) and (y represents the number of wheel turns before a pattern course is developed in the column adjacent to the starting column but on the side opposite to the direction of knitting) y is the lowest possible number.
Substituting the previous information, $4y = 39x - 1$.
$y = (39x - 1) \div 4$. If $x = 3$, y will be the smallest whole number possible, therefore $f = 3 \times F = 108$.

(b) Assuming $N = 1435$, $N \div T = 10\frac{1}{4}$, $P = N \div W = 41$.
Courses 1, 37, 73 and 109 will each be placed ¼ around the wheel making a fall of 36 courses. Using the equation $4y = 41x - 1$, $y = (41x - 1) \div 4$. $x = 1$, therefore $f = 36$.

Examples of a Pattern Area Calculation 11.12

1. Calculate the rectangular design area details from the following machine data. $N = 1470$; $T = 360$; $F = 36$; $C = 3$.
Calculation:
Factorize, $N = (2 \times 2 \times 3 \times 5) \times 29 = 1470$, $T = 2 \times 2 \times 3 \times 5 \times 6 = 360$.

W = hcf of N and $T = 2 \times 2 \times 3 \times 5 = 60$. $N = 60 \times 29$ therefore $P = 29$, $T = 60 \times 6$ therefore $d = 6$. $D = F \times d = 36 \times 6 = 216$ or $216 \div 3 = 72$ 3-colour pattern rows. As $d = 6$, feeder 1 wheel will produce courses $1, 1 + F, 1 + 2F, 1 + 3F, 1 + 4F, 1 + 5F$ or 1, 37, 73, 109, 145, 181. After the first machine revolution the wheel will have turned $N \div T$ or $29 \div 6 = 4\frac{5}{6}$, so that each selection will be placed 5/6ths further around the wheel in a clockwise direction and row 181 will be selected in the pattern column adjacent to 1 making a fall of 180 courses or 60 pattern rows. The fall may also be calculated in equation $dy = N/Wx - 1$, $6y = 29x - 1$, therefore $y = (29x - 1) \div 6$. When $x = 5$, the smallest whole number for y is achieved, therefore $f = Fx = 36 \times 5 = 108$ courses.

2. Calculate N, T and F given the following: $W = 36$; $D \div C = 36$; $C = 3$; $f = 24$ rows to right; estimated machine diameter 30 inches and gauge $\triangleq$ 16 npi.
Calculation: F = hcf of D and f, = hcf of 108 and 72 = 36.

$d = D \div f = 3$, each wheel will make 3 widths therefore $T = 108$. Feeder 1 wheel will make courses $1, 1 + F, 1 + 2F$, i.e. courses 1, 37 and 73. As $f = \frac{2}{3}T$, RT in the formula for $N = nT + RT$ is 72. Theoretically $N = \pi \times$ diameter $\times$ npi $= (22 \div 7) \times 30 \times 16 = 1508$. Theoretically $nT = 1508 - 72 = 1436$. Actual n must be a whole number $1436 \div T = 13$ remainder 32, n must be 13, therefore actual $N = 1404 + 72 = 1476$ at a gauge of 16 npi.

L-shaped, six- or eight-sided design areas

Design areas may be employed which have a bias relative to both wales and courses provided they fit into each other around the fabric tube. L-shaped areas provide a greater width and design areas potential than a rectangle based on the hcf of N and T, also the actual area tends to be disguised and this masks the appearance of spirality.
Example: $N = 1380$, $T = 130$, $F = 32$.

The hcf of N and T is only 10 in this case but the total design area consists of 13 rectangles each 10 wales wide and 32 courses deep. Any design may be utilized which is composed of all 13 rectangles being used only once and adjoining each other.

In an L-shaped area, two different pattern widths are utilized. There may be more than one primary or major width in each wheel but there is only one secondary width. In the equation $N = nT \pm RT$, RT is the primary width. In the example $N \div T$ = either (a) 10 + 80 or (b) 11 − 50.

(a) If 80 is chosen as the primary width, the secondary width will be $T - 80 = 50$. As nT is less than N the secondary width will be placed furthest from the direction of knitting and in the case of a clockwise revolving cylinder machine its starting wale will commence on the left in the starting wale of the primary width.

(b) If 50 is chosen two primary widths are obtained and the secondary width will be $T - 100 = 30$. As nT is greater than N the secondary width will be placed towards the right on a clockwise revolving cylinder machine and its finishing wale will coincide with that of the primary width below it.

11.13 Argyle Wheels

Argyle diamond designs may be produced by using two opposing diagonal stripes of design each occurring at alternate pattern rows using pattern wheels with $T + 1$ tricks to select for odd pattern rows and $T - 1$ tricks for even pattern rows where T is an exact factor of N. Example: 26-inch diameter machine 18 npi, $N = 1500$ and $F = 60$. 125 may be chosen as T, for two-colour there would be fifteen pairs of wheels having 126 tricks developing a stripe of design in one direction in odd rows and another fifteen pairs of wheels with 124 tricks developing a stripe in the opposite direction in even rows. During one machine revolution each wheel will turn twelve times and will be displaced by twelve wales for its next pattern row. To produce a smooth diagonal stripe, four out of every five pattern rows in the sequence of fifteen must be off-set by one wale, to achieve the correct final displacement for the next machine revolution.

11.14 Electronic Needle Selection

Electro-magnetic needle selection has now been introduced onto a number of types of knitting machines although it was first commercially used on circular rib jacquard machines.[9] The electronic impulse which energizes an electro-magnet is usually assisted by the field of a permanent magnet and the minute selection movement is then magnified by mechanical movements.

If all the needles or a block of needles were simultaneously selected, each would require its own actuator. It is much cheaper to select the needles at a single selection position in serial formation using between one and six actuators although the time interval between each selection impulse is shorter.

The Moratronic[10] was one of the first machines and was exhibited in 1963 (Fig. 11.13). For each feeder, a photo transistor scans its own track of an endless 35-mm film giving a selection for each jack control spring as it passes the control position of the feeder. If the position on the film has a transparent spot, light is transmitted to generate an impulse. If the position on the film is opaque no impulse is generated for that control spring. The impulse is magnified to energize a coil and thus neutralize its permanent magnet at the control position at the precise moment when the jack control spring is guided onto it. The spring is thus not held by the magnet and stands vertically to pass on the far side of a wedge-shaped control cam.

As the cam presses onto the spring it depresses the jack into a deep recess of the trick so that the jack butt is pushed away from the cylinder-raising cam and the needle above the jack is not lifted to knit. If no impulse is generated, the control magnet can hold the spring so that it passes in a bent position on the near side of the control cam and is held away from its jack which remains out of its recess with its butt remaining on the raising cam to lift the needle above to knit.

The film is driven in phase with the needle cylinder to make a selection in 0.5 milliseconds. Twelve million selections are possible – enough for a full width selection, 1565 pattern rows of three-colour design deep.

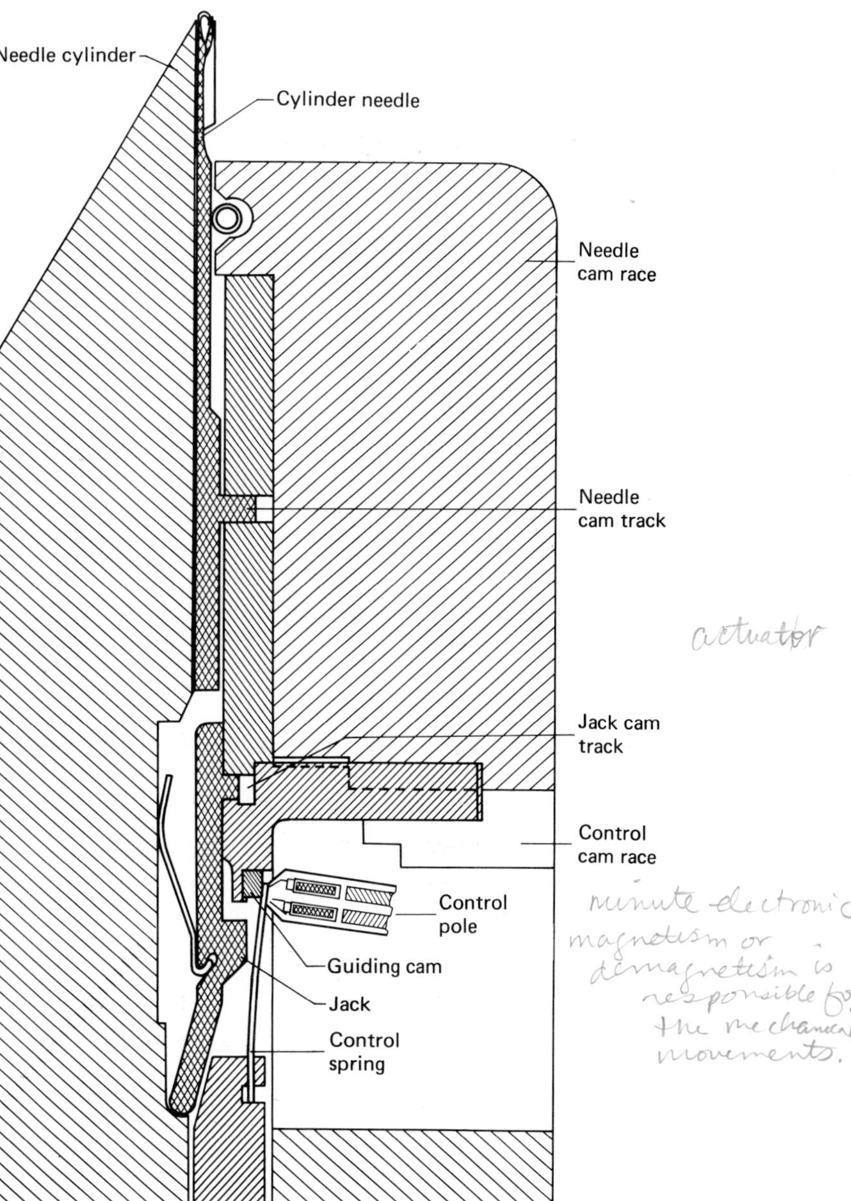

Fig. 11.13

Further Information

Pattern wheel designing

INNES, R., Rib jacquard yardsgoods knitting: a primer, *Knit. O'wr Times*, (1972) 13 Nov., 71–3.

LANCASHIRE, J. B., Figure designing on circular machines, *Hos. Trad. Journal*, (1958) July, p. 66.

LANCASHIRE, J. B., *Knit. O'wr Times*, (1967) 8 May, 133–7; 20 Oct., 34–5; (1970) 12 Jan., 30–2.

MISCHON, L. and ABRAMS, A., *Pattern Wheel Designing for Circular Machines*, Vanguard Supreme, North Carolina.

STEVENS, J. C., The potential of pattern wheel machines, *Knit. Times*, (1976) 9 Aug., 31–9.

Unusual aspects of pattern wheel designing, *Hos. Trade Journal*, (1964) April, 90–2.

General

LANCASHIRE, J. B., *Jacquard Design and Knitting*, (1969) Nat. Knit Outerwear Assoc., New York.

LANCASHIRE, J. B., Geometric patterning with multi-step mechanisms, *Knit. O'wr Times*, (1969) 18 Aug., 37–40.

LANCASHIRE, J. B., Patterning Elimination with the multi-step mechanisms, *Knit. O'wr Times*, (1969) 29 Sept., 33–34.

PAEPKE, H., New techniques in double knitting, *Knit. Times*, (1975) 26 May, 95–103.

1. STEVENS, J. C., Indirect patterning mechanisms: non-fixed selection, *Knit. Times*, (1977) 14 March, 33–6.
2. BOROWY, A. and KNAPTON, J. J. F., Full jacquard selection, *Knit. Times*, (1976) 3 May, 16–17.
3. GOADBY, D. R., Camber 40 G Cheminit, *Knit. Int.*, (1979) June, 106–7.
4. Background and specification for a viable multi-purpose double-jersey machine for the 1980s, *Knit. Int.*, (1980) July, 88–90.
5. New high-speed 72-feeder full area jacquard double-jersey machine, *Knit. Int.*, (1981) April, 36–8.
6. Patterning profile of a prize winner, *Hos. Trade Journal*, (1969) June, 111–117.
7. LANCASHIRE, J. B., Uses of punched film for needle selection on circular machines, *Knit. O'wr Times*, (1968) 30 Sept., 35–8.
8. BOROWY, A. S. and KNAPTON, J. J. F., Tape selection systems, *Knit. Times*, (1975) 3 Nov., 62–5.
9. KNAPTON, J. J. F., Electronic patterning in weft knitting, *Text. Inst. and Ind.*, (1974) 12 (7) 214–7.
10. ALEXANDER, W. V., *Hos. Trade Journal*, (1969) Feb., 79–80.
    MORAT, F., *Knit. O'wr Times*, (1967) 31 July, 22–25; *Knit. Times*, (1971) 11 Oct., 42–4.

GOTTSCHALL, G., *Knit. Times*, (1972) 19 June, 82–4.

12

Electronics in Knitting

The Advantage of using Electronics 12.1

Knitting machines have developed with mechanically-controlled and operated movements. The exacting requirements of modern knitting technology, however, tend to emphasize the limitations of mechanical movements which can be expensive in manufacturing costs, slow and cumbersome in operation, difficult to adjust or alter and subject to friction and wear. Alternative systems of power transmission and signal storage having the requisite speed and precision are provided by hydraulics, fluidics or electronics.

Of these three, electronics offers the decisive advantages of convenient power supply, compatibility with existing mechanical components and micro-miniaturization of circuitry. In addition, electronic systems do not require to be of a size proportionate to their task or to operate on a one-to-one relationship with it.

Electronics are increasingly being employed in stop motions, yarn feed systems, the design and preparation of knitting patterns, machine function control, pattern selection and striping (Fig. 12.1). The automatic monitoring and adjustment facilities provided by microprocessor control will obviously further reduce the manual attention involved in the operation of future knitting machines. Thus although knitting is still a mechanical action between the yarn and the knitting elements the design of tomorrow's machines will be increasingly influenced by the facilities offered by electronics.

Electronic Signals 12.2

Electronic devices process signals as binary digital logic which exists in two states 1 and 0, YES and NO, TRUE and FALSE. These states may assume, or be converted into, a wide variety of mechanical or electronic forms such as HIGH or LOW impulses, the PRESENCE or ABSENCE of a signal, an ON or OFF switch, MAGNETIC attraction or NO MAGNETIC attraction, MISSING or TUCKING, TUCKING or KNITTING, MISSING or KNITTING.

In electronic data processing or programming, the 1's and 0's (termed bits) are arranged in equal length series (words) each of which can be encoded and converted into a symbol, figure or letter which may be arranged to compose, for example, a knitting design, machine program or

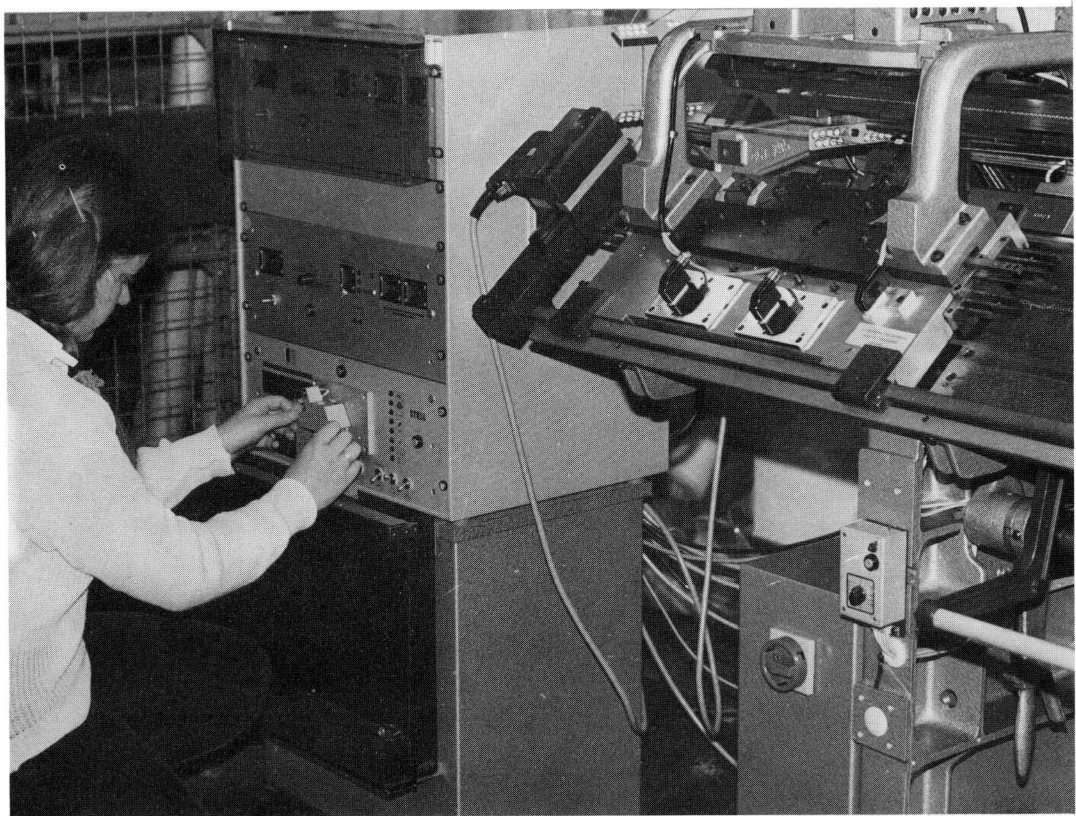

Fig. 12.1. Changing the pattern tape on a Stoll ANVH electronic V-bed flat machine.

set of operating instructions displayed on a printed paper roll, visual screen or any other convenient medium.

12.3 Computers

Probably the most important use of electronics is in computer systems. A computer can receive, store, manipulate and transmit large quantities of information. It performs arithmetical or logical processes accurately at high speed after receiving the instructions (program) and values (data) without the need for further intervention by the operator.

Flexibility in processing of data occurs because the system can be programmed to produce YES or NO decisions based on the result of comparing and testing monitored data which then determine the choice of two alternative courses of action in the program of the system. These alternative courses within the main program sequence may include counted loop sequences, branching or jumping out of the main sequence and selection of stored sub-routines. It is these facilities which give electronically-controlled knitting pattern preparation and needle selection their extensive capabilities as compared with existing methods.

Fig. 12.2. Pattern preparation for an Electronic Double Jersey Machine. 1 = Random digitizer; 2 = Cursor; 3 = Process Computer; 4 = Teletype; 5 = Electronically controlled Rib Jacquard Machine (Wildt Mellor Bromley).

Micro-miniaturization 12.4

The basic components of electronic systems are diodes which allow current to flow in one direction only (rectifiers), transistors which control the rate of current flow, resistors which impede its flow, capacitors which store electric charges and inductors which react to changes in levels of current. Micro-miniaturization has been achieved by combining these formerly discrete components into integrated circuits where all the components necessary for performing a function are chemically implemented on a tiny wafer of semiconductor material such as silicon which is bonded to a package containing pins for insertion into a circuit board. Large scale integration has enabled thousands of transistors to be implemented on a single chip so that in 1971, the first microprocessor chip containing all the components of the central processor of a computer could be introduced.

These chips use less than 5 millionths of the power, are a thousand times faster and have hundreds of times more capacity (with incomparable reliability) than the first generation of electronic valve computers (1945 to 1955). Standard chips and systems are now so cheap that they can be employed for end-users where their potential is not fully utilized.

12.5 Computer Hardware and Software

The electronic, electrical, magnetic and mechanical components of the system are termed 'hardware' whereas the programs and documentation for the system are termed 'software'. Software costs have not fallen in line with hardware costs and may therefore amount to many times those of the latter for a particular system. Programs are a series of procedural steps designed to solve a specific problem. As they are now often written in a high level language for easier comprehension and handling, more documentation is required and they occupy more of the system itself.

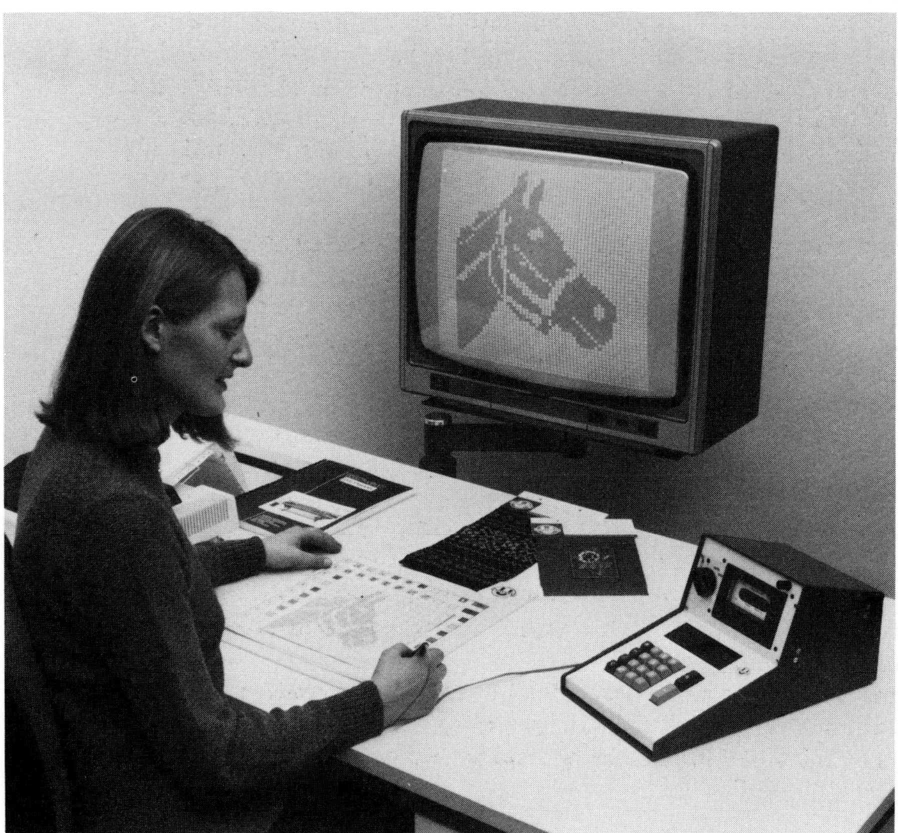

Fig. 12.3. Pattern preparation by means of a light pen and graphics tablet for the cassette control tape of an electronic flat machine (Universal Maschinen fabrik).

The Main Sections of a Computer 12.6

The three main sections of computer hardware are the central processor unit (CPU), the memory and the peripheral interface. A wired communications network known as a 'bus' transports signals and data to and from the various units of the system. The CPU coordinates and controls the actions of all the other units using timing pulses from a crystal clock to coordinate them into an overall schedule. The control unit of the CPU fetches program instructions in turn from memory, decodes them and causes them to be executed using its arithmetic and logical unit to carry out the processing on the bits which are temporarily stored in registers such as an accumulator.

Input and Output Devices 12.7

The addition of a peripheral interface converts the microprocessor into a computer system and enables it to monitor and selectively accept from and transmit signals to a number of external devices or mechanisms including inputs such as switches, sensors on knitting machines, keyboard, light pens, tapes and discs and outputs such as actuators on knitting machines, lights, digital and graphical displays, tapes and printers. Outside the system, the digital impulses may be changed from parallel to serial or even analogue form or be converted into light, sound, radio or carrier waves or mechanical movements.

The peripheral interface unit thus adapts the facilities of the microprocessor so that it can handle the technical requirements of a knitting machine (Fig. 12.4). It is a switching unit which matches the speeds of input and output units to that of the processor by acting as a buffer store (generally mechanical units operate more slowly than electronic devices) and changes their code format to the binary pulses of the CPU.

Although it is possible to directly program a system using switches, a matrix board, keyboard or other input device, the processor (and probably the knitting machine) will be held waiting during this time-consuming operation. It is therefore preferable to record the program and data on an auxiliary memory store such as a tape or disc whose contents can be rapidly inputted electronically into internal memory as required whilst using a direct input keyboard or switches for minor amendments or alterations during the running of the program.

Some systems are programmed to interact with the operative who is thus able (within specified and guided limits) to change values of data with the effects of the amendments being visually indicated by the system.

Fig. 12.4. The Gemini 200 microprocessor controlled straight bar rib-to-plain machine capable of running at twice the speed of a conventional Cotton's Patent frame. The microprocessor control may coordinate the actions of a number of these twin head units to achieve the production equivalent to a multi-head frame (William Cotton Group).

12.8 Storage

The bit length of the words handled by the system are generally four bits (a nibble), eight bits (a byte) or sixteen bits. This data is stored in memory locations as electrical or magnetic charges, current or voltage levels and given a coded location address for ease of recovery. Programs and data to be processed or in process are retained in the main internal memory store whose capacity is expressed in multiples of K where $K = 2^{10}$ words (1024 words). Data is transcribed into memory by 'writing' when it may replace the original data held at that location. 'Reading' is the ability to interrogate the contents of a memory location usually without physically destroying them. Volatile memory only retains as long as power is supplied to it.

ROM and RAM 12.9

Internal memory provides access, i.e. constant access time from any location addressed:

READ ONLY MEMORY (ROM) is non-volatile and cannot accidentally be corrupted or erased. It is used to hold programs essential to the efficient functioning of the system and is programmed during the manufacture of it. User programmable ROMs are available such as PROM which is programmable once only using a special prom blaster, EPROM which is erasable using ultra-violet light and EAROM which is electrically alterable. Both EROMs and EAROMs require re-programming after erasure and are much more expensive than ROMs.

READ AND WRITE MEMORY (RAM) (originally 'Random Access Memory') is volatile but its data can be amended and erased as required. It is therefore used to store programs and data during processing. RAM can be of two types, static RAM whose cells are flip-flop switches which hold their memory as long as the power is switched on, and dynamic RAM which has a higher density memory but stores data as capacitance charges which must be refreshed every 1 or 2 milliseconds by the system by reading out and writing back in again, otherwise the memory charge will leak away.

Bubble Memory 12.10

Bubble memory is a newly developed technique offering the advantage of very high packing density (about 1500 bubble domains per square millimetre), non-volatility and low power consumption with faster than serial access and an absence of mechanical movement. Minute cylindrical magnetic bubble domains are propagated to float with their axes lying perpendicular to a thin crystal film. Strings of bubbles are magnetically routed to pass through a stationary photo-diode reading head which converts the presence and absence of bubble domains into binary data impulses.

Tapes and Discs 12.11

Tapes provide access to data serially in the sequence in which it was stored and is thus a slower method than random access. Punched tape has been used as an input/output medium since the earliest computers, it is cheap, easy to handle and replace whilst the punched holes representing binary 1's are clearly visible but it cannot be amended and may be subject to stretching and atmospheric conditions. Light emitting diodes shine through the holes and are read by photo-electric cells on the other side of the reading head. Magnetic tapes and discs store data as magnetized spots

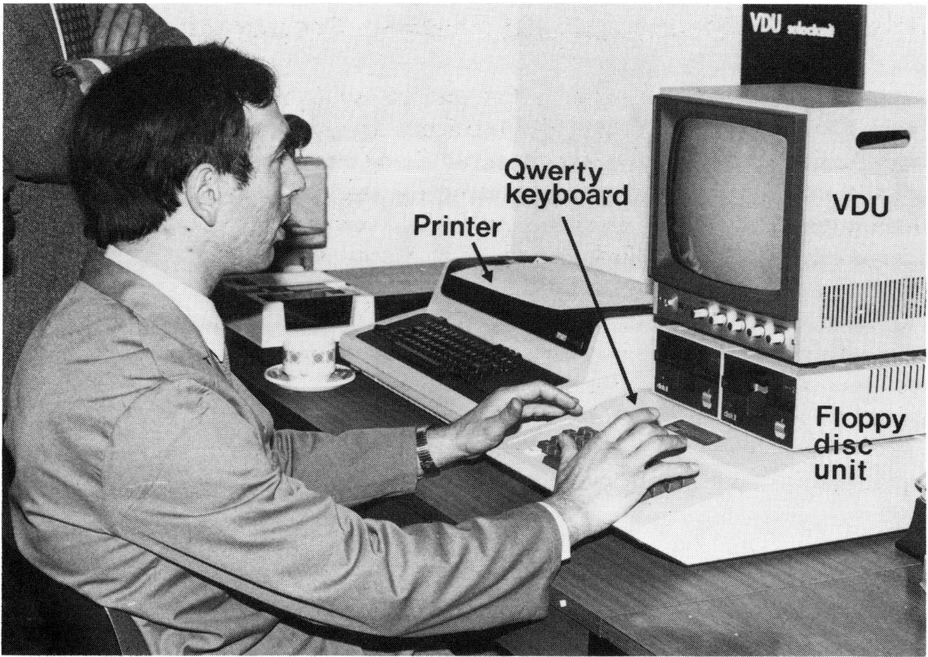

Fig. 12.5. Using an Apple microcomputer to prepare a knitting programme for a Stoll Selectanit machine (Walter Bullwer).

whose direction of magnetism is detected by electro-magnetic transducer read heads. Tape cassettes are simple, inexpensive, less affected by the atmosphere and can be modified. Magnetized floppy discs have a much faster access time and a greater storage capacity but must be protected from dirt and dust. They operate inside a sleeve having access for the read—write head. The data is recorded on concentric tracks.

12.12 Knitting Machine Programming and Control

Mechanical pattern and programming control for knitting machines stored by arrangements such as punched cards, chains, rackwheels, peg drums and element butt arrangements are expensive in material, bulky in space on the machine or in store, time consuming to handle and alter, slow in operation and offer restricted facilities. Electronic selection or machine control is compatible with higher running speeds, eliminates complex mechanical arrangements thus reducing supervisory requirements, provides greater versatility as regards design parameters, simplifies the modification of repeat sequences and pattern-changing operations and in some cases enables changes to occur whilst the machine is knitting.

Computer Graphics and Pattern Preparation 12.13

Interactive computer graphics enable a dialogue to occur between the operator terminal and the system with the resulting development of the design being immediately visually represented on the screen. The position of any point on the design is defined and located by two numbers in the Cartesian coordinate system. On the horizontal (X) axis the numbering increases positively from zero towards the right whilst on the vertical (Y) axis the numbering increases positively upwards from zero.

Generally an input device is employed which can be moved by hand in the direction of either axis with its location and movement over the screen being indicated by a special character symbol termed a cursor. The physical movement of input devices such as digitizers, joysticks and trackballs is converted by the system into the series of numbers whereas a light pen detects the presence of light whose position is being generated on the screen.

Enclosed areas of the design may be filled in with a colour (if this facility is available) and the locations of the colours may be exchanged. Stored sub-routines may also be recalled to assist with the development of the design.

By relating the coordinate points of the design to other coordinate points within the design area the design can be rapidly modified with motifs being multiplied in number or geometrically transformed. Each transformation may occur separately or as a combined effect, for example a motif may be reflected (mirror imaged) across the width (the X axis) or the depth (Y axis) of the design area. It can be translated – moved in a straight line without altering its appearance, rotated-moved in a circular path around a centre of rotation and scaled – increased or decreased in size along the X or Y axis or along both axes. Graphic capabilities are obviously dependent upon the type of system and its software.

Electronic pattern preparation thus provides the designer with an immediate visual representation of the design as it is being conceived, amended and edited without recourse to the knitting of trial swatches (Figs 12.2, 12.3). The grading of sizes[1] and the introduction, manipulation and placing of shapes and colours is achieved with the minimum of effort and the elimination of all tedious and repetitious actions. The program can be structured to guide and assist the designer and thus ensure that the resultant design is compatible with the knitting machine and the end-use requirements. Once a satisfactory design is achieved, a permanent record may be outputted onto hard copy and/or onto a carrier acceptable for controlling the knitting machine.

Further Information

1. COLES, G. M., Computer-aided lay planning and pattern-grading, *Text. Inst. and Ind.*, (1975) 13 (4), 108–10.

MAP Information Centre, Freepost, Department of Industry, Dean Bradley House, 52 Horseferry Road, London SW1P 2AG, pamphlets include – Microelectronics, The New Technology and Microelectronics – The Options.

ATKIN, K. J., *Basic computer science*, (1978) MacDonald and Evans Handbooks.

CHANDLER, A., *The Penguin Dictionary of Microprocessors*, (1981).

DEBENHAM, M. J., *Microprocessors: Principles and Applications*, (1979) Pergamon Press, Oxford.

FORESTER, T., (ed.), *The microelectronics revolution*, (1980) Basil Blackwell, Oxford.

LAURIE, P., *The Micro Revolution*, (1980) Futura Publications.

PARKER, M., Sophisticated flat beds create industry revolution, *Knit. Times*, (1982) **51**, (2), pages.

REICHMAN, C., *Electronics in knitting*, (1972) Nat. Knit. Outwear Assn., New York.

SCOTT, J. E., *Introduction to Interactive Computer Graphics*, (1982) John Wiley and Sons, New York.

Future impact of electronics in other knitting areas, *Hos. Trade Journal*, (1973) (Oct.) 71–73.

Microelectronics – A scientific American book, (1977) W. H. Freedman & Co., San Francisco.

13

The Production of Weft Knitted Fabric

Most weft knitted fabric in continuous lengths is knitted on large diameter multi-feeder latch needle machines and is slit into open width during finishing. The emphasis on productive efficiency and quality control in the manufacture, finishing and conversion of fabric into articles of apparel or other end-usage tends to encourage the establishment of larger units with longer production runs involving more capital intensive techniques than is necessarily the case in production of articles from garment lengths. Improvements in the quality control of knitted fabric and in the techniques of finishing and converting it have led to increased outlets for its products.

In handling operations during manufacture, the lengths of fabric must be maintained in as relaxed and tension-free a state as possible in order to reduce the problems caused by dimensional distortion and shrinkage. Apart from scouring, bleaching, dyeing and printing, the finishing process offers a wide range of techniques for modifying the properties of the knitted structure including heat setting, stentering, decating,[1] raising,[2] cropping, pleating[3] and laminating.

In the cutting room the lengths of fabric are layed-up many ply thicknesses deep onto long cutting tables using a traversing carriage to transport and lay the fabric. Cutting out techniques vary widely from marked lays whose outlines are followed by hand-guided cutting knives to press cutters whose blades are the outline of the garment part or cutting blades guided by a computerized programme.

In making-up, the lockstitch seam (type 301) is not as useful as it is for woven fabrics because it lacks extensibility. For jerseywear the double-locked chainstitch (type 401) is useful whilst in the making-up of knitwear the three-thread overlock (type 504) is popular because as well as being extensible it securely binds the cut edges of the fabric after neatly trimming them. For comfort in underwear and lingerie a flat-butted seam secured by a flat seam such as the five-thread flatlock (type 605) is generally preferred.[4]

Figure 13.1 illustrates some of the features of a modern circular fabric producing machine which ensure that high quality fabric is knitted at speed with the minimum of supervision.

The top(1) and bottom(2) stop motions are spring-loaded yarn supports that pivot downwards when the yarn end breaks or its tension is increased. The action releases the surplus yarn to the feeder thus preventing a press-off and simultaneously completes a circuit which stops the machine and illuminates an indicator warning light.[5]

Fig. 13.1. High Speed Four-Track Single-Jersey Machine.

3. Various spring-loaded detector points are carefully positioned around the cylinder according to their particular function. A pointer will be tripped to stop the machine by a fault or malfunctioning element such as a yarn slub, fabric lump, needle head, latch spoon, etc.

4A. The tape positive feed provides three different speeds (course lengths) and is driven and can be adjusted from the drive arrangement 4B.

5. The cylinder needle cam system for each feed is contained in a single replaceable section and contains an exterior adjustment for the stitch cam slide.

6. The automatic lubrication system.

7. Start, Stop and Inching buttons.

8. The cam-driven fabric winding down mechanism which revolves with the fabric tube.

9. The revolution counters for each of the three shifts and a pre-set counter for stopping the machine on completion of a specific fabric length (in courses).
10. Side creel (optional).
11. Lint Blower (useful when knitting with cotton spun yarns).

Although weft knitted fabrics may be approximately divided into single or double jersey according to whether they were knitted with one or two sets of needles, it is probably preferable to include some of these fabrics in two separate groupings of underwear and speciality fabrics. Pelerine eyelet, sinkerwheel mesh structures and float plated fabrics are mainly used for underwear whilst high pile and plush fabrics are speciality fabrics. Many of the jacquard structures have already been described (chapter 10).

Single-jersey fabrics are mostly knitted on sinker top machines. These machines have a simpler construction than cylinder and dial machines, are easier to supervise and maintain, have higher running speeds and more feeders and knit a greater range of structures with a wider tolerance of yarn counts. In Europe, double jersey was generally preferred to single jersey particularly for ladies' wear because of problems of dimensional stability, structural breakdown, air porosity and snagging of floating threads. However, fashion trends since 1973 towards prints, fine gauge lightweight fabrics and leisure wear have increased the popularity of single jersey to levels previously experienced in the U.S.A.

13.1 Simple Tuck and Float Stitch Single-Jersey Fabrics

Figure 13.2 illustrates the notations of some simple single-jersey fabrics whilst Fig. 13.3 illustrates a loop diagram of Hopsack, a single-jersey inlaid fabric.

In order to tie a lay-in yarn into the back of a single jersey structure, selected needles are raised to tuck height to receive the lay-in yarn at a point in advance of the ground knitting feeder, the needles are then raised to clearing height prior to receiving and knitting the ground yarn. Hopsack is a 1 × 1 inlay whose stability and appearance make it popular as a lady's suiting fabric when knitting staple spun yarns. In order to

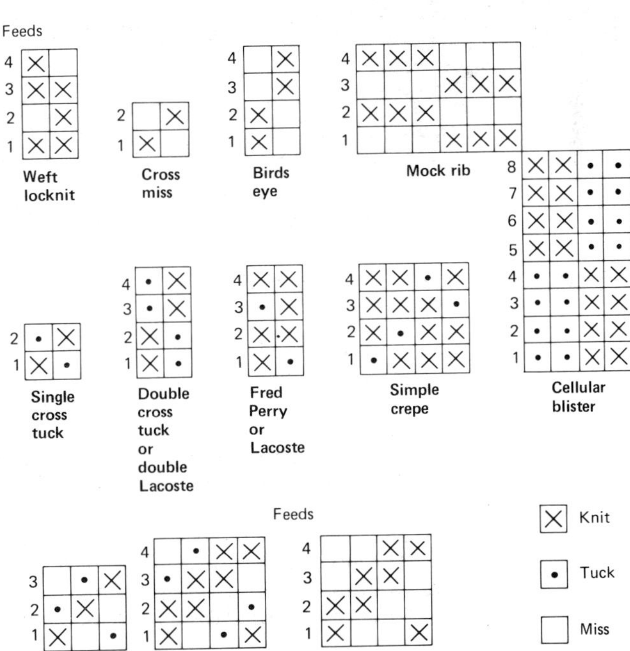

Fig. 13.2. Twill Effects.

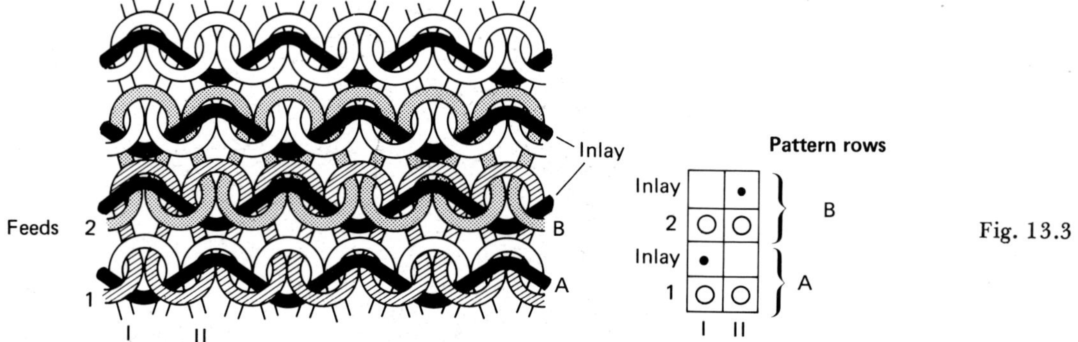

Fig. 13.3

spread the inlay across the back of the fabric it is the practice to centre the tuck on a different wale at the next inlay cycle. Another popular structure is a 2 × 2 inlay with a plain ground course between each ground inlay course. The tuck limbs of the lay-in yarns are crossed by the sinker loops on the technical back so they tend to grin through onto the technical face especially as they push the two adjacent wales slightly apart at these points. This problem may be overcome with a plated yarn arrangement as in the case of invisible fleecy. A 3 × 1 inlay structure used to produce a heavier fabric is shown in Fig. 13.4.

13.2 History of Double-Jersey

Double-jersey suiting fabrics evolved in France using French worsted spun yarns with miss stitches introduced to improve the stability of the interlock or rib base. In the early 1950s, Berridge of Leicester produced the first specific-purpose machine capable of knitting these modified structures. The twelve-feed machine had a revolving cam-box with interlock needle tracks in cylinder and dial and was the forerunner of the modern revolving cylinder double jersey machine which has changeable camming for knit, tuck or miss stitches and rib or interlock gating facilities.[6]

Double jersey achieved its success with 18-inch diameter machines knitting 1/36's worsted or acrylic fibre yarns for ladies' autumn or winter suiting and dresswear and 150 den. continuous filament textured polyester for spring and summer wear. Expansion commenced in Europe in the late 1950s knitting worsted or Courtelle yarns into an evolving range of stable structures which were finished on continuous finishing equipment adapted from woven cloth processes. Between 1963 and 1973, yarn consumption in double jersey increased from 6 Mkg to 90 Mkg of which 70 Mkg was continuous filament.[7]

Crimplene polyester yarn played a major part in this expansion taking nearly 50 per cent of the market in 1969. Being non-torque it could be used in singles form and had low shrinkage and low extension whilst the high 5 denier per filament 1/150/30 den. yarn provided a crisp resilient

Fig. 13.4. Dressing gown by W. G. Underhill. Fabric knitted on a Monarch, single-jersey 18-gauge multi-cam-track machine by Airedale Textiles using 1/5's Cotton Spun Courtelle for the 3 X 1 inlay and 167 dtex polyester for the plain backing, (Courtaulds, Hanover Place, London).

handle and was less prone to snagging. To mask the effect of feeder stripiness it was introduced in surface interest structures such as cloque (single-colour patterned blister) and bourrelet (horizontal relief stripes).

Soon bright package-dyed yarns were being used to knit patterned blister structures as fashion moved away from plain fabrics such as double pique to a demand for colour and surface texture with easy washability and lighter weights for centrally-heated environments.

In the early 1970s attempts were made with limited success particularly in the U.S.A. to break into men's leisurewear with a switch to 22 and 24 gauge machines using 120–135 denier textured yarn. This finer gauge was necessary in order to obtain lighter weights and achieve the more critical standards of stitch definition, and resistance to snagging, bagging, air porosity and shrinkage. However, 1973 proved to be the peak year of the narrowly-based double-jersey boom as an over-expanded industry failed to penetrate into new fields and at the same time received a rebuff from ladies' fashion which was turning to natural fibres and woven cloths as a change from textured polyester. Whereas the proportion of double-jersey to single-jersey fabrics was 1 : 0.4 in 1975, by 1981 it was 1 : 0.9. The industry is now smaller, using a wider range of yarn types and counts and gauges ranging as fine as 28 for rib jacquard and 40 for interlock print-base fabrics.

13.3 Types of Double-Jersey Structure

There are two types of double-jersey structures, non-jacquard produced mainly on the modified interlock machine and jacquard structures produced on the rib jacquard machine. Various modifications to the basic interlock machine have been necessary in order to produce the new structures. Originally only alternate tricks were fully cut through to accommodate long needles so that mock eight-lock was achieved by knitting normal interlock with every third dial needle removed, now all tricks may be cut through and inserts placed in tricks under short needles. Verge bits are required for knock-over during single-bed knitting, other modifications may include exchangeable or changeable knit, tuck and miss camming and variable needle timing, rib/interlock-gating and feeder guide positioning.

13.4 Non-Jacquard Double-Jersey Structures

Most interlock variation structures have six- or eight-feeder repeat sequences as only alternate needles in one bed are in action in a course, single pique or cross tuck interlock (Fig. 13.5a) was one of the first to be produced, by placing tuck cams in the dial at every third feeder. The tuck stitches throw the fabric out approximately 15 per cent wider than normal interlock to a satisfactory finished width of over 60 inches (1.5 m approx.), they break up the surface uniformity and help to mask feeder stripiness but they also increase fabric weight. Texi pique (Fig. 13.5b) is wider and bulkier and shows the same pique effect on both sides. Cross miss is the knit miss (Fig. 13.5d) equivalent of single pique but it is narrower and lighter in weight. Piquette (Fig. 13.5e) is a reversible knit miss structure with a light cord effect.

Bourrelet fabrics have pronounced horizontal cords at regular intervals produced by knitting excess courses on the cylinder needles, the cord courses may be in a different colour to the ground courses. There may be

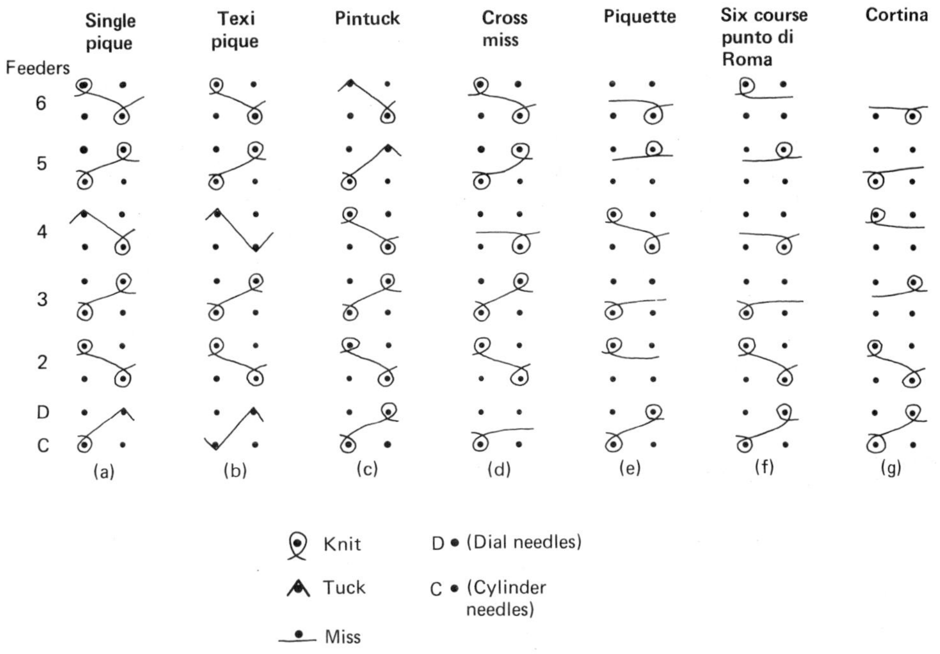

Fig. 13.5

half, more than half, or less than half the total number of feeders knitting the cord courses. Interlock rather than rib base bourrelet is usually preferred because it provides a softer, smoother more regular surface with less elasticity but it requires two feeders per cord row. Jersey cord (Fig. 13.6a) is an example of a miss bourrelet and super roma (Fig. 13.6b) is its equivalent in tuck bourrelet, the latter, sometimes termed horizontal ripple fabrics, tend to be heavier and to have a less pronounced cord than the former, which are termed ottomans in the U.S.A.

Double pique, wevenit and overnit are synonymous terms for the same stable knit miss rib gated fabric (Fig. 13.8) which is narrower and has a less pronounced pique appearance than single pique and tends to be rather heavy. Although it is now also produced on rib machines, it was originally produced by modifying the interlock machine as follows:

1. Rib gating.
2. Changing dial cam systems 2 and 3 over in every four-feed sequence.
3. Placing all long needles only in the cylinder if Swiss double pique is required, or all short needles only if French double pique is required.

This camming arrangement causes all cylinder needles to knit at every alternate feeder as there are no other length cylinder needles, whilst

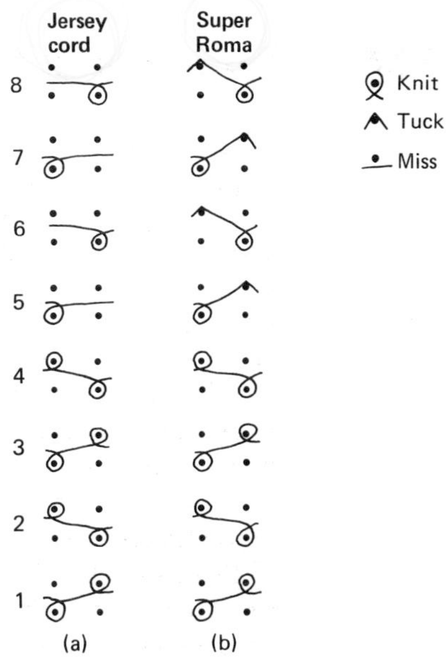

Fig. 13.6

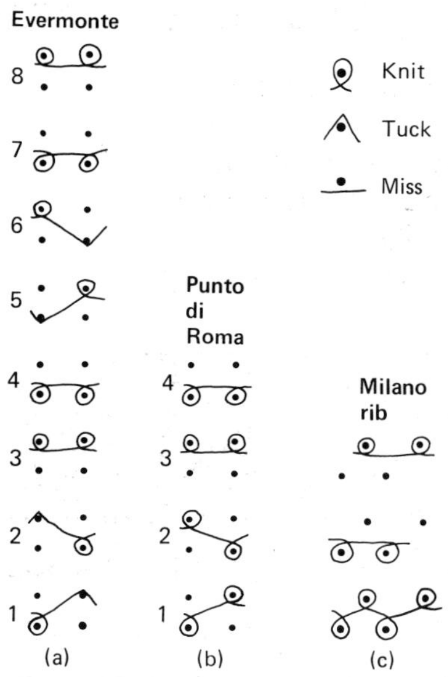

Evermonte

Knit

Tuck

Miss

Punto di Roma

Milano rib

(a) (b) (c)

Fig. 13.7

Swiss French

(a) (b)

Fig. 13.8

alternate length dial needles knit at two successive feeders because identical cam systems are placed in a two-feeder sequence in the dial. French double pique tends to be slacker and wider than swiss double pique because in this structure, the dial needle loops which are held for two feeders can rob extra yarn from the cylinder loops which are knitting in the same course thus producing long held loops. Rodier is a term sometimes applied to either double pique or texi pique and mock rodier to piquette.

Punto di roma (Fig. 13.7b) has replaced double pique as the most popular non-jacquard double-jersey fabric, it belongs to a group of structures which are reversible and have a tubular sequence of dial only and cylinder only knit. It has an acceptable weight and finishes with a width of about 70 inches (1.77 m). Cortina (Fig. 13.5g) is the six-feeder version of it, produced on interlock camming with run-through cams where missing is required. Milano (Fig. 13.7c) is the rib equivalent of punto with greater elasticity and width and 50 per cent greater production but there is a danger of yarn breakage causing a press-off at the all-knit course. It is also used in the production of fashioned collars. Evermonte (Fig. 13.7a) has a row of tuck stitches on one side after each tubular course which produces a slight ripple effect.

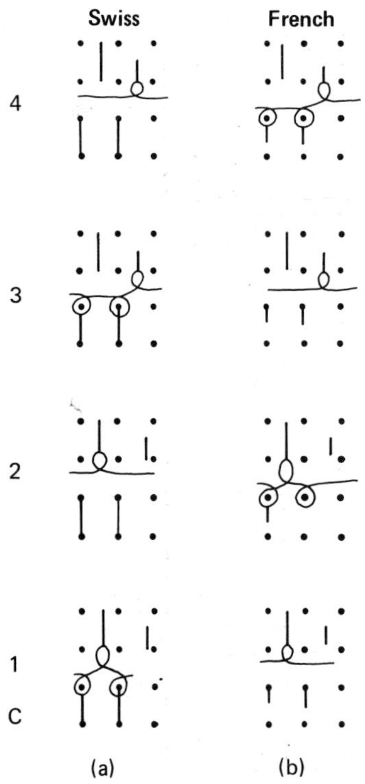

Rib Jacquard Double-Jersey Structures 13.5

Designs in these structures are achieved by cylinder needle selection, whilst the dial needles often operate in all-knit or alternate knit and miss sequences (Fig. 13.9) to produce the backing and eliminate floats which would occur when cylinder needles are selected to miss. There are two main groups of these fabrics, flat jacquards and relief designs.

Flat jacquards are described by the size of the design area, followed by

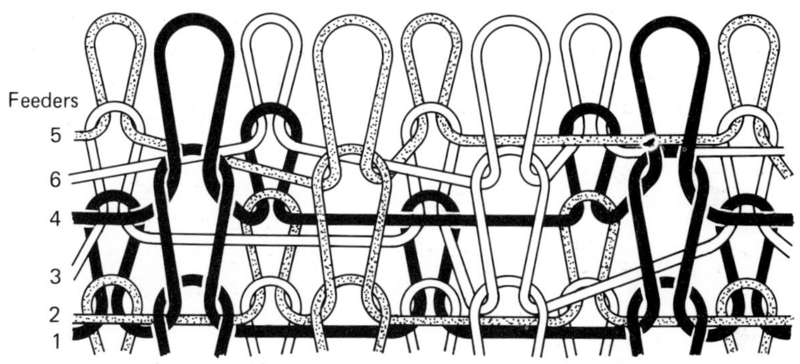

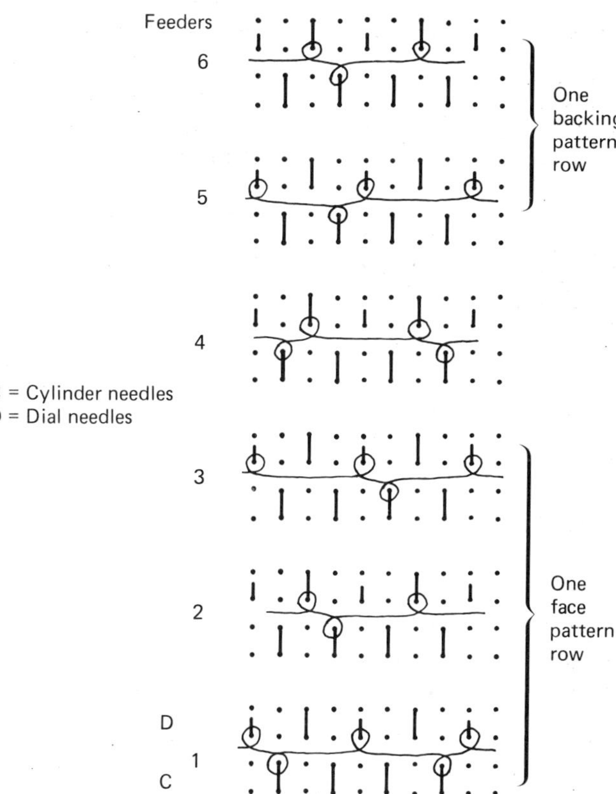

Fig. 13.9

the number of colours in one complete pattern row of loops and the type of backing.

The design area is controlled by the selection system of the machine, full jacquard implies unrestricted pattern depth in pattern rows and a width which may be the total number of needles in the machine, large area jacquard designs have a pattern depth which requires more than one machine revolution to be developed and therefore each feeder contributes two or more courses, the pattern width is usually more than forty-eight wales. A small area jacquard has a pattern depth which is developed in one machine revolution so that each feeder contributes only one course from a fixed selection and the pattern width is approximately forty-eight wales or less.

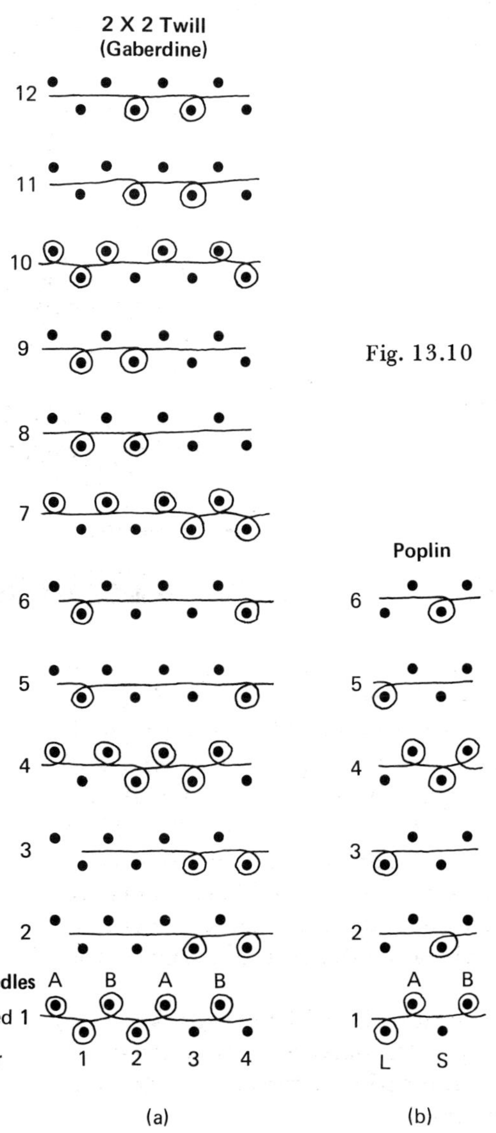

Fig. 13.10

Costa brava is a plain single-colour structure which requires individual needle selection on a width of four cylinder needles. A diagonal effect is developed on two adjacent cylinder needles which moves by one needle at the first of every three-feeder sequence, the third feeder complements this. These loops are extended by the dial-only course at every second feeder. Alternate dial needle knitting produces a twill backing.

Gaberdine (Fig. 13.10a) is a simple 2 X 2 twill double-blister fabric which is useful for fine gauge men's leisurewear. It has a four-needle width repeat with the dial needles all knitting the backing at every third (ground) feed. A flatter structure used for the same purpose is called poplin (Fig. 13.10b) and is a type of single blister with a two-needle width repeat.

The most popular relief designs are blister or cloque structures which are normally produced only on circular rib jacquard machines. Each cylinder needle is selected to knit either a ground yarn which also knits on alternate dial needles, or a blister yarn which only knits on the cylinder side and floats between blister loops inside the

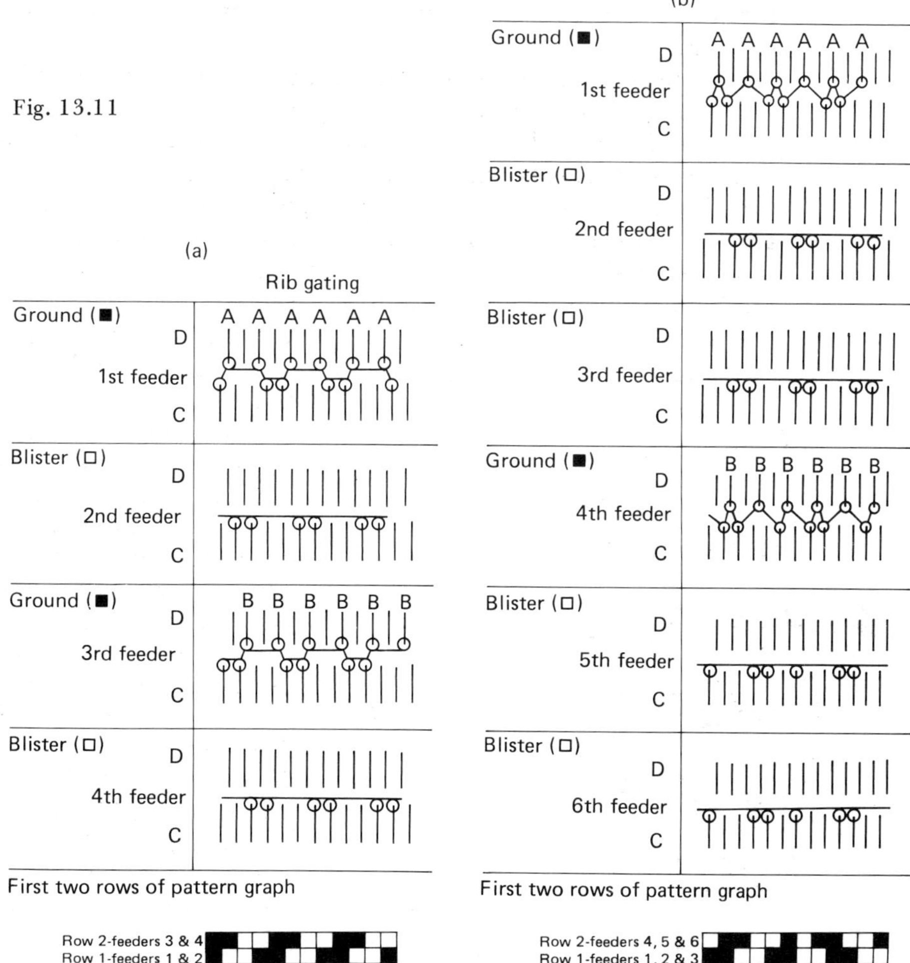

Fig. 13.11

structure hidden by the ground loops of the face and back. Double-blister structures have two blister feeder courses between each ground feeder course (Fig. 13.11b). This produces a more pronounced blister relief, with twice as many courses of blister loops to ground loops, it is heavier and has a slower rate of production than single blister. Blister loops at two successive feeders may not necessarily occur on the same needles. They may be in one or more colours with a self colour or a one- or two-colour ground. Single blister is also termed three-miss blister (Fig. 13.11a) because each dial needle misses three feeders after knitting, whilst double blister is termed five-miss. All blister structures only show the ground loops on the back.

Quilted structures are types of blister fabrics where blister yarn knitting occurs on a large number of adjacent cylinder needles so that enclosed pockets or quilts are formed by lack of connection between cylinder and dial courses. A number of colours may be used.

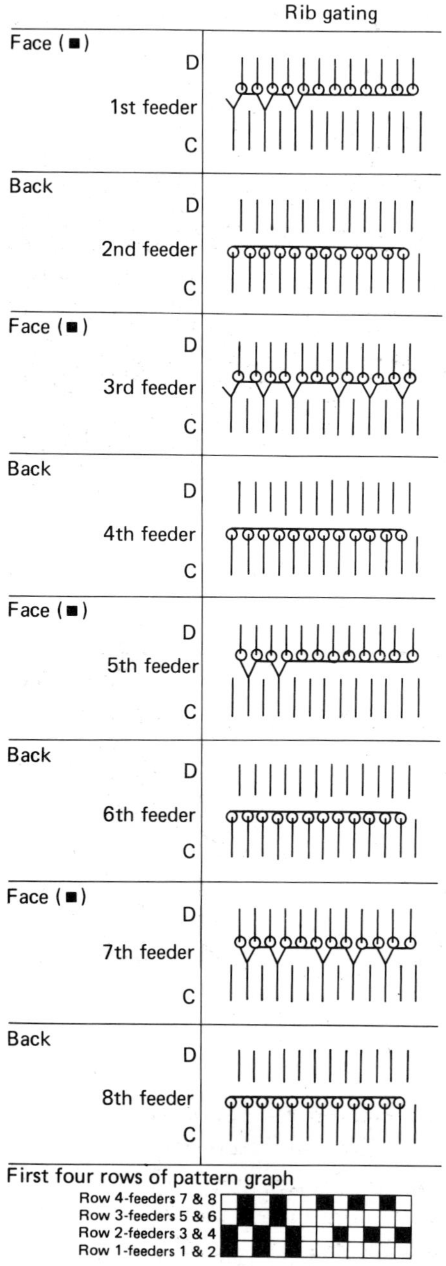

Fig. 13.12

Ripple designs show as figured rolls or welts on the all-dial knit side of the structure because there are more loops per wale on this side, every dial needle knits at every feeder but the cylinder needles are only selected to knit to balance the dial loops where the ripple is not required.

Tuck Lace or Mock Transfer (Fig. 13.12) designs consist of two fabrics knitted with different yarns or colours, one produced on the dial and the other on the cylinder. At the all dial knit feeders selected tucking may occur on alternate cylinder needles if required, often the selection is repeated at the next two-feeder sequence to emphasize the effect. The tucks produce a semi-breakthrough effect by displacing the wales of the dial side which is the effect side, so that the cylinder loops show through at these points as a different colour.

13.6 Double-Jersey Inlay

On double-jersey machines laying-in may be achieved by the tunnel inlay technique. The inlay is fed in advance of the knitting yarn at a feeder and is trapped as an almost straight horizontal yarn inside the fabric behind the cylinder and dial face loops. To reduce weight, the inlay is usually supplied at every third or sixth feed of a three-colour jacquard design, at feeders which always knit some loops on the cylinder. The tube inlay feed is attached to the feeder guide to supply its yarn low and in advance of the cylinder and dial needles moving out to clear for the ground yarn. To make the inlay visible and to reduce the fabric width and weight, alternate cylinder needles are removed and replaced by dummy or blank needles which prevent the tricks from closing-up or becoming clogged with dirt. Needle selection thus takes place on half-gauged cylinder needles with the inlay (either boucle or over fed yarn) protruding through between these wales.

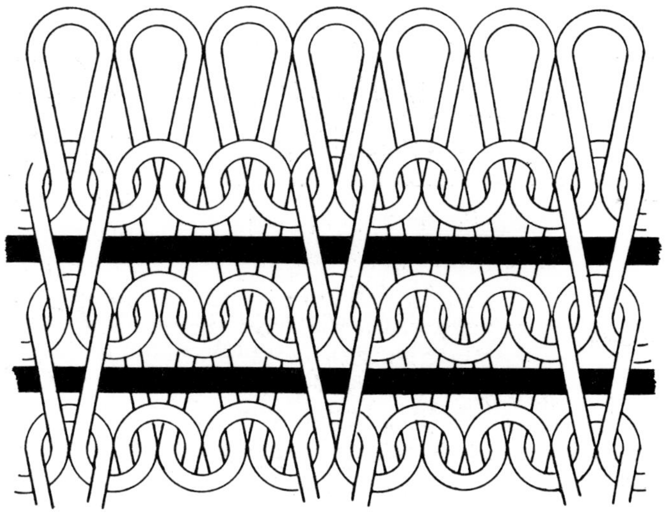

Fig. 13.13

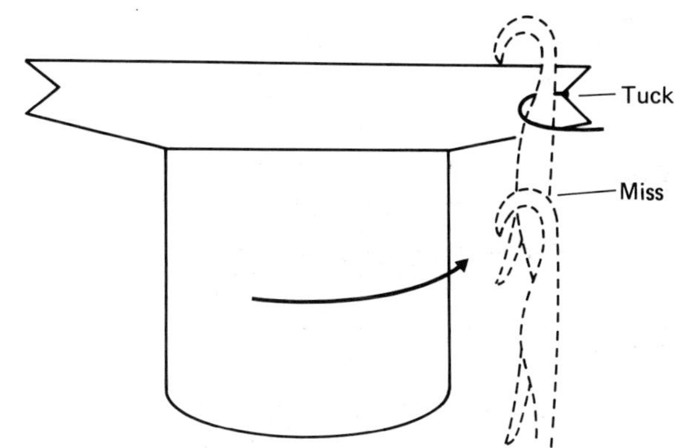

Fig. 13.14

Although tunnel inlay is a simple technique (Fig. 13.13), the yarn is not very secure when the fabric is cut into open width, also the yarn has a straight configuration with little surplus available for elastic extension. If an elastomeric yarn is employed there is widthwise but no lengthwise extension and recovery.

The alternative to tunnel inlay is to use a knitting feeder for inlay by missing and tucking on one or both needle beds. Texi pique (Fig. 13.5b) is an example but as tucking occurs on both beds and the cylinder needles are full gauged, the inlay is hidden inside the structure. The Faneknit device[8] (Fig. 13.14) achieves inlay by tucking only on one bed by employing a vee-bladed weft insertion wheel to which the inlay yarn is supplied and presents it in the correct position to the needle bed. The wheel may be gear-driven by the needle shanks so that its blades are set between either the dial or the cylinder needles depending upon its positioning. The device requires its own feeder where, if a needle is lifted to tuck height by means of a special butt position, the blades present the yarn into its hook. Needles not lifted miss the yarn as the blades take it past the top of their heads. The inlay length is 10 per cent greater than the machine circumference compared with only 4 per cent for tunnel inlay. Using an 18-gauge rib jacquard half-gauged on the cylinder yarns of up to 1100 denier or 1/8's worsted may be inlaid.

Worked Example

Calculate the length in metres of a plain single-jersey fabric knitted at 16 cpcm on a 26-inch diameter 28-gauge circular machine having 104 feeds. The machine operates for 8 hours at 29 revolutions per minute at 95 per cent efficiency.

Number of courses knitted in 8 hours

$$= 8 \times 29 \times 104 \times \frac{95}{100} \times 60$$

Therefore the total length of the fabric in metres

$$= \frac{8 \times 29 \times 104 \times 95 \times 60}{16 \times 100 \times 100}$$

$$= 859.6 \text{ metres.}$$

Further Information

Textbooks

BATCHELOR, C. W., Double jersey knitting and patterning, *Hos. Trade Journal*, (1972) (reprint of series of 9 articles published between April 1971 and June 1972).
BROWN, T. D., *Wool in Double Jersey*, (1973) Merrow Technical Library.
REICHMAN, C., *Doubleknit Fabric Manual*, (1961) *Nat. Knit. O'wr Assoc.*, New York.

Technical Articles

INNES, R., Camber single jersey machines, *Knit. Times*, (1977) 29 Aug., 22–9.
LANCASHIRE, J. B., Non-jacquard double jersey structures, *Hos. Trade Journal*, (1962) May, 92–4; (1965) Jan., 78–80; (1971) March, 92–5.
LANCASHIRE, J. B., Focus on fine gauge single jersey, *Hos. Trade Journal*, (1972) Sept., 118–23.
STEVENS, J., Fundamentals of single jersey knitting, *Knit. Times*, (1976) 29 March, 31–9.
WEBER, K. P., Theory of knitting (part 3), *Knit. Times Yr. Bk.*, (1975) 58–89.
Mayer single jersey machines, *Knit. Times*, (1977) 26 Sept., 20–3.
Single jersey, *Knit. Int.* (1981) Aug., 88–9.
50 years of circular yardgoods machinery, *Knit. O'wr Times Yr. Bk.*, (1968) 237–41.

1. HOWARTH, E. and SCOTT, P., A new approach to knit fabric decating, *Knit. Times*, (1979) 24 Sept., 12–14.
2. HOWARTH, E. and SCOTT, P., New techniques in fabric raising, *Knit. Times*, (1979), 9 July, 11–13.
3. HEMPEL, E., Pleated and folded, *Textile Asia*, (1980) June, 72–4.

4. The Clothing Institute Information Sheet Number 4, *Some Facts About Stitches And Seams.*
Fabricating knitted fabrics into garments, *Knit. Times Yr. Bk.*, (1977) 163–173.
Basic sewing stitches and seams to assemble knitted outerwear, *Knit. Times Yr. Bk.*, (1978) 182–3.
5. DARLINGTON, K. D., The functions and applications of knitting machine stop motions, *Knit. Times*, (1978) 24 July, 13–18.
6. HURD, J. C. H., Technical aspects of double jersey, *Hos. Trade Journal*, (1967) Aug., 78–82.
7. KNOBIL, H. E., Factors influencing the knitting industry, *Text. Inst. and Ind.* (1974) **24**, (4), 123–4.
8. FANE, K., Faneknit (ASKT Paper) *Knit. Int.*, (1979) May, 56–8, or *Knit. Times*, (1979) 16 April, 152–58.

14

Speciality Fabrics and Machines

Speciality fabrics include fleecy, plush, high pile and wrap fabrics. Although some constructions are unique to a single type of circular machine, others may be knitted by a range of machinery.

The surface effects of fleecy, plush or pile are developed during the finishing process. In fleecy fabrics, the fleece yarn fibres become entangled and indistinguishable from the base yarn on the effect side despite having been separately supplied during knitting. In pile and plush structures, the pile and plush is clearly distinguishable from the base. Pile is considered to stand out at right-angles to the base, whereas plush lies at less of an angle from the base suface. High quality three-thread invisible fleecy and sinker loop terry (plush plating) is still produced by the loopwheel frame and sinkerwheel machine respectively, despite intense competition from more productive machines. Both machines can also produce other structures.

Invisible fleecy (Fig. 14.1) is a plain plated structure composed of a face and binding yarn with a fleecy (backing yarn) being inlay tucked into the technical back at every fourth wale, to mesh only with the binding yarn. The face yarn prevents the arms of the fleecy tucks being visible between the wales on the face, which would spoil its clean appearance.

The fleecy inlay is spread across the technical back by centring the fleecy tucks of the next three-feed sequence on the middle of the three needles which missed the fleecy in the previous sequence.

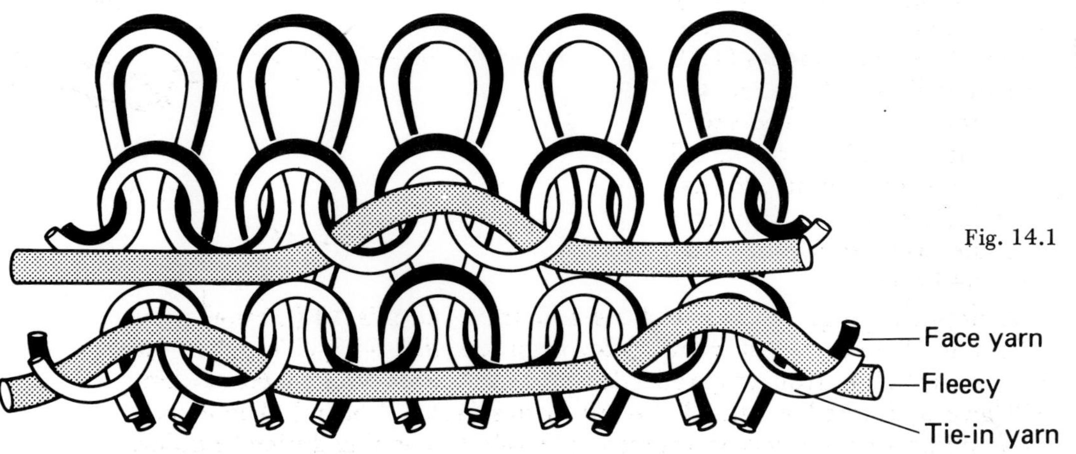

Fig. 14.1

The Loopwheel Frame 14.1

Since 1846, Tompkins in the U.S.A. have pioneered the development of the loopwheel frame and are now the only builders (Fig. 14.2). The bearded needles, which are in leads, are set vertically, with their beards facing outwards from an anti-clockwise revolving cylinder. Either one or two independently-revolving cylinders are supported on a table frame. A unique feature is that the fabric tube is drawn upwards and wound into a roll by a winding frame revolving high above the cylinder, driven from a vertical shaft coupled to the machine drive below the table. The knitting action is produced by angularly-set bladed burr wheels which transport the yarn and loops along the needle stems in conjunction with pressing wheels or shoes.

Gauges range from 5 to 32 needles per 1½ inches (3.8 cm) in cylinder diameters from 8 to 42 inches both of which are easily changed. There is usually one complete three-feed system to every 6 inches (15.2 cm) of cylinder diameter. On the latest machines the speed constant is 1380 diametral revolutions per minute, so that a 30-inch (76 cm) diameter machine will revolve at 1380 ÷ 30 = 46 rpm.

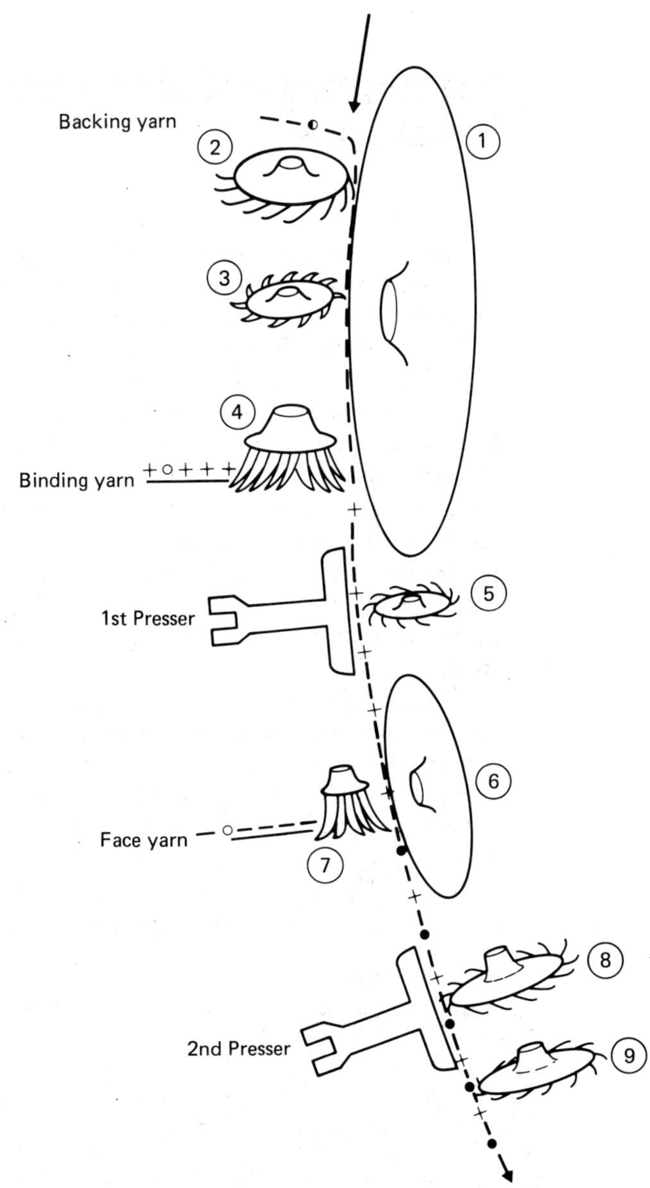

Fig. 14.2

A popular gauge for sweat shirts and track suits is 30 (20 npi) using 1/28's to 1/30's cotton count (cotton or acrylic) or 1/70's nylon and 1/9's to 1/12's cotton or acrylic fleece yarn. A 30-inch diameter machine will give a finished width of 54–60 inches (1.37–1.52 m). The loosely twisted fibres of the fleece yarn respond easily to napping during finishing.

14.2 The Knitting Cycle to produce one Course of Fleecy

Loop formation is achieved by burr wheels whose blades are of the same gauge and turn by contact with the revolving needles (Fig. 14.2). The blades are set at an angle on the hub so that as they turn they produce a helical or spiral effect, those fitted on the outside of the cylinder are set towards the needles to sink the newly fed yarns and those inside the fabric tube spiral away from the needles lifting the loops up the needle stems for landing and knock-over.

The cloth wheel (or shoe) (1) pushes the old loops down the needle stems as the knitting zone is entered. The burr wheel (2) has a steel insert in every fourth gap between its blades which causes that needle to be deflected backwards as the wheel introduces the backing (fleece) yarn, so that the yarn is tucked onto the beard of every fourth needle and inlaid behind the other three. A take-down burr (3) lowers the tucks onto the needle stems.

The burr wheel (4) feeds the binding yarn forming it into a loop underneath the beards of every needle. The first presser then closes the beards so that the landing wheel (5) lifts the tucks onto the beards and over the binding yarn loops trapped inside them, this action unintentionally also lifts the old loops which are lowered from the beards by the auxiliary cloth wheel leaving the fleecy tucks still on every fourth needle beard.

The burr wheel (7) feeds the face yarn to join the binding yarn loops in a plating relationship underneath the beards of every needle and at the same time, the fleecy tuck is cast-off and meshes only with the binding yarn. The second presser now closes the beards so that the landing wheel (8) can land the old course of loops onto the beards where the knock-over wheel (9) casts them off in a plating relationship.

14.3 The Production of Fleecy on Sinker Top Machines

Three-thread fleecy is increasingly being produced on open top latch needle machines in the manner first patented by Lestor Mishcon in the U.S.A. in 1937. Originally, pattern wheel selection was used for fleece yarn tucking. The preferred method today is to use a top needle butt and cam-track for knitting the ground (face) and tie-in (binding) yarns and four tracks and corresponding butt positions (which can be rearranged) for the fleecy tucking sequence.

Figure 14.3 shows a typical knitting sequence for producing three-thread fleecy:

1. Selected needles are raised to tuck height to receive the fleecy (usually one out of four). The sinker then moves forward for its top throat to control the fleecy tuck whilst the lower throat controls the previous course.

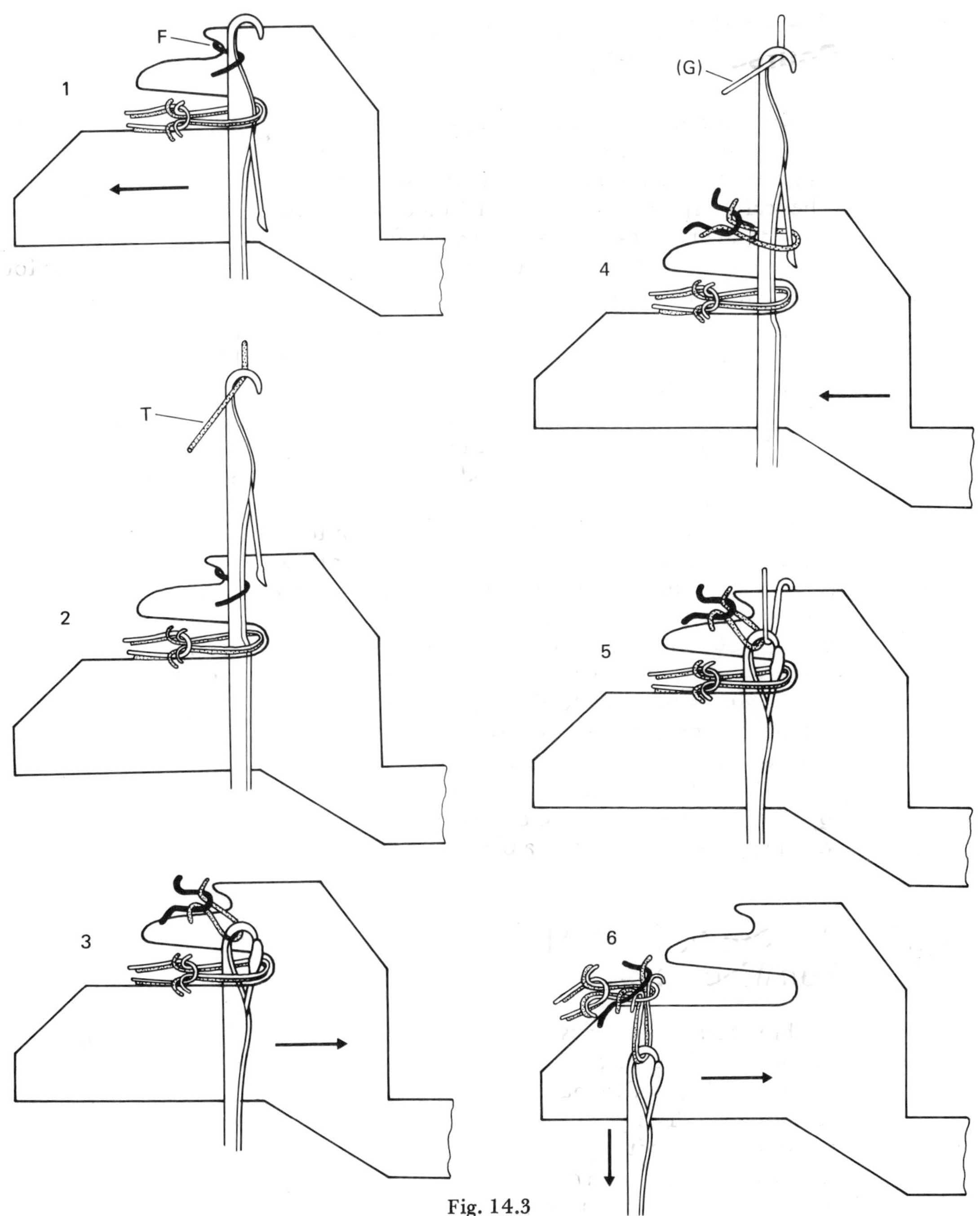

Fig. 14.3

2. All needles are raised to clear the previous course and receive the tie-in yarn.
3. The needles descend to normal tuck on the latch position so that the previous course remains on the outside of the closed latch but the fleecy tuck which is higher slips off the needle head and the tie-in yarn is drawn through it on the upper sinker belly as the sinker withdraws.

4. The upper sinker throats hold the tie-in loops on the open latches whilst all needles rise to receive the ground yarn.
5. The needles again descend to the tuck on the latch position to form loops from the tie-in yarn over the sinker crowns.
6. The sinker finally withdraws and as the needle descends the new plated course slips onto the lower sinker belly and the old course is knocked-over. Very carefully adjusted cam settings encourage the ground yarn to plate on the technical face (the underside) of the structure.

14.4 Fleecy Interlock

This is plated fleecy fabric consisting of a main yarn which is fed to knit on both needle beds and a fleecy yarn which is fed first and at a lower level below the latches of the dial needles whilst they are at clearing height, so that it does not enter their hooks or show on the dial side of the fabric (Fig. 14.4).

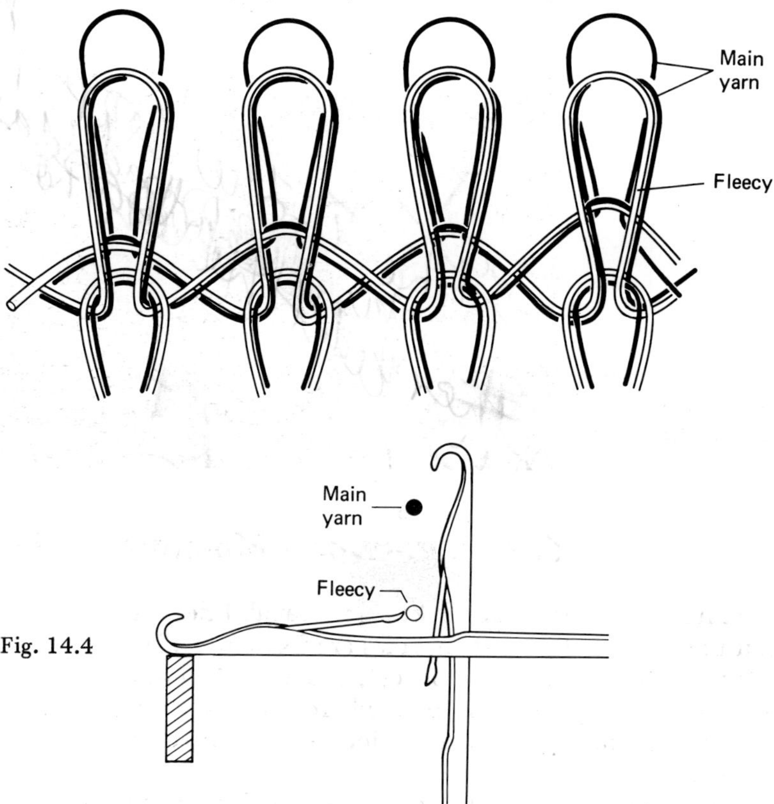

Fig. 14.4

14.5 Plush Structures

Single-sided plated plush or terry is a popular leisure and sportswear structure found in both fabric and sock form having the form fitting elasticity of single jersey. The elongated plush sinker loops show as a pile between the wales on the technical back as a result of having been formed over a different surface to that of the normal length ground sinker loops with which they are plated (Fig. 14.5). Henkel plush or velour is achieved during finishing by cropping or shearing the loops in both directions, to leave the individual fibres exposed as a soft velvety surface whilst the ground loops remain intact. It requires a fine gauge structure and involves a considerable loss of cropped yarn. The bearded needle sinkerwheel has long been renowned for this type of fabric construction.

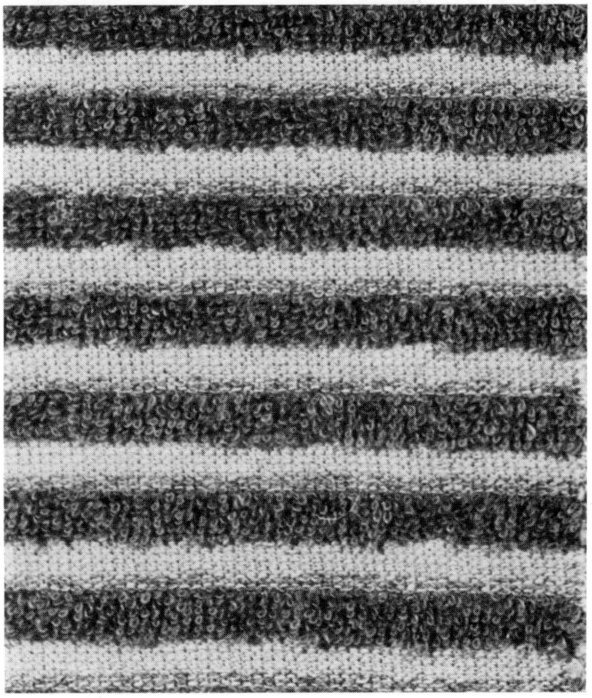

Fig. 14.5. Horizontal ribs with an ottoman effect on two-tone towelling (Alwin Wild, Switzerland).

The Sinkerwheel Machine 14.6

In construction, knitting action and fabric knitting capabilities the sinkerwheel machine is unique[1] (Fig. 14.6). Its needles are fixed, to radiate horizontally outwards with their beards uppermost, from a clockwise revolving cylinder whose central axle (A) is suspended from an overhead beam as the machine has no supporting frame. Machines may be driven as sets but have separate clutches.

At each feed around the needle circle periphery and meshing into it, is a vertically mounted sinkerwheel (S) whose sinkers form and control the loops cooperating with other elements in a gentle knitting action as they are individually cammed down in sequence between the needles. Wire cards (W) mechanically rising and falling inside the fabric tube draw it downwards towards a container revolving at floor level.

Fig. 14.6. A sinkerwheel machine knitting A Jour Knupf fabric.

The machine's productivity is low with a speed factor of 500 and only four to a maximum of twelve feeds in a diameter range of 10–44 inches. It can, however, knit weak yarns or very high quality tightly-knitted structures including plus, inlay and unique loop transfer stitches (it is the only circular single-jersey machine capable of automatically transferring or spreading needle loops to the left or to the right). Gauges are expressed in zoll or French inches (1/36 metre or 1.09 inches) at the point of needle location. Fein or fine gauges (per zoll) range upwards from 20 fein (15 npi) and includes the popular 26 fein (18 npi). Gross or coarse gauges (per 1½ zoll) range downwards from 27 Gross (14 npi).

14.7 Knitting Action

Figure 14.7 shows the knitting action of the sinkerwheel machine:

1. *Yarn presentation*. The gear-wheel (g) fed yarn is positioned by its guide under the sinker throat.
2. *Loop formation*. An adjustable stitch cam inside each sinkerwheel causes the sinkers to descend in sequence between the needles to form the new loops just below the beards.
3. *Beard covering*. The sinkers are guided to take the new loops under the open beards.
4. *Pressing and landing*. The platines situated between each needle, are cammed forwards to land the old loops resting against them onto the beards which are pressed closed by a wheel.
5. *Knock-over*. The platines are cammed fully forwards to knock-over the old loops. At this point, the sinker retires releasing the new loop it has been retaining to the forward platine.

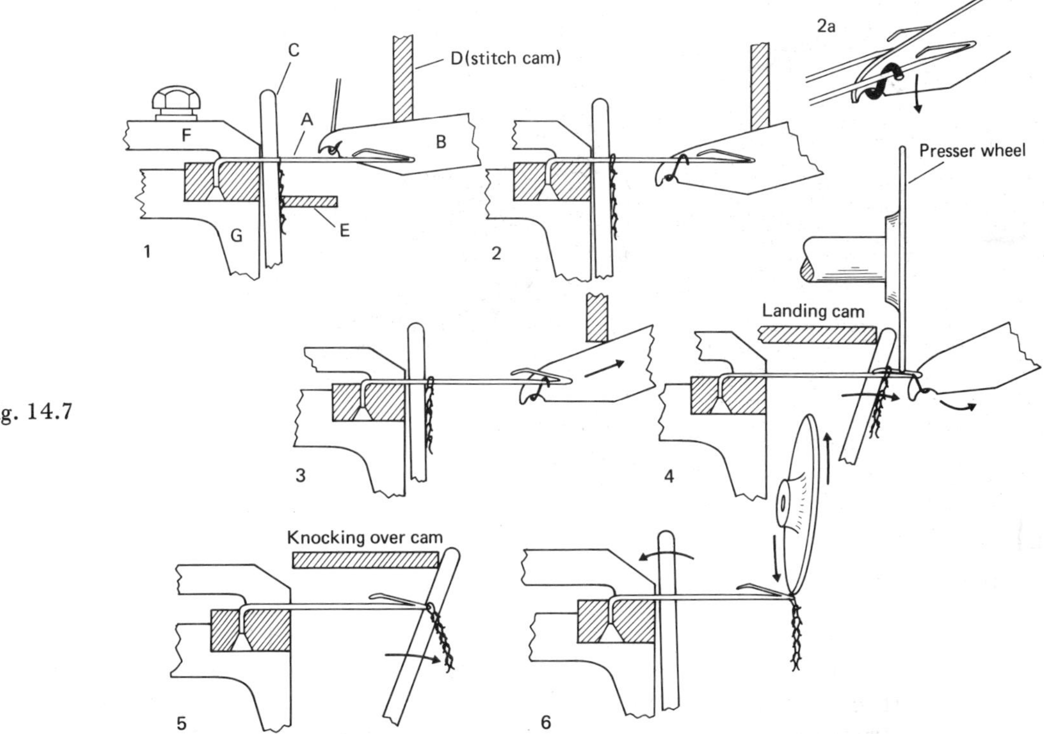

Fig. 14.7

6. *Beard clearing*. An inclined wheel knocks-over any loops still hugging the needle head. The platines, no longer under cam control are withdrawn by their spring band whilst the new loops are pushed from under the beards up to them by a serrated wheel and push-back blade.

The gradual and controlled loop formation cycle of the sinkerwheel machine prevents plush yarn robbing and produces the highest quality plush in terms of fineness of gauge, tightness of knitting, uniformity of pile and accuracy of plating without the plush yarn bubbling onto the face and creating pilling problems. Sinkers with two throats are employed (Fig. 14.8), the shallow throat draws a long sinker (A) loop with the plush yarn which is fed nearest to the needle head whilst the deeply cut throat draws a normal length sinker loop (B) with the ground yarn fed lower on the needle stem. Sinkers with different cuts of throat are available for different lengths of plush. If plain (Fig. 14.9) and plush sinkers are employed in the same wheel sculptured designs may be developed based on pattern wheel design area principles.

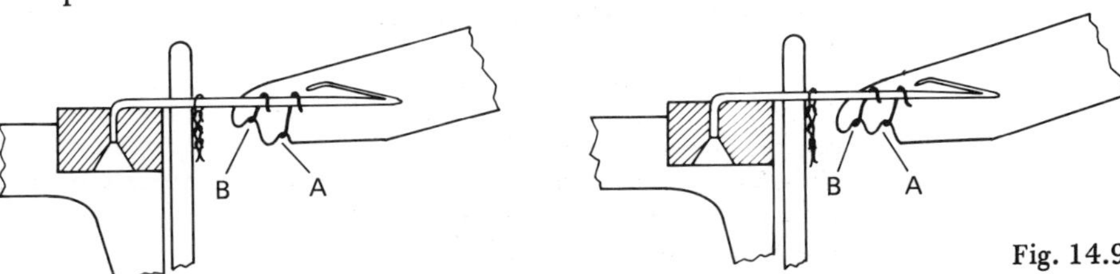

Fig. 14.8

Fig. 14.9

14.8 Plush on Sinker Top Latch Needle Machines

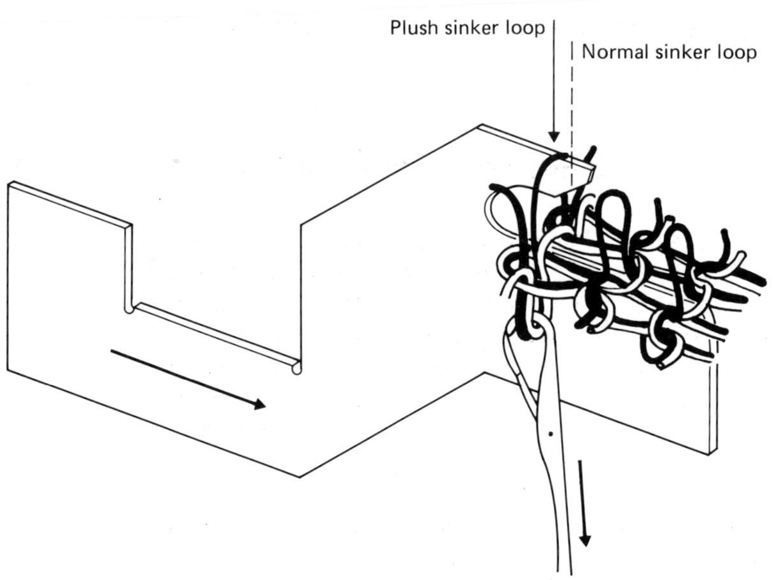

Fig. 14.10

On the more productive sinker top latch needle machine, the ground yarn is fed into the sinker throat and the sinker is then advanced so that the plush yarn fed at a higher level (Fig. 14.10) is drawn over the sinker nib. If the sinker is not advanced the two sinker loops will be of equal size. Horizontal pattern wheels may select onto the backs of sinkers and thus produce designs in plain and plush stitches. A range of plush heights from 2 to 4 mm is possible using different sinker heights. Precise camming of needles and sinkers, sharper angles of stitch cams and control of loops such as by sinker nib penetration methods after formation, are all being employed to improve accuracy of plating and reduce plush loop robbing.

On a 20 npi machine 1/30's cotton might be used for the plush with a ground of 2/70 denier S and Z twist nylon alternating at each feeder in a weight of approximately 285 gm per metre[2], whereas for 24 npi the more expensive 1/30's cotton and 100 denier nylon is required. The speed factor is about 500–600 with between 1.3 and a maximum of 2 feeders per diametral inch.

Other less conventional methods of knitting plush are possible. On the Multiwaga machine, compound needles are employed together with loop-forming and knock-over sinkers to achieve high production with multi-feeders.[2] Double-sided plush can be obtained on the Jumberca RDC machine with the face plush yarn being drawn by the throats of a second, specially shaped, sinker placed alongside the plush sinker in each dial trick.[3] Babygro – a special two-way stretch babywear structure is knitted on a loopwheel frame by pressing-off the plated cotton yarn at odd needles of odd feeds and even needles of even feeds to obtain float pile loops. A wide range of plush fabrics in single-jersey construction can also be knitted on modified rib machines by drawing loops with the second set of needles and then pressing them off to form the plush loops.[4,5] Sometimes plush points are employed.

Sliver or High-Pile Knitting 14.9

This single-jersey circular machine has sliver feeds where the stock- or dope-dyed slivers are drawn from cans at ground level and then prepared by mini three-roller drafting card units followed by two wire-covered rollers (Fig. 14.11). At each sliver feed the needles are lifted to an extra high level where they rise through the wires of the doffer roller to collect a tuft of staple fibres. Air jet nozzles over the knitting points ensure that the tufts are retained in the needle hooks and that the free fibre ends are orientated through to the inside of the fabric tube (the technical back) which is the pile side. As the needles start to descend, the ground yarn is fed to them, so that each has a ground loop and a tuft of fibres which are drawn through the previous loop. A variety of machines altogether provide opportunities including up to sixteen roller speed settings, the use of two different fibre lengths and mechanical or electronic needle and sliver selection. Electronic selection can cause needles to take fibres from one of four different coloured slivers.

Borg Textiles pioneered specialized sliver knitting in the 1950s in cooperation with Wildman Jacquard although J. C. Tauber obtained U.S. patents as early as 1914. A typical machine now has a diameter of 24 inches in a gauge of 10 npi and runs at 45 rpm with 12–16 sliver feeds, the fabric finishes 54–58 inches wide in a weight of about 450 g per metre^2, knitting 360 denier fibrillated polypropylene ground yarn and a modacrylic sliver having a 3-denier $1\frac{1}{8}$ inch staple. However, fibre staple

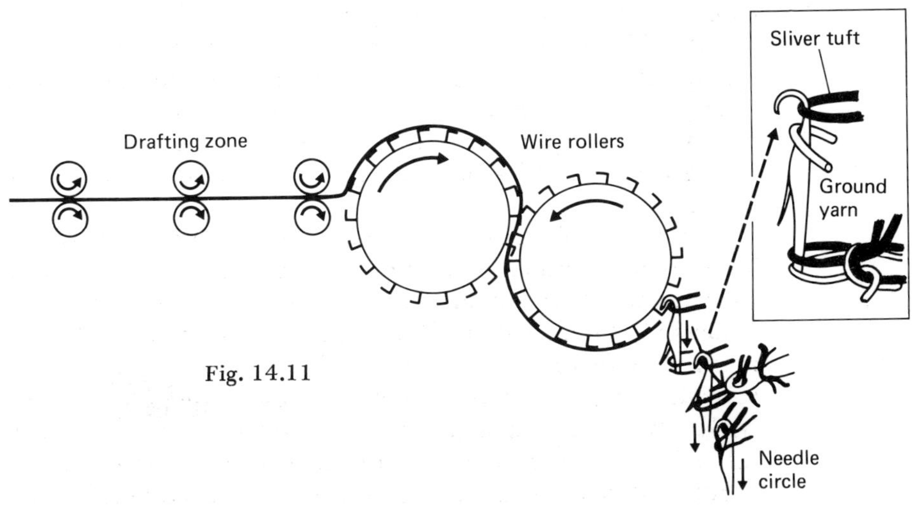

Fig. 14.11

lengths can range from 20 to 120 mm. in sliver weights from 8 to 25 g/metre giving greige (unfinished) weights of 300–2000 g/metre^2 for end-uses such as fun furs, linings, gloves, cushions, industrial polishers and paint rollers.

A typical high pile finishing route is: rough shearing, heat setting and back-coating, pile cropping, electrifying or polishing (to develop the lustre and remove crimp from the fibre ends), tiger framing (to distribute the pile effect) and controlled torque winding (to further develop the pile uniformity).

14.10 Wrap Patterning

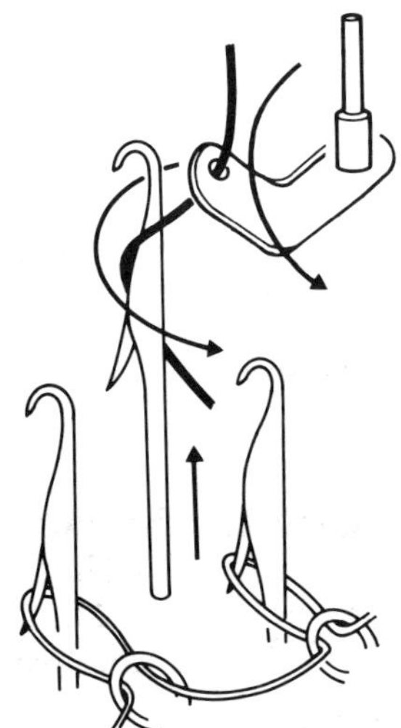

Fig. 14.12

Wrap patterning is popular in single jersey, especially underwear, for producing vertical stripe effects often in conjunction with horizontal patterning (Fig. 14.12). *The fingers or wrapping jacks with their warp yarn pins must rotate in unison with the cylinder in order for each to remain with its section of needles.*

Solid-colour warp insertion is achieved with the Camber wrapping method which may be used on any of their needle selection machines. The first selection system of the sequence selects needles to receive the wrap yarn and the second selects the remaining needles to receive the weft ground yarn. According to machine model, diameter and gauge (5–32 npi), up to 100 or more fingers will successively pass through each section and be capable of wrapping across up to eight or more selected adjacent needles.

As each finger in turn contacts a stationary cam at the wrapping section it pivots out of the cylinder and rises up its clockwise moving post wrapping its warp yarn into the passing hooks of those needles selected to rise to take it. It is then cammed to return to its inactive position inside the cylinder whilst the needles pass to the next system where those previously unselected rise to take the ground yarn. On a 28-gauge machine 70–200 denier yarn might be used for the warp and 30/1 cc–50/1 cc for the ground.

On the Mayer Vilonit machine wrapping and striping is incorporated into fabrics in the form of tuck-miss inlay patterns thus providing an opportunity to use a wide range of yarn counts. A 26-inch diameter machine has twenty-four feeders, six have four-colour striping and six use the forty-six wrapping fingers. Needle selection is by punched tape controlled peg drums. Cam sections are in sequences of eight. At feeders 1 and 5, needles are selected to tuck the striping yarn and at 3 and 7 they are selected to tuck the wrap yarns whilst at feeds 2, 4, 6 and 8 needles are selected to knit the ground yarn.

Further Information

General

BRINKER, R., Wildman jacquard, *Knit. Times*, (1975) 20 Oct., 20–22.
GOADBY, G. R., Tompkins loopwheel frames, *Knit. Int.*, (1976) May, 45–8.
HURD, J. C. H., Developments in single jersey machines and fabrics (IFKT paper), *Knit. Int.*, (1975) Nov., 53–58.
LOMBARDI, V., Patterning potentials in sinker top machines (ASKT paper), *Hos. Trade Journal*, (1961) June, 106–107.
SCHMID, W., Single jersey variations for the '80s (IFKT paper), *Knit. Int.*, (1981) June, 48–52.
VETTER, S., Single jersey pattern possibilities, *Int. Text. Bull.*, (1977) 1, 9–14.
WUSTROW, K. D., Single knit machinery, *Knit. Times*, (1978) 10 July, 16–27.
Knitting Times (1979) 2 April, papers presented at the conference on Creating Surface Interest:
MAASEIDE, J. O., Mayers Vilonit wrap machine, 26–8,
SCHERER, K., Double faced terry, 29–31.
ALLIBONE, D. B., Camber wrap insertion principle, 32–5.
LITTLETON, J. T., Another look at double jersey
Text of NKOA Conference Papers on: The fine cut look in knitted fabrics and garments, *Knit. Times*, (1975) 15 Dec, 45–49.

Fleecy

GOADBY, D. R., Camber fleece machine, *Knit. Int.*, (1981) July, 83.
LOMBARDI, V., Knitting fleece fabrics; alternate methods of production, *Knit. Times*, (1981) 20 April, 155–66.
BENTLEY TTF Model, *Knit. Int.*, (1980) 20 Aug, 82–3; *Knit. Times*, (1981) 20 April, 167–70.
Mellor-Bromley fleecy, *Knit. Int.*, (1980) Aug., 82–3.

Pile, High-Pile or Sliver Knitting

FREEDMAN, H. A., High pile knitting: a review (ASKT paper), *Knit. Times*, (1978) 15 May, 48–51.
GOADBY, D. R., Camber single-jersey pile machines, *Knit. Int.*, (1978) May, 51–2.
MODIG, N., Sliver knit fabrics; finishing methods reviewed (IFKT paper), *Knit. Times*, (1980) 8 Dec., 46–48.
MODIG, N., The production and finishing of knitted pile fabrics, *Int. Text. Bull.*, (1981) 2, 9.
REICHMANN, C., Sliver knitting machinery, *Knit. Times*, (1975) 20 Oct., 18–19.
Monarch XL PL/2 loop pile machine, *Knit. Int.*, (1978) July, 73.

Wrap Patterning

GOADBY, D. R., Camber wrap insertion, *Knit. Int.*, (1981) July, 101–102; (1980) Sept., 84–85.

1. INNES, R., Waga sinker wheel machine, *Knit. Times*, (1979) 15 Oct., 25–31.
2. Multiwaga, *Knit. Int.*, (1980) Jan., 40–2.
3. LOMBARDI, V., Double faced terry, *Knit. Times Yr. Bk.*, (1978) 77–87; *Knit. Times*, (1978) 30 Oct., 28–30; *Knit. Times Yr. Bk.*, (1980) 96–9.
4. SORENSEN, N., Creating plush fabrics via the IWS Bentley attachment, *Knit. Times*, (1979) 16 April, 162–8.
5. DARLINGTON, K. D., How to produce velour on double knit machines, *Knit. Times*, (1976) 9 Feb., 36–40.

15

Loop Transfer Stitches

Both bearded and latch needle weft knitting machines offer considerable scope for the transfer of a full or part needle or sinker loop onto an adjacent needle either in the same bed or in an opposing bed with the objective of achieving shaping, producing a design or changing the stitch structure. In addition, loop transfer is used in ladies' stocking knitting when producing the double-thickness plain fabric inturned welt, in running on and doubling rib loop fabric onto the needles of a straight bar frame to form the rib border of a garment part and when running the loops of two separate fabrics onto the points of a linking machine for linking these fabrics together.

Loop transfer by hand-controlled points is a tedious and skilled operation but automatic loop transfer requires a specific arrangement of specially-shaped needles and/or transfer points.

There are four main types of transfer stitches;

1. Plain needle loop transfer stitches produced by transference from one needle to another in the same bed.
2. Fancy lacing stitches produced by modification of the plain loop transfer stitch.
3. Rib loop transfer stitches produced by transferring a loop from one needle bed to the other.
4. Sinker loop transfer stitches.

15.1 Plain Loop Transfer Stitches

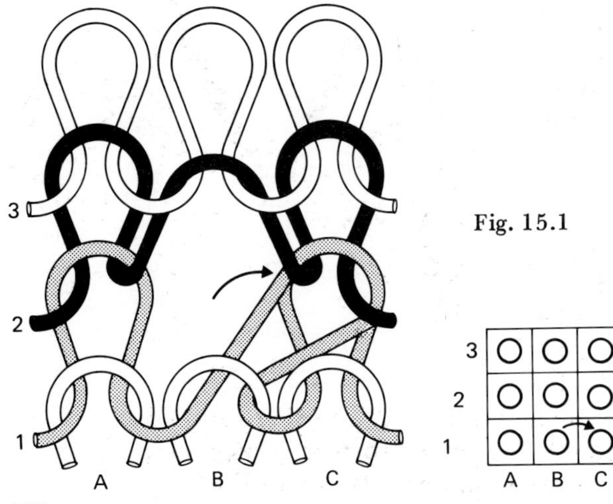

Fig. 15.1

Needle loop transfer on plain fabric is most commonly achieved on straight bar frames using specially shaped rackably controlled transfer points (Fig. 15.1). In designs it is termed a lace stitch[1] whereas in selvedge shaping it is termed fashioning. When crossing over transfer stitches or narrowing it is possible to transfer a loop to the next but one adjacent needle but when the needle loses its loop and is required to knit at the next cycle it will form a tuck stitch which when widening, may require filling in. Two-needle widening is not possible because a faulty stitch would be produced by two adjacent empty needles commencing knitting at the same time.

Loop transfer to adjacent plain wales in rib structures is seldom achieved automatically by means of transfer points and even then it tends to be restricted to the narrowing of collars and sleeves. The method is mechanically complex and slow, there are few straight-bar rib frames and automatic V-bed rib machines usually employ simpler methods of shaping. One latch needle machine, the Stoll 220, has had a limited use, it employs grooved base L-shaped points working in narrowing boxes at each selvedge. To collect a loop, the base of the point fits into a recess below and on the hook side of the needle, so that as the point lifts the needle in its trick, the loop slides down onto the base of the L, after lifting the loops clear of the needles. The points are narrowed inwards and transferred back as the receiving needle rises up the groove on the underside of the base of the L point.[2]

Fancy Lacing Stitches 15.2

The bearded needle sinkerwheel machine (Fig. 14.6) produces the largest range of fancy lacing stitches.[3] Some of which are unique to it, these have the term à jour in their description which implies a sequence of samples. À jour C or knupf (Fig. 15.2) – also termed Filet lace, weft knitted net and knotted stitch – has square apertures in an all-over effect which is popular for men's athletic underwear. On a 16 fine gauge machine 1/18's cotton or 2/70 den. nylon might be used. A course of long loops are knitted and the two side limbs of every second needle loop 'B' are spread side-ways onto the needle loops 'A'. The second course is knitted with a short stitch length and tucking occurs on needles 'B' to make the aperture wider.

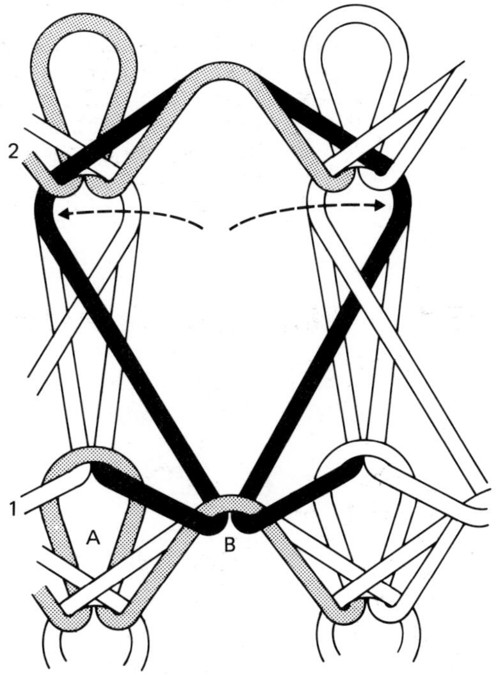

Fig. 15.2

Another stitch known as à jour B has a twisted transferred loop produced by deflecting the beard of the receiving needle across into the eye of the delivering needle so that as the loop is pressed off the delivering needle it twists over. The effect is achieved by using toothed lacing wheels with the upper wheel teeth coupling two beards together, these teeth are arranged according to pattern requirements. À jour H is loop displacement without transference and is produced by deflecting alternate needles (receiving needles) underneath and past the loops on the delivering needles so that when the receiving needles spring back into position they draw the limbs of the adjacent needle loops sideways over their heads.

15.3 Rib Loop Transfer Stitches

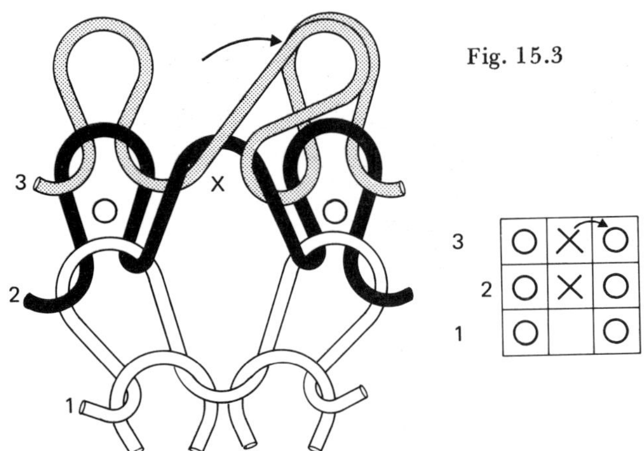

Fig. 15.3

Figure 15.3 illustrates an example of a rib loop transfer stitch. At the first course needles are only knitting in one bed. At the second course an empty needle in the opposite bed commences knitting producing 1 X 1 rib and at the third course this needle transfers its loop.

The rib loop transfer stitch is a very popular stitch and many automatic V-bed flat machines have needle selection facilities and camming for transfer as well as knit, miss and tuck, often from both needle beds. The RTR type circular garment length machine has a similar arrangement at transfer cam sections in the cylinder with collective dial to cylinder transfer on some underwear machines for changing from 1 X 1 rib to 2 X 2 rib needle set-outs (knitwear machines tend to use press-off cam facilities onto the back butt of every third dial needle).

Whereas the RTR type of machine produces designs involving selective transfer of cylinder needle loops onto dial needles which already have a loop of their own, V-bed flats can select needles to transfer their loops to empty needles in the opposite needle bed thus providing increased design possibilities for purl stitch effects, cable and other crossed over stitches and selvedge edge shaping.

The basic requirements for rib loop transfer on any rib machine are:

1. A needle bed rack of between 1/3 and 1/2 needle of a needle space so that the stems of the delivering and receiving needles will be close together during transfer.
2. Specially-designed latch needles with a ledge for lifting the delivering loop and either a recess or a spring clip in the side of its stem to assist entry of the receiving needle hook into the spread loop.
3. A delivering needle cam which lifts its needle higher than clearing height spreading and lifting its loop so that the hook of the receiving needle can enter as its cam lifts it to approximately tuck height. Normal needle selection arrangements can thus be employed to select those needles required to be lifted by the delivering needle cam to transfer their loops.

Figure 15.4 illustrates the transfer action together with its associated cam system. There is a receiving cam (R) and a delivering cam (D) in each

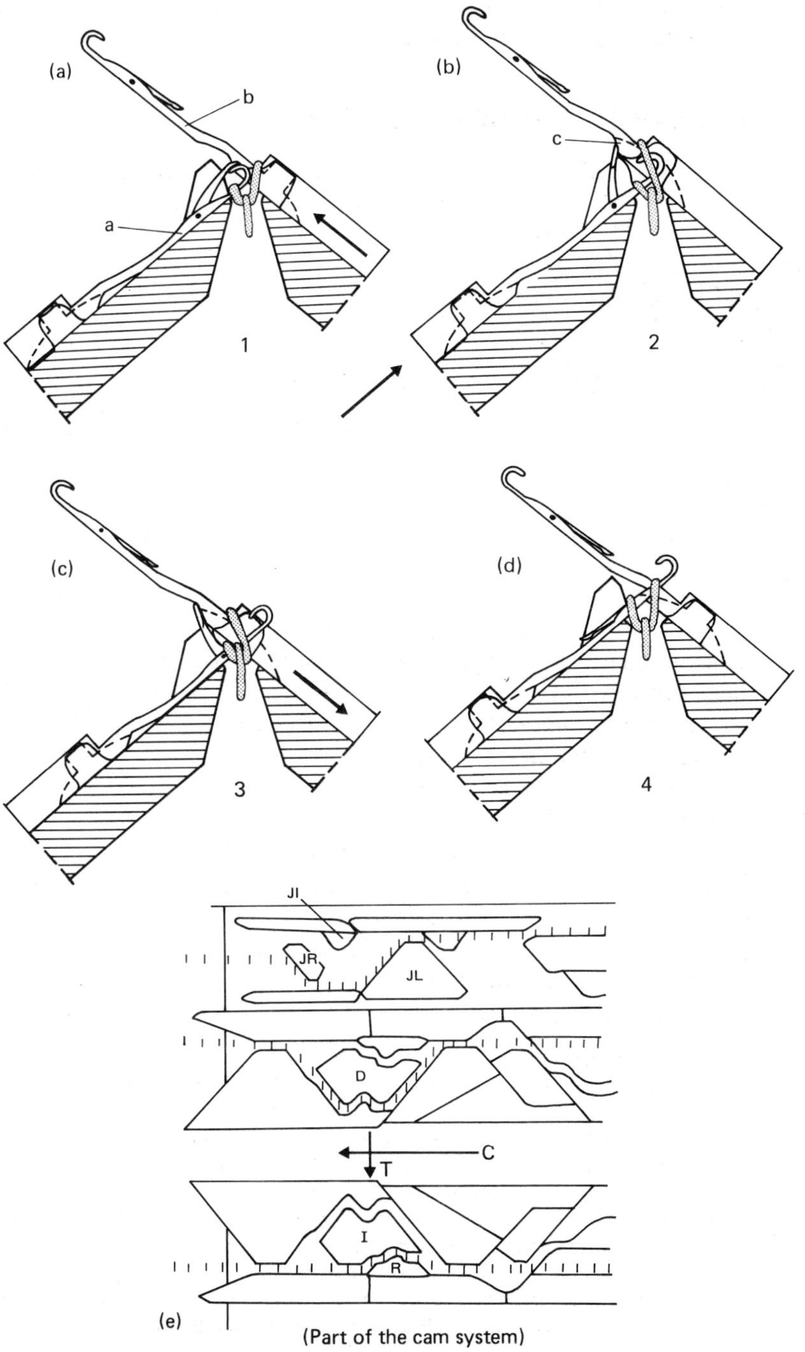

(Part of the cam system)

Fig. 15.4

needle cam system at each end of the system thus providing the possibility of two-way loop transfer in the leading system in each direction of carriage traverse. The delivering needle cam has a double peak, the first peak lifts the loop to stretch and open it ready for transfer on the second peak, the receiving needle cam in the opposite bed is aligned with it and the under-edge of the delivering cam in its system acts as a guard cam for the receiving needle butts.

In Fig. 15.4a the delivering needle (b) is moving towards transfer height with the receiving needle (a) about to enter the recess on its under-side. At this point (Fig. 15.4b) a stop ledge (c) on the rising delivering needle (b) contacts and opens the latch of needle (a) (this arrangement is necessary for opening the latches of empty receiving needles).

In Fig. 15.4c needle (b) is cammed to full transfer height lifting the loop to be transferred and needle (a) is cammed into it with its hook open.

In Fig. 15.4d transference is completed by lowering needle (b) so that its loop is knocked-over and fully transferred into the hook of needle (a). Single-bed knitting is possible whilst the beds are racked for transfer.

15.4 Rib Loop Transfer on a Circular Garment Length RTR Type Machine

The dial is shogged so that the cylinder needle is closer to the dial needle on its right but as the cylinder needle is raised a gear-type deflecting mechanism rotating with the cam-box deflects the needle to the right so that the dial needle can now enter its recess on the left side and penetrate the lifted cylinder loop. The cylinder needle now descends casting off its loop into the hook of the dial needle and returning to its undeflected position. At the next knitting section the empty needle may be selected for miss or to receive the new yarn.

Collective dial to cylinder rib loop transfer usually occurs on every third cylinder needle when changing from 1 X 1 to 2 X 2 rib in the knitting of stitch shaped vests. Dial needles with back butts are cammed out so that the ledges on their stems align their loops with the cylinder needle hooks. An angular cam face deflects the dial needle against the direction of knitting so that the cylinder needle normally on its right enters its expanded loop on the left aided by the recess in the back of the dial needle and a part shog of the dial. The dial needles then withdraw transferring their loops and not taking part in knitting again until 1 X 1 rib is required.

15.5 Pelerine or Eyelet

Eyelet is a cellular structure whose elliptical apertures are formed at courses where adjacent plain wales move outwards, as a result of the absence of connecting sinker loops. Specially shaped pelerine points consisting of two shaped members occupying a single trick are employed to gather the sinker loops, usually at two successive courses, transferring them back at the next knitting cycle to the hooks of the two needles between which they were originally formed.

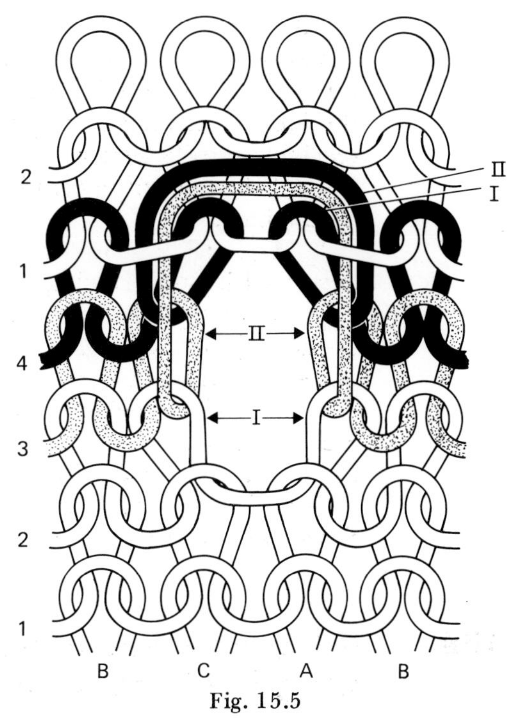

Fig. 15.5

Pelerine is produced in the form of continuous fabric on circular plain web eyelet machines when it is used for lightweight underwear, as rib eyelet in one set of the 2 X 2 rib wales of ladies' body length stitch shaped underwear and as eyelet designs in some types of socks.

Although the diameter of web eyelet machines range from 9 to 22 inches (23–56 cm), 16 inch (40 cm) tends to be popular in a common gauge of 16 npi using cotton counts between 2/28's and 2/35's. The points are normally set-out in the cylinder for convenience of selection and rearrangement and the plain knit base structure is produced by a full set of needles in the dial.

Figure 15.5 illustrates standard all-over plain web eyelet which has a repeat area of three wales by four courses. After every three needles A, B, C, in the dial a pair of points are placed in the trick of the cylinder. Courses 1 and 2 are knitted as plain fabric with the points merely rising to act as holding down sinkers when the dial needles move out to clear.

Before the start of the third course a cam lifts a butt of the points causing their head to protrude between the two dial needles in the gather position. Thus as the needles knit courses 3 and 4 extended sinker loops are drawn around the raised head of the points. The butt of the points now enters the transfer section and the points are cammed to a higher level so that the ledges on either side lift the gathered sinker loops which are spread by the wider eye shape of the head. The needles are then cammed outwards by a tuck cam so that the two adjacent needles enter the eye of the points (Fig. 15.6) just beneath the gathered sinker loops. The points now descend and the two members spring apart (Fig. 15.7) as they pass the outward dial needles, fully transferring the gathered sinker loops into the hooks of the two needles.

Diagonal eyelet has alternately staggered eyelet holes produced by odd pairs of pelerine points operating through their long top butt at the first four-feed cycle and even pairs of pelerine points operating at the second four-feed cycle by means of their long bottom butt, and so on with each butt position having its own cam-track.

Patterned eyelet can be produced by using a pattern wheel to select points for collection at every third feeder (the friction of the sinker

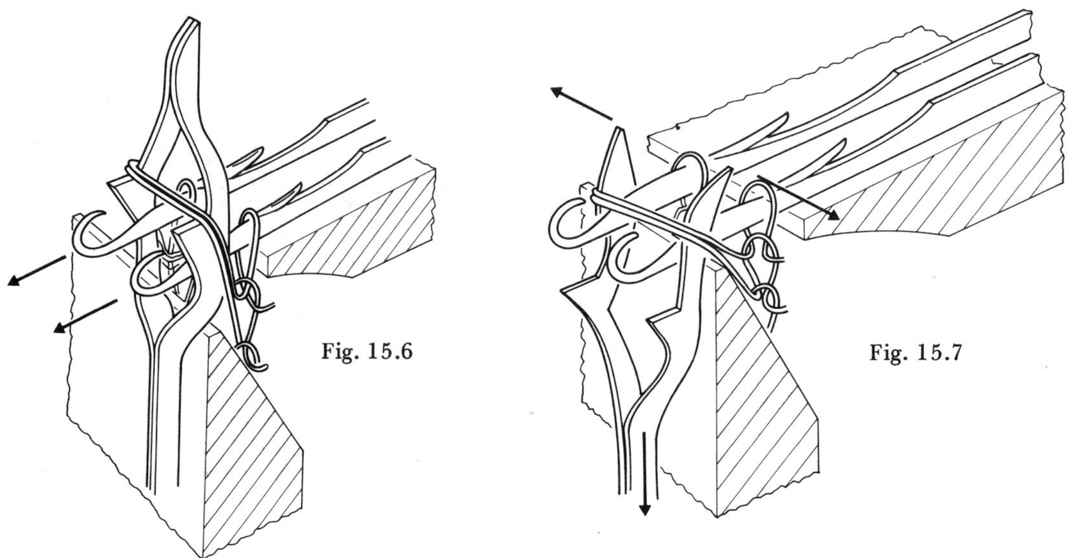

loop will hold the points in action at the fourth feeder). Dummy points engage the wheel from the other cylinder tricks and as only every third pattern wheel trick is in use, three different pattern selections may be loaded. Designs may either be in the form of eyelet motifs on a plain ground or plain motifs on an eyelet ground.

Some of the newer eyelet structures employ two needles to a pair of points. Fine eyelet has a four-feed repeat sequence, close eyelet has a two-feed collect and transfer sequence using odd points at the first sequence and even points at the next, whilst pin point is a patterned eyelet having two plain courses and selection for a single collect and transfer course.

For standard eyelet a 16-inch diameter machine might have twenty feeds and five transfer stations and for close eyelet sixteen feeds and eight transfer stations.

Occasionally, points with one straight member and one curved member have been employed to produce half sinker loop transfer stitches.

Further Information

LANCASHIRE, J. B., Stitch transfer fabrics, *Hos. Trade Journal*, (1968) April, 62–6.
REICHMAN, C., Fundamentals of loop transfer, *Knit. O'wr Times Yr. Bk.*, (1966) pp. 77, 81, 371.
Knitted fabrics for modern underwear, *Hos. Trade Journal*, (1963) Jan., 78.
Web eyelet fabrics, *Hos. Trade Journal*, (1961) Aug., 108–9.

1. LANCASHIRE, J. B., Patterning with points in full fashioned knitting, *Hos. Trade Journal*, (1959) May, 90–100.
2. SMITH, L. A., The role of flat fashioning machines, *Hos. Trade Journal*, (1970) Oct., 124–5.
3. Filet Lace sinker wheel machines, *Hos. Trade Journal*, (1962) Oct., 102–5.

16

Welts, Garment Sequences and Knitting to Shape

As previously mentioned (8.3), the production of a firm starting welt and the introduction of shape during knitting are often features of garment length knitting sequences.

The Welt 16.1

A welt is an attractive and secure edge of a knitted article which helps to prevent laddering or unroving of a structure. It is either formed during the knitting sequence (usually at the commencement and parallel to the courses) or as a later seaming operation during making-up. On machines with no facilities for rib welt sequences the plain fabric is formed into either a turned over welt or a mock rib welt. The ability to produce a knitted welt sequence usually distinguishes an article-producing machine from a fabric-producing machine. Some machines commence at the closed toe end or finger-tip and terminate with the welt end of the article.

The inturned welt is used particularly for manufacturing ladies' hose on circular (Fig. 16.1) and Cottons Patent (Fig. 16.2) machines. Jacks or hooks collect the sinker loops of the third course or the set-up course and hold them, drawing the fabric away until sufficient has been knitted for

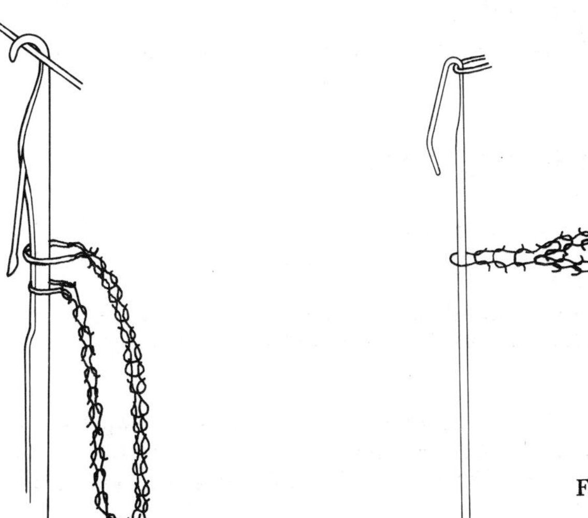

Fig. 16.1

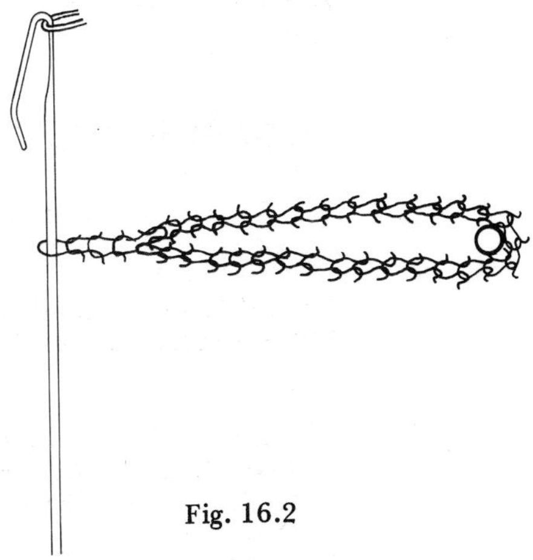

Fig. 16.2

the double-thickness welt. The welt is then turned by transferring the held course back onto the needles, which knit it into the structure. A picot edge at the turn of the welt is achieved either by an alternate needle tuck sequence or by alternate needle loop transfer. Cottons Patent Plain Machines often produce garment panels by knitting onto the rib border, which has been run onto the needles having been previously knitted on a V-bed rib machine or by rib to plain knitting with an ancillary set of needles.

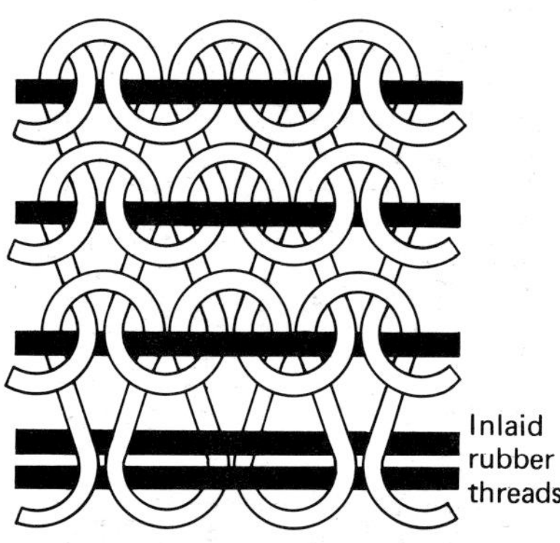

Fig. 16.3

An *accordion top* (Fig. 16.3), *welt* and mock rib can be produced on single-cylinder half-hose and sock machines and on other machines using a single set of needles in a tubular arrangement. Elastomeric yarn is laid-in to odd needles only for a few courses so that when the first plain course is knitted by the textile yarn the straight contracted elastomeric yarn lies through its sinker loops, forming a neat roll edge. The elastomeric yarn is then usually inlaid on a two-tuck two-miss or a one and one basis at each course or alternate courses for a number of courses. As the elastomeric yarn relaxes, it causes alternate wales to be displaced into a mock rib configuration. Sometimes, the second course of textile yarn is only knitted on alternate needles.

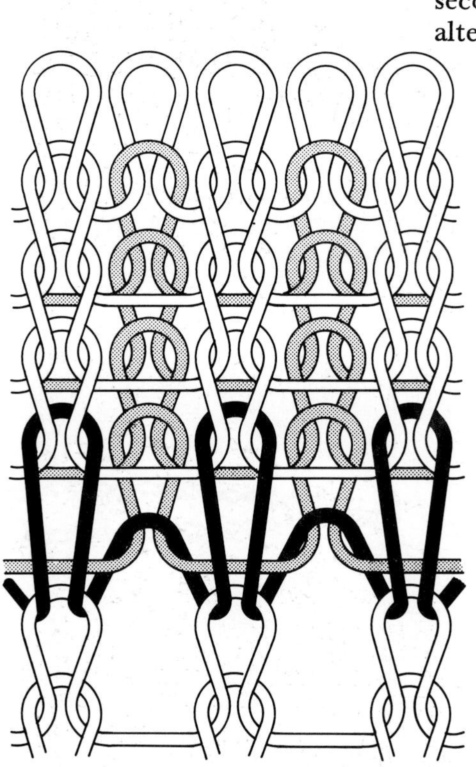

Fig. 16.4

Most fully-fashioned and stitch-shaped underwear and outerwear garments and half-hose and socks have ribbed borders containing a welt sequence, which is produced by causing the sets of needles to act independently of each other after the 1 × 1 rib set-up course. When the rib border is to be knitted in 2 × 2 rib the needle bed is either shogged to form a skeleton 1 × 1 rib needle arrangement or it is knitted on a normal 1 × 1 rib needle set-out followed by rib loop transfer to achieve 2 × 2 rib for the border. Three types of welt are possible when needles are arranged in 1 × 1 rib set-out, these are:

1. The Tubular or French Welt.
2. The Roll or English Welt.
3. The Racked Welt.

The Tubular Welt (Fig. 16.4) is the most popular because it is a balanced structure, which is reversible, lies flat, can be extended to any depth and is elastic. Its only disadvantage is that it can become baggy during washing and wear unless knitted tightly. Apart from some Cottons Patent Rib Machines, most garment producing machines can produce this welt.

The Split Welt is actually a tubular welt knitted at the end instead of at the beginning of the article sequence. It is used as an open tube for a collar or stolling to fit over the cut edge of a garment to which it is then linked by a through stitch.

The Roll Welt (Fig. 16.5) is produced by knitting approximately four courses on one set of needles only, whilst continuing to hold the setting-up course of loops on the other set of needles. It is bulkier and less elastic than the tubular welt and has the disadvantage of long held loops. This welt is produced particularly on half-hose and links-links machines. A reverse roll welt is produced for sleeves with turn-back cuffs and turn-over top socks. In this case the opposite set of needles (bottom cylinder needles on half-hose machines) are caused to hold their loops so that the roll of the welt appears on the other side of the structure but it is on the face when the fabric is folded over.

The Racked Welt (Fig. 16.6) is neat and inconspicuous rather like the set-up course of hand knitting in appearance and is favoured for collars and other trimmings, but it is not as elastic as the other two welts and is normally only produced on flat machines. It is produced by racking the needle bed by one space after the set-up course and retaining the arrangement.

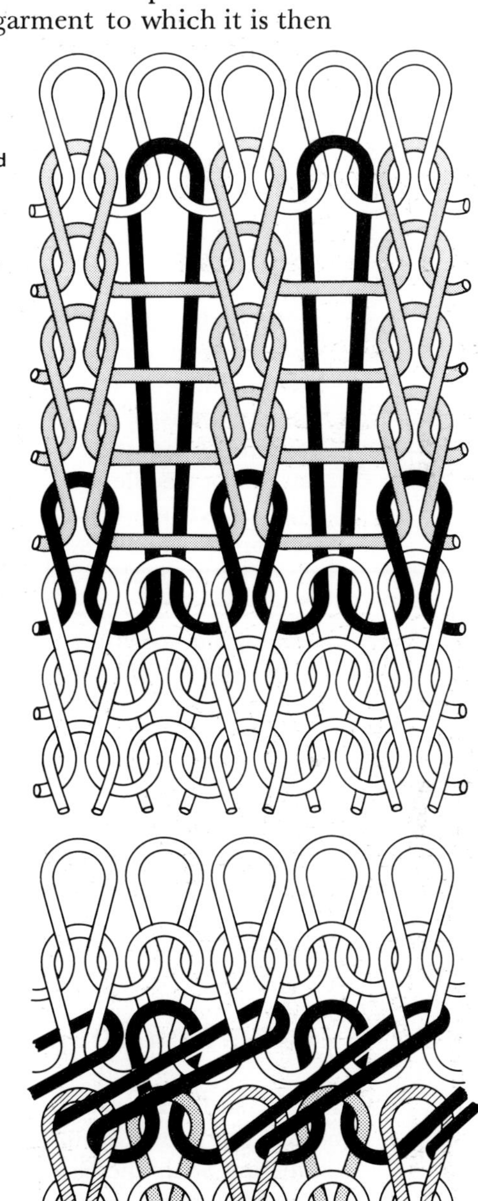

Fig. 16.5

Fig. 16.6

16.2 Separation

Whereas articles are often produced separately on single-cylinder machines and Cottons Patent machines, articles are mainly produced in continuous string formation on many flat and circular rib and purl machines because fabric tensioning is dependent on a continuous length of fabric between the needles and the take down rollers, and there would be a danger of latches not being open at the start of a new garment sequence.

If the string of garments is separated by cutting there is a danger of either the welt being damaged or of unwanted yarn not being removed, for these reasons some form of separation course is usually provided, normally in the form of a draw thread course, preceding the first course of the new garment.

The draw thread is usually a smooth strong yarn which may be knitted as a slack, plain tubular course to facilitate easy removal. The tubular draw thread course does not unrove accidently during wet processing. A second method is the press-off draw thread construction, which although more expensive in time and yarn, tends to be more popular. The course preceding the start of the new garment is knitted in 1 × 1 rib and then one set of needles presses off its loops leaving a single plain course of extra long drawthread loops which can be quickly and easily removed. Prior to the press-off course, locking courses are produced by knitting three or more additional courses only on the set of needles which are to press-off. These help to reduce tension in the structure after pressing-off and thus reduce the possibility of laddering back.

A popular alternative to a draw-thread which is employed on half-hose and sock machines is to knit a number of courses in a soluble yarn such as alginate, the socks are separated by cutting and the remaining courses of yarn are dissolved away during finishing to leave a neat edge to the welt.

Most garment length machines using two needle beds have a butt arrangement of two long, one short for each bed, enabling 2 × 2 rib knitting after pressing off the loops of a 1 × 1 rib set-out and recommencing knitting on only long butts on each bed in turn.

16.3 Imparting Shape During Knitting

In addition to facilities for garment length sequence knitting, weft knitting provides unique opportunities for width-wise shaping during knitting with the sequence being initiated and coordinated from the same central control mechanism.

The three methods of width shaping are:

1. By varying the number of needles in action in the knitting width.
2. By changing the knitting construction.
3. By altering the stitch length.

Wale Fashioning 16.4

This is the normal manner of shaping (symmetrically or asymmetrically) on straight bar frames (Figs 16.7, 16.8). It involves the transfer of loops from one needle to another within the same needle bed either transferring onto selvedge needles which are to commence knitting (widening) or transferring from needles which are to cease knitting (narrowing). The fashioning technique is generally restricted to plain fabric structures although there are a few rib straight bar frames and also a limited number of automatic V-bed flat machines with facilities for narrowing by fashioning. (It can also be achieved by rib loop transfer, racking and transferring back (Fig. 16.9)).

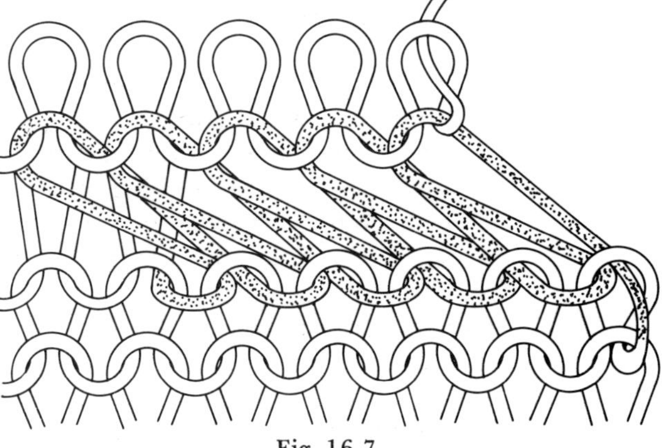

Fig. 16.7

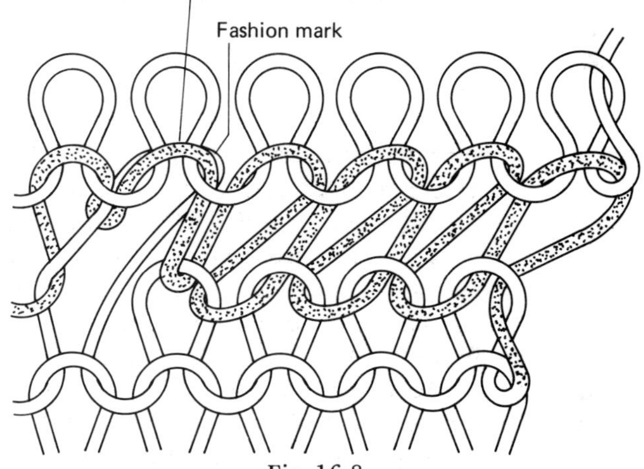

Fig. 16.8

The firm fashioned selvedge edges can be point- or cup-seamed together without the need for cutting and seaming to shape with consequent loss of expensive fabric. The shaping angle is varied by changing the fashioning frequency (i.e. the number of plain courses between each fashioning course) aided by the possibility of four-needle or two-needle as well as single-needle narrowing. A block of loops are transferred at a time so that the transferred loop effect (fashion mark) is clearly visible in the garment away from the selvedge as this is a hall-mark of classic full-fashioned garments.

Widening involves transferring the loops of a group of needles outwards by one needle thus leaving a needle without a loop which would produce a hole if it was not covered by the action of filling-in. Figure 16.8 shows the effect of using a single filling-in point which is set slightly in advance of the innermost fashioning point. It has an independent vertical movement and takes a stitch from the previous course placing it onto the empty needle. Another technique is to use two half-points to transfer the half limbs of two adjacent needle loops sideways in order to cover the hole.

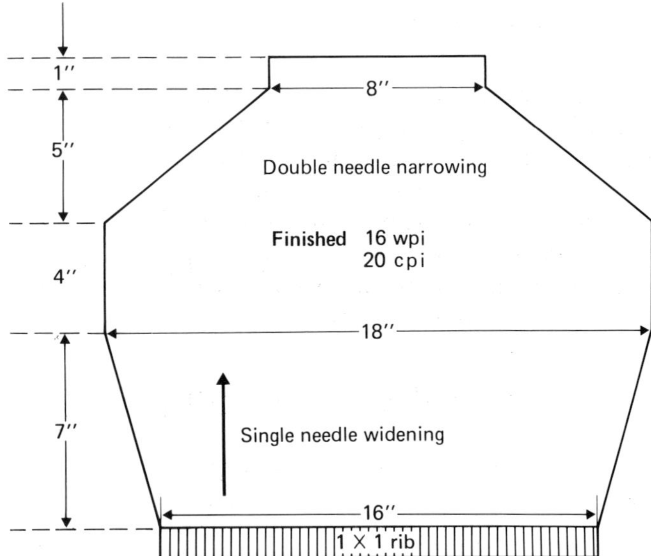

Fig. 16.9

16.5 The Calculation of Fashioning Frequencies

Using the details indicated in Fig. 16.9 as an example, the following sequence is necessary in order to calculate the required fashioning frequencies from the dimensions of a garment part:

1. Convert the length dimensions in each section to total number of courses by multiplying the length measurement by the cpi. Thus 7 X 20 = 140; 4 X 20 = 80; 5 X 20 = 100 courses.
2. Convert the width dimensions at the start of each section to total numbers of needles by multiplying the width measurement by wpi. Thus 16 X 16 = 256; 18 X 16 = 288; 8 X 16 = 128 needles.
3. Calculate the total number of needles increased or decreased from one section to another by taking one total from the next.
4. Divide the totals obtained by 2 in order to obtain the increase or decrease of needles at one selvedge, thus 288 − 256 = an increase of 32 needles. 32 ÷ 2 = 16 single needle widenings; 288 − 128 = 160; 160 ÷ 2 = 80 needles, 80 ÷ 2 gives 40 double-needle narrowings.
5. There are 16 single-needle widenings occurring during the knitting of 140 courses, assuming the first fashioning occurs in the first course, there will be 15 fashionings in 139 courses, 139 ÷ 15 = 9 and a remainder of 4. Thus 4 fashionings must occur at 10 course intervals and the remaining 11 at 9 course intervals.

Forty double-needle narrowings occur during 100 courses, again assuming the first fashioning occurs in the first course, 99 ÷ 39 = 2 and a remainder of 21, thus 21 fashionings occur at 3 course intervals and the remaining 18 fashionings occur at 2 course intervals.

Three-Dimensional Wale Fashioning 16.6

Shaping of this type occurs within the width of needles, using an additional pair of independently controlled fashioning boxes to shape stocking heels or bosom pouches. In the centre of the pouch, a number of needles knit plain fabric whilst on either side of them the extra sets of points widen outwards and later narrow inwards again. During widening, each needle which loses its loop and does not receive a new loop will commence a new wale in the next course whereas during narrowing when a needle receives two loops, two wales will be caused to converge into one.

Needle Selection Shaping 16.7

In this case, the selvedge needle(s) is introduced or withdrawn from the knitting width by means of needle selection. It is more convenient on automatic V-bed flat machines to employ the jacquard selection to introduce empty needles for widening and to take needles out of action for narrowing (i) by transferring and re-transferring rib loops in conjunction with needle bed racking, (ii) by pressing off loops or (iii) by causing needles to hold their loops for large numbers of traverses (Fig. 16.10)[1]. It is even possible during tubular plain knitting on a V-bed flat machine to introduce or remove a selvedge needle from the knitting action thus achieving a certain amount of shape in the tube.

The full shaping potential of the V-bed flat machine can only be fully exploited if the conventional roller take-down system is replaced by a presser foot device or variable take-down arrangement capable of accommodating itself to fluctuating fabric widths.

Reciprocating Knitting of Pouches 16.8

Three-dimensional shaping of pouches can be achieved on small-diameter hosiery machines by using held loop shaping in a similar manner to flat knitting so that the number of courses knitted by adjacent needles is varied, in order to knit a pouch for a heel and, if necessary, for a toe. During pouch knitting the rotating movement of the cylinder changes to an oscillatory movement. In the first half of the pouch knitting sequence only half the needles commence knitting and during the reciprocating knitting a needle at each edge is lowered out of action (narrowing) to join (in the case of heel pouch knitting) the instep needles which are already holding their fabric loops. When only one-third of the needles remain in action, widening commences too so that needles are successively brought back into action at the edge of the pouch. When all the pouch half of the needles have recommenced knitting, the cylinder returns to rotary knitting and circular courses are knitted with all needles in action. A small

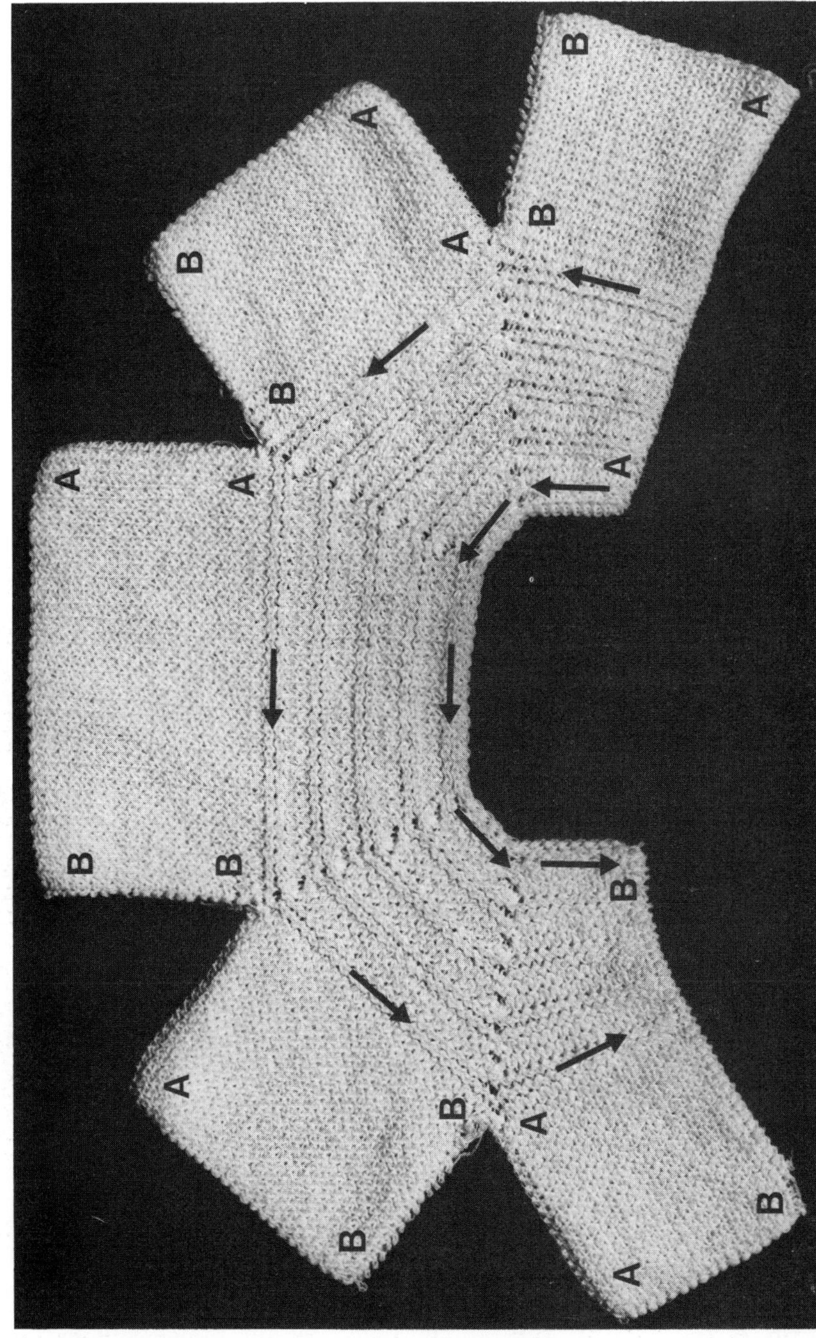

Fig. 16.10. Garment shaping by holding loops on a V-bed Flat Machine thus knitting wales with different numbers of courses. (A) is the commencing course and (B) the pressed-off course. A presser foot device was employed (Knitting International).

diameter garment machine has been successfully developed to produce shaping for the bust or shoulder section of integrally knitted garments using the reciprocated pouch principle.[2]

As oscillatory knitting is a much slower and more complicated process than circular knitting, the toe is produced as a tube on many stocking and tights machines which is seamed to shape later. The heel may also be knitted as a part of the leg tube being boarded out and heat-set shaped during finishing. One method of producing a heel pouch in completely circular knitting is to knit circular courses at the first feeder and to select needles for heel section knitting at the second feeder in conjunction with striping, cutting and trapping of yarn. With this method, a part circular course is sandwiched between each full circular course for the heel section.

Shaping by Changing the Knitted Structure 16.9

Stitch shaping is the imparting of shape into selvedged or tubular weft knitted structures by changing the nature of the stitch structure without altering the number of needles which are in action. It may be used for garment shaping sequences in knitwear, jerseywear and underwear produced on latch needle machines. It is a simpler and faster method than fashioning and does not require specially shaped elements but it can only be used for a few definite step changes of shape rather than the graduated shaping technique of fashioning.

In the sleeve and body panels of knitwear the tuck stitches will cause half and full cardigan to throw out wider than the 1 X 1 rib border (Fig. 16.11) and in ladies' stitch-shaped vests patterned rib eyelet will produce a similar effect in the bust and skirt sections compared with the 2 X 2 rib waist and border (Fig. 16.12). In plain tubular fabric articles such as some socks and gloves, elastic may be inlaid on an alternate tuck miss basis on the same needle sequence so that the fabric concertinas into a narrower elastic mock rib effect for the tops.

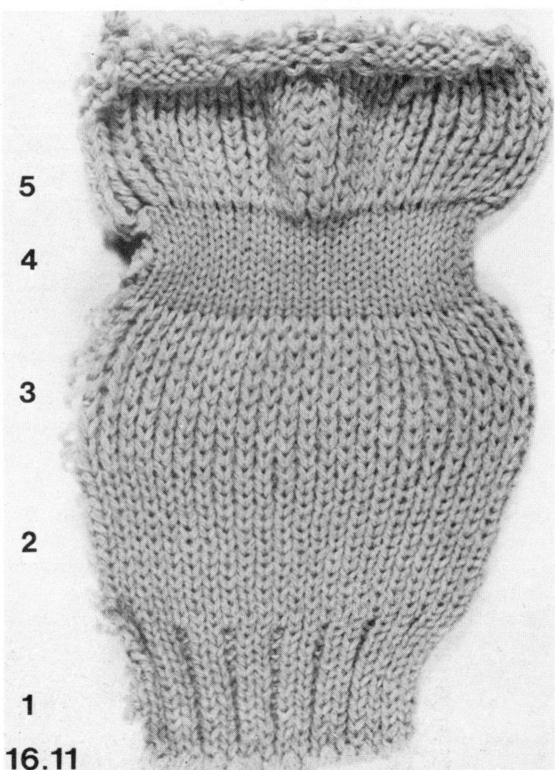

Fig. 16.11. Stitch-shaping (1 = 2 X 2 Rib; 2 = 1 X 1 Rib; 3 = Half-Cardigan; 4 = Tubular Courses; 5 = Full Cardigan).

Fig. 16.12. Stitch-shaped thermal underwear in 1 X 1 rib with rib loop transfer and cylinder needle pick-up design knitted in 1/28's cotton spun 50/50 Viloft/Polyester on a 10-gauge RTR (13-, 15- and 17-inch diameters) by Twinlock (Courtaulds, Henrietta House, London).

16.10 Shaping by Altering the Stitch Length

Changes of stitch length by alteration of stitch cam positions are carried out at particular points in a garment-knitting sequence, flat machines usually have at least five pre-set positions which can be automatically obtained during traversing. On both circular and flat machines it is also possible to change from synchronized to delayed timing in 1 X 1 rib knitting and thus produce tighter and more "elastic" rib courses suitable for rib borders. In ladies' hosiery a graduated stiffening or tightening of the stitch length occurs to obtain a certain amount of shape between the thigh and the ankle.

The introduction of a certain percentage of elastane yarn into the construction of a weft or warp knitted fabric improves the extension and recovery properties and therefore its form-fitting properties. The percentage elongation of the elastane yarn may be controlled during fabric finishing by heat-setting.[3]

Further Information

BERESFORD, G., Three dimensional knitting on the FCM, *Knit. Int.* (1974) Oct., 80–3; *Knit. Times*, (1975) 15 Sept., 67–73.

CANZLER, R. and HIEMANN, K. H., 3D and other effects in F/F outerwear and underwear, *Hos. Trade Journal*, (1964) Nov., 104–10.

CARR DOUGHTY, J., Steps in integral knitting, *Hos. Trade Journal*, (1970) Feb., 109–13.

CARR DOUGHTY, J., Research and developments in knitwear and knit fabrics (Part 1), *Hos. Trade Journal*, (1971) Sept., 103–10.

GOADBY, D. R. and MILLINGTON, J., Aspects of integrated garment production, *Knit. Int.*, (1975) March, 61–2.

LANCASHIRE, J. B., Stitch constructions of knitted welts, *Hos. Trade Journal*, (1964) Jan., 110–11.

OFFERMANN, P. and TAUSCH-MARTON, H. H., Knit to shape and full-fashioned knitting procedures, *Knit. Times*, (1971) 12 April, 47–55.

WIGNALL, H., The bifurcated garment: new production techniques, *Knit. Times Yr. Bk.*, (1974) 101–3.

WIGNALL, H., Garment engineering for knitted goods, *Text. Inst. and Ind.*, (1977) 15, (5), 171–3.

1. The Basque beret; A survey of manufacturing processes, *Hos. Trade Journal*, (1962) July, 92–3.
2. WIGNALL, H. and KLEE, J., Circular garments with integrally knitted sleeves, *Text. Inst. and Ind.*, (1965) 3, (6), 143–8.
3. REIDER, A., New trends in elastic knitted fabrics (IFKT paper), *Knit. Int.*, (1981) 50–2.

17

The Straight Bar Frame

17.1 Development of the Straight Bar Frame

Like all knitting machines, the straight bar frame is, with a number of later improvements and developments, a direct descendant of William Lee's hand frame. Firstly, Aston, a former apprentice of Lee's, arranged the sinkers into alternating sets and thus obtained better uniformity of loop length and much finer machine gauges. The jack sinkers continued to be individually raised and lowered but the lead or dividing sinkers were moved down *en bloc* afterwards to equalize the loop lengths. The principle of sinkers and dividers is still employed on fine gauge straight bar frames.

Credit for the development of the first acceptable power-driven rotary frame is given to Samuel Wise, who in 1769 replaced the foot pedals with a power-driven rotary shaft whose tappets caught against arms and levers to move the working parts. To increase productivity it was now necessary to simplify the knitting action and introduce automatic mechanisms to replace hand-controlled operations. In 1857 Luke Barton introduced a self-acting narrowing mechanism to replace hand-controlled loop transfer points in fashioned shaping and in 1861 Paget produced a movable needle bar.

It was, however, William Cotton of Loughborough who transformed the hand-controlled power driven rotary frame into the high-speed automatic fashioning multi-head straight bar frame and thus encouraged the transition of knitting from a cottage-based industry into mass production. Between 1846 and 1864, he obtained patents which have caused the term Cottons Patent or Cotton Machine to be synonymous with that of the straight bar frame and the company he founded continues to build and develop his frames. Cotton invented the vertically-moving needle bar, developed the use of screw-controlled fashioning points for automatic widening and narrowing and placed the driving shaft for the elements towards the base of the machine to reduce vibration. The replacement of the end controls by a central control unit in 1953 paved the way for the modern automatic straight bar frame with its fully programmed garment-knitting sequence (Fig. 17.1). Balanced and simplified motions together with variable draw have increased knitting speeds, whilst automatic actions have reduced standing time and labour allocation.[1]

Fig. 17.1. A sixteen-head plain straight bar frame having a conveyor for transporting the rib ends to each head (Iropa).

17.2 Fully-Fashioned Articles

Excepting knitwear which is a comparatively recent development, fully-fashioned or wrought products have suffered a considerable decline in fashion demand during the twentieth century as the result of the improvement of cheaper manufacturing techniques in other sectors of weft knitting including, more recently, the development of heat set shaping based on the use of thermo-plastic fibre yarns such as nylon.

Fully-fashioned half-hose and socks were the first to be replaced by circular knitted products between 1900 and 1920.

Stockings

Fully-fashioned nylon stocking production reached a peak in the 1950s with automatic machines having up to forty divisions, each 15 inches (38 cm) wide, in usual gauges of 51 G and 60 G (needles per 1½ inches/38 mm). Each stocking blank which has a turned welt top, shaped leg and foot, round heel pouch and diamond point toe was completed in 30 minutes and pressed off from the few needles still knitting. The stocking blank selvedges were then cup-seam joined together with a seam which passed straight down the back of the leg and underneath the foot. By the end of the fifties, however, fashion was swinging over to the bare leg look of the cheaper, heat-shaped circular knitted seamless stocking and production of the fully-fashioned stockings declined rapidly during the early 1960s.

Underwear and knitwear

Fully-fashioned underwear such as men's undershirts and pants (union suits) and women's vests, panties and combinations were popular until fashion changed during the 1920s, from then onwards the surplus machine capacity was used for knitting outerwear. Attention was concentrated on women's twin-sets and men's pullovers. Classic knitwear styles became very fashionable after the second world war and production was aided by new machine attachments such as that producing the V-neck shape.[2]

Today, outerwear straight bar frames with sixteen knitting sections, each 32 or 34 inches wide, may be as long as 77 feet or almost 23.5 metres, and weigh 70 tons. The gauge is still expressed in needles per 1½ inches so that the popular 21-gauge is actually $21 \times 2/3 = 14$ needles per inch. The normal gauge range is from 9 to 33, typical yarn counts for 9, 21, 24 and 33 gauges respectively are 2/10's, 2/24's, 2/28's and 2/40's worsted count or 175, 74, 64 and 44 tex. Knitting section widths range from 28 to 36 inches for bodies and 20–22 inches for sleeves, the wider sections are useful for knitting higher shrinkage synthetic yarns.

17.3 Knitting Motions of the Straight Bar Frame

The three directions of motion required for the knitting action are provided from two separate sources. The rotary motion of the cam-shaft produces the vertical and horizontal movement of the fashioning points and the needle bar. The sideways reciprocating movement for the yarn carriers and for introducing the sinkers in seriatim sequence via the slur-cock is obtained from a coulier or draw cam attached to a shaft set at right angles to the main cam-shaft at the back of the machine, which oscillates a draw lever. A variable draw ensures that the stroke of the draw is related to the varying knitting width thus more courses per minute are knitted on narrower widths. Operating speeds of a hundred courses per minute can be achieved.

Knitting Action of the Plain Straight Bar Frame 17.4

Figure 17.2 shows the cross-section of the knitting head containing the following elements:

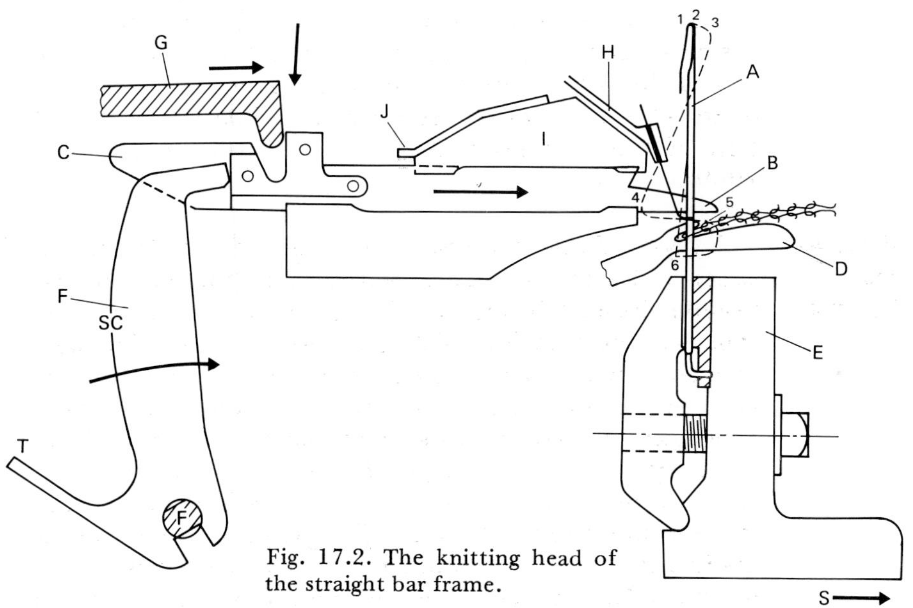

Fig. 17.2. The knitting head of the straight bar frame.

A. *Bearded Needle* having a cranked end for location in the tricked and drilled needle bar.
B. *Sinker*, only one between every other needle space, with a reinforced back and at the front, a catch to sink the yarn around the needles, and a Neb to separate the old and new loops until knock-over.
C. *Divider*, occupying each remaining space, usually having the same shaped front as the sinker but with an extended tail at the back.
D. *Knocking-over Bit*, one directly beneath each sinker and divider, having a 'throat' for holding the loops and a 'nose' for knocking-over.
E. *Needle Bar* having a compound horizontal and vertical movement.
F. *Striking Jack*, fulcrummed at its lower end, each with its nose resting on a sinker back, and a 'spring' exerting pressure on its 'tail'.

G. *Catch Bar*, extending the full width of the knitting head, having forward and backward, as well as vertical movement.

H. *Yarn Carrier*, which traverses in alternate directions across the head from one course to the next, up to six carriers may be available. The carrier is connected to a reciprocating carrier rail by friction and when the carrier is arrested by its carrier stop, the carrier rail completes its full traverse, driven by the Coulier Cam by punching through the carrier friction.

J. *Falling Bar*, is a stop which cushions the advance of the sinkers and dividers.

Figure 17.3 a–f shows the movement of the knitting elements to produce one course of loops:

(a) *Thread Laying*. The carrier moves across the knitting head laying the yarn on the noses of the sinkers and dividers and the beard side of the needles.

(b) *Sinking*. The slurcock (one for each knitting head) travelling behind

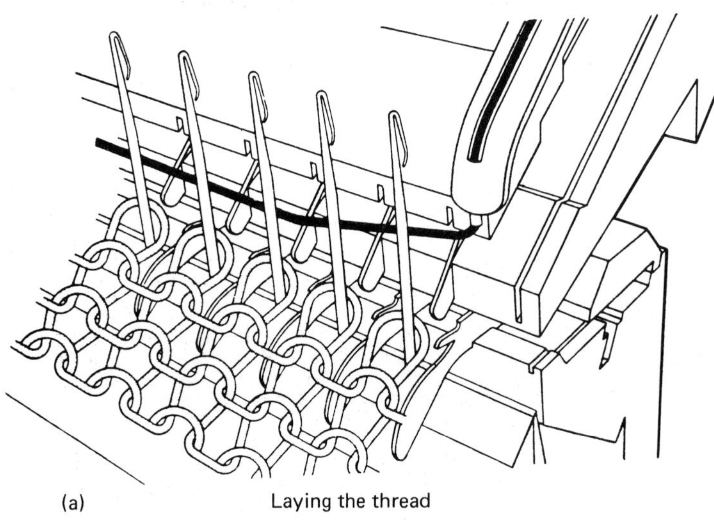

(a) Laying the thread

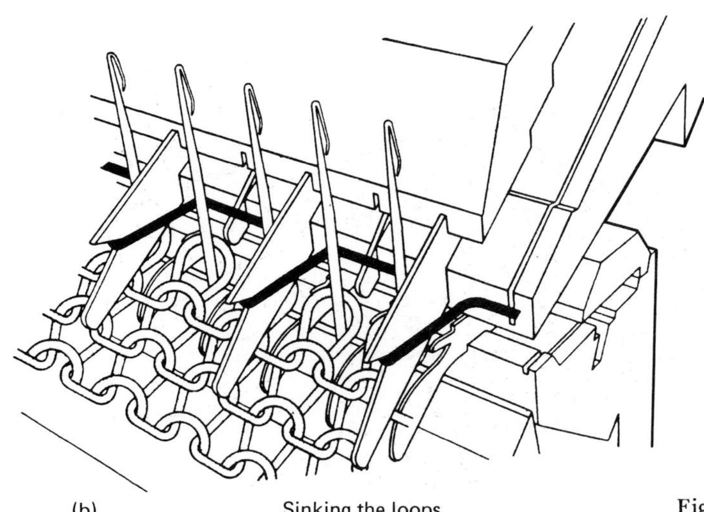

(b) Sinking the loops

Fig. 17.3 a,b

the carrier, contacts the jacks (Fig. 17.2) and is shaped so that each jack in turn pushes its sinker forwards to kink a loop around every two adjacent needles.

(c) *Dividing*. The catch bar moves the dividers forwards collectively, whilst the needle bar tips slightly outwards to allow the double loops to be divided into equal sized needle loops around every needle.

(d) *Pressing and* (e) *Landing*. The needle bar descends placing the new loops inside the hooks of the beards. The catch bar is now lowered so that the sinkers as well as the dividers are collectively controlled by it for the rest of the knitting cycle. They now start to withdraw. The needle bar moves towards the sinker verge causing the beards to be pressed. A further downward movement of the needle bar lands the previous course of loops, resting on the knocking-over bits, onto the closed beards.

The Drop-Off. As the needle bar moves away from the pressing edge,

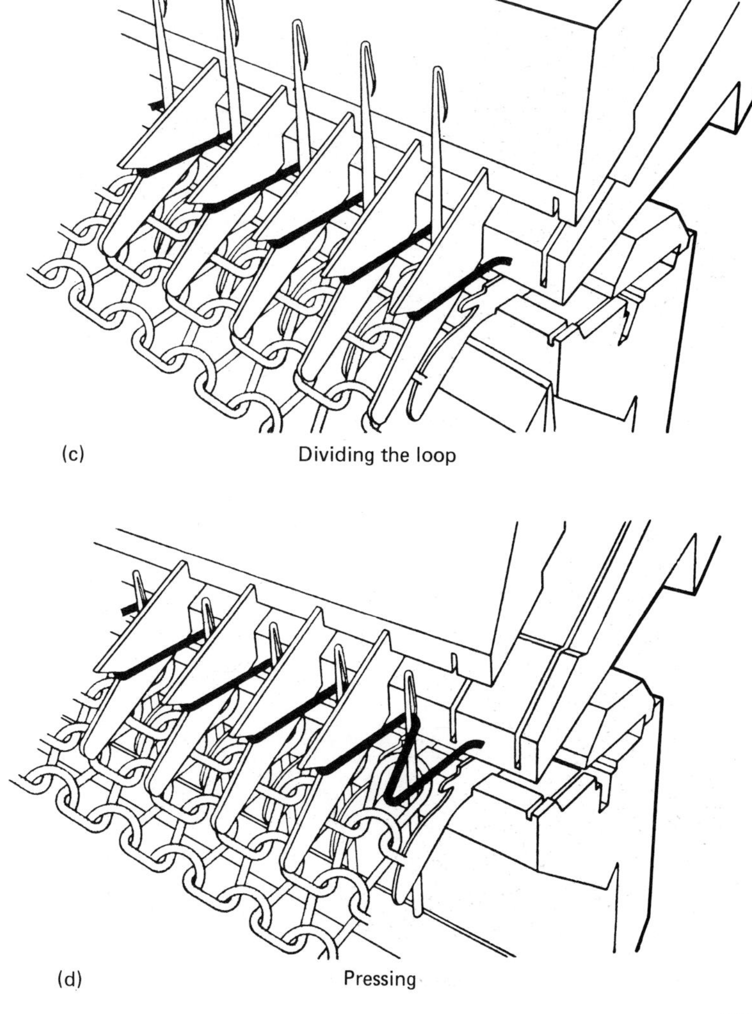

(c) Dividing the loop

(d) Pressing

Fig. 17.3 c,d

the sinkers and dividers withdraw so that the newly formed course of loops drops off their noses onto the knocking-over bits.

(f) *Completion of Knock-over.* The needle bar descends to its lowest position. As the heads descend below the belly of the knocking-over bits, the old course of loops is collectively knocked-over.

Holding-Down. As the sinkers and dividers move collectively forward to hold down the fabric, the needle bar rises to the thread-laying position. The catch bar is slightly raised to release the sinkers for individual movement at the start of the next course.

On coarser gauge machines it is possible to accommodate sinkers with reinforced butts between every needle space thus eliminating dividers and their action. Some machines have selvedge dividers with a lower forward ledge so that when the yarn carrier stops over one divider the next divider

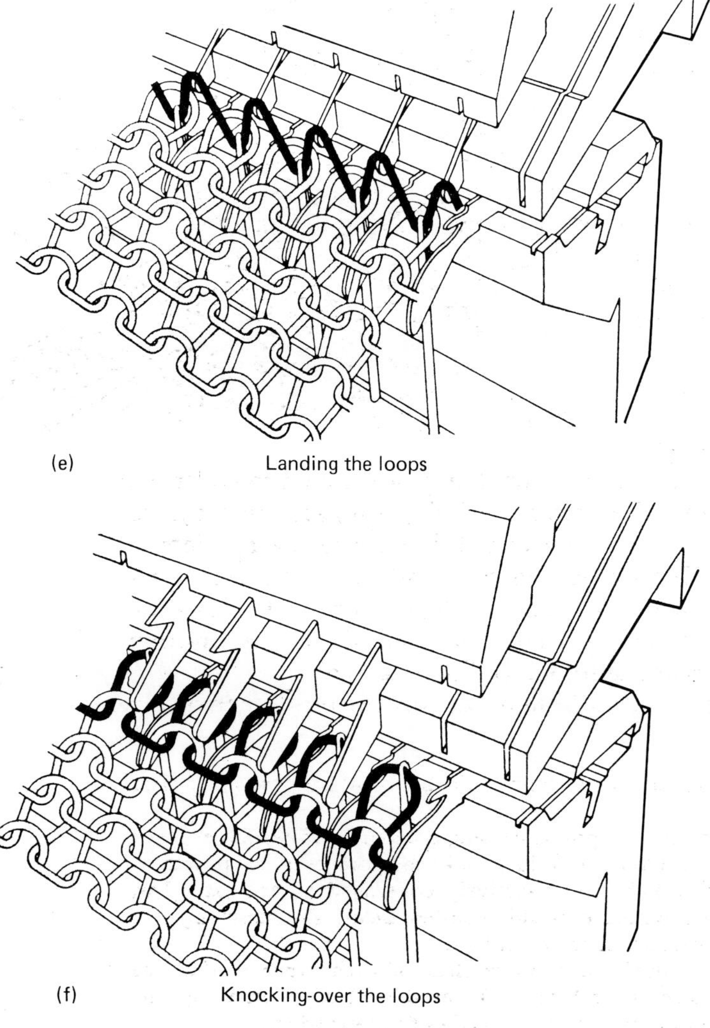

(e) Landing the loops

(f) Knocking-over the loops

Fig. 17.3 e,f

inwards from it will be the last to take that traverse of yarn which will slide into its specially-shaped lower throat and form a tight selvedge.

Loop Transfer 17.5

Loop transference is used not only for fully fashioning on straight bar frames but also for making lace stitch patterns and for introducing marking stitches or drop stitch effects. The positioning and sideways traverse of the points will depend upon the effect required. This sideways traverse of the points is usually achieved by some type of screw thread (Fig. 17.4). To produce a drop stitch, the tip of the point is turned away from the needle so that, for example, when knitting a cardigan front the loop is collected from the centre needle towards the end of the cycle sequence and is cast off from the point to form a ladder as a guide for cutting.

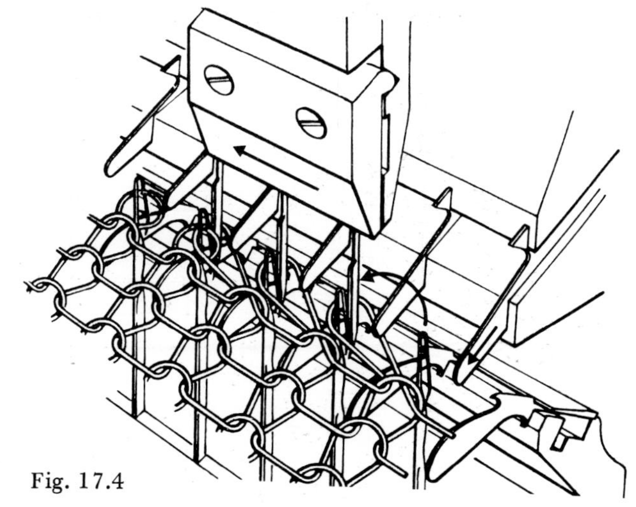

Fig. 17.4

A fashioning course or 'dip', like the knitting action, requires one revolution of the main cam-shaft but the speed of production is lower with about 50–60 revs/min being achieved during fashioning instead of 60–100 revs/min during straight knitting. Fashioning involves a set of points being positioned to cover the needles of each selvedge and the cam-shaft being shogged sideways to present a set of fashioned cams to the cam followers or lever rollers in place of the knitting cams. The fashioning cams only take the needle bar to an intermediate height and the needles are slightly tipped to allow the points to descend to cover them. At the same time, the coulier motion which drives the yarn carriers and slurcock is disconnected.

Figure 17.5 a–f illustrates the fashioning action for either narrowing or widening.

(a) The fashioning points descend and the needle bar tips backwards to clear them.
(b) The needle bar moves towards the points causing the beards of needles engaged with points to be pressed and 'boxed' or located in the grooves of the points.
(c) The sinkers and dividers, which are collectively contrôlled by the catch bar, retire and the needles and points descend together below the knocking-over bits so that the loops are cast off onto the points.
(d) The needles and points now rise and move clear of each other so that the points can make the sideways 'fashion rack' at the selvedge either by one needle for widening or by one, two, or four needles for narrowing.
(e) The needles and points now descend and the needles box with the points

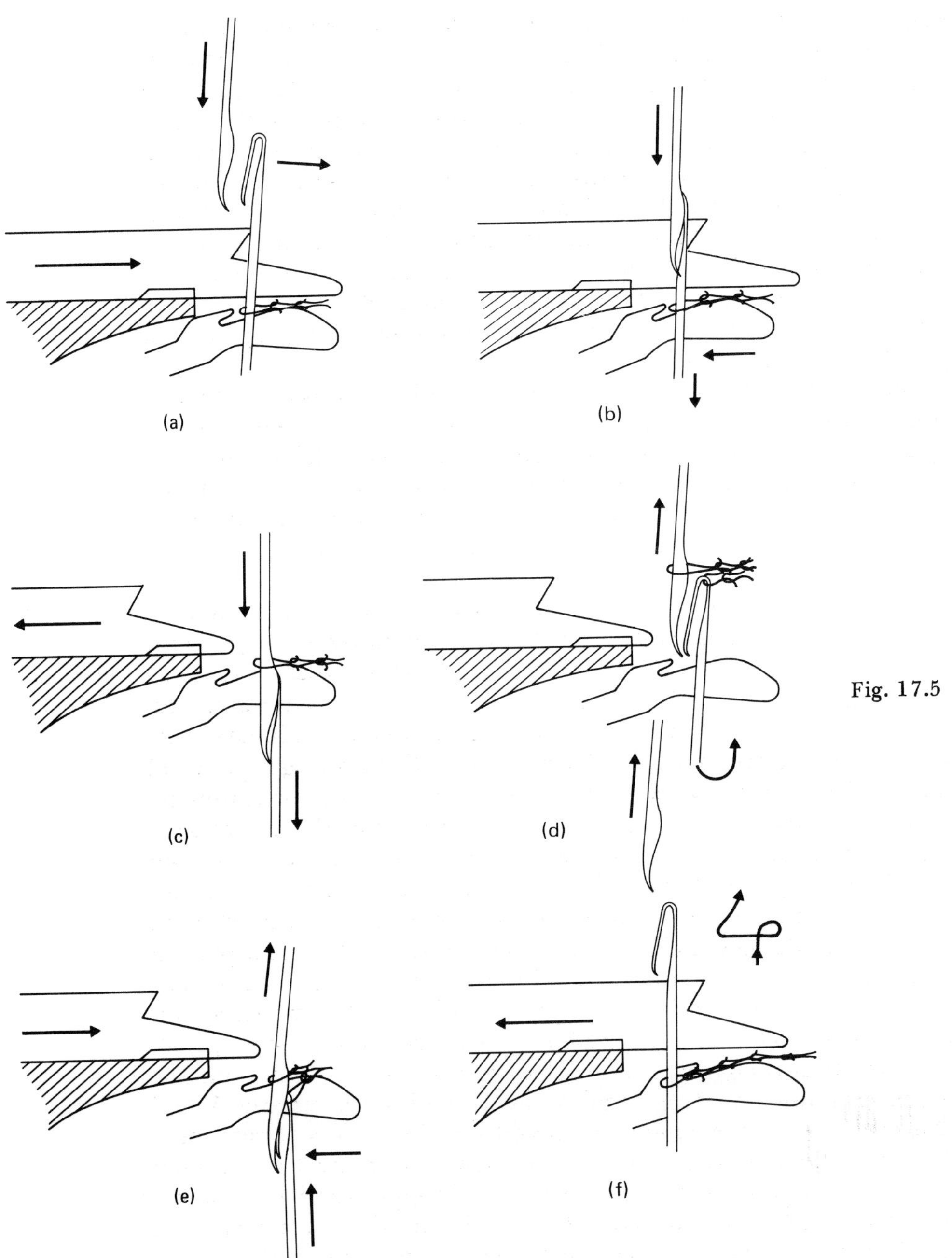

Fig. 17.5

again so they receive the transferred loops. As the needles and points descend below the sinkers the sinkers and dividers move forwards to hold down the loops.

(f) Once the needles have slid up into the grooves of the points to receive the loops, the points rise to their high inoperative position. The needle bar rises causing the transferred loops to slip down onto the stems and the cam-shaft is shogged back to the left again so that knitting can restart.

On earlier straight bar frames, a ratchet selector was employed which could, through the introduction of racking pawls and a choice of rack-wheels having different numbers of teeth, turn a shaft to produce (usually) two fashioning actions during each of its revolutions. Each rackwheel thus provided a different fashioning frequency. The operator, however, had to set the machine for widening or narrowing, choose the frequency, count the number of fashionings and terminate the action. A control chain was later introduced which could automatically initiate the fashioning, insert a slack course, control the machine speed and operate a chain saver. Soon the demand for a cheaper, simpler and quicker method of changing styles or sizes led to the development of an electronic console unit programmed from a punched plastic card film.

To become fully automatic, control of the following was necessary: counting of courses and fashioning; changing from widening to narrowing; initiating the rib transfer or welt turning; stopping the machine on completion of the set; racking back the carrier and stops for the next starting width; laying the yarn for the start of the next garment; controlling the machine speed; inserting the initial draw-off and severing connecting yarns after pressing-off the previous garment piece.

On the card film there is provision for twenty-three punched hole positions across its width, each position being scanned by a dropper pin. When the dropper enters a hole it trips a micro-switch for a circuit to produce the required action. The first four hole positions are for counting the number of courses in binary units, the next four count in binary tens, a similar arrangement occurs for the fashionings in the next eight punched hole positions. The remaining seven hole positions are used for automatic controls such as machine speed, striping, control for the V-neck, racking the automatic control shaft, setting the fashioning screws, etc. Once the last couse of knitting or fashioning has been completed, the droppers are collectively raised and the drum carrying the film is advanced to the next position. For fancy designs such as lace, cable, tuck and intarsia the pattern may be taken from a separate card control to that of the garment sequence.

As the turned welt of the doubled plain fabric which is produced on stocking frames is usually less acceptable for the start of a garment panel, a rib border is often preferred. Straight bar rib frames have been built but they have proved uncompetitive against faster and more versatile V-bed flat machines. A popular technique, is to knit the rib borders or cuffs on a V-bed flat machine and then to transfer them, using the last required course, loop by loop onto the points of a special topping-on bar (running-on). The fabric is then transferred off onto the needles of the straight bar frame (barring-on). Six ribs may be transferred at a time but only the topmost is placed on top of the knocking-over bits and underneath the sinkers ready for knitting the plain onto it. It is a common practice to employ doubling, i.e. to have more wales in the rib than in the plain so that during running-on sometimes two rib loops are run onto the same points. In this way, the rib is in a more relaxed state and gives a better fit.

Rib transfer has been automated by using a conveyor to transport loaded rib transfer bars from one end of the machine to individual knitting heads (Fig. 17.1). Each bar is then transferred to the holders of automatic rib transfer mechanism in readiness for rib transfer at the commencement of the next garment cycle. Arms then advance the rib transfer holder and present the new rib to the needles. Empty bars are replaced on the conveyor which automatically returns them to the loading station for refilling. This operation has reduced standing time between sets from an average of five minutes to a matter of a few seconds and has enabled the knitter to supervise more knitting heads. At the commencement of knitting on the straight bar frame an initial draw-off engages the ribs or welt rods whilst sufficient courses are knitted for them to be engaged by the main draw-off arrangement.

Special V-bed flat machines have been designed for automatic rib knitting and magazine bar loading. A four-head machine can knit an average body rib in 1 min 25 secs at 60 cpm or in less time without doubling. The machine is pre-programmed to knit a cotton course which is taken by the hook-up bar of the take-down mechanism followed by the tubular welt and rib in 1 × 1, 2 × 1 or 2 × 2. On completion of the rib a separate mechanism actuated by a cam on the main cam-shaft causes the front bed loops to be transferred to the back bed. A transfer bar then descends to collect these loops and transfer them onto the points of the magazine bar. A maximum of sixteen ribs can be accommodated. Doubling on every seventh needle on a 14 npi machine can be achieved, if desired, for a 21 G garment.

17.6 Rib-to-Plain Machines

Despite automation in transferring rib border fabric from the V-bed flat machines onto straight bar frames, the operation requires the co-ordination not only of the fabric but also of extra labour and machinery and involves additional factory space. The rib-to-plain technique pioneered by S. A. Monk involves a straight bar frame which can knit an integral rib border start without the need for the complex mechanical action of the conventional rib frame.[3] During rib border knitting, an ancillary set of horizontally-arranged latch needles (machine needles) cooperates with only the even needles of the vertical bearded needle bar (frame needles). At the commencement of the fully-fashioned panel, the machine needles transfer their loops onto the re-introduced odd frame needles so that a full set of plain needles is in action (Fig. 17.6).

The Bentley Cotton CRP has twelve or sixteen knitting heads in a gauge range from 9 to 24. Its frame needle bar is composed of short even needles which are attached to the needle bar and longer odd needles which extend through this bar and are attached to a ledge below it. When the ledge is in its lowest position odd frame needles are out of action and the gaps are occupied by machine needles for rib knitting. When the ledge is raised to

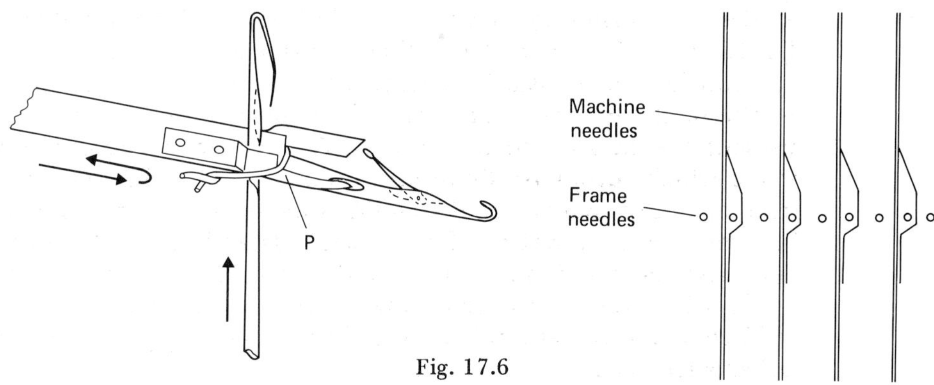

Fig. 17.6

its highest position the heads of odd and even needles are at the same height for normal plain knitting.

During rib knitting loops are formed by the sinkers around even frame needles and the machine needles collect the yarn for their loops later as it drops into their hooks from the withdrawing sinkers. The machine needles have a simple horizontal movement and their knitting action is assisted by a movable knock-over slide which pushes the old loop in the opposite direction to the needle movement. On the side of each latch needle is a spring expander which assists in the transference of the loop to the frame needle during rib transfer.

The machine makes 'doublings' at pre-determined wales in the last course of the rib using two wider sets of transfer boxes, one from each selvedge, which continuously dip and transfer inwards (before the machine needles have received their loops). At first, a one-needle space transfer action occurs which later changes to a two-needle space movement. The latter hides eyelet holes formed by the first action as well as producing doubling. As loops are transferred off the selvedge needles the carrier stops are adjusted inwards.

Two balanced cam-shafts which shog in opposite directions instead of a very long and heavy single shaft are employed, it also has two draw cams, one for plain and the other for rib, which are brought into operation by shogging the cam-follower from one to the other. A 2 X 2 rib needle set-out can be achieved as well as tucking on the frame needles for half-cardigan. However, it can only knit a roll welt and not a tubular welt because the machine needles are incapable of knitting alone without the frame needles.

The possibility of controlling the knitting heads on separate machines from a single microprocessor has encouraged Cottons to produce their Gemini model as a possible alternative to a long multi-head frame (Fig. 12.4). This rib-to-plain machine is of single section size but has two knitting heads working back-to-back. The number of shafts has been reduced, the leverages rationalized and the ancillary mechanisms miniaturized. A shorter knitting motion and accurate conjugate camming enables speeds up to 200 cpm to be achieved when knitting on narrow widths giving the production of a four-section machine for a quarter of the space.

Machine control for shaping and patterning from a microprocessor eliminates the need for punched cards, control chains and automatic control shafts with programming being taken from a magnetic tape cassette. The modular construction offers flexibility in the acquisition of units as regards time and gauge, downtime is restricted to two heads each time a stoppage occurs and the machines can be accommodated in a more restricted space than can a conventional straight bar frame.

17.7 Patterned Structures

Although noted for the production of plain classic fully-fashioned knitwear, the straight bar frame is capable of utilizing stitch patterns whose scope is dependent upon the particular machine's facilities, these may include lace, coloured designs, tuck stitches and combinations of these stitches.[4]

Lacing points operate in a similar manner to fashioning points. Sets of points fixed in boxes will produce symmetrical effects whereas individually-controlled points may be used to produce motifs. Between transfer actions, the points are racked sideways for re-positioning. Lace effects are determined by the type of pattern control, the number and type of points available, the point set-out, the direction and extent of the transfer movement, and the number of plain knitted courses between transfer actions.[5]

Cable stitch designs, in two-cord cross-over of three wales each, are possible on some machines with the cord being emphasized by removal of a number of needles on either side of it leaving a gap up to the adjacent wales.

Coloured designs are achieved with a number of carrier rods having different-coloured yarns. The designs range from simple horizontal stripes to plating and elaborate intarsia patterns. One machine also uses wrap guides in order to make tartan designs.[6]

Tuck stitch designs are generally achieved by replacing the leading pressing edge of the sinker bed with individual presser bits, one for each needle beard. The presser bits are carried on slides which receive their forward pressing movement from steel strips on a tambour or drum. Punched positions in the steels do not advance their slides and thus produce tuck stitches. After each course, a different selection may be produced by racking the drum.

Further Information

BRADLEY, S. B., *Fully Fashioned Hose Manufacture*, (1953) Harlequine Press.

INNES, R., Fully fashioned developments, *Knit. Times*, (1981) 7 Sept., 8–9; 21 Sept., 8–9; 5 Oct., 10–11; 26 Oct., 10–11; 2 Nov., 10–11.

MILLS, R. W., *Fully Fashioned Garment Manufacture*, (1965) Cassell and Co. Ltd.
WEBER, K. P., Theory of knitting (Part 4), *Knit. Times Yr. Bk.*, (1976) 90–109.
Symposium on Fully-Fashioned Knitting, articles published in the *Hosiery Trade Journal* between August and October 1970 also available in booklet form.

1. START, E., Developments in automatic fully fashioned outerwear machines (IFKS Paper), *Hos. Trade Journal*, (1961) Nov., 115–18.
2. Full-fashioned knitting. A 50-year survey, *Knit. O'wr Times Yr. Bk.*, (1968) 225–230.
3. Monk ultramatic rib-to-plain fully fashioned machine, *Hos. Trade Journal*, (1968) Nov., 86–7; (1969) March, 87–8.
4. CANZLER, R., Novel effects in full-fashioned knitting, *Knit. O'wr Times*, (1969) 22 Sept., 84–97.
5. LANCASHIRE, J. B., Patterning with points in full fashioned knitting, *Hos. Trade Journal*, (1959) May, 90–100.
6. Scheller BSW, *Knit. Times*, (1980) 21 April, 12–13.

18

Flat Knitting Basic Principles and Structures

18.1 History

The first flat bar machine (section 8.6) was demonstrated in 1862 and patented in 1865 by the Rev. Isaac Wixom Lamb, an American clergyman. Although he later changed the arrangement to the inverted V-bed shape patented by Eisenstuck, the term 'flat bar' has been retained as the generic name for both rib and purl flat machines. In 1867, Henri Edouard Dubied acquired the European rights for Lamb's machine at the Paris Exhibition and established his knitting machine building company. Similarly, in 1873, Heinrich Stoll, a German engineer began to build and repair Lamb machines and by the early 1890s he was not only building improved versions of the rib machine but also flat bed purl machines of a similar standard of perfection. The two companies founded by Dubied and Stoll continue to play a dominant part in the development of flat knitting machinery.[1,2]

In the early 1960s, Kenneth Macqueen unsuccessfully attempted to develop a revolutionary computer-controlled V-bed flat machine having compound needles.[3] The idea was to use the basque beret technique of knitting wedge-shaped garment parts in a sideways manner with held loops, part course knitting and sections separated by waste yarn segments. The machine was to use a variable traverse, magnetically energized raising cams to lift the needle butts, tape control for the design selection and garment sequence, with computer control of up to six 'slave' knitting machines. Although Macqueen's concept failed through being too ambitious, the advent of micro-electronic technology and presser-foot shaping have enabled some parts of his far-sighted dream to be realized.[4]

18.2 Flat Machines

Flat machines (Fig. 8.2) are normally gauged on the English system of needles per inch. However, the Metric system, which is based on the distance in tenths of a millimetre from the centre of one needle to the next, is also used. This is a direct system with a higher gauge number indicating a coarser yarn, i.e. the opposite of the English system. An English gauge of 10 needles per inch or 2.54 cm would therefore have a distance of 2.5 mm between needles giving a metric gauge of 25. It is therefore possible to convert from one gauge to the other by dividing 254 by the given gauge number.

Generally flat machine gauges range from 5 to 12 npi but there are coarse gauge machines of only 2½ npi and some machines which are as fine as 14 or 16 npi. Strapping machine needle bed widths tend to range from about 14–50 cm, hand-operated garment width machines from about 80–120 cm and power-driven automatic garment length machines from about 66–200 cm or more. In recent years there has been a general trend towards wider machines and this has been accentuated on the electronic machines.

V-bed machines have two rib gated, diagonally approaching needle beds, set at between 90 and 104 degrees to each other and giving an inverted V-shape appearance. Flat bed purls or links-links machines are mainly employed knitting simulated hand knitted constructions of a speciality type. They use double-ended latch needles which are transferred to knit in either of two directly opposed needle beds. The non-knitting hook is controlled in the manner of a needle butt by a slider which hooks onto it. There is a set of sliders in each needle bed whose butts are controlled by the traversing cam-carriage to produce knitting or transfer of the needles (see 7.14).

Many intarsia machines employ only one needle bed for knitting the plain solid colour designs although another bed is required in order to produce the rib border for the garment. Intarsia garments tend to be expensive and their demand is subject to the vagaries of fashion (10.3).

Yarn Counts 18.3

An indication of an approximately suitable count for a flat machine may be calculated using the formula: worsted count = gauge^2 ÷ 9.

The following are typical count ranges for particular gauges.

12 npi 2/26's to 2/42's
8 npi 2/14's to 2/22's
5 npi 6/14's to 6/18's
2 npi 8/7's to 8/9's

It can be seen that a characteristic of the flat machine is the large number of ends of yarn which may be knitted at the same time. However, if light-weight structures are required, the number of ends may be much fewer.

Simple Hand-Manipulated V-Bed Rib Flat Machines 18.4

Figure 18.1 shows a cross-section of a simple, hand-manipulated V-bed rib flat machine:

1. The knock-over bits

The trick walls are replaced at the needle bed verges by fixed, thinner, polished and specially shaped knock-over bit edges. In rib gating, a knock-over bit in one bed will be aligned opposite to a needle trick in the other

KT-N

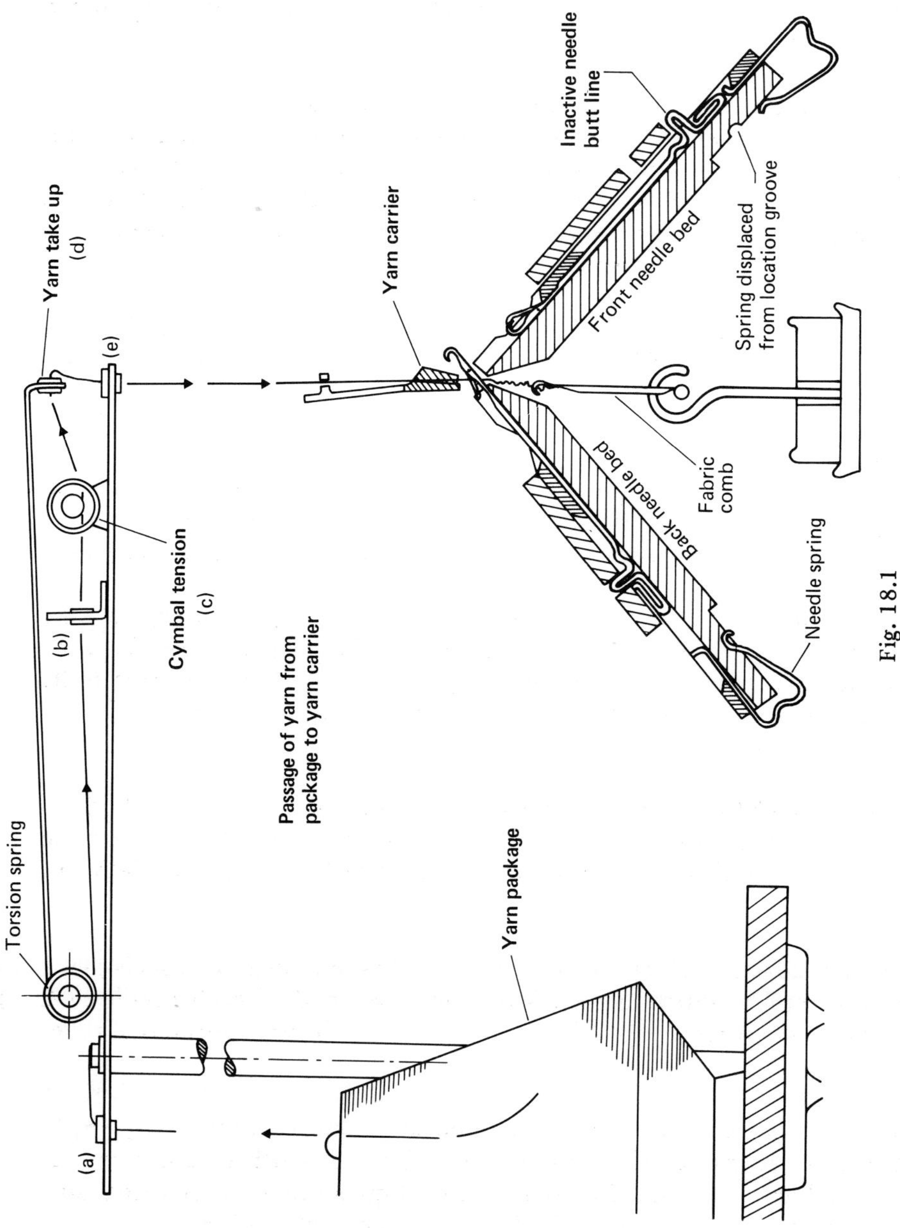
Torsion spring
Yarn package
(a)
(b)
Cymbal tension
(c)
Yarn take up
(d)
(e)
Passage of yarn from
package to yarn carrier
Yarn carrier
Inactive needle
butt line
Front needle bed
Spring displaced
from location groove
Fabric
comb
Back needle bed
Needle spring

Fig. 18.1

bed. During knitting, the edges of the knock-over bits restrain the sinker loops as they pass between needles and thus assist in the knocking-over of the old loops and in the formation of the new loops. Flat machines do not normally employ holding-down sinkers as the take-down tension and the loops on the needles in the other bed help to hold the old loops down on the needles stems.

2. The cover plate

This is a thin metal blade located in a slot across the top of the needle bed tricks which prevents the stems of the needles from pivoting upwards out of the tricks as a result of the fabric take-down tension drawing the needle hooks downwards, whilst allowing the needles to slide freely in their tricks. The plate can be withdrawn sideways out of the needle bed to allow needles to be removed.

3. The security spring

Supporting the tail of each needle is a security spring which fits over the lower edge of the needle bed. When the spring is pushed fully into position it locates into a groove on the undersurface of the needle bed and the butt of the needle which it supports is aligned with the knitting cam-track on the undersurface of the traversing cam-carriage. When a needle is not required to be in action, its security spring is not located in the groove, so that the needle is nearer to the lower edge of the needle bed and its butt is by-passed by the cam-carriage as it traverses across the trick.

On machines employing jacquard selection the positioning of the security spring is replaced either by the thrust of a jacquard steel onto the tails of the elements or by the raising or depressing of the knitting butts into the tricks, in order to position the needle butts for each carriage traverse.

4. The latch brushes

Latch brushes are attached to the cam-plates of both needle beds to ensure that the needle latches are fully opened. The supports of the brushes are adjustable to ensure precise setting of the bristles relative to the needles.

The carriage guide rails

The cam-carriage either slides or runs on ball-bearings or wheels along guide rails, one of which is fixed over the lower end of each needle bed. It is propelled either by hand or from a motor-driven continuous roller chain.

5. The yarn carriers

Each yarn carrier is attached to a block which slides along a bar, which, like the carriage guide rails, passes across the full width of the machine. The carrier bar may be of the double prism type so that yarn carriers may be attached to slide along both the front and the back surfaces.

The yarn carriers are picked up or left behind by the carriage as required, by means of driving bolts or pistons which are attached to and are controlled from, either manually or automatically, the carriage bow. There is a bolt for each carrier bar track, which when lowered, entrains with a groove in the shoulder of a yarn carrier guide block. Stop plates having inclined edges are positioned on the carrier bars at the knitting selvedges. On contact with a stop plate, the base of the bolt rises and is lifted out and disconnected from the groove of the carrier block so that the carriage continues its traverse without that carrier.

18.5 The Cam System

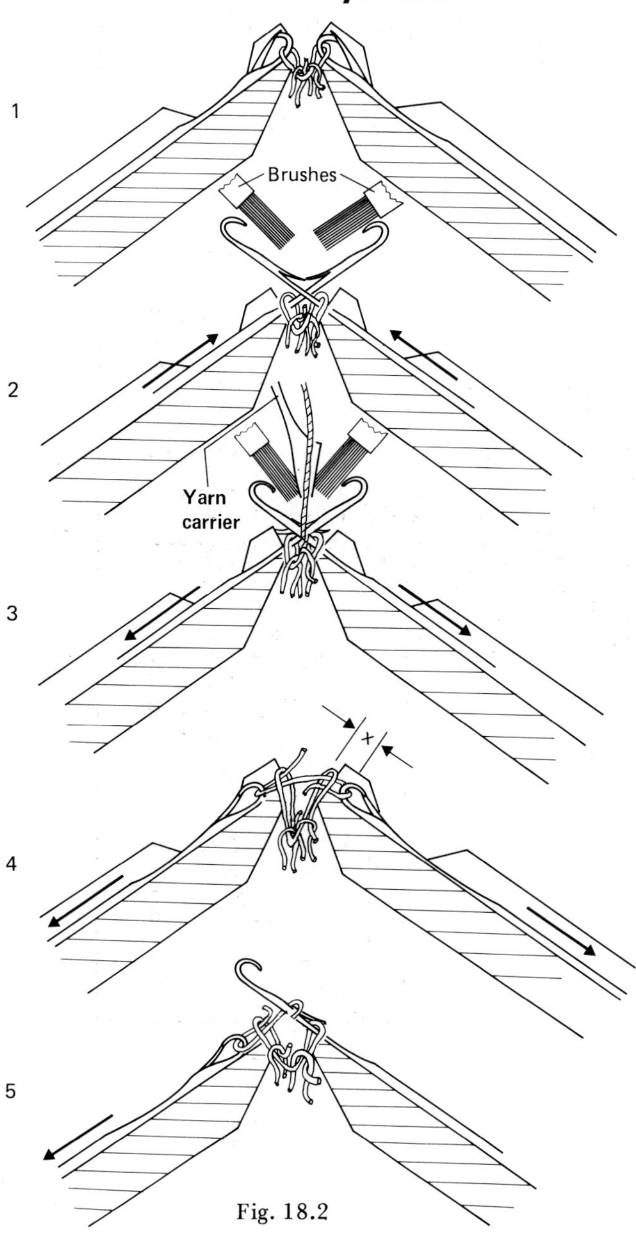

Fig. 18.2

Figure 18.2 illustrates the knitting action of a hand flat machine and Fig. 18.3 shows the underside of the cam-carriage and the cams forming the tracks which guide the needle butts through the knitting action.

A set of cams – raising cam (S) (clearing cam), guard cam and two stitch cams necessary in order to knit a course of loops on one bed of needles in either direction of carriage traverse – is termed *a lock*.

The symmetrical camming arrangement is typical of many V-bed machines as it enables a similar action to be achieved in both directions of carriage traverse in each needle bed. The needle butts will enter the system from the right during a left to right carriage traverse and from the left during a right to left traverse so that two raising cams (on most machines) and two stitch cams are required for each knitting system. Only one cam of each type carries out its function during a traverse, the other acts as a guard cam by forming part of the cam-track for the butts. In the traverse in the opposite direction, the roles of the two cams are reversed.

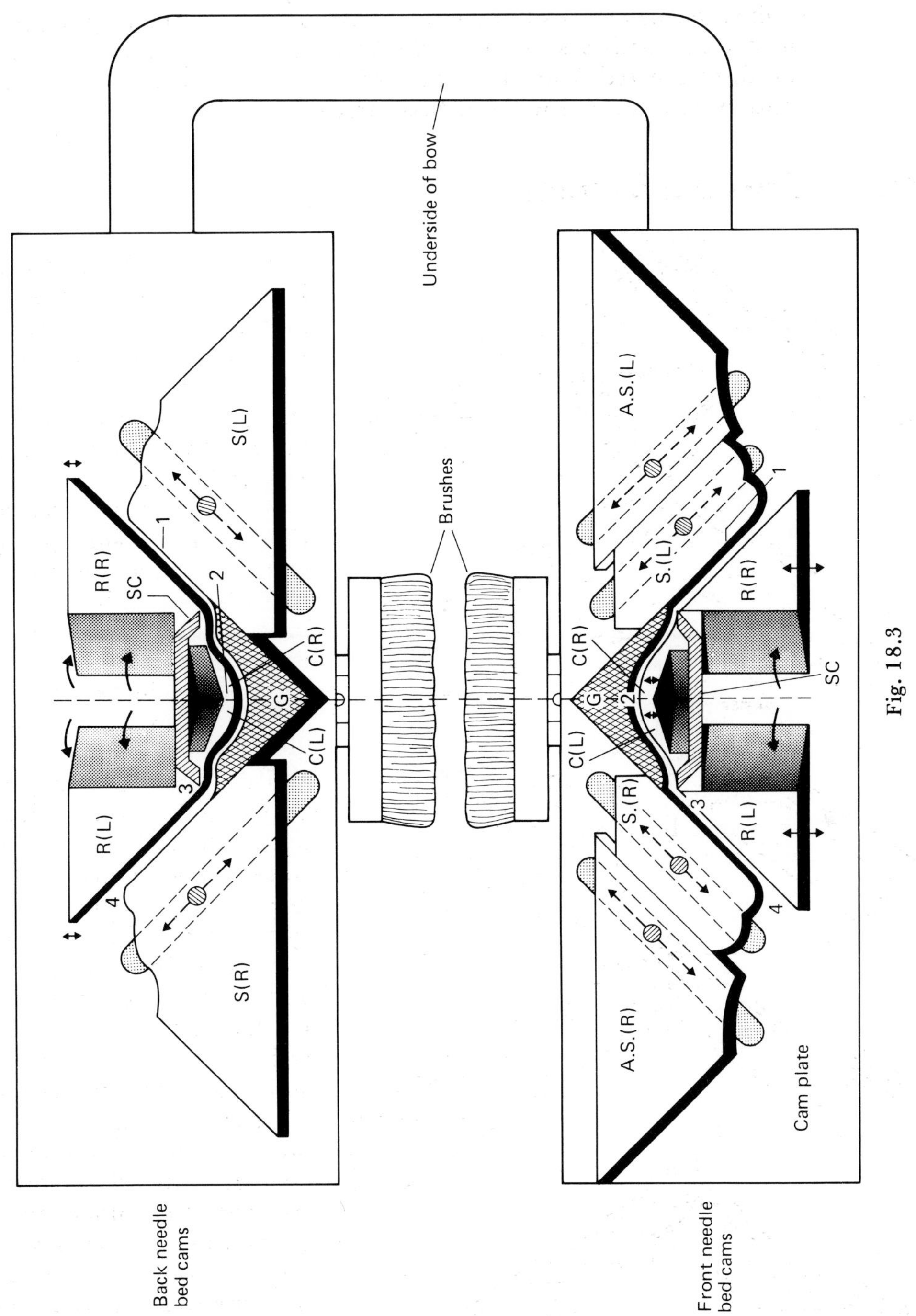
Underside of bow
Brushes
Back needle bed cams
Front needle bed cams
Cam plate
S(L)
S(R)
R(R)
R(L)
SC
C(R)
C(L)
G
A.S.(L)
A.S.(R)
S.(L)
S.(R)
1
2
3
4

Fig. 18.3

The numbers 1 to 4 correspond to the numbers of the knitting action illustrations assuming a carriage traverse from left to right. Similar positions may be plotted for the return traverse using the cams given an (L) designation to provide the positive movements.

1. The rest position The tops of the heads of the needles are level with the edge of the knock-over bits. The butts of the needles assume a straight line until contacting the raising cams R (R) because the leading stitch cams S (L) and A.S (L) are lifted to an inactive position. The lifting action is an alternating action, which always lowers the trailing stitch cams and raises the leading stitch cams in each system as the traverse commences. This action prevents needles from being unnecessarily lowered and a strain being placed on the old loops prior to the commencement of the knitting action.

2. Clearing The needle butts are lifted as they contact the leading edge of cams R (R) which raise the needles to tucking in the hook height with the undersurface of cams S (L) acting as guard cams. The needles are lifted to full clearing height as their butts pass over the top of cardigan cams C (R) and C (L).

3. Yarn feeding The yarn is fed as the needles descend under the control of guard cam (G) and the required loop length is drawn by each needle as it descends the stitch cam S (R).

4. Knocking-over To produce synchronized knocking-over of both needle beds simultaneously, the stitch cam S (R) in the front system is set lower than the auxiliary stitch cam A.S (R) so that the latter is thus rendered ineffective. If, however, delayed timing of the knock-over is employed, knock-over in the front bed will occur after knock-over in the back bed. In this case stitch cam S (R) is not set as low as A.S (R), so that the depth setting of the latter cam produces the knock-over action. Delayed timing is only normally used on gauges finer than 8 npi and cannot be used for broad ribs.

Stitch cam settings The stitch cams are located in slots by studs and they may be raised or lowered to a different setting position by moving the stud along the slot. Unless the rate of yarn feed is controlled, the setting of the stitch cam at knock-over will determine the stitch length because it controls the distance the head of the needle descends below the knock-over bit edge from the rest position. The alternating stitch cam settings are indicated by pointers on a calibrated scale on the outside of the cam-plate. On hand flats the adjustment of the settings is obtained by hand controls whilst on automatic flats as many as five different stitch cam settings can be achieved during a garment sequence once the initial adjustments have been made.

Spring-loaded cams Raising cams R and cardigan cams C are of the spring-loaded type which can be depressed into the undersurface of the cam-plate against the action of a spring. The leading edge of a leading raising cam is straight so that it causes the butts to follow its profile. However, the inner edges of these cams which are the leading edges when the cams are trailing, have gently sloping edges. Needle butts deliberately not raised by the leading cam thus ride up this edge depressing the cam into the cam-plate and then follow an undisturbed path across its face. Immediately after the butts have passed across, the cam springs outwards to its active position for the return traverse.

The cams are often of the sinkable setting type so that they can be set:

1. Fully out of the cam-plate so that they act on every needle butt.
2. Partly withdrawn into the cam-plate so that they miss the low or short butts which pass undisturbed across their face.
3. Fully withdrawn into the cam-plate so that all butts pass undisturbed across their face.

Set-out of long and short butts

The standard set-out when using different lengths of butts is two long and one short in each bed, which enables changes from 1 X 1 to 2 X 2 rib knitting to occur.

Control of cam settings and alterations

Changes of cam settings are achieved by movement of controls which are placed on the outside of the cam-plate. In the case of automatic power flats these controls consist of metal push slides (S in Fig. 12.1) each corresponding to a different cam and whose sideways movement produces the required change of cam setting. At each end of the machine is a contact post containing striking plates aligned to contact the slides as the cam-carriage reaches the end of its traverse so that the cams may be set for the return traverse. Control of the plates is achieved from the main garment control of the machine.

On hand flat machines it is useful to have split cardigan cams so that a different setting can be achieved in each direction without having to stop the carriage at the end of each traverse, however, as the automatic machine can change the cam settings for each traverse, split cardigan camming is unnecessary and these machines usually have a single cardigan cam for both traverse directions.

Double Cam Systems 18.6

Although hand flat machines have single cam system carriages, many automatic power flat machines have double cam systems with two complete sets of knitting cams being arranged side by side in the same cam-plate each working with a separate yarn carrier. Thus in one carriage traverse two courses of knitting can be produced. Although a double-system machine might be assumed to have double the productivity of a single-system machine, the rate of carriage traverse is often reduced firstly because of the heavier carriage and secondly because it is longer and therefore must traverse further in order to be clear of the needle bed at each end, thus making the machine longer. There is also a problem of vertical float threads at the selvedge edges of the fabric. Improved machine construction and the use of lightweight alloys has, however, encouraged some machine builders to produce models having three or even four cam systems.

18.7 Direct and Indirect Yarn Feed

Direct yarn feed is often used on hand flat machines as it allows weak yarns to be knitted because the yarn is supplied directly down from the centrally-positioned yarn tensioner to the reciprocating yarn carrier so that the tension is kept fairly constant at a minimum level. With this arrangement, the carrier must always remain on one side of the carriage bow, for example on the right, and not pass underneath it as the yarn path would be disturbed. Yarn carriers can therefore only be collected and left by the carriage at the right side of the machine so that only double course striping can be produced. The pick-up device for the yarn carrier is located on the outside of the low bow.

Indirect yarn feed is used on power flat machines and has a high carriage bow passing over the carrier bars and the yarn path is parallel with them from guide eyes at the end of the machine to the yarn carriers. The yarn is deflected in its downward path from the tensioners across to the guide eyes thus increasing the tension on the yarn and tending to cause fluctuations depending upon whether the carrier is traversing away from, or towards, the guide eye end of the machine. However, it does enable the yarn carrier to be picked up or left on either side of the machine using plungers which operate down onto the carrier blocks from the underside of the carriage bow.

The *yarn carriers* are arranged to slide on both sides of double prismatic guiding bars and there are usually six or seven carriers operating on two or three double bars. When two carriers operate on the same track of the same bar it is essential to arrange the sequence so that if the two carriers are deposited on the same side, the one nearest to the cam-carriage will be the one first required to traverse back in the opposite direction.

There are two methods of entraining carriers with cam systems on double system machines: uncrossed and crossed. With the uncrossed arrangement, the same yarn carriers operate with the same cam systems in both directions of traverse. This simplifies the control and is essential when two carriers are on the same track, but it causes problems with vertical yarn floats at the selvedges, because the yarn with the leading cam system will finish the first course, but will not knit the return traverse course immediately after the trailing yarn has knitted its course as the trailing system becomes the leading system in the return traverse.

With the crossed arrangement, one yarn carrier will always be entrained with the leading cam system and the other with the trailing system, so that if the carriers are of different colours each will knit alternate courses.

In *carrier positioning and traversing for jacquard* (Fig. 18.4) the yarn carriers must be carefully positioned initially in order to keep their number to a minimum whilst ensuring that empty traverses (without knitting a course) are avoided whenever possible, as they reduce productivity. By drawing a plan of traverses and colours and indicating each time a new carrier is picked-up, the initial positions can soon be established. For double-system knitting in two- or three-colour jacquard, each system will require as many carriers as there are colours but the two carriers of the same colour can use the same track. Only in the case of single-system two-colour jacquard is it necessary to alter the sequence of coloured

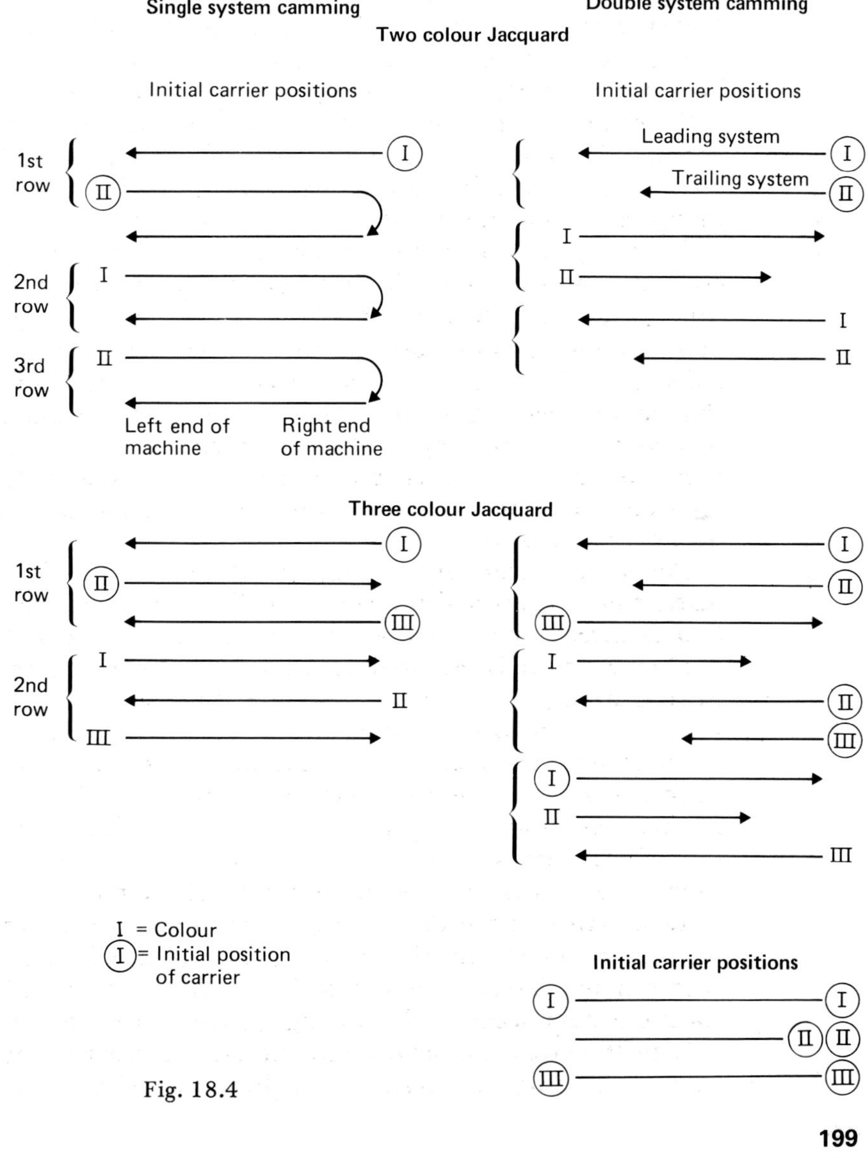

Fig. 18.4

courses. This is because after their first course, each colour is knitted at two consecutive courses.

18.8 Cardigan Stitches

Cardigan stitches are two-course repeat, tuck rib knitwear structures widely used in the body sections of heavy-weight stitch shaped sweaters. The tuck stitches cause the rib wales to gape apart so that the body width spreads outwards to a greater extent than the rib border. The tuck loops increase the fabric thickness and make it heavier in weight and bulkier in handle although the rate of production in rows of loops will be less than for normal 1 X 1 or 2 X 2 rib. The greater the proportion of tuck to cleared loops, the heavier and wider the finished relaxed structure (see Fig. 16.11).

In the production of a knitted stitch the leading raising and cardigan cams for that bed and direction of traverse must be in action, whilst for a tuck stitch, the raising cams remain in action but the cardigan cam is taken out of action. It is important to arrange the camming for the needle beds so that at the start of the traverse when tucking, the first needle is tucking and the last needle in action is in the opposite bed and is thus knitting. If the last needle is tucking the selvedge tuck loop will withdraw from the needle hook as the reverse traverse commences.

Half-cardigan or Royal Rib (Fig. 18.5) is produced on a 1 X 1 rib base

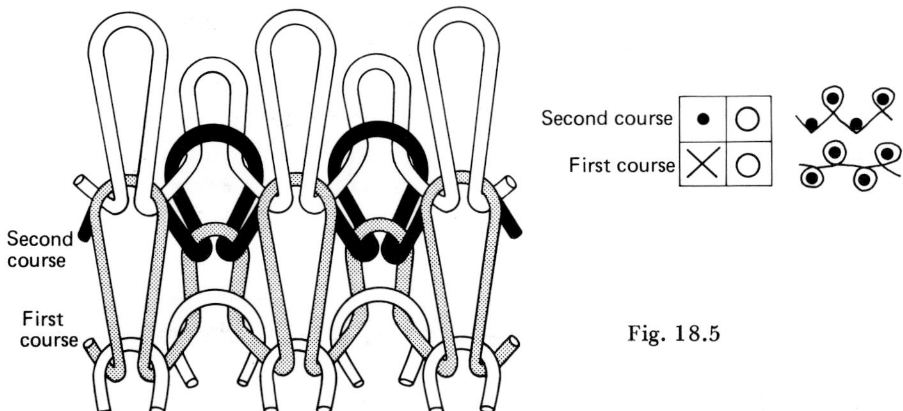

Fig. 18.5

having tuck loops on one bed only at alternate courses; it is therefore an unbalanced structure with a different appearance on each side and with twice as many cleared loop courses per unit length on the all-knit side to the tuck loop side. On the all-knit side one course of loops are very large and rounded. This is because they receive yarn from the tuck loops on the other side, the other course of loops on this side are, in contrast extremely small and insignificant because they are robbed of yarn by the elongated held loops on the other side which consists only of held loops as the tuck loops, i.e. behind them. A two-tuck variation of half-cardigan based on a four-course repeat with each sequence repeated at two consecutive courses is useful as it produces rounded loops on the knit side as a result of yarn passing across in the second tuck course.

Full cardigan or Polka Rib (Fig. 18.6) has the same appearance on both

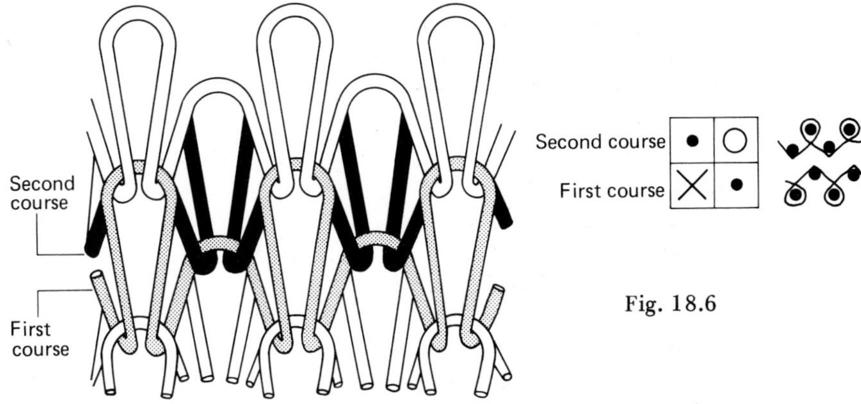

Fig. 18.6

sides as it is a balanced structure. If different coloured yarns are knitted at alternate courses a 'shot rib' will be produced which in the relaxed state will show one colour on one side and the other colour on the opposite side. In open width a 1 × 1 rib fabric will relax by about 30 per cent, half-cardigan by only 5 per cent and full cardigan will show no width shrinkage compared with the knitting width. On a single-system hand flat making half-cardigan, only one of the four cardigan cams is put out of action so that in one direction of traverse a tuck stitch is produced on one needle bed instead of the 1 × 1 rib of the opposite traverse. To produce full cardigan, diagonally opposite pairs of cardigan cams are taken out of action, so that in one direction of traverse, the front needle bed will tuck and in the reverse direction of traverse the back needle bed will tuck.

The 2 × 2 rib version of half-cardigan is termed Fishermans Rib and the full cardigan version is termed the Sweater Stitch.

Racked Rib Structures 18.9

The V-bed flat machine is capable of producing a unique range of racked rib (inclined loop) structures based on the facility of racking one needle bed by one or more tricks past the other in either direction as and when required. Usually the needle set-out is 1 × 1 rib or its modification, with a half- or full cardigan knitting sequence.[5]

The basic principles are as follows:

1. The structure must be rib based so that the loop of a wale of one bed *is racked past a loop of a wale in the opposite bed.*

2. When a single-needle rack occurs after a 1 × 1 rib knitting course, the 45-degree inclination would be shared between the loops on both sides

producing an insignificant effect unless the rack is increased to two needles.

3. A single-needle rack after a course of tuck loops on one bed and knitted loops on the other will produce a full 45-degree inclination of the knitted loops irrespective of which bed was racked (Fig. 18.7). The open legs of the tuck loops resist the effect of racking causing the tension to incline only the knitted loops. Half- or full cardigan sequences are thus an ideal base for racked structures.

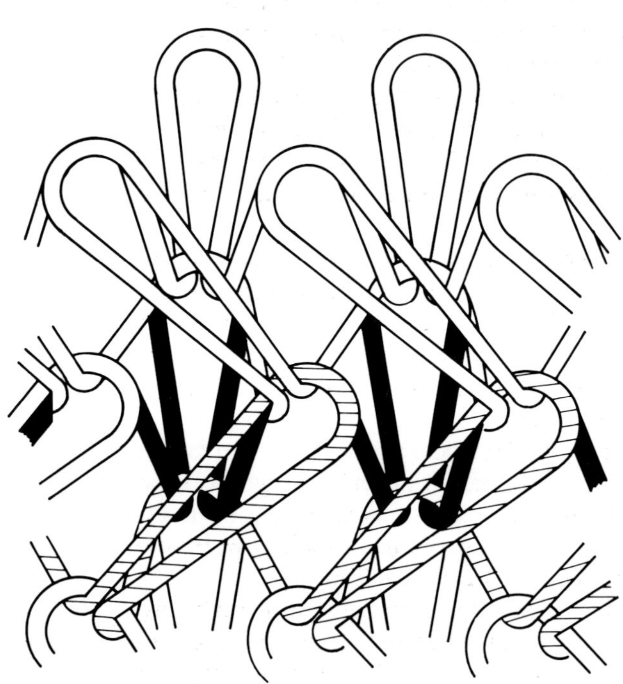

Fig. 18.7

4. With the half-cardigan sequence, racking will occur after the tuck course (every second course). The effect will show on the all-knitted loop side on alternate courses; in between, the 1 × 1 rib courses will appear as minute upright loops.

5. *The full cardigan sequence provides the possibility of having racked loops on both sides of the fabric when racking occurs at every course.* When racking occurs at every second course, the effect will be on one side only but the non-racked courses will hide the tucks behind the racked loops whilst providing the necessary knitted loops for the opposite bed.

6. If in a full cardigan sequence, racking occurs in one direction after odd courses and a return rack occurs after even courses, all loops on both sides of the fabric will be inclined towards the same direction. The reason is that, for example, a loop will incline towards the right if its bed is racked towards the right or if the bed containing the tucks is racked past it towards the left. The first loop inclination will show on the front bed if this has the knitted loops and the second on the back bed because this will contain the knitted loops at the return rack.

The wales will thus be inclined in the same direction at an angle of 45 degrees. If the colour of the yarn is changed at fixed intervals of courses and the fabric is cut in rectangular pieces at right angles to the inclined selvedges, diagonal rather than horizontal stripes will be produced relative to the selvedge.

7. If in a full cardigan sequence, racking occurs in the same direction at two successive courses and is followed by racks in the opposite direction

at two successive courses, alternate courses will show loops inclined in opposite directions on each side of the fabric because the first and third racks will affect one side and the second and fourth racks will affect the other side of the fabric.

8. A Vandyke or zig-zag selvedge edge will be produced if the principles explained in 6 and 7 are combined. For example, sixteen courses might be knitted with a rack to the right after each odd course and a rack to the left after each even course. A course without racking will then put the sequence out of phase so that loop inclination is in the opposite direction during the next sixteen-course racking sequence which is then followed by a further course without racking and so on. On each side courses will incline in one direction in eight-course sequences and every sixteen courses there will be one course of small insignificant upright loops.

9. The previously explained principles assume both beds to have a full complement of needles so that all wales on one side of the fabric have an identical appearance of inclination. When the repeat set-out includes empty tricks, knitted loops racked past these will not be under tension and will thus not become inclined whilst adjacent loops which have passed tuck loops in the opposite bed will be inclined as usual.

To produce a racked and straight wale effect on one side of the fabric of a full cardigan knitting sequence, racking will occur after every alternate course, for example, once right and later once left. A straight wale will be produced by racking past the same empty trick, whilst a racked wale will be produced by racking past the same needle with a tuck loop.

If after a number of repeats of this sequence, two successive racks are made in the same direction before continuing the sequence, the racking sequence will be out of phase so that needles formerly racking across an empty trick will now be crossing a tuck loop and vice versa so that racked wales will show upright loops and straight wales will show racked loops. The changeover can be produced whenever required.

10. Racked loops are more prominent if the needle bed is half-gauged with every alternate needle removed.

Knop Structures 18.10

Knop fabrics are relief structures in rib where successive tuck stitches on all the needles or certain needles of one bed produce a three-dimensional effect. Sometimes the all-knit foundation courses are produced in a different colour and sometimes racking occurs after the knop sequence so that the next knop is off-set.

The Cable Stitch 18.11

This is a traditional hand-knitted stitch pattern incorporated into fisherman's sweaters in the islands of Jersey, Guernsey and particularly

Aran where it is one of a range of stitch patterns (Fig. 19.10) which include ladder, blackberry stitch and honeycomb.[6] Traditionally the yarn is partly scoured wool in its ecru (undyed and unbleached) colour. The cable stitch is a three-dimensional design of cords of face loop wales centred in a panel of reverse loop stitches bordered on either side by rib wales of face stitches. Each cord is usually three wales wide which move as a unit when they are crossed over (twisted) another cord. The direction of twist of cords is always the same relative to the surface of the design. Cables are normally either two-cord or three-cord. In machine knitting, the cords are knitted from one needle bed and the background panel from the other. The cable loops are longer to reduce the tension where the cords twist. At this point, the loops of one cord are transferred over to the other bed so that the two cords can be racked past each other before they are transferred back to recommence knitting. Cable stitches are knitted on some automatic flat rib and purl machines as well as on a double-cylinder machine with the facility for shogging the top cylinder.

Further Information

LANCASHIRE, J. B., *Hos. Trade Journal*, The versatility of flat frame knitting, (1956) Aug., 58–62. Fancy trimmings for outerwear, (1955) Feb., 72–4. V-type strappings and stollings, (1970) April, 74–7.

WEBER, K. P., Theory of knitting (part 2), *Knit. Times*, (1975) 14 April, 141–163.

Flat Machines, (1979) ITF Maille, France.

The Dubied Knitting Manual, (1967) Edouard Dubied and Cie, Neuchatel.

1. Recalling a century of flat progress, *Knit. Int.*, (1982) April, 36–40.
2. LANCASHIRE, J. B., 50 years of V-bed flat knitting machinery, *Knit. O'wear Times Yr. Bk.*, (1968) 221–4.
3. MILLINGTON, J. T., The Macqueen knitting technique, *Hos. Trade Journal*, (1961) May, 97–100.
4. MILLINGTON, J. T., The continuing electronic revolution, *Knit. Int.*, (1978) Aug., 28–32.
5. LANCASHIRE, J. B., Racked ribs/focus on racked rib fabrics, *Hos. Trade Journal*, (1958) May, 66–9; (1969) Dec., 80–4.
6. LANCASHIRE, J. B., The cable stitch, *Hos. Trade Journal*, (1959) Oct., 96–100.

19

Automatic Power Flat Knitting

The basic principles of flat knitting have already been outlined in Chapter 18, the main difference between the simple hand flat and the automatic power flat is that the latter can be programmed to knit through a garment length sequence at high speed and often has greater patterning facilities.

Mechanically-Controlled Jacquard Knitting 19.1

Figure 19.1 illustrates the arrangement of elements in the needle bed of a machine having full mechanical selection. A separately controlled arrangement may also be available on the other bed. In the tricks beneath each needle are selectors (two in the case of the double-cam system machine) whose tails are supported by a jacquard steel which extends across the full width of the needle bed. There is a possible punched hole position for each selector on each jacquard steel. The steels are hinged together to form an endless 'chain loop' which passes over the prism. Whilst the cam-carriage is clear of the needle bed at the end of its traverse, the prism can turn, bringing another steel onto its upper surface and thrusting it upwards into contact with the protruding tails of the selectors thus producing a simultaneous selection at every needle trick for the next carriage traverse. The prism can dwell to repeat a selection, or rack forwards or backwards by one or two positions.

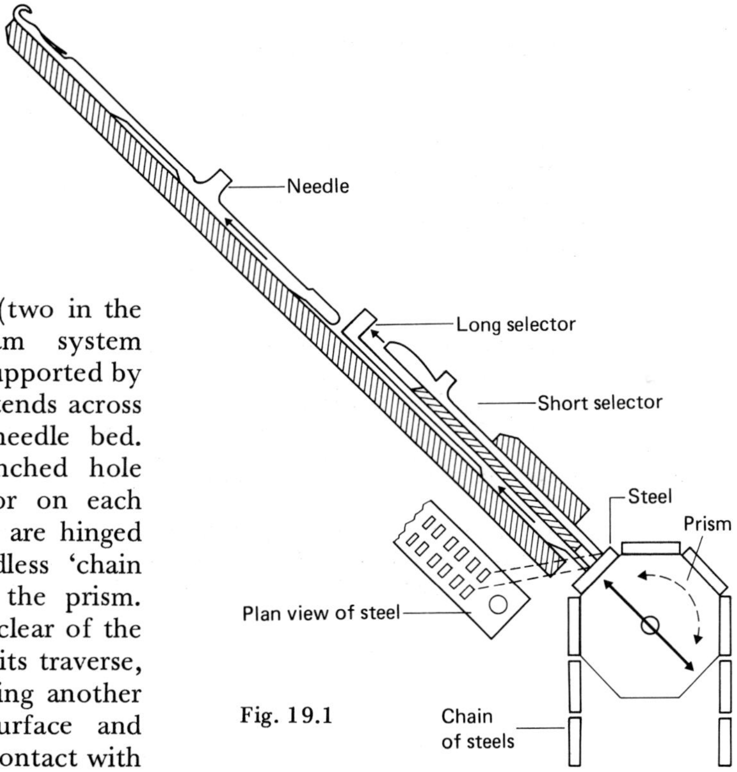

Fig. 19.1

An unpunched portion in a steel causes the corresponding selector to be pushed upwards in the trick aligning its butt with a raising cam in the carriage so that eventually the needle above it will be lifted possibly to knit. A punched hole allows the selector tail to sink through it into the groove in the prism and thus be unaffected by the thrust of the prism so that its needle is left at the inactive level. If the needle bed is racked the jacquard apparatus moves sideways to keep in alignment with it.

Selected long selectors act directly into the needles when lifted by cams whereas short selectors act onto the long selectors in order to lift the needles.

During jacquard knitting, long selectors act as principal selectors making the selection in the leading cam system and short selectors (auxiliary selectors) select for the trailing cam system. Only the stitch and guard cams are in action in the needle cam-race as the selectors and their cams cause the needles to be lifted.

Figure 19.2 illustrates the symmetrical arrangement of a double-system machine having mechanical selection on both beds with two knitting systems and two rib loop two-way transfer sections with a cam-race for each of the three elements.

The arrows illustrate the direction from which the butts will enter the cam-races, on the left when the carriage is traversing towards the left and on the right when traversing towards the right. Level 'a' represents the selected butt level and 'b' represents its unselected or base level. The shaded cams are those permanently in action. Any cams 'R' will cause the needle to be lifted to tuck height and if cam 'C' is also in action the needle will be lifted to clearing height. Guard cams (G) begin lowering the butts after knitting. Cams 'L.C' lower the butts back to the active butt line, whilst cams 'S.C', when in action, take the butts down to the base level so that the selection which occurred in the previous knitting system is not repeated in the following system.

The Long Selector Cams

A punched hole in the steel allows a long selector butt to remain in the base (inactive) position below cams 'W.X' and 'Y'. It will thus not cause its needle to be lifted from miss height.

A solid portion in the steel lifts the long selector so that its butt passes in the active position over cams 'W.X' and 'Y'. For a knitting selection cam 'T' is in action so that the butt is lifted onto the permanent cam (Z) and passes onto the clearing cam (C). For a tucking selection cam 'T' is taken out of action so that the butt passes across and is lifted as it passes over cam 'R' taking its needle to tuck height.

The Short Selector Cams

If a hole is punched in the steel, the short selector butt will pass in the base position below cams 'A' and 'T.R' and it will not be lifted to contact and lift the long selector.

The short selector butts are arranged in 2 × 2 formation; two long butts and one short butt so that if the 2 × 2 cam is introduced the long butts only will be lifted producing 2 × 2 rib without using selection.

If there is no hole punched, the butt will pass over cam 'A' in the active position and for jacquard knitting none of the short selector cams are in

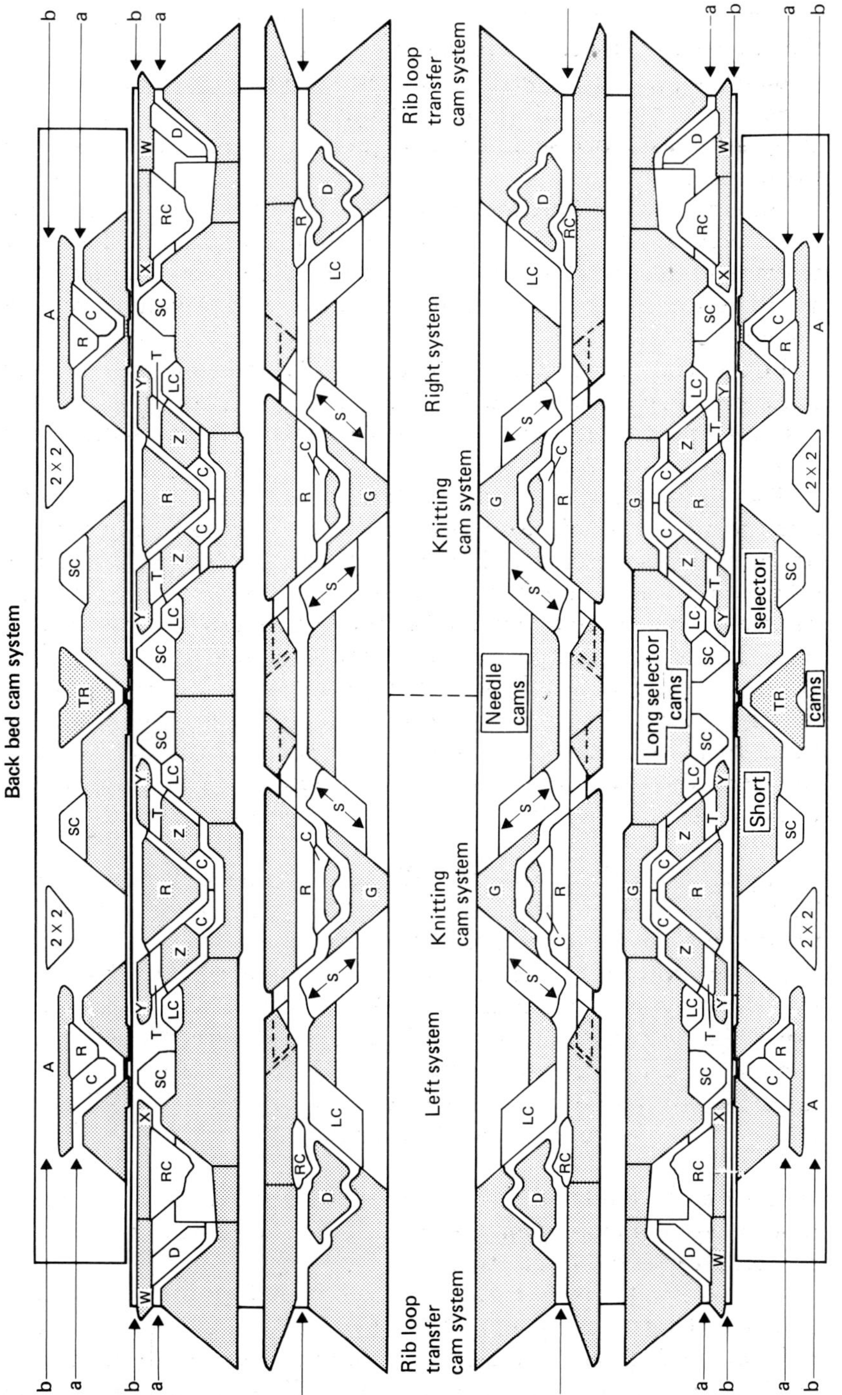
Back bed cam system
Rib loop transfer cam system
Right system
Knitting cam system
Needle cams
Knitting cam system
Left system
Rib loop transfer cam system
Long selector cams
Short selector cams
Front bed cam system
A
C
R
SC
2 X 2
TR
RC
D
W
X
Y
T
LC
Z
G
S
a
b

Fig. 19.2

KT-O

action so that the butt will contact on 'T.R' and be raised lifting the long selector above into action in the trailing system.

A miss, tuck and knit selection in the same system may be obtained by using the long selector for tuck and the short selector for knit. It is also possible to select for knit or for tuck on the short selector whilst using the long selector for rib loop transfer selection. If the cancellation cams are out of action, the selection may be repeated in the following cam system.

19.2 The Pasteboard Movement Card Reader Unit

This is situated either towards or at the end of the machine if it is a mechanically-controlled power flat. The pasteboard cards provide the unit with the data in order to control and coordinate the machine's functions in the garment length knitting sequence. Each card may have between sixty and ninety punched hole positions arranged in rows each corresponding to a spring-loaded pin. Amongst the movement functions provided by particular hole positions are; yarn carrier selection from either side of the machine, positioning of raising cams and stitch cams, needle bed racking, speed changes, jacquard prism rotation and cancellation of jacquard selection, and the starting and stopping of the disc counter which economizes on the cards.

Figure 19.3 shows a typical unit arrangement. The horizontal spring

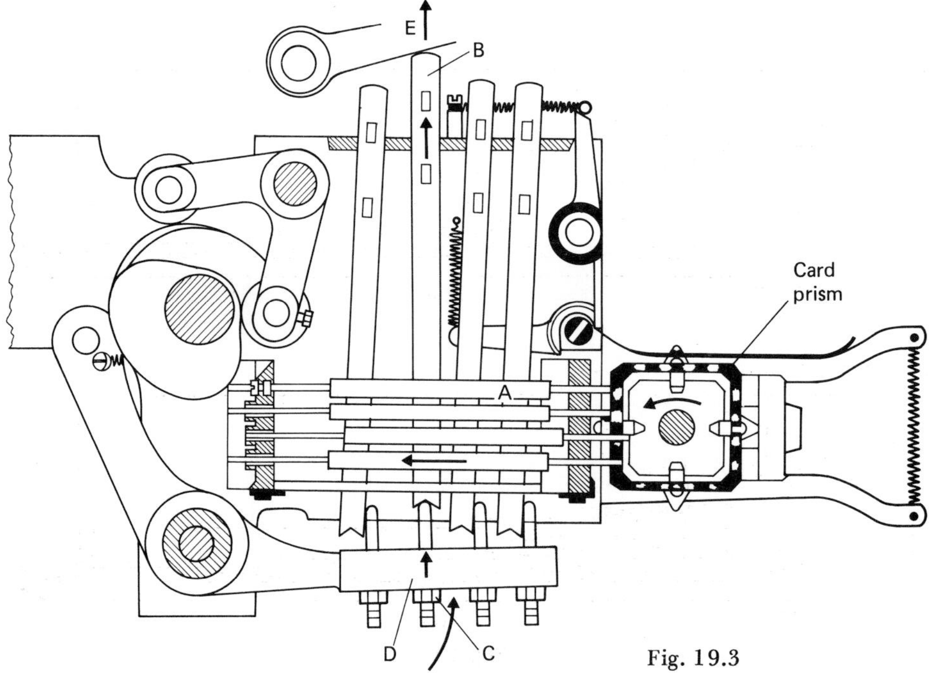

Fig. 19.3

loadêd pins (A) are moved towards the left by the solid parts of the card each moving its associated rod (B) out of the vertical plane. Where a hole is punched in the card, the rod 'B' will be undisturbed and will be aligned with a set screw (C) in platform 'D' which is raised by a cam. As a result, rod 'B' lifts lever 'E' causing the required movement to take place.

The card movement (forwards or backwards by one or two cards or dwell) occurs whilst the carriage is clear of the knitting width.

The chain of pasteboard cards is composed of cycles of two, four, six or eight cards whose sequence is used a number of times with the aid of the economizer disc. In between the cycles are passage cards.

Stoll Selectanit Electronic Selection 19.3

In 1975, the ANV was the first commercial flat machine to utilize punched tape electronic control in place of both the mechanically-operated movement card apparatus and the needle selection mechanism of jacquard steels. Stoll have since produced a range of V-bed and flat bed purl machines incorporating the Selectanit electronic control system.

Needle selection (Fig. 19.4) is through tipping platines (P) placed in front of the jacks (J) with butts at one of six heights in echelon repeat set-outs across the needle bed. In the platine cam system of the carriage below each knitting cam system is a vertical set of six flat-plate rocker cams corresponding to the butt set-out. Without selection, the field of a permanent magnet holds these cams in the ground position so that they contact the butts causing the platines to be tipped into the tricks ('B' in

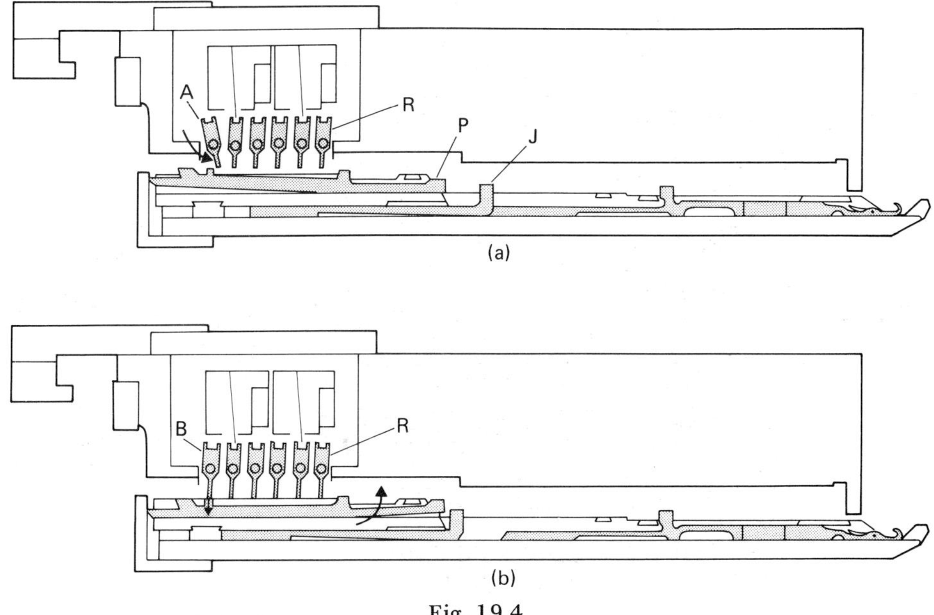

Fig. 19.4

Fig. 19.4b) so that their base butts miss the platine raising cams and they therefore fail to lift their jacks (and needles) onto the raising cams at the succeeding cam system.

As the carriage traverses, a needle detector in each of the jack tuck cams senses the passing needle tricks to ensure that the selection impulses are correctly timed. An impulse decision for each rocker cam will occur once for every six needle tricks traversed. When the magnetic coil for a cam is impulsed, the effect of the magnet is cancelled and the cam is swung out of action ('A' in Fig. 19.4a) leaving the corresponding platine in its working position, so that the needle is raised in the succeeding cam system. After selection, the platines are lowered and re-aligned for the next selection.

19.4 The Dubied Actuator Selection Post

This form of electro-magnetic selection is employed on both the electronically controlled C48 Wevenit circular rib jacquard machine and the newer JET double-system electronically-controlled jacquard V-bed flat machine. On the circular machine, the posts are in a stationary position in advance of each feeder cam system with the selector heads passing through them as the cylinder revolves. On the flat machine, three posts (P) are arranged: one in advance, one in between and one trailing behind the two raising cam systems of each needle bed and are attached to a bar below the cam-plate of the cam-carriage so that they select onto the heads of the selectors in the stationary tricks in both directions of traverse (Fig. 19.5b).

The light-weight selectors (S) (Fig. 19.5c) have a magnetically sensitive head (H) so that each can be selected to slide in either direction in a special dust-free trick beneath each needle trick. As they slide, one of their feet (F) is pointing in the direction of movement and the other is trailing. During the selection, the selector heads are funnelled through the narrow throat (T) of the actuator post where, at its narrowest constriction, an electronic impulse (one for each selector) produces an attraction from one wall and a repulsion force from the other so that the selector slides by a distance of a few microns. The walls diverge at the exit from the throat but at this point permanent magnets ensure that the heads of selectors are still held by them so that selection movement is magnified sufficiently to transmit a mechanical movement to the knitting elements.

On the flat machine, a fixed preparation cam (PC) (Fig. 19.5a) at the actuator post position presses down onto the heads of jacks (J) placed on top of the flexible needle tails. This depresses the needle tails and their raising butts into the tricks and out of action and causes the jacks to pivot so that their tails are lifted. At this moment, selectors may be selected to slide towards the jack tails so that their feet slide under and hold this element arrangement with the needle butts sunk into the tricks and out of action, missing the raising cam system (RC). If the selectors slide in the

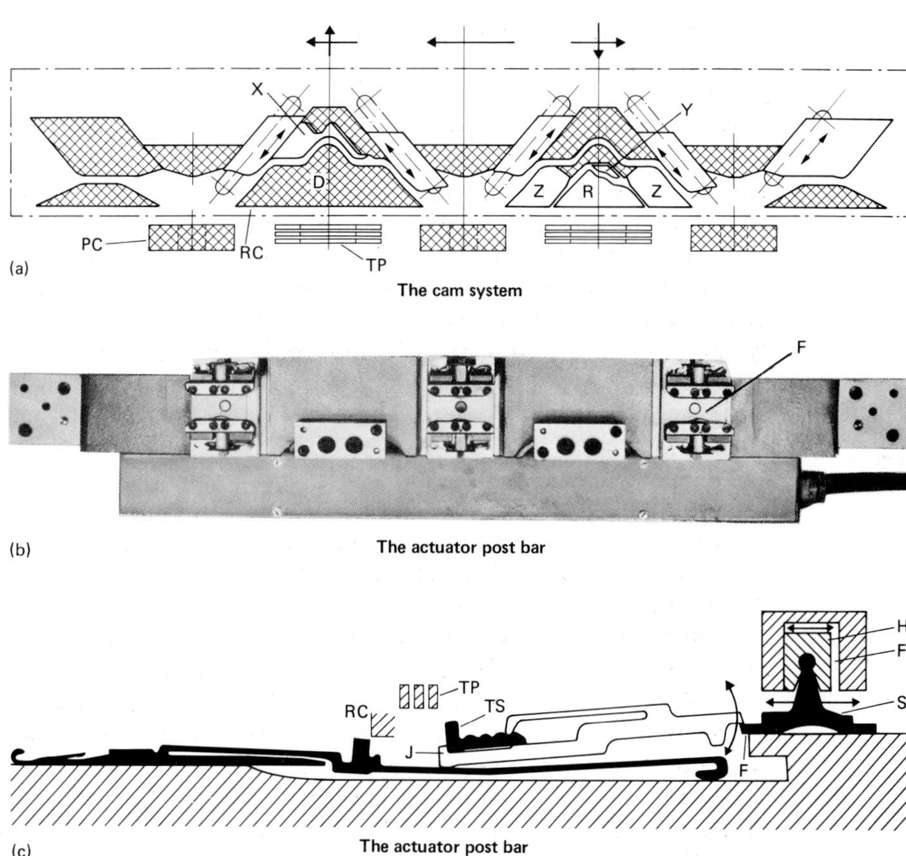

The cam system

The actuator post bar

The actuator post bar

Fig. 19.5

opposite direction the jack tails are unsupported and as soon as the preparation cam is passed, the needle tail springs upwards placing the needle butt into action on the raising cam. Two of the posts select in advance of the raising cam systems and the trailing post merely selects all needle butts into action for checking purposes.

Once a needle butt is selected onto the raising cam, it may be sunk out of action when tuck height is reached, by means of a separate superimposed mechanical selection. Clipped on top of each jack is a tuck selector (TS) which can be placed so that its butt is aligned with one of the three tuck presser (TP) cams positioned below each raising cam. These cams may be put into action to produce tucking at their corresponding needles when required.

Figure 19.5a illustrates the cams for transferring rib loops with the delivering cam arrangement in the left system and the receiving cam arrangement in the right. When cam 'X' is lowered onto 'D', the double-humped delivering cam is formed with the fixed cam above acting as a guard cam. In the right system, the receiving cam arrangement is achieved by taking cams 'Z' out of action so the track is formed between cams 'R' and 'Y'.

19.5 Multi-Carriage Flat Machines

Introduced by Textima in 1950, the Diamant machine has two separate pairs of needle beds each 72 inches (183 cm) wide arranged parallel to each other on either a rib or a purl basis. Each pair of beds is capable of producing a garment length having straight cut end selvedges by means of 15–18 cam-carriages which achieve 10–15 clockwise circuits of the beds per minute, transporting their own yarn packages, stripers and selection drums. At one end of the machine, the movement changes required for the next circuit are mechanically or electro-magnetically initiated as each carriage in turn passes by the main control section.

The Shima Seiki company has perfected a *fully automatic method of glove knitting in tubular plain on a small width V-bed machine*. Each finger is knitted in turn from its tip with its loops then being held until the palm sequence commences.[1] The glove is completed and pressed-off with an elasticated mock rib cuff. Control of knitting across the varying width is assisted by holding-down sinkers and a variable traverse of the cam-carriage (Fig. 19.6).

19.6 The Presser Foot Concept

The object of the presser foot and other similar devices is to push the old (fabric) loops down the needle stems whilst the needles rise for clearing or yarn feeding and thus to ensure a 'clean' knitting action *irrespective of the variable tensions within the knitted structure or the lack of take-down tension operating onto the fabric from below*. Interest in this concept was regenerated in 1968 by the development work of Frank Robinson and Max Betts of Courtaulds whose patents have now been licensed by Dubied, Bentley and Mitsubishi for use on their flat knitting machines. Other companies have also employed stitch pressing down devices of various types on their machines, including Wildt Mellor Bromley who have used presser foot wires on their coarse gauge circular garment machines to obtain multiple tuck patterning.

In the conventional take-down system of the automatic V-bed flat machine, the fabric is drawn downwards from the needle beds and passes between the grip formed by the roller and counter roller. The roller is composed of freely-turning sectional rollers on a common shaft. Each roller is pre-set, spring-tensioned as the shaft turns under the influence of racking pawl controlled by a lever, and weight arrangement. The pressure grip is maintained by adjustable pressure rollers.

The conventional take-down requires a continuous flow of knitted structure from the needles to the roller grip so that garment pieces must be knitted in string formation held one to the next by a course knitted with a draw-thread which is removed after knitting in order to separate the individual garment pieces. Furthermore, the system operates most successfully on a fabric having a consistent knitting width and a balanced

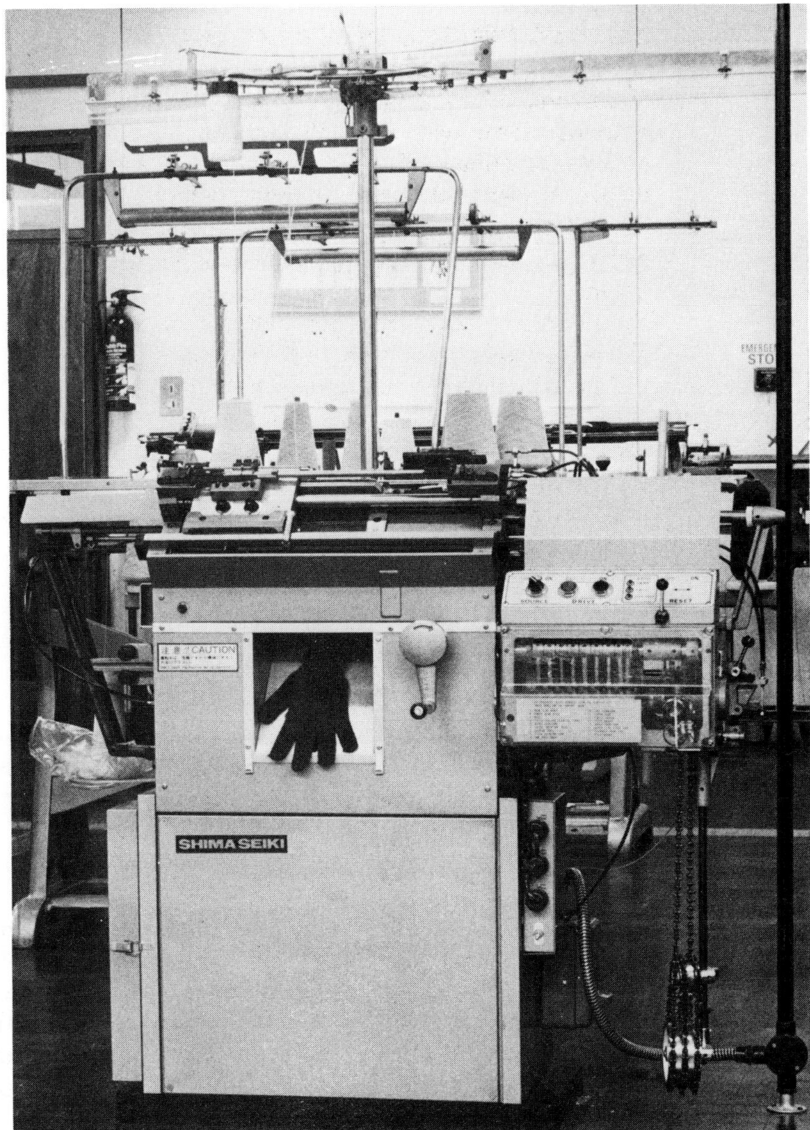

Fig. 19.6. Automatic V-Bed Glove Knitting Machine which knits gloves in tubular plain commencing with the closed finger tips and terminating with the mock rib elasticated cuff section (Walter Bullwer, Leicester Polytechnic).

course and knitted loop arrangement both between the two needle beds and within each bed. As tension is exerted equally on all wales within the roller grip, those not gripped (if the fabric is being widened) will be untensioned, held loops will receive excessive tension, whilst other wales, where more continuous knitting occurs, tend to receive insufficient tension. Thus the conventional arrangement tends to inhibit both shaping and also types of designs which involve multiple tuck accumulation and holding loops over a number of courses.

The presser foot which was patented by Courtaulds, consists of a piece of wire which is bent at either end to form a foot (Fig. 19.7). The centre of the wire is carried on the underside of a pivoted arm which hangs downwards from a cross member so that it brushes against the fabric loops as it moves with the cam-carriage. At the end of each traverse, the pivoted arm is tilted to incline in opposite direction, lifting one foot out of action and lowering the foot on the other end to trail across the needle beds for the return traverse.

← Carriage traverse

A–In active foot
B–Foot lowered into action

Fig. 19.7. The Action of the Presser Foot. The foot is shown during a right-to-left traverse pressing down the loops on the needles in advance of the yarn carrier. (The cam carriage has been removed for purposes of clarity) (*Knitting International*).

There is a device working with each cam system and its yarn carrier. Different diameters of wire may be employed for varying machine gauges and yarn counts and it is possible to fit specially-angled feet of triangular cross-section for use during single-bed knitting or loop transferring if necessary. It has been necessary in some to modify the shape of the knock-over bits and stitch cams to obtain maximum advantage.

The foot acts slightly in advance of the yarn carrier and the rise of the needles for tucking or clearing. It enters the space between the needle beds to gently stroke the old loops down the needle stems as it trails, set at a slight decline to their upper surface. Accommodation to differing degrees of knitting tightness can be achieved with a spring-loaded, self-compensating presser foot which rides up the support arm when the structure is knitted to a tighter quality. Large fluctuations in the yarn length between the last knitted loop and the yarn carrier position which occur during shaping have led to the development of a more sensitive yarn take-up. A presser foot set at an angle and having a flat surface is employed for single-bed knitting. Most machines also have a conventional roller take-down system to provide complete versatility.

As the presser foot does not create tension on loops already formed, loops may be held on inactive needles for many knitting cycles and stitch concentrations can be varied across the fabric width. It also enables separate garment panels to be commenced on empty needles and to be pressed off on completion. The lack of take-down tension removes the problem of shape distortion and the bowing of courses caused by relaxation of the structure thus often eliminating the need for the operation of first pressing. The structures do, however, tend to be heavier and, in the case of rib knitted on a double system, tend to show a slightly racked appearance because the presser foot causes yarn to flow into the first limb of each loop which it contacts and two courses are made in the same direction of traverse each time thus emphasizing the inclination of the loops.

The presser foot provides scope for the use of the holding of loops, pressing-off and part course knitting in the production of unconventional integrally-knitted garments, which require less seaming and virtually no cutting. Amongst the garment shapes are cruciform, articles in tubular plain and garment parts of varying course sizes, knitted as shaped single pieces of fabric in a spiral formation similar to the principles of the basque beret or the ideas of Macqueen or Pfauti. Integrally-knitted garments have, so far, received limited acceptance except for babywear but in the production of garment panels by held stitch shaping and in multi-tuck designs such as the blackberry stitch, the presser foot knitting technique has proved particularly successful.

Flat Bed Purl Knitting 19.7

There are far fewer hand- or power-operated flat bed purl machines than V-bed flat machines as this is a more specialist technique. Figure 19.8 illustrates the cam system of the popular mechanically-controlled Stoll LIUM machine which now has an electronically-controlled version termed the LNCU.[2] The LIUM has needle bed widths of either 59 inches (150 cm) or 67 inches (170 cm) and the LNCU has a width of 82 inches (205 cm). Machine gauges are 6, 8 and 10 n.p.i. with the carriage traverses running at approximately 15–17 per minute.

The machine has a single-knitting system for each slider bed together with needle transfer as well as loop transfer facilities onto special jacks in the front bed. Loop transfer to adjacent needles for cable stitch and crossed wale effects is thus possible by racking the front bed up to six needle

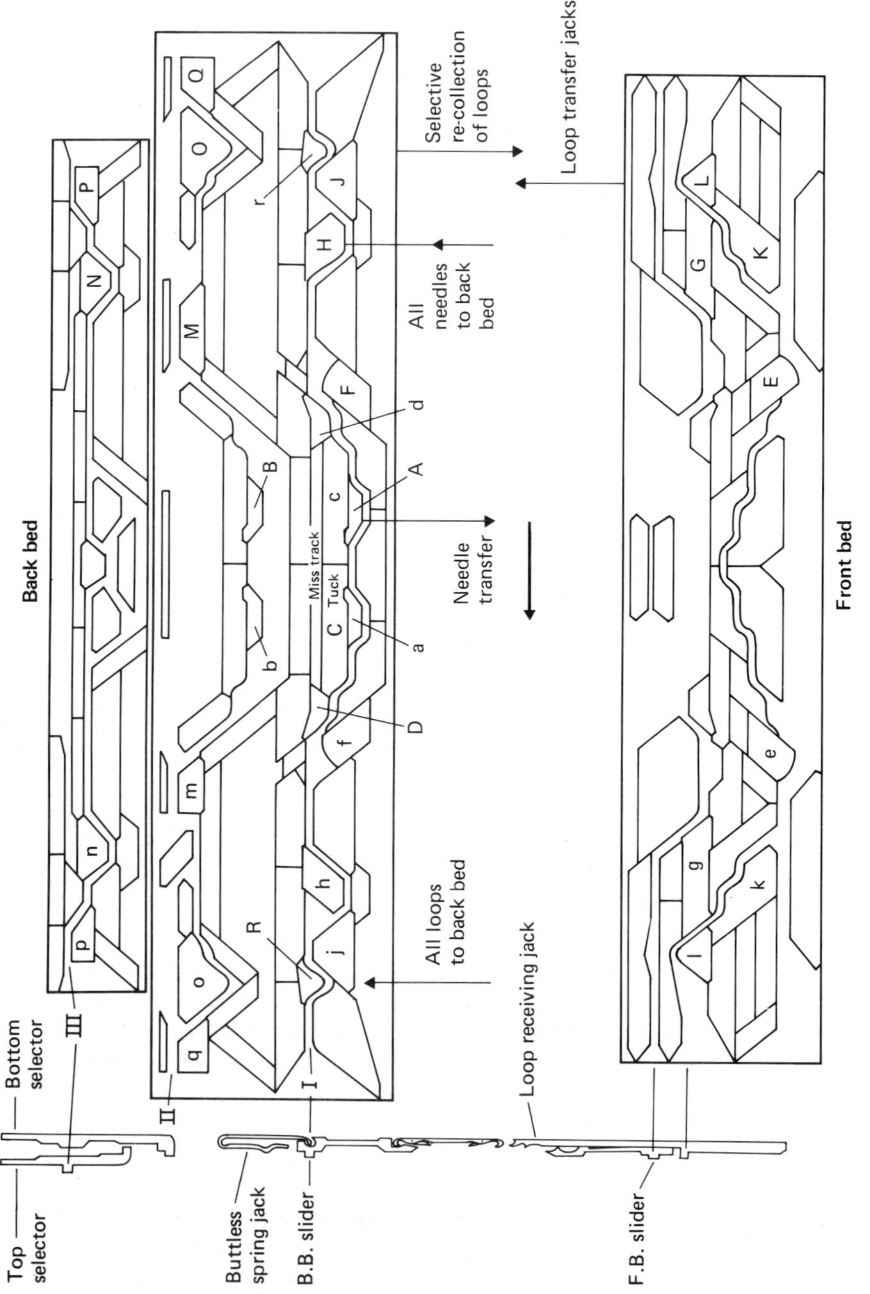

Back bed
Front bed
Top selector
Bottom selector
Buttless spring jack
B.B. slider
F.B. slider
Loop receiving jack
All loops to back bed
Needle transfer
All needles to back bed
Selective re-collection of loops
Loop transfer jacks
Miss track
Tuck

Fig. 19.8

spaces. Selective control of all these facilities is achieved by means of two-row jacquard card steels which operate onto the selectors in the back slider bed. The prism can turn to change the selection at the end of each carriage traverse.

As the cam system has a balanced arrangement for traverse in either direction, it is convenient to explain the action in only a right to left direction. Collective action of back bed sliders is produced by cams contacting their butts in track I. At the commencement of each traverse, all needles will be engaged with back bed sliders (even those which actually knitted a stitch with the front bed sliders in the previous traverse), whilst some loops may have been retained on the loop receiving jacks as shown in Fig. 19.9i; with racking of the front bed occurring at the end of the previous traverse.

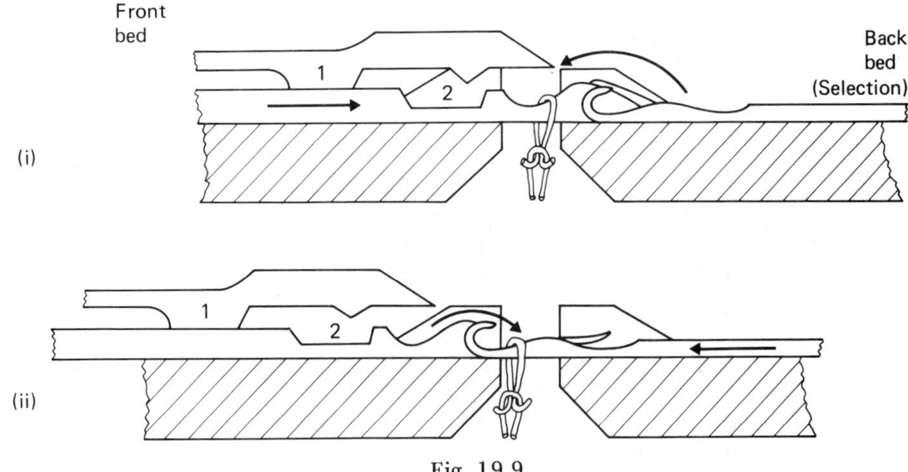

Fig. 19.9

As the back bed slider butts pass over cam 'R' in track 'I', their needles are moved out of the tricks to contact the loop receiving jacks and collect any loops from them (Fig. 19.9ii). Cam 'D', when out of action, opens the track for missing in the back bed unless the bottom selector is lifted by a solid portion in the steel so that it passes in the active track 'II' and thus lifts its slider across the gap to Cam 'C'. Cam 'C' itself may be out of action to produce collective tucking unless the slider butt is lifted by its selector, depending on the setting of the bottom selector cams in track II position. Cam 'A' is the purling cam which collectively causes back bed sliders to transfer their needles across to knit in the front bed, when 'A' is out of action, cam 'B' can perform the same function by means of bottom selectors.

Sliders holding needles retained to knit in the back bed have stitch cam 'F', whilst front bed sliders holding needles use stitch cam 'E'. During the garment sequence the stitch cams may be positioned at any one of seven settings when required and the leading stitch cams in each direction of traverse are automatically lifted out of action. After the needles have knitted in their respective slider beds, all needles in the front bed are transferred to sliders in the back bed by the action of cams 'G' and 'H' with cam 'J' causing back bed sliders to withdraw with their needles.

At this point, cams 'K' and 'L' cause the loop transfer jacks to collectively move across to take the loops from the needles as shown in Fig. 19.9i. Top selectors corresponding to unpunched sections in the steel follow an active track III over cam 'N' lifting their bottom selector butts over cam 'O' so that these cause the selected sliders to advance their needles to take their loops back from the transfer jacks, the selectors are then levelled by cams 'Q' and 'P'.

In the return traverse, cams with small case letters perform the same functions as described above.

It should also be noted that butt 'I' of the front bed slider (Fig. 19.9) fits into recess 2 of the jack so that a withdrawal of the jack can be used to withdraw the slider and an advance of the slider can cause the jack to advance thus reducing the complexity of the camming.

Figure 19.10 shows an Aran pullover knitted on a JDR flat bed machine.

Fig. 19.10. Aran crew-neck pullover knitted by T. W. Kempton on a 5-gauge JDR flat machine from 2/6's worsted count woollen spun yarn (Courtesy of the British Wool Marketing Board/Marks and Spencer).

Further Information

AGGUS, G., The presser foot: a new design tool, *Knit. Times*, (1977) 3 Jan, 24, 25, 40; 4 April, 30–2.

BUSWELL, D. A., The application of electronics to flat knitting machines, *Text. Inst. and Ind.*, (1979) 17 (10) 62–4.

COOKE, W., The programming system for the JET 2F, *Knit. Int.*, (1980) Nov., 48–50.

MICHEL, P., Electronic control, *Int. Text. Bull.*, (1980) 3, 95–6, 101–6.

MILLER, T.D.W., Jacquard effects, *Knit. Times*, (1974) 15 July, 52–57.

REICHMAN, C., Classification and guide to V-bed flat machines, *Knit. Times*, (1977) Aug., 21–30.

REICHMAN, C., The electronic flat machine, *Knit. Times*, (1980) 9 June, 35–9.

SPENCER, D. J., Flat machinery developments at ITMA, *Text. Inst. and Ind.*, (1980) 18 (3) 70–2.

TOLLKUHN, D., A new programming system for flat machines, *Knit. Int.*, (1979) Oct., 56–60.

JET 2, *Knit. Int.*, (1978) Nov., 62–4.

Knitting fashioned collars on V-type machines, *Hos. Trade Journal*, (1970) Aug., 89–92.

Pattern preparation on the ACE machine, *Knit. Int.*, (1980) June, 54–5.

Presser foot portfolio – a series of 14 articles published in *Knitting International* from Jan. 1981 to April 1982, reproduced in booklet form.

The presser foot system. Is this the shape of things to come? *Text. Monthly* (1980) Feb, 22–3; March, 23–4.

1. The development and potential of automatic glove machines, *Knit. Int.*, (1979) Dec., 41–5.
2. Stoll LNCU, *Knit. Times*, (1981) Part I, 30 March, 10–11; Part 2, 6 April, 10–11.

20

Circular Garment Length Machines

Fig. 20.1. RTR circular garment length revolving cam-box rib machine. The peg drum control unit and timing drain are clearly visible. Also note the slipping belt take-down mechanism which draws down the stationary fabric (Walter Bullwer).

Circular garment length machines are of the rib cylinder and dial type (Fig. 20.1) or the double-cylinder purl type. Although more restricted in patterning capabilities than flat machines, they may offer advantages in productivity and fineness of gauge. Many are of the revolving cam-box type whose cams, selection units and striper units are altered when their externally positioned levers are contacted as they pass the control position on the periphery of the machine (Fig. 20.2).

The peg drum control unit for the garment length programme is now tending to be replaced by an endless film loop which is driven by a horizontal perforated roller. The film is advanced by one row of holes for each feed or transfer section which passes per cam-box revolution. When no changes are required, an economizer rack-wheel operates.

On Bentley machines the Mechatape Pattern Control Unit has been introduced to replace peg drums or trick-wheels providing a virtually unlimited pat-

Fig. 20.2. Close-up of RTR Revolving Cam-box showing the Exterior Striking Levers (A = striper box; B = dial stitch cam adjustment and levers; C = cylinder stitch cam and adjustment levers; D = stationary striking lever post) (Walter Bullwer).

tern depth, faster running speeds, easier pattern preparation and more rapid pattern changes. The control unit consists of a drum whose perforations correspond to the staggered rows of punched hole positions on plastic film loop. Each row operates through the bank of horizontal levers onto the levers of a passing selection unit. The arrangement in the selection unit is fixed for a complete circuit of the machine whilst it selects onto the jack pressers arranged around the cylinder.

The fabric take-down mechanism cannot be driven directly by the machine rotation as the length of fabric knitted per machine revolution can vary in different parts of the garment sequence. The slipping-belt system is an efficient arrangement which accommodates itself to the rate of fabric production.

The take-down rollers and the belt pulley which drives them via worm gearing are attached to a pivoted lever. The rollers are driven faster than the rate of knitting so that as soon as the surplus fabric has been drawn away, they tend to climb up the fabric lifting the pivoted lever together with the belt pulley so that the belt becomes slack stopping the drive to the rollers until sufficient fabric has been knitted to lower the lever again. This self-adjustment occurs so smoothly that a consistent take-down tension is ensured.

20.1 Double-Cylinder Garment Length Machine

Spiers produced a successful machine of this type in 1930, termed the Spensa Purl machine. It has a revolving cylinder and internal sinkers and is capable of knitting garment lengths with a tubular welt and rib border. In 1956, Wildt (Mellor Bromley) replaced it with the model SPJ which has an anti-clockwise revolving cam-box, no dividing cams or internal sinkers and sliders with pointed noses for opening the latches of needles knitting in the opposite cylinder. As well as being mechanically more reliable for purl knitting, the patterning potential of this model has been improved over the years.

The main gauges are 6–12 npi with 2/16's worsted being an average count for 10-gauge. Machine diameters are now 16–20 inches (40–50 cm approx.) with six feeds, 22 inch (56 cm) (which has replaced the 11-inch diameter for infantswear) with eight feeds and a 33-inch (84 cm) diameter model with twelve feeds.

The machine produces knitwear garments for adults, children and infants with a separating course, welt, 1 × 1 or 2 × 2 rib border and a body or sleeve panel sequence. Stitch patterning may include any of the following in plain colour or striped-in colours: plain and purl; tuck rib; tuck purl; float stitch jacquard or rib jacquard.

The machine has the standard knitting element arrangement for a purl machine of one set of double-ended needles which can be controlled for knitting or transferring by either of two sets of sliders which operate from opposing tricks of the top and bottom cylinders. The tricks of the top cylinder are held in alignment with the bottom cylinder by a dogless head whilst the cam-boxes for the two cylinders are rotated in unison by means of a vertical cam-shaft and two pinions.

Figure 20.3 illustrates the basic arrangement of the elements and cams which are subject to the machine builder's modification. Each set of sliders has a single operating butt position and is controlled from a knitting cam-box. The butts are alternately arranged long and short with long butts in one cylinder opposite to short butts in the other for obtaining a 1 X 1 needle arrangement.

Controlled by a cam-box below the bottom knitting cam-box is a set of intermediate jacks having single operating butts. Each intermediate jack is supported at its base by the ledge of a spring-tailed jack placed behind

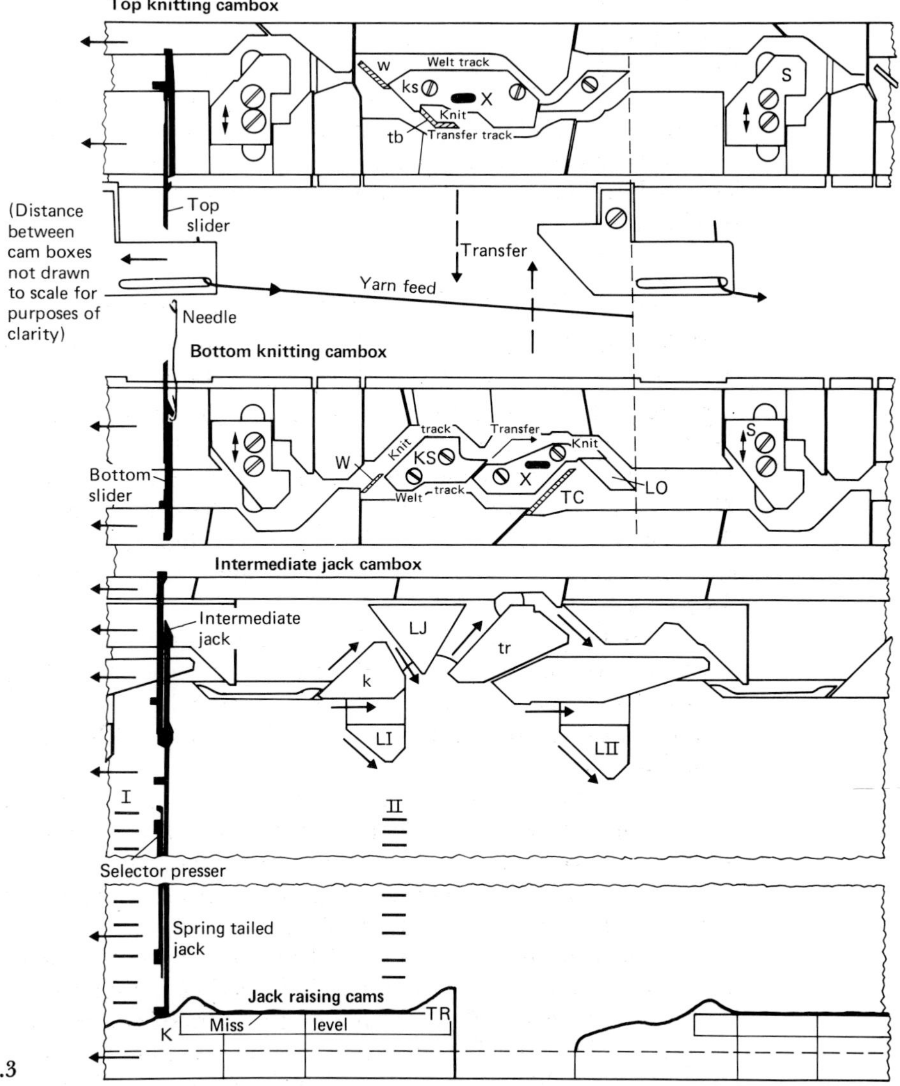

Fig. 20.3

KT-P

and below it in the same trick and which has a tail butt controlled by raising cams when not selected (the indirect selection principle was described in section 11.8). The intermediate jacks thus translate the selection into a movement causing the bottom sliders to be lifted for knitting or transferring their needles.

The presser selectors have seventy-nine butt positions corresponding to the pattern units (or presser brackets) which have batteries of seventy-nine slides. Of these, seventy-five are available for patterning and of the bottom four which are used for isolation purposes, three are controlled by the Cardomatic film with set-outs of 1 out 1 in, 2 out 2 in and cancelling out the knitting selection, whilst the other line of all-in butts can be selected from the Mechatape for cancelling all transferring.

Two full size pattern units may be provided for double selection on the bottom cylinder at each feeder. At selection I, needles are selected to remain at miss height whilst the remainder are raised to clearing (knit) height. At selection II, of those needles taken to clearing height some are selected to remain at that height, whilst the others are raised to be transferred to the sliders in the top cylinder.

Thus at selection I, the tail butts of non-selected jacks pass over the raising cam (K) to lift their intermediate jacks onto cam 'k'. As the intermediate jacks pass over 'k' they lift their bottom sliders onto the clearing cams (KS) putting them into the knitting track. The butts of non-lifted sliders will pass through in the welt (miss) track below 'KS' cams. S are the stitch cams for the knitting sliders which can be automatically changed to any one of four pre-settings of "quality" during the garment cycle.

Prior to selection II, the non-selected intermediatę jacks are lowered by cam 'LJ' and their spring-tailed jacks by cam 'LI'. These jacks therefore have their bottom butt aligned with raising cam (TR) if non-selected by selection II, they are raised over cam 'TR' and lift their intermediate jacks over cam 'tr' raising their bottom sliders to transfer their needles to the top cylinder. At this moment, the tails of sliders which are transferring needles pass across the spring-loaded cam (X) which presses down on them causing the front of the slider to pivot upwards and unhook itself from the transferred needle. Needles of jacks non-selected at I but selected at II will pass through the upper cam track at knit height. Cam LII lowers the spring-tailed jacks ready for the next double-selection sequence.

In the knitting cam-boxes, certain cams are bolt cams of the plunger type which are introduced or withdrawn out of the track as required for any cam-box revolution. When fully in action they deflect all sliders passing through, when half in action they only deflect long butt sliders and when out of action the cam-track is clear.

Cams 'W' are the welt bolt cams which guard the entrance to the welt tracks and when fully in action cause all sliders with needles to knit. Cam 'W' is in for knitting or transferring of all needles in the bottom cylinder but is out of action for selected knit miss or knit tuck stitches. In the top cylinder, there is no selection so therefore those bolt cams are used during pattern selection. Cam 'W' is employed when knitting, transferring down or receiving transferred up needles in the top cylinder, half in action it is employed for knitting or transferring on a 1 X 1 arrangement and when fully out of action needles in the top cylinder will miss. Cam 'tb' is the bolt cam for transferring needles down from the top cylinder and works in conjunction with spring loaded cam (X).

In the bottom cylinder, the bolt cam (TC) can be introduced to cause needles controlled by sliders in the welt track to be lifted to tuck. When employed in conjunction with cam 'LO' the needles are immediately lowered to miss but their latches are opened.

Figure 20.4 shows part of a purl garment knitting sequence.

Some SPJ machines are equipped with shogging facilities for the top cylinder in order to knit *true six-needle cable*. The top cylinder slider butt set-out is altered with long butts only used for the sliders controlling the cabling needles. Thirty-six of the selection-height positions are used for the cabling selection which is controlled from the Mechatape whilst the profiled shogging cams are controlled from the Cardomatic. The sequence involves five revolutions for an eight-section machine during which time a fail-safe sensing mechanism ensures that the tricks are precisely aligned, the bolt cams are correctly positioned, the needles are inoperative when necessary and that the film punching is correct.

The cable is commenced with the cabling needles knitting in the bottom cylinder and at least three needles either side knitting in the top cylinder in order to make the cable stand out from the reverse knit ground. The operations at each of the five revolutions of the cam-box are as follows:

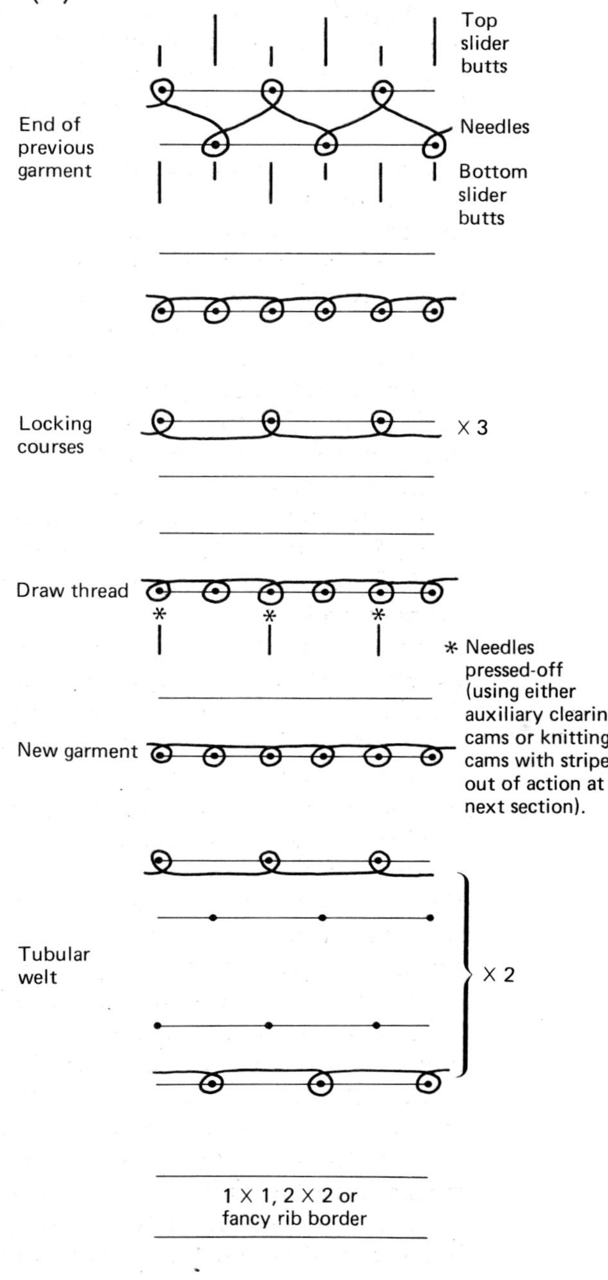

Fig. 20.4

1. The yarn is striped out at all feeders whilst non-knitting on all needles.
2. The top cylinder is shogged three needle spaces and the three cable needles opposite to empty tricks are transferred to the top cylinder.
3. The cylinder is shogged six needle spaces in the opposite direction and the remaining three cabling needles are transferred up to the top cylinder.
4. The cylinder is shogged back three needle spaces to its original position.
5. The yarn is striped in at all feeders.

On a 6½-gauge 22-inch diameter machine knitting 2/10's Shetland the cabling speed is reduced to 12 rev/min instead of the usual 18 rev/min, this is still estimated to be 50–100 per cent faster than on a flat knitting machine.[1]

20.2 RTR Garment Length Machine

This fully-automatic garment length rib machine was introduced in 1938 by Wildt (Mellor Bromley) as a replacement for their RSB model of 1936 which had no facilities for rib loop transfer. Its anti-clockwise revolving cylinder and dial cam-box has cam sections of equal size whether they are for knitting feeders or rib loop transfer. A unit set in advance of the section can select the cylinder needles for the knitting or transfer action. The original RTR has six cam sections four for knitting (2 and 3, 5 and 6) and two for transfer (1 and 4). Section 4 also has facilities via the back butt set-out of the dial needles for changing the rib either by collective dial to cylinder loop transfer or by dial needle loop press-off. Four Brinton trick-wheel units provide selection for the cylinder needles, with one for each transfer section and one for every two knitting sections, with the selection at section 2 being repeated at 3 and the selection at 5 being repeated at 6.

In Figs 20.5 and 20.6, section 4 contains the cams for selective cylinder to dial loop transfer cams R and Y and collective dial to cylinder loop transfer cams X, P and Q.

In section 1, cam T may be set to raise cylinder needles to clearing height and as there is no feed position in this section when they are lowered by cam U they will press-off their loops (for the end of the garment sequence). In a similar position at section 4 are raising and lowering cams P and Q which act as receiving cams for the collective transfer of dial loops when cam I acts on the back transfer butts of dial needles.

It soon became apparent that the machine's garment length knitting sequence of drawthread separation course, tubular welt, 1 × 1 or 2 × 2 rib border or waist, body panel section and press-off locking courses could be used for knitting jacquard, double-jersey or coarse-gauge knitwear as well as stitch-shaped underwear. A six-knitting section model, each with its own selection unit thus became available for jacquard with interchangeable transfer sections, whilst for double jersey, the dial shogging was adapted for interlock knitting. Depending upon the end-use of its model, body panels can thus be knitted in 1 × 1 rib, dial only knit, interlock, milano rib, rib jacquard or half- or full-cardigan with selective patterning in rib loop transfer, coloured stitches, miss, tuck, knit or raised cloque relief stitch. Articles which can be knitted include vests and panties, cut and sewn sweater dresses and trouser suits, jumpers and coarse gauge cardigans and sweaters.

As well as the original 13- and 15-inch diameter models other diameters have been introduced including 18, 20 and 22 inches to cater for more than one panel width (with a needle out between) high shrinkage synthetic yarns and coarse gauges. This concept has been extended to a 33-inch diameter machine where flexibility of knitting width and economy of wasted yarn is achieved by removal of non-required needles in a block thus leaving a panel of float threads.

Machine speeds now range from about 16 to 32 rpm according to diameter, machine design and type of stitch being knitted, with the number of cam sections being between eight and twelve in body diameters and up to eighteen in the 33-inch diameter model. Gauges extend to 16 npi for underwear or jerseywear down to 7 for knitwear with the coarse gauge model having gauges of 3 and 6 npi.

Dogless Drive and Dial Shogging 20.3

It is essential to hold the dial in a steady relationship with the cylinder whilst providing the facilities for dial shogging by half a needle for rib loop transfer and by one needle for changing the rib set-out from 1 × 1 to 2 × 2. In the past 'dogs' were used to hold the dial steady, these are small metal lugs which project downwards from the dial and upwards from the cylinder and thus rest against each other. However, the fabric as it leaves the needles must pass down in between these two types of dogs. To reduce damage to the fabric, 'vibrating dogs' were used on RTR machines. With this arrangement, the dial dogs (usually four or six) were each at the end of a fulcrummed lever so that as a cam on the underside of the dial revolved, they were swung away from the fixed cylinder dogs in turn. At any one time, only one steadying dog is engaged with its cylinder dog, the dial is thus not very positively held and damage can still be caused to the fabric surface.

A dogless dial arrangement is now employed with the dial being held in position by means of a central machine shaft. When dial shogging is required, a hole punched in the appropriate track of the Cardomatic film causes a lifting lever and cable to raise one of two starwheels situated at the front of the dogless head so that it is in the path of the striking levers revolving with the cam-plate. When the starwheel is struck by its striking lever it causes a heart-shaped cam attached to it to turn, moving the dogless head turning the control machine shaft and shogging the dial by a half or one needle position. The dial remains shogged until the same starwheel is struck again.

20.4 The Basic Elements and Camming Arrangement of the RTR

The geometric selection employed on this machine has been previously described (11.8). Figures 20.5 and 20.6 illustrate the arrangement of cams for a six-section machine, other models are similar. On the 33-inch diameter model, however, each presser has seventy-nine butts with a maximum of seventy-three available for patterning, one is removed to leave a gap and the remaining five are used for isolation purposes as

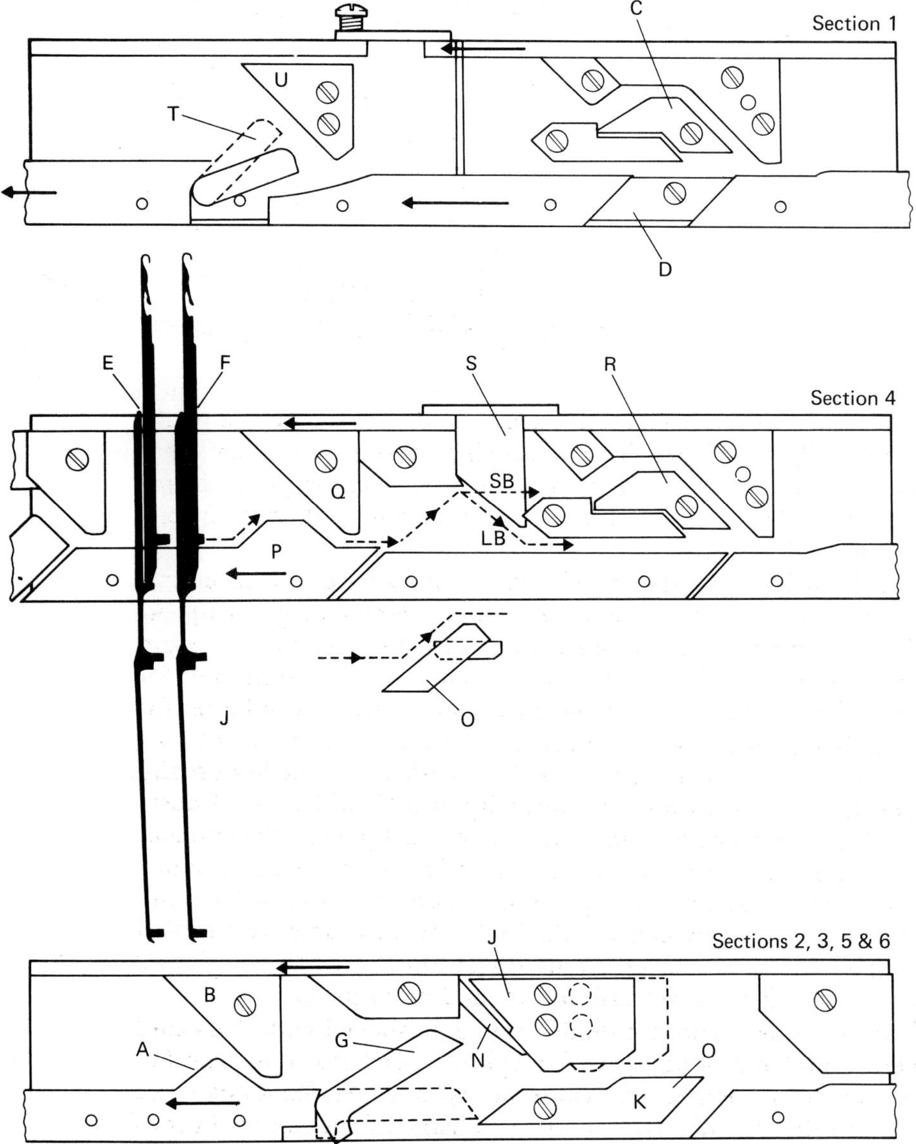

Fig. 20.5

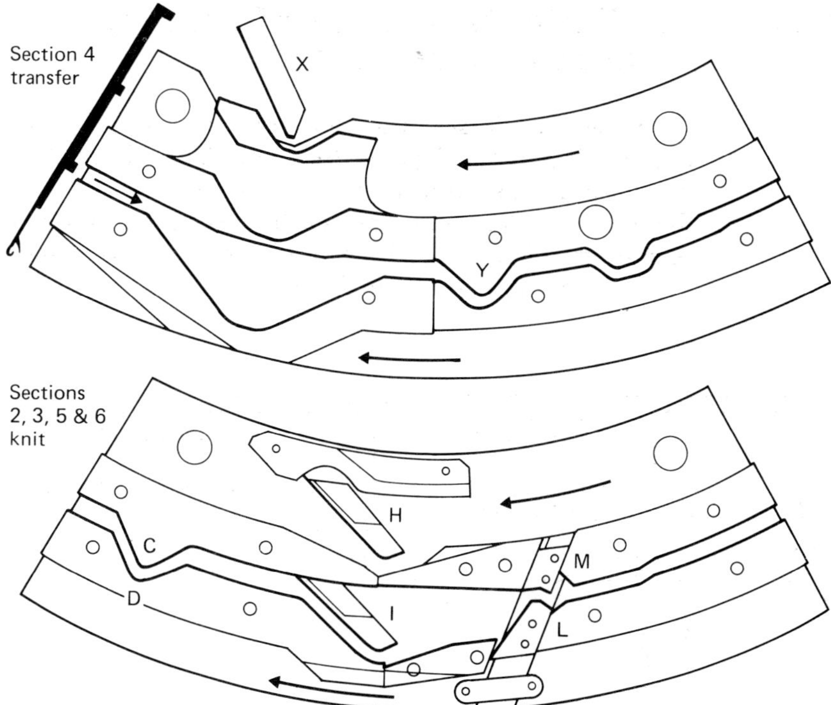

Fig. 20.6

follows: all butts on, two out of three, one out of three, odd needles only, even needles only. The dial needles are usually set-out with every third needle having a back butt for dial to cylinder transfer or press-off for achieving 2 X 2 rib. Cylinder needle butts may be set-out 1 short 2 long butt for 2 X 2 rib in the waist.

There is a jack-raising cam associated with each cylinder selection unit raising any jack butts whose pressers are not selected (Fig. 11.6). As empty needles may be required to re-start knitting, in sections 2, 3, 5 and 6, cams A and B, C and D raise and lower the cylinder and dial needles for latch opening. Cylinder cam G is a swing-clearing cam which can be set for knit or miss and is split into two sections, the top section acts on all butts, the bottom section only acts on long butts. In the dial, odd needles usually have long back knitting butts and are raised by cam H, whilst cam I raises even needles with long front knitting butts. The front part of the cylinder cam N is fixed, the back part J is shown in a solid line for delayed timing and in a dotted line for synchronized timing, its upthrow cam is K. L and M are the stitch and upthrow cams in the dial. The two cams are adjusted together and have three pre-set positions for automatic alteration during the garment sequence for the welt, rib border and body panel.

In both cam sections 1 and 4 cylinder cam R is aligned with dial cam I as the delivering and receiving cams for cylinder dial rib loop transfer. In section 4, cam O in action will cause all cylinder needle loops to be transferred to the dial for dial only knit, by means of the middle butt of the jack, if cam S is in action long butt jacks will be lowered before transfer can occur, it is used for producing a 2 × 2 rib set-out for the waist at section 4.

20.5 The Mecmor Variatex

This is a circular revolving cam-box cylinder and dial garment length machine having a knitting bed around 300 degrees of the machine's circumference. The machine has a diameter of 28 inches providing a maximum knitting width of 70 inches (180 cm). The remainder of the machine's periphery consists of a command sector containing a multi-track Mylar film loop with insertable plastic studs and a master control drum to control each knitting or transfer station as it passes. The knitting width may be reduced according to requirements thus economizing on yarn. The garment length is of constant width with fringes produced as each course is striped into and out of action for the knitting width.

Further Information

GOADBY, D., Where next with garment making machines? *Knit. Int.*, (1978) Sept., 79–82.

LANCASHIRE, J. B., Garment making interlock machines, *Hos. Trade Journal*, (1955) Nov., 62–64.

LANCASHIRE, J. B., Sweater knitting on superimposed cylinder machines, *Knit. Times*, (1973) 17 July, 49–51.

REICHMAN, C., Merits of the circular technique and guide to sweater-strip machines, *Knit. Times*, (1978) 30 Jan., 21–23, 39.

50 years of circular sweater-strip machinery, *Knit. O'wr Times Yr. Bk.*, (1968) 231–36.

RTR/MU, *Knit. Int.*, (1979) May, 110.

RTR 33, *Knit. Times*, (1973) April, 94–95.

RTC, *Knit. Int.*, (1975) May, 94–95.

RTC 8D, *Knit. Int.*, (1981) Oct., 42–43.

1. Knitting true cable on a circular purl machine, *Knit. Int.*, (1979) June, 100–101.

21

The Manufacture of Hosiery on Small Diameter Circular Machines

For centuries the production of hosiery was the main concern of the knitting industry, emphasized by the fact that the prototype machines for warp, circular, flat and full fashioned knitting were all originally conceived for this purpose. Nowadays, however, hosiery production is almost exclusively centred on the use of small-diameter circular machines.

The term 'hosiery' specifically refers to knitted coverings for the feet and legs but it may generically be applied to all types of knitted goods and fabric. Most hosiery articles are knitted with integral tubular legs and feet on small diameter circular machines. These machines have a master control which automatically times and initiates the mechanical operations and changes of stitch length necessary to produce the garment length knitting cycle although later making-up and finishing operations may still be required.

Hosiery is usually available for a range of foot sizes and in the case of staple fibre spun yarns such as cotton or worsted, different foot lengths are obtained by knitting them with differing total numbers of courses. However, hosiery knitted from continuous filament stretch nylon yarn may have an extension of 50 per cent so that a standard foot length is capable of accommodating itself to a range of foot sizes.

The following types of hosiery articles are particularly common: *Hose* which have a leg length extending above the knees; *three-quarter hose*, which are of knee length (which is approximately twice the foot length; Men's *half-hose* which are usually in two leg length ranges of between 7 and 9 inches or between 11 and 15 inches (18–23 and 28–38 cm); *Tights*, which have a body section which, although having an elasticated waist band is composed of the same knitted structure as the leg sections and designed to be worn over briefs or panties; and *panty-hose*, which are designed to replace briefs and be worn as an integral underwear and legwear garment.

Classes of Hosiery Machines 21.1

Except for the few Griswold type hand-turned machines (Fig. 4.4), all hosiery machines are of the rotating cylinder type. This arrangement offers the advantages of high revolution speeds, a simplified drive and the possibility of selectively striping-in yarn from stationary packages placed at fixed feed positions around the cylinder. The garment sequence control must, however, be linked by means of cables and rods by the shortest possible routes to the various mechanisms at the knitting points around the needle cylinder without interfering with accessibility to the machine (Fig. 21.1).

Fig. 21.1. Close-up view of the knitting head of a 4-feeder seamless hose machine (D = Dial) (Walter Bullwer).

The three types of machine in order of their increasing complexity and needle bed arrangement are single cylinder, cylinder and dial and double cylinder. Whereas ladies' seamless hose, tights and panty-hose are produced on single-cylinder machines, men's half-hose have been almost exclusively produced on double-cylinder machines.

21.2 Development of Seamless Hosiery

Circular machinery entered hosiery production inauspiciously during the nineteenth century by knitting fabric which was then cut and seamed into cheap 'leg bags' onto which heels, soles and toes were later hand or hand-frame knitted. The development of specifically designed circular hose machines followed from patents such as those of Newton in 1857 and McNary in 1860, which described how seamless heel and toe pouches could be knitted as part of the tubular leg structure by selectively taking needles out of action. Thus during the 1870s, the patents granted to Henry Griswold virtually perfected the hand-powered sock machine. This world famous small-diameter latch needle machine has a single rotating cam system (feeder) which can be oscillated for heel and toe pouch knitting and has an attachable dial needle holder for knitting the integral rib tops at the commencement of the sock.

Much of the early development of both large- and small-diameter single-cylinder machinery occurred in the U.S.A. because for many years, both in Britain and the rest of Europe, the products of these machines were considered to be inferior in quality to those knitted on bearded needle machinery or (later) latch needle machines with two needle beds. Major developments in circular hosiery machinery included:

> the introduction of power, the use of holding-down sinkers, the automatic control of mechanical changes and operations, a change of design from rotating cam-boxes to revolving cylinders and the gradual replacement of bearded needles by latch needles as their fineness of manufacture was improved.

The first powered circular hose machine was produced by Shaw in 1879 and in 1887, pickers were added to automatically knit heel and toe pouches. By 1900, most mechanical operations could be automatically controlled by the machine apart from welt turning and toe closing (Scott and Williams patented the former on their Model 'K' machine in 1915 and the latter, over forty years later, in 1967).

However, with only yarns such as rayon, silk, cotton and worsted available for knitting, bagginess (particularly around the ankle) of the circular hose caused it to be regarded as a cheap but inferior rival to the more shapely fully fashioned hose knitted on the straight bar frame, even when the former was provided with an imitation of the fashionable seam at the back of the leg. There was thus little encouragement for circular hose manufacturers to re-equip and in 1946, only a quarter of circular hose machines knitting in British factories could produce an automatic inturned welt and most machines had only a single feed. In the same year, nylon, the ideal stocking yarn became plentifully available. Not only was it cheap, strong, fine and uniform yarn, it had the major asset of being thermo-plastic so that articles knitted from it could be heat set into shapes whose form they would permanently retain, provided that the setting temperature was never exceeded during washing and wearing.

The straight bar frame was, at first, the main beneficiary of the huge demand which was unleashed for nylon stockings and this caused gauges to become progressively finer and productivity to rise dramatically, as operations became more automated and efficient and knitting speeds increased. For the circular hose machine, however, the advent of nylon meant that a combination of stitch- and heat-shaping could now produce a stocking with satisfactory leg-fitting properties provided ladies' fashion would accept it.

Fashion intervened in the late 1950's, when with skirts getting progressively shorter, the younger and then all generations, opted for the 'bare leg' look in preference to the seamed leg. Similarly, in 1966, the advent of the 'mini skirt' brought the welted tops of seamless stockings into view and the conversion from stockings to more comfortable and less noticeable self-supporting panty-hose commenced.

For the seamless hosiery industry, the period from 1956 has been one of dramatic and revolutionary changes in knitting, making-up, dyeing and finishing, marketing and fashion. Although hiccups are produced by swings of fashion, the following trends are noticeable:

- the simplification of styles, knitting machines and make-up
- increasing automation of operations, handling and transportation
- higher knitting speeds and/or numbers of feeders (in twenty years there was a five-fold increase in productivity per knitting machine)
- increasingly fierce competition and drastic reductions in the prices of stockings and panty-hose which have transformed the overall image from one of fashionable luxury and glamour to that of a mass-produced commodity article.

Amongst specific developments occurring during this period were the following: The slow and expensive reciprocated and linked-closed toe was replaced on a twin feed machine in 1956, by all-circular knitted courses of spliced fabric, which was later cut and seam shaped into a toe. In the same year, the Reymes Cole patent described how the reciprocated heel might also be replaced, in this case, by part-circular knitted splicing courses on selected heel section needles.

In 1961, the four-feed Billi Zodiac machine popularized the tube stocking with a patch heel by knitting a stocking in 2 minutes 10 seconds compared with the 12 minutes taken to knit a stocking with a reciprocated heel and toe on a single-feed machine in 1953. Speeds and numbers of feeds were then gradually increased with a six-feed machine running at 210 rpm in 1963 and by 1971, a twelve-feed machine running at 260 rpm.

Demands for higher quality and more versatility led to a reduction in the number of feeds so that by the 1979 ITMA exhibition, there were eight-feed machines running at over 400 rpm, high-speed four-feed machines running at over 1000 rpm and much slower four-feed machines knitting reciprocated heels. Machines are now capable of producing 1000 dozen pairs of panty-hose per month and there are indications that even this productivity may be doubled in the future. At the same time, machine manning has been improved so that one man may now run 60—80 machines whilst 5 kilogram yarn packages can reduce yarn package replacement to 5-day intervals. The reduced number of mechanical parts mean less mechanical attention is necessary.

One rather unsuccessful development has been the closed toe which was almost immediately replaced by the automatic toe sewing equipment used in making-up the panty-hose. In seamless hosiery finishing equipment, the dyeboarder, introduced in the early 1960s, replaced, in a single cycle, the separate operations of scouring, pre-boarding, dyeing and post-boarding, thus reducing labour content as well as drawthreads caused during handling.

Ladder-Resist Structures 21.3

The fine smooth filaments in ladies' hosiery structures make them very susceptible to laddering. It is therefore important to reduce this tendency without impairing either the appearance or the extension and recovery properties of the structure too greatly.[1] Any stitch which reduces the likelihood of one loop being withdrawn through another (for example tight knitting) or which spreads the tension (knitting on alternate needles) will produce ladder-resist properties from the end knitted last whereas an alternate knit and miss or knit and tuck structure will be ladder-proof from the end knitted first.

Float-plated fishnet (9.8) is one popular structure, all needles take the fine yarn (for example 15 denier) whereas alternate – or in the case of patterned fishnet – selected needles rise high enough to take the thicker yarn (for example 30 denier). The two yarns are knitted in a plating relationship. This structure is popular for use in stockings to produce an anti-ladder band to prevent ladders from running down from the top of the leg.

1 × 1 cross tuck is another ladder-resist structure, alternate needles tuck at alternate courses. Micromesh is similar although less effective because it contains less tuck stitches. In this structure, the tuck stitches spiral around the leg reducing light reflectance and presenting an attractive appearance. There is usually a course of all-knitting in between each course of tuck stitches, the notation (Fig. 21.2) shows the popular 3 × 1 micromesh.

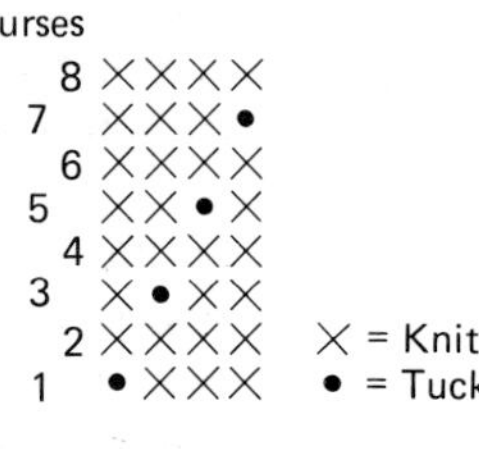

Fig. 21.2

Development of the Double-Cylinder Machine 21.4

The first double-cylinder machine was the model XL patented by Stretton and Johnson of Leicester in 1900, employing double-headed latch needles patented by Townsend in 1849 and internally-controlled sinkers patented by Spiers and Grieves in 1895. Using dividing cams for disengaging the sliders from the needles, it eliminated the need to knit the rib tops on a separate machine and then to transfer the fabric on a quill ring to the needles of another machine, in order to knit the leg. In 1912, the machine was converted to a revolving cylinder type and in 1920 the first of over 100,000 Komet machines was produced. From that year onwards a wide range of double-cylinder machines have been developed from high-speed plain models, to highly complex machines with extensive patterning capabilities.[2]

Amongst the range of patterning effects available are the following: three-feed jacquard, links-links, embroidery plating and terry.

21.5 The Slider Butt Set-Out

If a broad rib set-out is used whose repeat is not an exact factor of the total cylinder tricks, the extra non-standard panels must be carefully arranged to balance at the heel centre (back of the leg) so that they are less noticeable. It may also be necessary for the foot bottom to be slightly less or slightly more than half the cylinder tricks in order to balance the rib panels on either side of the foot.

As previously mentioned (7.15), sliders have a needle knitting butt towards their head and a needle transfer butt towards their tail. Generally, the knitting butts are *long* in the instep half (which are raised out of action during reciprocation) and *short* in the heel half in both cylinders.

When arranging the transfer butts it is necessary to understand that the *transfer bolt cams are gradually introduced in stages so that the longest butts will be used for the first transfer actions*, whilst the shortest butts will be unaffected until the cam is fully in action for the last required transfer.

The 1 × 1 rib top arrangement is obtained by transferring up alternate needles using alternate *long* butts in the bottom cylinder. When a broad rib leg is required, a second up-transfer may be necessary using *short* butts on the bottom sliders. In a minimum movement only the necessary needles will be transferred up whereas with a links-links movement, all needles are transferred up. The broad rib wales are achieved by transferring down using long top cylinder butts, medium butts are used to transfer down for the heel and later short butts are used to transfer down the instep needles still in the top, in order to finish by knitting the toe in plain.

21.6 Timing and Control of Mechanical Changes on Circular Hosiery Machines

Although the technical details of specific machines may vary, the essential principles of the mechanical timing and control of changes on circular hosiery machines is as described below.

The changes are timed by the links of a forward racking chain which also control the racking of a forward-turning control shaft to which are attached the cam-drums and wheels which initiate the major mechanical machine changes (Fig. 21.3). The starting link is marked and one complete racking of the chain together with one complete revolution of the control shaft is necessary to produce the length knitting sequence for each hosiery article.

The timing chain consists of square ring metal links, hooked one onto the next for easy rearrangement, which pass as an endless loop over a sprocket wheel which turns freely on the cam shaft and is racked by means of a clawker. Plain links are used purely for providing time between major changes whereas movement links have projections or studs to initiate mechanical changes usually by causing the cam shaft to be racked.

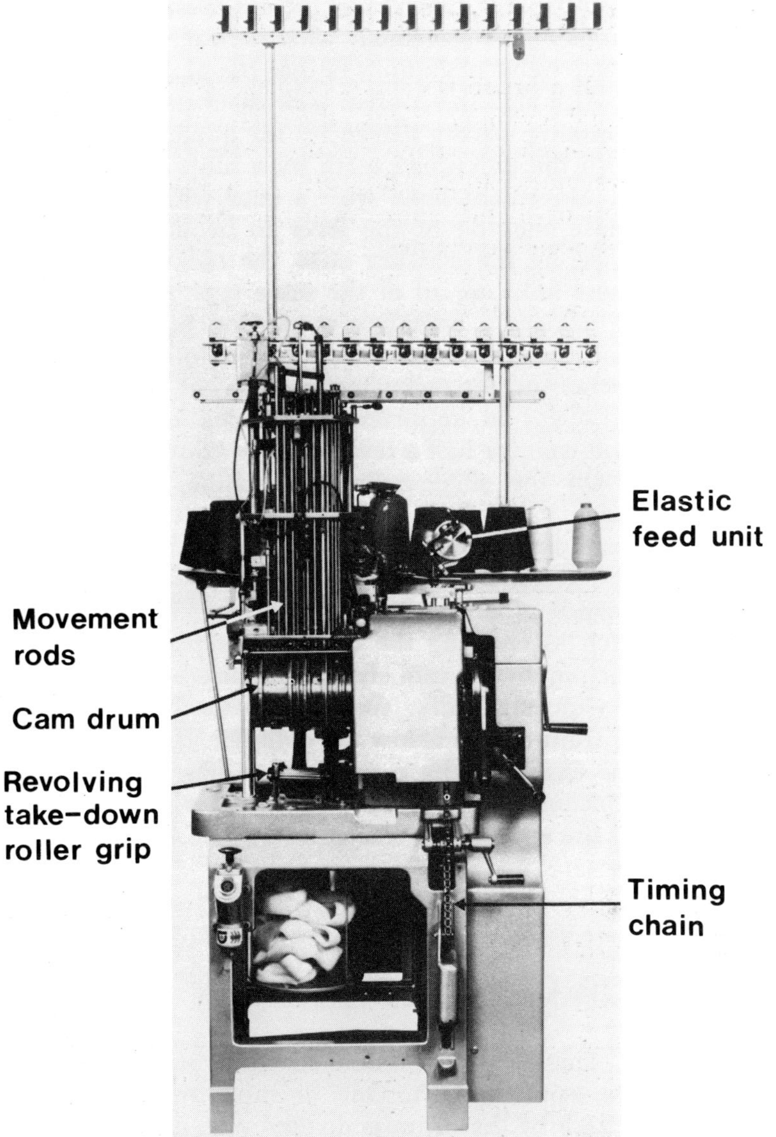

Fig. 21.3. Double cylinder half-hose machine (Bentley).

Typically, chains on double-cylinder machines are racked forwards by half a link and on single-cylinder machines by one third of a link at a time. On the former, chain saver links may be employed. These have pins which project across and engage with a cut-away section of the circumference of an economizer wheel placed alongside the chain rackwheel turning the wheel so that its toothed circumference section moves under the rackwheel clawker. Thus as the clawker moves, it causes the wheel to turn and fails to engage with the chain rackwheel for forty-six racks (equivalent to twenty-three links) until the cut-away section is reached when the clawker drops into engagement with the rackwheel teeth again. There must be at least twelve plain links before the next pin link.

Although the control rackwheel clawker continuously reciprocates horizontally, usually driven by the quadrant, it is held away from engagement with the rackwheel teeth by a bluff lever which is positioned underneath it. Movement links with a stud which projects upwards from one limb cause the toe of the lever to be lifted allowing the lever to pivot and lowering the clawker onto the rackwheel. On double-cylinder machines these links are all of the same type and twenty-four are required in order to achieve a complete revolution of the cam-shaft. A rotary cam action can cause the clawker to make a long rack followed by three short movements and the rackwheel may be cut with long and short teeth. A long rack produces an important mechanical change, a short rack may introduce a bolt cam for half a revolution to contact long element butts.

On the single-cylinder machine, movement links may be of three heights: low links which introduce the clawker for the shortest time, for example for introducing the heel pickers; medium height links for yarn and speed changes; and high links which introduce the clawker earlier and keep it in action for the longest rack for complicated mechanical changes such as entering the heel. The versatile control of drum racking reduces the number of cam changes required.

Conventionally, the intermittently-racked control shaft is positioned in front of and below the cylinder. However, on some Billi Matec machines, for example, the control drum has been positioned vertically below and concentric with the needle cylinder in order to simplify the transmission of the mechanical changes.

21.7 The Cam Drums

These are large-diameter drums which are attached to and revolve with the control shaft. One or more may be employed on a machine. The length of the drum is divided into a number of tracks each corresponding to a lever or rod which scans its section and is contacted and moved by any long narrow cams screwed into position in its track. The cams have a tapered leading and trailing edge to transmit a smooth movement to the machine.

Amongst functions which may be controlled from the tracks are: speed changes, knitting cam changes, pickers, the verge, take-down splicing and pattern drum racking. On seamless hose machines, a number of drums may be joined together by the shaft, these may be used for speed control, quality control (stitch control in various parts of the hose) selector control and feed changes.

Adjustment of Loop Length 21.8

On hosiery machines without positive feed, the distance between the top of the needle head at knock-over and the loop-supporting belly of the sinker will determine the length of loop which is drawn. On single-cylinder machines this distance is altered by raising or lowering the sinker position, whereas on double-cylinder machines it is achieved by adjusting the stitch cams and thus the needle height.

In single-cylinder machines, the sinkers are in a bed fixed to the head of the needle cylinder so that any raising or lowering of the cylinder will affect the loop length. Levers scanning tracks on the control drum operate through adjustable set screws to raise or lower the cylinder. Separate tracks on the drum may be responsible for adjustment of the loop length for the waste courses, toe, heel, panel, ankle and foot, graduated stiffening, etc. Graduated stiffening is operated from a rotary eccentric cam which is racked independently of the control shaft and allows the cylinder to be gradually lowered during the knitting of the calf so that loops gradually become smaller and the leg tube is narrowed.

Production of Heels and Toes 21.9

Three-dimensional turned heel and toe pouches (Fig. 21.4) are knitted in plain so that, in the case of double-cylinder machines, the heel section needles must be transferred down to knit from the bottom cylinder. A spring take-up holds the surplus yarn as the needles traverse towards the feed on the return oscillation, whilst a pouch tension equalizer ensures that the pouch fabric is held down on the needle stems. The pouch is usually knitted in single feed so that the other feeds are taken out of

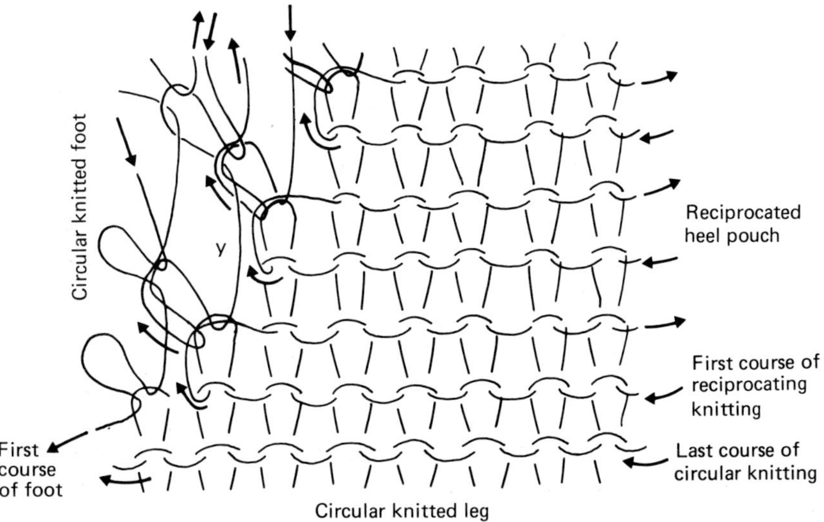

Fig. 21.4

action but an additional splicing yarn is striped in for reinforcement. The shape and extent of the spliced section may extend beyond the pouch. Reciprocation of the cylinder is produced by the drive at this point being taken from the forward and backward oscillation of the quadrant. As the changeover is mechanically complex oscillatory knitting takes place at approximately two-thirds of the speed of circular knitting. In socks with reciprocated heels and toes in single feed, over a third of the courses will be in oscillatory knitting and may require over 60 per cent of the machine's operating time thus making this operation time-consuming and expensive.

During the oscillatory knitting of the pouch, the remaining needles (approximately half) are raised into a high inactive cam-track by the introduction of a cam which operates only on the long knitting butts allocated specifically to them so that they retain their loops from the last course of circular knitting. During narrowing, the leading needle in each direction of oscillation is lifted up to join the other needles in the inactive track by the action of one of two side pickers which are alternately in action according to the direction of oscillation. These pickers operate throughout the oscillatory motion. During widening, a down picker is introduced which lowers two needles at a time thus cancelling the effect of the up picker and putting an extra needle into action.

Each of the side pickers has an L-shaped recess and they are positioned facing outwards at the approach into the cam system so that in either direction of oscillation the knitting butt of the leading heel needle or slider is caught by the recess. The continued movement of the cylinder causes the picker to be moved backwards and as its movement is restricted, it pivots upwards in its holder to place the butt into the high inactive track, the spring attached to the picker then pulls it down again. The down picker, when brought into action moves down from the inactive track bringing two butts down with it each time. It has a recess on each side of its undersurface so that two butts can be accommodated in each direction of oscillation. Lonati use only one picker which is turned over to act as a down picker during widening. Some of the Bentley machines knit a twin feed heel and toe, during narrowing two needles at a time are lifted, whereas during widening this up picking continues with only one needle at a time whilst three needles are lowered into action at each side. With this method, a twin feed heel or toe with acceptable sutures can be knitted in 22 seconds.

In the production of a standard small heel, half the needles knit in the heel section with narrowing occurring at each side until only one-third of the needles are left in action. As each needle is lifted out of action the yarn is automatically wrapped over it in the form of a tuck stitch which makes the heel join stronger. Widening then takes place until all the heel section needles are brought back into operation when circular knitting recommences. A toe pouch is knitted in a similar manner, if the heel section needles are used again the seam will be on top of the toe (as is the case in most socks) but if the instep needles are used instead, a reverse toe is knitted with its seam being underneath (usually preferable in hose).

Many modifications to the basic pouch sequence have been employed, particularly on hose, in order to improve the fit and appearance. In the Y heel, extra fabric is knitted in the centre of the inverted Y suture-line by widening for twelve courses after narrowing to the one-third needles then narrowing back to the one-third needles before commencing normal widening. The gusset toe is a reverse toe knitted in a similar manner except that when the one-third needles are left, a group are re-introduced collectively after which single-needle narrowing occurs for twelve courses and then the rest of the needles previously collectively widened are lifted out of action and the normal widening picker is introduced. In the ballet toe, all the needles are brought collectively into action for a few courses of circular knitting after the needles have been narrowed to one-third, all except the one-third are then collectively raised out of action as normal widening commences.

In the conventional closing of toes during making-up, an individual loop of the instep is joined to an individual loop of the toe pouch by stitching on a linking machine. This is, however, an expensive relatively slow and skilled operation. In Rosso linking the fabric to be joined is guided by a conveyor guide onto dial points and is seamed from opposite sides but the join is not exactly on one course nor is there an individual loop-to-loop join. In the case of the run-down toe, the toe fabric is knitted in normal circular knitting (possibly with 40-denier instead of 15-denier yarn), it is later seamed from under the foot in an upward curve towards the top of the toe in a single or two-needle three-thread seam. Automatic toe seaming units can automatically turn the hose inside out (by means of compressed air), position the hose and then convey it to a seaming head, after seaming the hose is turned back to its correct side, the complete cycle only occupies a few seconds.

Many novel methods have been devised for knitting closed toes or one-piece panty-hose but have achieved very limited success in competition with modern automated seaming and handling techniques which have considerably reduced the labour content and time required. The main disadvantages of these knitting methods have been one or more of the following: the necessity of a complex adaptation of the knitting machine and its knitting sequence with reduced production speeds and poor comfort, wearing properties and appearance of the resultant article.

Two automatic toe-closing methods which have achieved some acceptance are the Scott and Williams method and the Dura Vent method which is jointly patented by the Bentley and Billi companies. Both methods employ the similar technique of knitting a form of welt in circular courses at the toe with the mid-courses of this fabric being constricted during knitting whilst holding the last knitted loops. A small rosette of fabric or minute open vent is thus formed which is smoothed down and 'popped through' to the inside so that during wear it fits in the archway between the big and second toes. Both methods have been adapted to the normal toe knitted last sequence and can be produced on either hose or half-hose.

In the Scott and Williams method, the drive to the dial (hose) or top cylinder (half-hose) is disconnected for between 200 degrees and one complete revolution half-way through the circular toe fabric knitting sequence so that a twist is imparted to the fabric at that point. In the Dura Vent method, the constriction is obtained by taking needles in the bottom cylinder to a low position whilst the cylinder revolves so that the yarn, under tension, wraps around the fabric a number of times underneath the top cylinder or dial. To ensure that the run-off tab is inside the half-hose, the article may be withdrawn upwards through the top cylinder.

21.10 Automatic Separation

The automatic separation of half-hose and socks was introduced on Bentley double-cylinder machines in 1967. Pressing-off occurs at the point where the draw-thread would normally be introduced when the needles are engaged with bottom cylinder sliders. The first few needles are raised to non-knit height in advance of the loop-forming position of the main feed so that the yarn from the previous article passes across them under tension and is severed as the sinkers move radially inwards and kink it with their throats. At the main feed, the yarn for the new article is taken into every needle hook in the bottom cylinder. To ensure that all hooks are open, the needles have extended latches which are opened by the extended pointed ends of the sliders which receive a rocking motion from cams at the transfer position. During this revolution, alternate needles are transferred to the top cylinder where they knit one course, whilst the needles in the bottom cylinder remain in the non-knit track. For the next course, the rib needles enter the welt track and the plain needles are cleared to knit at the main feed for the commencement of the welt.

The Bentley–Solis arrangement[3] employs vacuum suction complemented by a mechanical system to withdraw the separated article from the knitting zone. For reversed take-up, an inner plastic delivery tube then sucks the article upwards through the top cylinder where it drops onto a hinged trap exit door which automatically opens to allow it to fall into a collection container. The revolving take-down arrangement consists of two independently-operated sleeves positioned one with the other at the lower end of the top cylinder with the inner sleeve protruding below the outer. The fabric is alternately held and pushed downwards by the sleeves which are lifted and dropped once per revolution by cam action. The inner plastic delivery tube is slightly shorter than the inner sleeve so that it can suck the article upwards and away from the sleeves. The system has not been incorporated into any form of downstream collection as in some stocking plants because of the need to keep the many styles separated and the fact that the force of the vacuum necessary to convey a half-hose is much greater than for a stocking.

Panty-Hose 21.11

The concept of the modern panty-hose has been derived from earlier designs of tights seamed together from two slit legs and a fabric gusset or from panty-hose produced by seaming two hose legs to the bottom of the legs of a pair of panties. The cost of handling and seaming, combined with the static price of the finished article, has encouraged alternative methods of production in the form of one piece panty-hose knitted on the machine or the more successful, at present, automated panty-hose seaming techniques.

The various one piece panty-hose methods normally involve using a hose machine of 3¾ to 4 inches (9.5–10 cm) diameter with approximately 400 needles and knitting a modified tube of fabric. It is necessary to obtain a width of 4–5 inches (20–22 cm) for the ankles and a lateral stretch of 16–20 inches (40–50 cm) for the body which may be achieved with textured yarn. The main problems have involved the time and the cost of the knitting sequence, fabric breakdown under tension at the leg joins and insufficient extension of fabric at the thighs with an excess of fabric in the crotch section.

One of the first commercially-produced panty-hose was patented by Pretty Polly in 1968, it consisted of a tube started at one toe and leg with a wider body section in the centre and terminating with the other leg and toe. A slit is made down the wales on one side of the body section which forms the opening for the elasticated waist section whereas the other side of the body section becomes the under leg-crotch section as the tube bends into a banana shape. Billi (Matec) modified this concept to achieve a better shape by introducing part course sections on the crotch side of the body section combined with graduated sections of multiple tucks on a 1 × 1 knit tuck basis which decrease in number towards the waist opening which is a rectangle with a knitted-in elastic waist band. With this technique a 'complete' panty-hose can be knitted on a Zodiac eight-feed machine in approximately 3 minutes.

Other methods have involved reciprocation in the body section and in the case of the Samo Panty-Sol one half of the waist band and panty is knitted in each of the two cylinders of a special double-cylinder machine, afterwards one leg is knitted in each cylinder with normal circular knitting. Other methods have involved slitting and rejoining either on the machine or later during seaming.

Further Information

CANZLER, R., Developments in seamless hose manufacture (IFKS paper), *Hos. Trade Journal*, (1961) Nov., 118–21.

GOADBY, D. R., Lonati introduce micro-electronics, *Knit. Int.*, (1979) Nov., 54–56.

GOADBY, D. R., Conti-panty, *Knit. Int.*, (1980) Oct., 54.

GOADBY, D. R., Single-cylinder sock machines survey, *Knit. Int.*, (1980) Nov., 61–77.

GOADBY, D. R., The Brematex Zero, *Knit. Int.*, (1980) Nov., 51–52.

GOADBY, D. R., The Bentley H54, *Knit. Int.*, (1980) Dec., 52–53.
GOADBY, D. R., The development of one-piece panty-hose and future prospects, *Knit. Int.*, (1982) April, 44–49.
HURD, J. C. H. and WOOD, G., Sock knitting types compared, *Knit. Int.*, (1980) July, 51–55.
IMBODEN, W. H., Elements for producing panty-hose in one, *Knit. Times*, (1970) 22 Nov., 52–53.
INNES, R., Billi range of seamless machines, *Knit. Times*, (1973) April, 208–15.
JOHNSON, M. R., Concepts of future one-piece tights and briefs, *Knit. Int.*, (1974) June, 52–53.
KIRKLAND, J., Milestones in the stockings and tights revolution, *Knit. Times*, (1978) Oct., 36–37.
LANCASHIRE, J. B., Focus on seam-free stockings, *Text. Recorder*, (1961) Aug., 50–51.
LANCASHIRE, J. B., Circular hosiery machines, *Hos. Trade Journal*, (1969) Jan., 85–6.
MILLINGTON, J., Projecting a technological tights scenario, *Knit. Int.*, (1978) June, 39–40.
MORLUNGHI, R., The two-minute stocking story, *Hos. Times*, (1962) Jan., 25, 27, 81.
NEGRI, E., New methods for producing panty-hose, *Knit. Int.*, (1974) Jan., 67–69.
NEGRI, E., Complete: one-piece panty-hose, *Knit. Times*, (1974) April, 28–33.
PEEL, R., Aspects of closed-toe stocking production, *Hos. Trade Journal*, (1969) Oct., 125–28.
REICHMAN, C., The closed toe for sure, *Knit. O'wr Times*, (1969) 26 May, 31–33.
WOOD, G., Recent developments in knitted footwear, *Text. Inst. and Ind.*, (1968) July, 184–85.
WRIGHT, K., The decline in world tights machines (IFKT paper), *Knit. Int.*, (1980) Dec., 63; *Knit. Times*, (1980) 8 Dec., 49.

Textbooks

ELEY, A. W., *Stockings*, (1953) Hos. Trade Journal.
WIGNALL, H., *Hosiery Technology*, (1968) Nat. Knit. O'wr Ass., New York.

1. LANCASHIRE, J. B., Ladder-resist stitches, *Hos. Trade Journal*, (1962) July, 108–110.
2. HURD. J. C. H., Developments in double-cylinder knitting machinery, *Knit. Times Yr. Bk.*, (1974) 92–98.
   LANCASHIRE, J. B., Knee-length stockings on double-cylinder machines, *Knit. Times* (1970) 28 Sept., 52–53.
3. Bentley automatic separation, *Hos. Trade Journal*, (1967) March, 98–100.
   Reverse take-up for Komets, *Knit. Int.*, (1977) June, 119.

22

Aspects of Knitting Science

Knitted Loop Shape and Loop Length Control 22.1

Weft knitted structures, especially those used for hosiery, knitwear and underwear have unique properties of form-fitting and elastic recovery based on the ability of knitted loops to change shape when subjected to tension. Unfortunately dimensional changes can also occur during production or washing and wearing when problems of shrinkage and size variation can cause customer dissatisfaction and increase production costs.

During the 1950s, H.A.T.R.A. (the Hosiery and Allied Trades Research Association) investigated the problems of knitted garment size variation and created a much clearer understanding of the influence of stitch length on knitted fabric dimensions which led both to further research in this field and to the practical application of this knowledge in production. Doyle emphasized the relationship between stitch length and fabric dimensions when, in plotting stitch length against stitch density for a wide range of dry, relaxed, plain weft knitted structures, he showed that, irrespective of yarn type or count and of machine type or gauge, the points lay close to a general curve. H.A.T.R.A. was thus able to establish three basic laws governing the behaviour of knitted structure:

1. *Loop length is the fundamental unit of weft knitted structure.*
2. *Loop shape determines the dimensions of the fabric and this shape depends upon the yarn used and the treatment which the fabric has received.*
3. *The relationship between loop shape and loop length may be expressed in the form of simple equations.*

The acceptance of these rules has encouraged the introduction of yarn-length measuring and yarn-feed control devices, accelerated improvements in shrink-resist and fabric relaxation treatment and provided a basis for the theory of knitted fabric geometry.

Loop Length 22.2

Loop lengths exist in course lengths and it is these which influence fabric dimensions and other properties including weight. Variations in course length between one garment and another can produce size variations, whilst course length variations within structures (particularly when using continuous filament yarns) can produce horizontal barriness and impair the appearance of the fabric.

With the exacting demands of modern knitting technology the need to maintain a constant loop length at one feeder for long periods of time, between one feeder and another on the same machine and between different machines knitting the same structure, has become of major importance in the control of fabric quality. This requirement has encouraged the development of yarn feed measuring and control devices.

Under normal circumstances about 15 per cent of the yarn drawn into a newly-formed loop is actually robbed from already-formed neighbouring loops and although a machine may be set to knit a specific stitch length, fluctuations in yarn or machine variables can affect yarn surface friction or tension and ultimately influence yarn input tension at the knitting point so that the ratio of 'robbed back' to newly-drawn yarn changes, thus altering the knitted loop size.

Course length measurements can be obtained by unroving the yarn from a knitted fabric but this is time consuming, destructive of material and only provides the information after knitting. Two types of meter may be employed to monitor at a feeder during knitting – yarn length counters and yarn speed meters – which may be considered to be respectively analogous to mileometers and speedometers in cars.

The *yarn length counter* is simplest in construction providing a reading of the amount of yarn fed during a certain time period. It is particularly suitable for attaching to a moving feeder on a revolving circular cam-box machine. After a specific number of machine revolutions, the machine is stopped to enable the yarn length reading to be taken which is then divided by the number of knitting machine revolutions to obtain the course length for that feeder.

The *yarn speed meter* may require calibrating and provides a direct reading of the rate of yarn feed, usually in metres per minute, whilst the machine is running. The meter may be hand held and can be used on revolving cylinder machines without the need to stop it. To obtain the course length it is necessary to divide the reading by the number of knitting machine revolutions per minute.

Monitoring every feed of a large-diameter multi-feeder is time consuming and provides no guarantee that the course length will remain constant after measuring. *Positive feed devices are designed to overcome this problem by positively supplying yarn at the correct rate under low tension to the knitting point* instead of allowing the latch needles or loop-forming sinkers to draw loops whose length could be affected by varying yarn input tension. H.A.T.R.A. introduced the nip roller positive-feed device during the early 1960s consisting of a lower roller driven by gearing at a speed directly proportional to the machine drive with an upper, freely-running, weighted roller turning in contact with the yarn surface completing the nip. Devices of this type tended to have complicated drive linkages, provided a complex yarn path and required careful adjustment of each device if uniformity of course length was required at a number of feeders.

For the above reasons, the cheaper, simpler and more adaptable tape positive-feed system developed by Isaac Rosen proved to be more acceptable. A continuous tape, driven from the machine drive by a single pulley, encircles the machine above the feeders and provides identical and constant rate of feed for any yarn threaded through the nip it forms with a free-running wheel at each feed position (Figs 13.1, 22.1). On clockwise revolving machines, the yarn passes from its package into the right hand side of the tape/wheel nip and on leaving the nip on the left passes down through a detector to the feeder. The faster the tape speed relative to the machine speed the faster the rate of yarn feed and the longer the resultant course length. This is altered by adjusting the scrolled segments of the drive pulley to produce a larger or smaller working diameter.

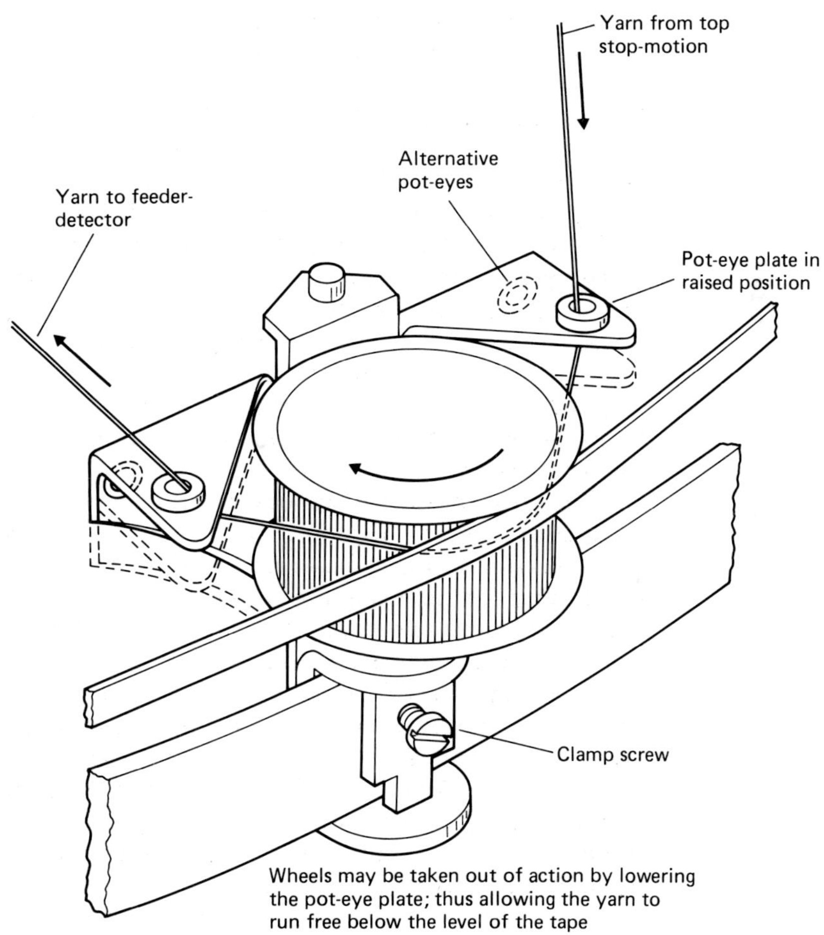

Fig. 22.1

Punto di roma, milano rib and double pique require much longer course lengths at the feeders where most needles knit than at the other feeders. For structures of this type, up to four tiers of tapes, each driven at a different speed by a different diameter drive pulley, can be accommodated. Facilities for yarn disengagement are provided and sometimes the yarn is guided around the wheel in a coil to prevent slippage.

Tape positive feed is generally only suitable for structures having a maximum of four different course lengths requiring a constant course length at each feeder, but some small area jacquards and diagonal twills can be produced with it. Large area jacquards and similar structures whose individual needle selection causes large fluctuations in feed rate requirements, both between feeders and at the same feeder from one machine revolution to the next, cannot be supplied from positive-feed devices.

The other type of yarn furnishing device is the *storage feeder* (Fig. 17.1) which supplies yarn at a *uniform tension rather than at a uniform rate of feed* and is thus suitable for a wide range of yarn feed. It may also be used for supplying patterning and weft insertion yarns on some warp knitting machines. Yarn is withdrawn from the package and wound tangentially as equally-spaced coils on a 'store'. Demand at the knitting point causes axial withdrawal of yarn from wraps at the opposite end of the store.

On one design the spool rotates to wrap the yarn at the top of the store and a light-weight circular plastic comb ensures controlled take-off tension from the base of the store. An inclined disc resting over the wraps senses when they have reached a minimum and switches on the electric motor for the spool drive, it later switches the motor drive off when the required maximum number of wraps have been produced. On another design, the yarn input is through the centre of a stationary spool with a rotating disc winding the yarn on at the base of the store, the coils being moved upwards by reciprocation of the spool surface. Yarn stop motions and indicator lights are fitted to most units.

A further development is the combination of positive feed and storage feed with a choice of mode available by means of a clutch. With this design, even for positive feed, the tape, which has punched holes, never contacts the yarn; instead it is used to drive a studded wheel and thus to wind the yarn onto the store.

Storage feeders provide a store of yarn as the machine stops after a yarn breakage so it is possible to simplify the yarn path and eliminate the top stop detectors. It is also possible to place packages on supply creels separate from the machine because the storage feeds can compensate for a variation in yarn tension produced by a difference in the angle of the yarn path.

Structures produced with constant and identical course lengths may have a differing or impaired appearance if the allocation of the course length between the knitting elements, and therefore between the components of the stitch structure, varies. Factors which can cause a variation include element timing, element gauge in relation to machine gauge and the depth of knock-over of one needle bed compared to the other. The effect can be magnified or minimized by the type of structure and yarn, the machine gauge and the type of relaxation and finishing treatment.

Warp Let-Off 22.3

Loop length is equally as important in warp knitting where, in the form of run-in, it is determined by the warp let-off which is either negative or positive. In the first arrangement, tension on the warp causes it to be pulled from the beam as it turns against a controlled friction. It is self-compensating releasing warp on demand. An overall increase of run-in is obtained by increasing the speed of the fabric take-up rollers which increases the tension. In the second arrangement, the warp beams are positively driven to deliver a pre-determined run-in. The surface speed of the beam is monitored so that as the beam circumference decreases the beam drive speed is increased to maintain a uniform rate of let-off. The arrangement must also be capable of catering for fluctuating let-off requirements in patterned fabrics. Tension fluctuations which occur during the knitting cycle are compensated by spring-loaded tension bars over which each warp sheet passes in its path to its guide bar.

On multi-guide bar Raschel and tricot lace machines, the spot beams which supply the partly-threaded pattern guide bars are completely negatively turned. These light-weight beams turn easily and have a three-spoked star attached to one end on which small weights are placed and positioned in order to ensure balanced rotation. At the other end, weights attached to a collar provide controlled friction.

An intermittent negative-brake-type let-off may be employed on slow speed machines (below 600 cpm) which are knitting fabrics from full-sized beams. The friction of a belt brake restrains the beam rotation until the warp tension is sufficient to cause the tension bar to be lowered which in turn lifts the belt allowing the beam to turn freely.

On high-speed Raschel and tricot machines, the light-weight tension rails are completely separate and can oscillate rapidly at high knitting speeds. Each warp beam shaft has a separate positive drive and warp speed to machine speed adjustment arrangement (Fig. 22.2). A machine

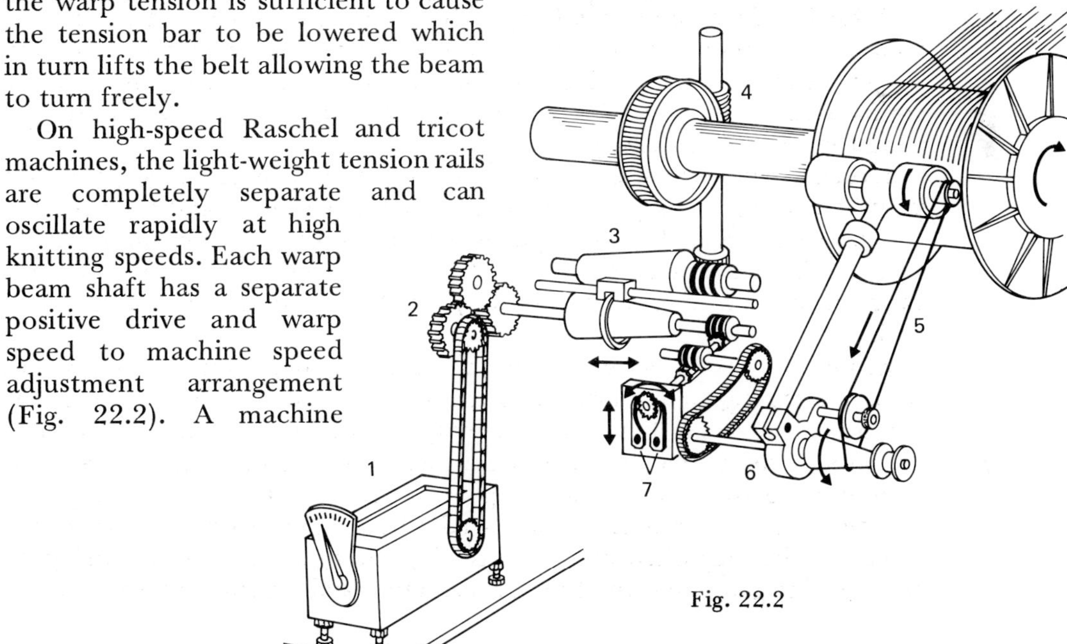

Fig. 22.2

driven 'nut' and a warp driven 'bolt' are 'fast screwed' together, so that when the bolt turns at a different speed it moves sideways moving a steel ring sideways as it transmits the drive between two opposed cones (3). The slowest beam speed is achieved with the ring on the smallest circumference of the lower (driver) cone transmitting to the largest circumference of the higher (driven) cone. As the warp beam decreases the ring is gradually progressed towards the largest circumference of the lower cone. The upper cone shaft drives a vertical shaft through bevel gearing and its worm (4) then drives the worm wheel of the warp beam shaft.

The ring can adjust in either direction controlled by a two-way rack-wheel and dependent upon one of two side racking pawls on a slide (7) which is moved by the 'bolt'. The bolt spindle shaft (6) is driven by a belt (5), from a metering roller driven by contact with the warp of the beam surface. The 'nut' shaft is driven at a constant machine speed by the lower cone shaft.

A change gear system (1) positioned between the main machine drive shaft and the lower cone shaft enables the gearing to be altered to produce different run-in rates. A clutch arrangement can be employed to alter warp drive speed if required for patterning purposes or to disconnect the drive in interrupted warp let-off sequences.

Karl Mayer have now developed a computer control unit which, from fabric parameters inputted via a keyboard, automatically regulates the warp let-off of the machine. The computer receives the machine data as pulses from encoder emitters on the warp beam shafts and the main machine shaft. Control data computed by the system is then transmitted as pulses to the individual warp beams to drive series wound d.c. motors and worm gearing.[1]

22.4 Weft Knitted Fabric Relaxation and Shrinkage

Changes of dimension after knitting can create major problems in garments and fabrics especially those produced from hydrophilic fibres such as wool and cotton. Articles knitted from synthetic thermoplastic fibres such as nylon and polyester can be heat set to a shape or dimensions which are retained unless the setting conditions are exceeded during washing and wear.

In the case of wool fibres, this effect can be magnified by felting shrinkage. When untreated wool fibres are subjected to mechanical action in the presence of moisture, the elasticity and unidirectional scale structure of the fibres causes them to migrate and interlock into a progressively closer entanglement. Eventually the density of the felted fabric restricts further fibre movement but long before this point the fabric properties, including appearance, will have been severely impaired. Fortunately, it is now possible to achieve a shrink (felting)-resist finish in wool yarns during spinning so that, as with cotton yarns, little yarn shrinkage will occur during washing and wearing.

Knitted fabrics tend to change in width and length when taken from the machine, even without yarn shrinkage, indicating a change of loop shape rather than of loop length. During knitting, the loop structure is subjected to tension from sources such as the take-down mechanism and in the case of fabric machines the width stretcher board of approximately 15–25 grams per needle. Unless the structure is allowed to relax from its strained and distorted state at some time during manufacture, the more favourable conditions for fabric relaxation provided during washing and wearing will result in a change of dimensions leading to customer dissatisfaction.

In theory, knitted loops move towards a three-dimensional configuration of minimum energy as the strains caused during production are allowed to be dissipated so that eventually, like all mechanical structures, a knitted fabric will reach a stable state of equilibrium with its surroundings and exhibit no further relaxation shrinkage. Unfortunately there are a number of states which may be achieved by different relaxation conditions such as dry relaxation, steaming, static soaking and washing with agitation, centrifuging and tumble drying. These states are difficult to identify, define and reproduce as friction and the mechanical properties of the fibres, yarn, and structure can create high internal restrictive forces and thus inhibit recovery. However, agitation of the knitted structure whilst it is freely immersed in water appears to provide the most suitable condition for relaxation to take place as it tends to overcome the frictional restraints imposed by the intermeshing of the structure.

A satisfactory relaxation technique applied during the finishing of cotton fabric in continuous length form is the compacting or compressive shrinkage technique. The fabric is passed between two sets of roller nips with the feed rollers turning at a faster rate than the withdrawal rollers so that the courses are pushed towards each other and the fabric is positively encouraged to shrink in length. This technique can create difficulties with interlock fabric which tends to buckle outwards three-dimensionally to produce ripples on the surface known technically as 'orange peel'.

Knitted Fabric Geometry 22.5

Early concepts of fabric geometry were based on models having maximum cover so that adjacent loops touched each other with a constant ratio of stitch length to yarn diameter. Doyle initiated a new approach to fabric geometry by deriving his concepts from an interpretation of experimental data. He showed that for a range of dry, relaxed, plain weft knitted fabrics stitch density could be obtained using the formula $S = ks/l^2$, where S is stitch density, l is loop length and ks is a constant independent of yarn and machine variables.

Munden took this work a stage further in 1959 with experimental results that indicated that the linear dimensions as well as the stitch density for a wide range of thoroughly relaxed, plain knitted worsted yarn fabrics were uniquely determined by their stitch length and that all other variables influence dimensions only by changing this variable.

He suggested that in a relaxed condition, the dimensions of a plain knitted fabric are given by the formulae:

$$\text{cpi} = \frac{kc}{l},$$

$$\text{wpi} = \frac{kw}{l},$$

$$S = \frac{ks}{l^2},$$

$$\frac{\text{cpi}}{\text{wpi}} = \frac{kc}{kw} = R$$

where R = loop shape factor

His k values for plain worsted fabrics in dry and wet relaxed states were supplemented later by values proposed by Knapton for a 'fully-relaxed' state which required agitation of the fabric. To achieve this state it was suggested that the fabrics be wetted out for 24 hours in water at 40°C, briefly hydro-extracted to remove excess water and tumble dried for 1 hour at 70°C.

The k values for the three states were as follows:

	Dry Relaxed	Wet Relaxed	Fully Relaxed
ks	19.0	21.6	23.1
kc	5.0	5.3	5.5
kw	3.8	4.1	4.2
R	1.3	1.3	1.3

It is now thus possible to pre-determine the fully relaxed dimensions of a shrink-resist (felting-resistant) treated plain knitted wool fabric before knitting. Similar experimental work has been carried out on the relaxed dimensions of rib, interlock and some double-jersey structures as well as some structures knitted from cotton yarns. It is suggested that for complex structures the loop should be replaced by the structural knit cell as the smallest repeating unit of the structure.

Most theoretical models of knitted loops are based on an adaptation of a geometrical shape known as an 'elastica'. This is the shape which a slim body such as a uniform elastic rod will assume when buckled by the action of forces.

Munden has suggested that in a relaxed configuration, so as to achieve minimum bending of the yarn, the widest part of the loop coincides with the narrowest part of the feet of the loop above it. The theory is, however, complicated by such factors as the three-dimensional shape of loop structures, the jamming of loops, yarn friction and the pre-setting of loop shapes. *Fabric tightness or compactness when expressed as a factor is the ratio between the yarn diameter and its loop length in the structure.* It is not an absolute value and does not refer to the area occupied by the loop, so the state of relaxation of the structure does not affect the ratio. It is thus possible to have two fabrics with the same compactness, one with a small loop length and fine yarn count and the other with a large loop length and heavy yarn count. Compactness is an important fabric property which influences durability, drape, handle, strength, abrasion resistance, dimensional stability and, in the case of wool, felting behaviour.

Tightness Factor 22.6

Munden first suggested the use of a factor to indicate the relative tightness or looseness of plain weft knitted structure to be used in a similar manner to that of the cover factor in the weaving industry. Originally termed the cover factor but now referred to as the tightness factor (TF), he defined it as the ratio of the area covered by the yarn in one loop to the area occupied by that loop.

The total area covered by yarn is: $S \times l \times d$, if l is loop length in mm and d is yarn diameter in mm (assuming the yarn to have a circular cross-section and the fabric to be theoretically flat and not three-dimensional).

Introducing the expression $S = ks/l$, the area covering 1 cm^2 of fabric is:

$$\frac{ks \times l \times d}{l^2 \times 100} = \frac{ks \times d}{100\,l}.$$

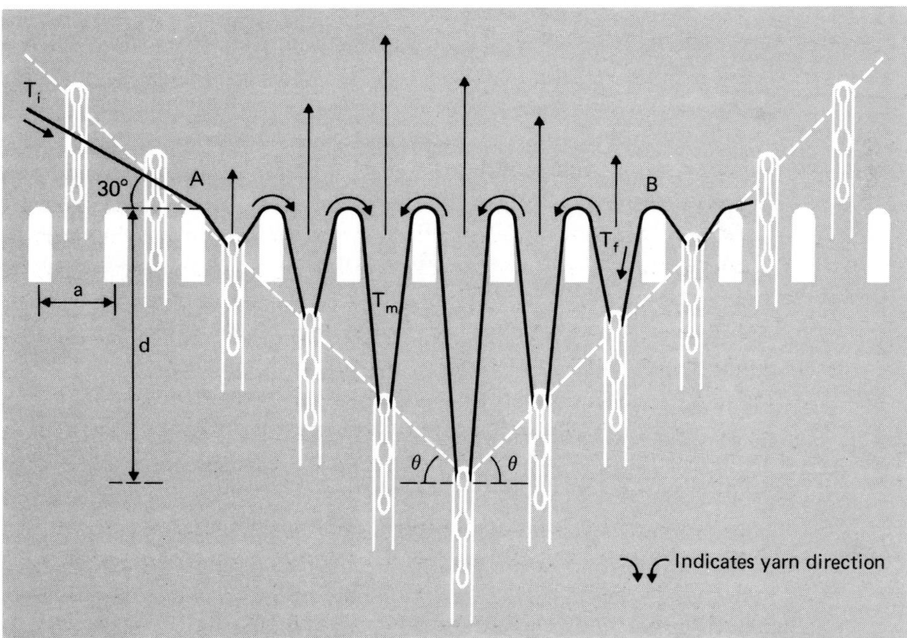

Fig. 22.3. Model of weft-knitted loop formation indicating the mechanism of 'Robbing-Back' and the build-up in yarn tensions acting on the needles.

A correction for the four areas of each stitch covered by two thicknesses of yarn is then necessary together with an expression of yarn diameter in terms of linear density.

When comparing structures of the same type and yarn in similar states of relaxation it is possible to use the simplified formula;

$$\text{TF}, K = \sqrt{\frac{\text{tex}}{l}} \quad \text{in SI units}$$

For most plain fabrics knitted from worsted yarn the TF ranges between 1.4 and 1.5.

The TF in Imperial Units is:

$$K = \frac{1}{l\sqrt{N}}$$

where N is the worsted count and l the loop length in inches.

22.7 Robbing Back

Knapton and Munden suggested the phenomenon of 'robbing back' to be the reason why the measured loop length in a knitted structure is smaller than the theoretical loop length when calculated from the depth of the stitch cam setting as well as the reason for fluctuations in yarn input tension producing large variations in loop length. As the needles descend the stitch cam, the tension required to pull yarn from the package increases rapidly and *it becomes easier to rob back yarn in the opposite direction from the already formed loops of needles further back which are now beginning to rise from their lowest (knock-over) position.*

With reference to Fig. 21.4 it was suggested that under the dynamic conditions of loop formation yarn tension increases according to Amonton's Law of Friction as it passes over the knitting elements from point A, robbing back occurs from needles on the other side of the stitch cam and the lowest point of tension is reached at B. The tension on the yarn is determined by the yarn/metal friction and the number of angles of yarn wrap, thus a two-fold increase in yarn/metal friction can cause a six-fold increase in maximum knitting tension. As robbing back reduces tensions, flat-bottom cams would obviously be undesirable and a cam angle-shape of 60 degrees was preferable to one of 45 degrees because the number of yarn/metal contacts was reduced. It was further proposed that smoothly-designed non-linear camming with a pressure angle of greater than 50 degrees could provide smooth acceleration of needles for much higher knitting speeds. Camming of this type has been incorporated into some simple high-speed single-jersey machines but it requires adaptation for more complex and alterable cam arrangements.

Needle Bounce and High-Speed Knitting 22.8

On circular knitting machines, higher productivity involves faster needle movements as a result of an increase of knitting feeds and machine rotational speed. On fabric machines the machine revolutions per minute have almost doubled and the number of feeders have increased twelve-fold in the past 25 years, so that as many as 4000 courses per minute can be knitted on some plain machines, whilst in some high-speed seamless hose machines the tangential speed of the needles can be more than 5 metres per second. To achieve this productivity, research and development has been necessary into machine, cam and needle design. The horizontal cam track sections have been reduced to a minimum, whilst needle hooks and latches have been reduced in size whenever possible, in order to reduce the extent of the needle movement between the clearing and knock-over points.

'*Needle bounce*' is a major problem in high speed knitting. This *is caused by the needle butt being suddenly checked by the impact of hitting the upper surface of the up-throw cam after it has accelerated away from the lowest point of the stitch cam.* At this moment, inertia at the needle head may cause it to vibrate so violently that it fractures, also the up-throw cam becomes pitted in this section. Needles passing through in the miss track are particularly affected, as their butts contact the lowest part of the stitch cam only, and at a sharp angle which accelerates them downwards very rapidly. To reduce this effect, a separate cam is often used to guide these butts at a more gradual angle. The smoother profiles of non-linear camming help to reduce needle bounce and a braking effect is achieved on the butts by keeping the gap between the stitch and up-throw cams to a minimum. For this reason on some hose machines the up-throw cam is horizontally adjustable in conjunction with the vertically-adjustable stitch cam.

The Reutlingen Institute of Technology has carried out a considerable amount of research into this problem and as a result, a new design of latch needle with a meander-shape stem, a low smooth profile and a shorter hook is now being manufactured by Groz-Beckert for high-speed circular machines. The meander shape assists in the dissipation of the impact shock before it reaches the needle head whose shape improves resistance to stress as does the low profile, whilst the gently-shaped latch is designed to open more slowly and fully onto a cushioned position produced by a double saw cut.

The Cadratex Unit[2] 22.9

During take-down, a fabric tube changes its shape from a circular section at the needle bed level to a flattened form at the take-down rollers, whilst to reduce creasing at this point, it is also spread outwards by a former placed inside the fabric tube. Unfortunately, the conventional system creates fabric distortion such as the bowing of striped designs and as the take-down tension is not equal around the needle bed, a higher take-down tension is necessary to prevent tuck stitches occurring where tension is low during knock-over. The high take-down tension leads to a greater incidence of cuts and holes in the fabric as well as wear on the knitting elements, problems when knitting weaker yarns and a greater length-wise deformation and consequent shrinkage after knitting.

The Cadratex unit, now being commercially fitted to machines, has been developed by ITF Maille of France. It replaces the conventional spreader with two complementary elements one inside and the other outside the fabric tube which cause the tube to adopt a square cross-section and then a gradually flatter configuration but of constant circumference right into the nip of the take-down rollers. The distance from any needle to the take-down rollers is the same so that wale and course density remains constant around the fabric tube and throughout its length whilst enabling a lower uniform take-down tension to be employed. During adjustment, the outer guide frame is maintained in an exact relationship with the inner frame.

Experiments by ITF Maille have demonstrated the possibility of employing a second pair of take-down rollers above the first so that the unit may be placed 12 inches (30 cm) higher than for a conventional stretcher board, thus enabling the fabric roll diameter to be increased from 19 to 32 inches (47 to 82 cm) increasing the potential fabric length in the roll by over 350 per cent.

Further Information

BLACKMAN, B. F. and HOPKINSON, J. C., The application and impact of HATRA positive feed, *Journal Text. Inst.*, (1962) 53 (a), 590–609.

BOOTH, J. E., *Textile Maths, Vol III*, (1975) Textile Inst. pp. 487, 499.

DANGEL, S. C., Cam action in weft knitting, *Knit. O'wr Times Yr. Bk.*, (1968) 278–83.

GAN, L. R., Dimensional stability of wool knitwear, *Hos. Trade Journal*, (1968) Jan., 109–114; (1969) Nov., 117–120; (1969) Dec., 89–92.

GAN, L. R. and BROWN, J. M., Determination of dimensional changes of wool-containing knitted fabrics, *Text. Inst. and Ind.*, (1968) July, 187–91.

GOADBY, D. R., IRO positive feed, *Knit. Int.*, (1977) Sept., 62–4.

GOADBY, D. R., IRO storage feed, *Knit. Int.*, (1977) Oct., 50–2.

GROSBERG, P., *Contributions of Science to the Development of the Textile Industry*, (1975) Textile Inst., 179–89.

HURT, F. N., Stabilisation of knitted fabrics, *Text. Inst. and Ind.*, (1966) Aug., 230–33.

KNAPTON, J. J. F., Possible future developments in high-speed knitting, *Knit. Times Yr. Bk.*, (1972) 87–91.

KNAPTON, J. J. F., The economic benefits of high-speed weft knitting, *Text. Inst. and Ind.*, (1975) 13 (4), 100–102.

KNAPTON, J. J. F., How to knit spun yarns efficiently, *Knit. Times Yr. Bk.*, (1977) 111–15.

LAWSON, J., The art of knitting, *Knit. O'wr Times Yr. Bk.*, (1968) 172–77.

MUNDEN, D. L., *HATRA Research Report, No. 9,* (1959) April.
MUNDEN, D. L., The dimensional properties of plain knit fabrics, *Knit. O'wr Times Yr. Bk.*, (1968) 266–71, 480.
MUNDEN, D. L., Geometry of knitted structures, *Textile Inst. Review of Text.* Progress, (1963) Vol. 14, 250–56; (1967) Vol. 17, 266–69.
RICHARDSON, G. A., Mechanical shrinkage control, *Text Inst. and Ind.,* (1977) **15** (2), 55–59.
SHELTON, W. E. A., Yarn furnishing devices. A survey and review of current practice, *Text. Inst. and Ind.,* (1973) **11** (6), 150–53.
WHEATLEY, B., Knitting outerwear fabrics on tricot and Raschel machines (part 14), *Knit. Times,* (1973) Oct., 108–16.
Knitting properties of wool yarns and fabrics, *Wool Science Review,* (1973) Nov. (47), 2–13 (part 1); (1974) March (**48**), 33–41 (part 2).
The geometry and properties of all-wool weft knitted structures, *Wool Science Review,* (1971) Jan. (**40**), 14–27 (part 1); (1971) March (**41**), 14–27 (part 2); (1971) (**42**), 42–60 (part 3).
Positively speaking Isaac Rosen to John Gibbon, *Hos. Trade Journal,* (1972) June, 90–93.

1. *Kettenwirk Praxis* (English Translation) (1981) 3, 1–2.
2. COOKE, W. D., *Knit. Int.*, (1980) Aug., 94–95.
   Technology Week, *Knit. Times,* (1981) 1 June, 8–9.

23

Basic Warp Knitting Principles

23.1 Construction of Warp Knitted Fabrics

In a warp knitted structure, all ends supplied from the same warp sheet normally have identical lapping movements because each is lapped by a guide attached to the same guide bar (Fig. 23.1). Beams supply the warp sheets in parallel form to the guide bars whose pattern control determines the timing and configuration of the lapping movements in the form of overlaps and underlaps. The needles intermesh the new overlaps through the old overlaps to form the intermeshed loop structure.

23.2 The Warp Beams

To ensure uniform conditions of warp feed and tension, the ends are supplied from flanged beams attached to shafts which turn to unwind the warp sheet in parallel formation. For convenience of handling, a number of beams may be attached to a beam shaft to achieve the full width of warp sheet, for example, a warp sheet 84 inches (213 cm) wide might be supplied from a full width beam, two beams each 42 inches (106 cm) wide, or four beams each 21 inches (53 cm) wide.

23.3 The Guide Bar

Each guide bar is normally supplied with a warp sheet from its own beam shaft to suit its requirements of threading and rate of warp feed for its particular lapping movement. Occasionally, two partly-threaded guide bars may be supplied from the same full-threaded beam provided they make lapping movements of the same extent to each other whilst moving in opposite directions. The minimum number of guide bars and warp sheets for commercially acceptable structures is usually two.

23.4 The Guides

Warp guides are thin metal plates drilled with a hole in their lower end through which a warp end may be threaded if required, they are held together at their upper end in a metal lead and are spaced in it to the

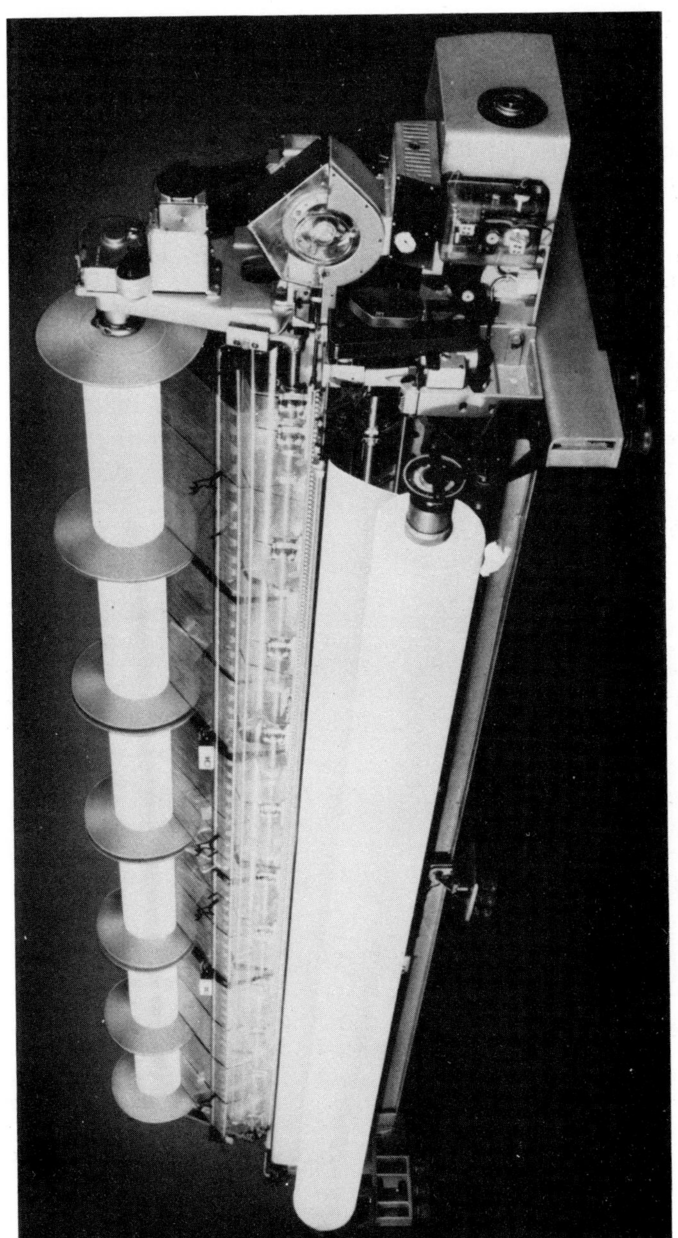

Fig. 23.1. Two guide bar compound needle tricot machine (Karl Mayer).

same gauge as the machine. The leads in turn are attached to a guide bar so that the guides hang down from it with each one occupying a position at rest midway between two adjacent needles, in this position the warp thread cannot be received by the needles and it will merely produce a straight vertical float. *The needles only receive the warp thread in their hooks if the guide bar overlaps across their hooks*, or across the side remote from their hooks when the guide bar underlaps. *All guides in a conventional guide bar produce an identical lapping movement at the same time* and therefore have identical requirements of warp, tension and rate of feed, although the threads may differ in colour or composition from each other.

23.5 Single Needle Bar Structures

In the following description, for purposes of simplicity, it is assumed that only one needle bar is being employed. Essentially the principles remain the same for double needle bar machines which are described later in the book.

When the needle bar is observed in plan view from above, it can be seen that *the guides of a guide bar are required to execute a compound lapping movement composed of two separately derived motions* (Figs 23.2, 23.3).

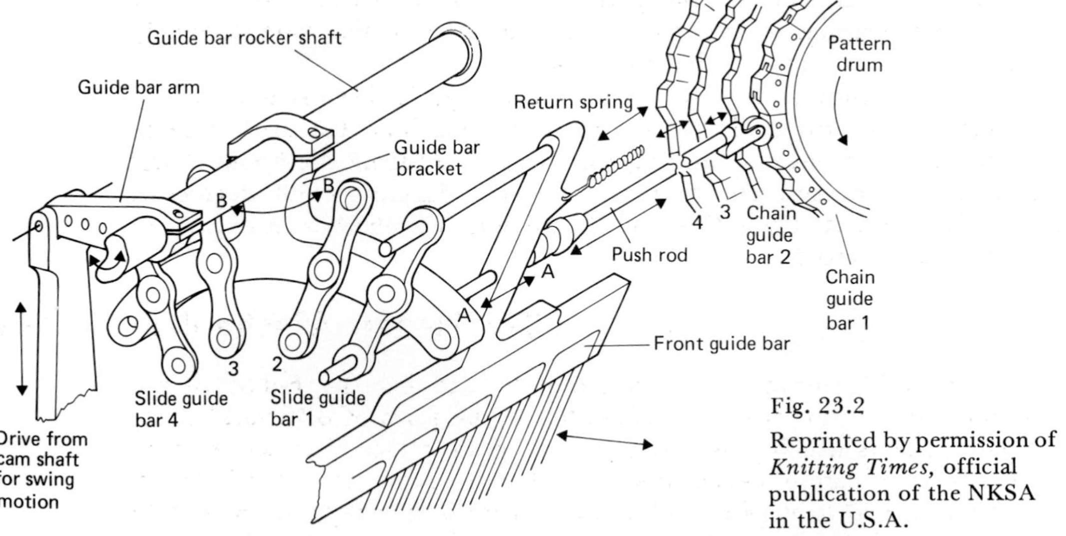

Fig. 23.2
Reprinted by permission of *Knitting Times*, official publication of the NKSA in the U.S.A.

A swinging motion (A—A) *and a shogging movement* (B—B) *act at right angles to each other in order for their threads to form overlap and underlap paths which are joined together around the needles.*

The swinging motion is in an arc from the front of the machine to the hook side and a later return swing. It occurs between adjacent needles and is a *fixed, collective and automatic action for all the guide bars as they pivot on a common rocker-shaft.* It is derived in a similar manner to the needle and other element bar motions from the main cam-shaft and is adapted via levers, pivots and linkages. The two swinging movements produce the two side limbs when combined with the overlap shog. When the overlap is omitted the guides swing idly between adjacent needles and achieve no useful purpose.

On some machines such as jacquard Raschels and some multi-guide bar and double needle bar machines it is more convenient to swing the needle bar and trickplate between the guide bars after they have shogged for the overlap and underlap as this considerably reduces the complexity of movement of the heavy guide bar assembly to only that necessary for shogging and thus increases the speed and efficiency of the machine.

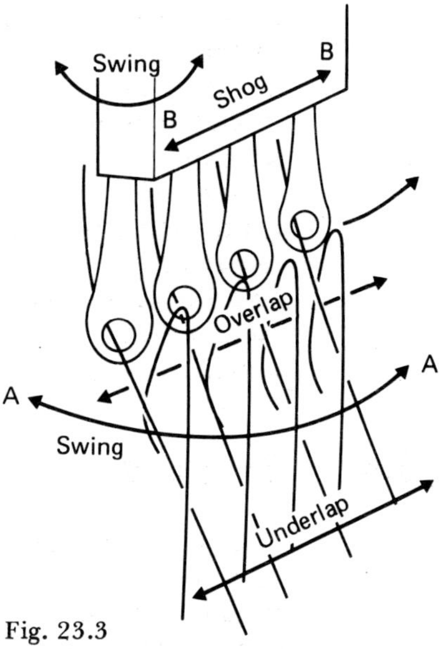

Fig. 23.3

The sideways shogging movement which occurs parallel to the needle bar produces the underlaps and overlaps. The occurrence, timing, direction and extent of each shog is separately controlled for each guide bar by its pattern chain links or pattern wheel attached to a horizontal pattern shaft driven from the main cam-shaft but set at right angles to it at one end of the machine. The guide bars are shogged independently sideways parallel to each other along linear bearings which support them in the swinging frame assembly which is keyed to the guide bar rocker-shaft.

A shogging movement can occur when the guides have swung clear of the needle heads on the back or front of the machine. On the hook side it will produce an overlap and on the side remote from the hooks it will produce an underlap. The timing of the shog during the 360 degrees of the main cam-shaft revolution will thus determine whether an overlap or underlap is produced.

The Pattern Mechanism 23.6

The shogging movement is initiated by varying the radius of the continuously-turning pattern shaft either in the form of different heights of pattern links which pass over a pattern drum attached to the shaft, or in the form of carefully-shaped solid metal circular cams, termed pattern wheels, attached to it (Fig. 23.2). *An increase in height from one link to the next produces a thrust against the end of the guide bar shogging it positively into the machine, a decrease will produce a negative shog towards the pattern shaft as the result of the action of a return spring.* A constant height will produce no shog and the guide bar will continue to swing through the same needle space. The periphery of the pattern wheel or chain track is scanned by a roller which is linked by a flexible ball-jointed push-rod to the end of a guide bar, the underside of the rod near the roller is supported on a slide which moves freely on a metal surface as shogging occurs.

The drive for the pattern shaft is obtained from the main cam-shaft via bevel gears and a universal joint to a worm which drives the wormwheel of the pattern shaft. The ratio of cam-shaft speed to the pattern shaft speed is usually 16 : 1, therefore 1/16th of the surface of a pattern wheel would represent one course or knitting cycle.

Pattern wheels provide accuracy and smooth running at high speeds but they are only economical for long production runs of the common simple repeat structures; for fancy structures, frequent changes of pattern and long pattern repeats, the shogging movements are obtained by assembling a chain of re-usable pattern links.

23.7 Chain Links

In plan view the identically Y-shaped chain links are similar in appearance to a tuning fork with the fork end leading. The tail of the preceding link fits into the fork of the succeeding link and the links are held together by pins which are pushed through holes in the sides of the fork and tail, the pins pass through all the tracks and chains and the ends fit into grooves in the serrated flanges of the pattern drum so that as the drum turns the chain links are advanced in unison, in correct timing.

Chain links require accurate grinding at the fork and/or the tail if they are higher than the preceding or succeeding link so that a smooth transition and an accurately timed shog occurs (the ground ends of two successive links must never be adjacent to each other). Too sharp a gradient will produce an early timed shog and too gradual a gradient a late timed shog for the knitting sequence. There are four types of link: plain unground, fork ground, tail ground and fork and tail ground.

With direct *transmission of the shogging movement* from chain links to guide bar, as described, *the exact distance shogged is the difference in heights between the two successive links.* This method is employed on most high speed machines and on the ground guide bars of many multi-bar Raschels. A second method, the indirect method, magnifies or adapts the thrust derived from the links by transmitting it through a pivoted lever whose leverage can be adjusted thus altering the throw of the shog. This is a versatile method used on the pattern guides of multi-bar machines which enables links of one gauge to be employed for a range of maching gauges and also for arrangements to be used which economize on chain links.

Chain link numbering commences with '0' height and every guide bar chain sequence must contain at least one of these '0' links because when the guide bar is on this link it will be in its nearest position to the pattern mechanism, during that particular lapping movement. Tricot links are numbered 0, 1, 2, 3, 4, 5, etc., and with direct shogging, each will be successively one needle space higher than the previous link, so that on a 28-gauge tricot machine, a '2' link will be 1/28th inch (0.9 mm) higher than a '1' link which will be 1/28th inch higher than a '0' link. If a '1' link is placed after a '0' link, a one-needle space shog away from the pattern mechanism will be produced. If a '0' link is placed after a '3' link a three-needle space shog towards the pattern mechanism will occur. If two links of the same height are placed next to each other, for example '3' followed by '3' a shog will not be produced and the guides will remain between the same needle spaces.

It must be understood that *a height of link, for example '0', does not represent a fixed position between two needle spaces, it represents the nearest position each guide in a particular guide bar approaches the pattern mechanism during that lapping movement*. When a guide bar is on a '0' link, all guides in that bar will be in their '0' position but each will occupy a different space between needles across the width. Likewise, two guides from different bars may occupy the same space between two adjacent needles and yet be at different heights of links at that point.

A chain notation is a list in correct sequence of chain link numbers spaced into knitting cycles for each guide bar necessary to produce a particular structure (Fig. 23.4b). The difference between the first two links is normally the overlap. It must be remembered that the links are joined together in a closed loop with the starting link for each bar joined to its last link. For this reason, underlap movements towards left and right tend to balance each other.

The *number of links per course* is fixed for each machine, a minimum of two is usually required with the overlap occurring between the second link of one course and the first link of the next. On tricot machines, a third intermediate link is often used so that the underlap is also spead between the second and third links giving it more time and coinciding more closely with the knitting cycle requirements.

Development of Lapping Diagrams and Chain Notations 23.8

Lapping diagrams are drawn around horizontal rows of points which represent needles in plan view, usually assuming the pattern mechanism to be on the right. As the guides position themselves in the spaces between needles, the positions between the vertical columns of points can be given chain link numbers commencing with '0' position which is to the right of the right hand column of points.

Provided the direction and extent of the overlaps are correctly indicated in the lapping diagram and chain notation, the underlaps will always be correctly positioned as each extends from the end of one overlap to the start of the next.

Figure 23.4a represents a diagrammatic plan view of a two-course repeat sequence. S_1 and S_2 represent the swinging motions and O and U represent the overlap and underlap shogs at each course.

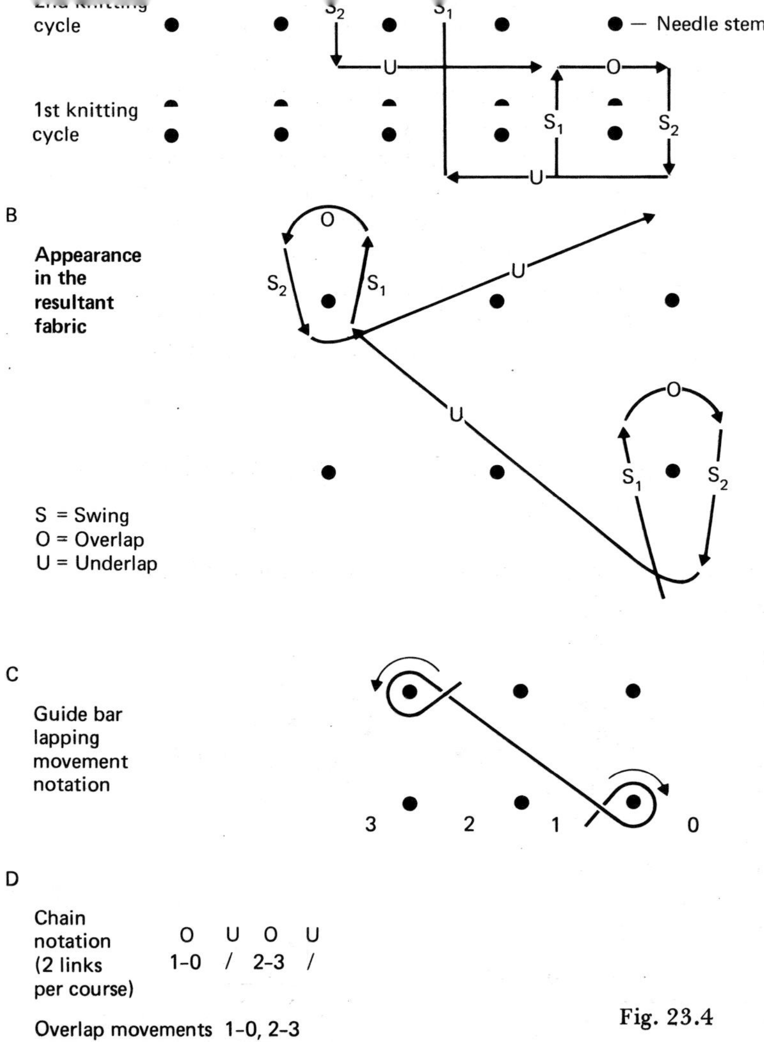

Fig. 23.4

In the lapping diagram (Fig. 23.4c), the first overlap will be drawn in a curve over a point from space 1 to space 0 and the second from space 2 to space3. The lapping diagram is completed by joining the overlaps together with underlaps and the chain is notated as 1—0/2—3/ where — represents an overlap and / an underlap. *Whereas the shogging movements are produced by the transition from one link to the next, the swinging motions occur whilst the push-rod roller of the guide bar is in the centre of a link so that no shog is produced.*

Single- or Double-Needle Overlaps 23.9

Overlap movements are normally across only one needle space as a double-needle overlap would cause both the warp thread and the needles to be subjected to the severe strain of two simultaneous adjacent knock-over actions, whilst different tensions on the two loops in the structure will adversely affect their appearance. The underlap between the double overlap loops has the appearance of a sinker loop. Only in a few Raschel structures is the double-needle overlap used and here the needles are less easily deflected and there are no knock-over sinkers over which to draw the loops. *A single full-threaded guide bar making a double-needle* overlap will cause each needle to receive two overlapped threads at that course.

The greater the extent of the underlap in needle spaces, the heavier the fabric and the more horizontal the path of the thread as it crosses the structure.

The Five Basic Overlap/Underlap Variations 23.10

All guide bar lapping movements are composed of one or more of the following lapping variations (Fig. 23.5):

1. An overlap followed by an underlap in the opposite direction (closed lap) (Fig. 23.5a).
2. An overlap followed by an underlap in the same direction (open lap) (Fig. 23.5b).
3. Only overlaps and no underlaps (open laps) (Fig. 23.5c).
4. Only underlaps and no overlaps (laying-in) (Fig. 23.5d).
5. Neither overlaps nor underlaps (miss-lapping) (Fig. 23.5e).

Movements 4 and 5 require the overlaps of another guide bar in front in order to hold them into the structure.

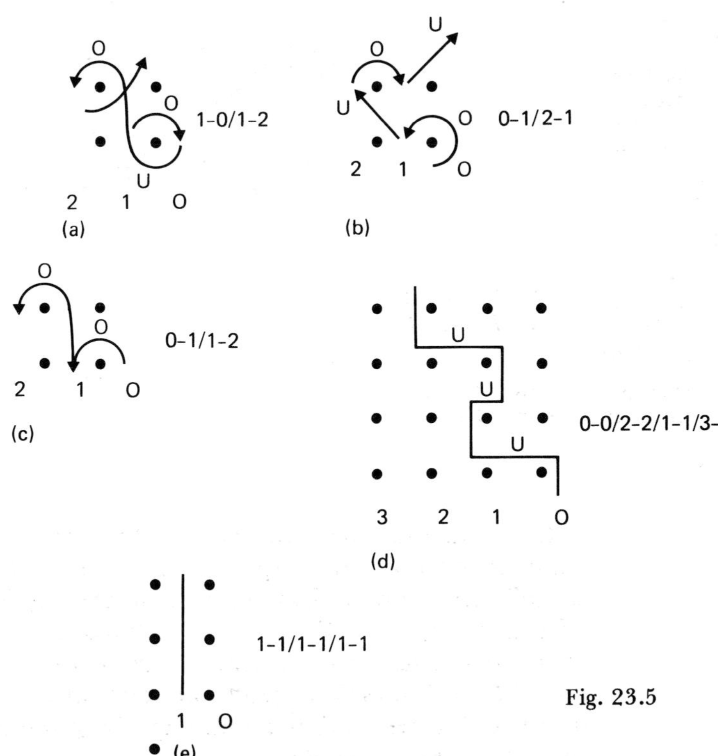

Fig. 23.5

23.11 Direction of Lapping at Successive Courses

When using either open or closed laps there are three possible arrangements of lapping at successive courses which may be used alone or in combination:

1. *The pillar stitch. In the pillar or chain stitch, the same guide always overlaps the same needle.* This lapping movement will produce chains of loops in unconnected wales which must be connected together by the underlaps of a second guide bar. Generally, pillar stitches are made by front guide bars either to produce vertical stripe effects or to hold the inlays of other guide bars into the structure. *Open lap pillar stitches are commonly used in warp knitting.* They can be unroved from the end knitted last. Closed lap pillar stitches are employed on crochet machines because the lapping movement is simple to achieve and is necessary when using self-closing carbine needles although a false twist is introduced into the yarn (Fig. 23.6).

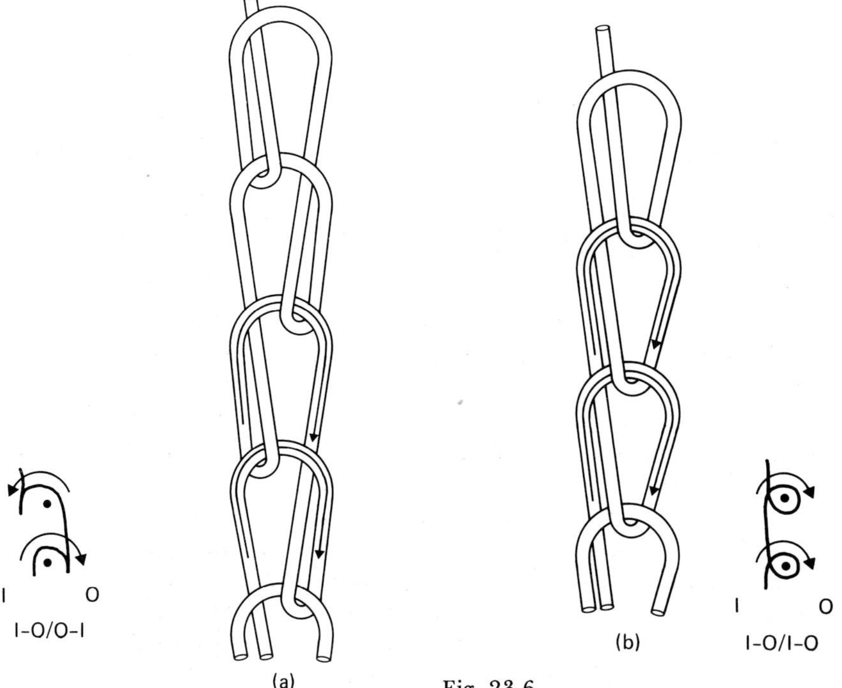

Fig. 23.6

2. *Balanced advance and return lapping in two courses* (Fig. 23.5a). Many tricot structures are based on this type of lapping movement. Its extent may be described by indicating the number of needles underlapped, followed by the number of needles overlapped (usually one). *With a fully threaded guide bar, every one-needle space increase in the underlap movement will cause an extra warp thread from that bar to cross between each wale.*

1 X 1 or tricot lapping is the simplest of these movements producing overlaps in alternate wales at alternate courses with only one thread crossing between adjacent wales. Two threads will cross between wales with a 2 X 1 or cord lap, three threads with a 3 X 1 or satin lap, four threads with a 4 X 1 or velvet lap and so on. *Each increase in the extent of the underlap tends to make the structure stronger, more opaque and heavier, with the increasing float of the underlap having a more horizontal appearance, whilst overlaps produced by the same thread will, at successive courses, be separated by an extra wale.*

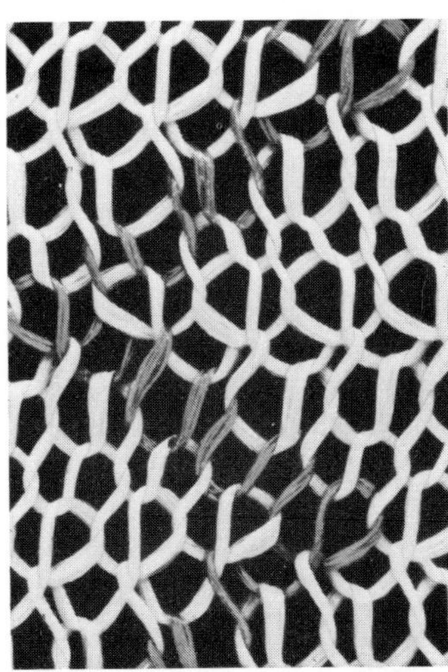

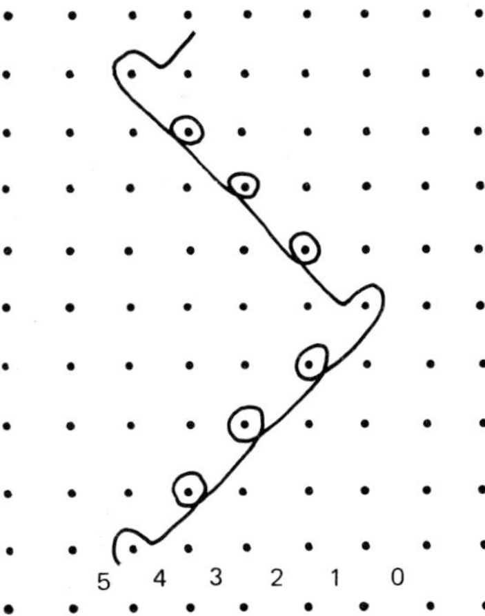

Fig. 23.7

3. *Atlas lapping* (Fig. 23.7). This is a *movement where the guide bar laps progressively in the same direction* for a minimum of two consecutive courses normally followed by an identical lapping movement in the opposite direction. Usually the progressive lapping is in the form of open laps and the change of direction course is in the form of a closed lap, but these roles may be reversed. From the change of direction course, tension tends to cause the heads of the loops to incline in the opposite direction to that of the lapping progression. *The change of direction course is normally tighter and the return progression courses cause reflected light to produce a faint transverse shadow stripe effect.* The underlaps on the technical back give the appearance of sinker loops in a spirally weft knitted structure. With a single guide bar having different coloured warp threads, zig-zag effects can be produced. It is sometimes termed single Atlas or Vandyke. More elaborate geometrical patterns can be achieved with patterned warps using Atlas lapping on two or more guide bars. Atlas is also the base for many Simplex and all Milanese fabrics.

Single guide bar structures (Fig. 23.8a,b). Although cohesive structures may be produced by a single full-threaded guide bar producing underlaps and overlaps, these are seldom commercially viable because of their flimsiness, low strength, lack of stability, poor covering power, and

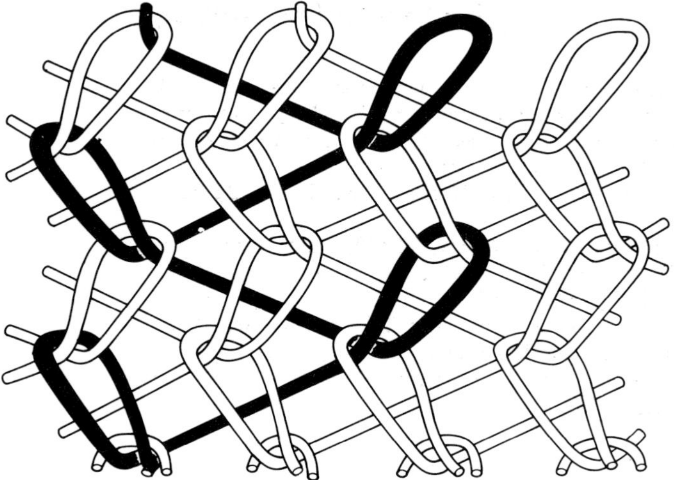

(a) Technical Face

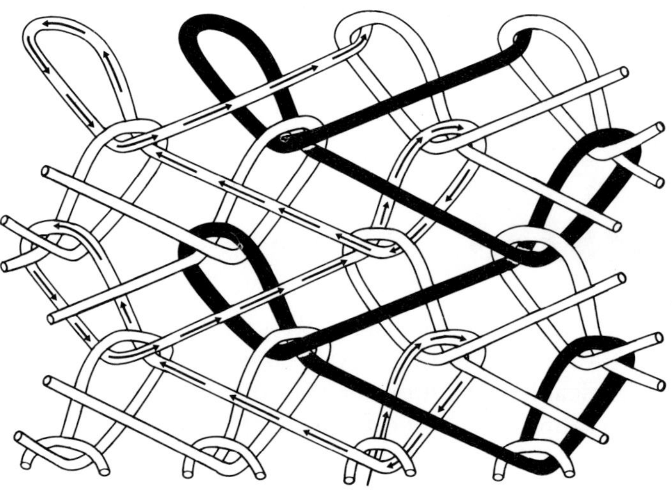

(b) Technical Back

distortion caused by loop inclination as well as limited patterning potential. Loop inclination is caused by the underlaps of the guide bar entering and leaving the head of the needle loop from the same side and thus producing an unbalanced tension from that direction (unlike weft knitting where the sinker loops enter and leave from opposite sides of the head of the loop). *A more balanced tension is achieved by having two sets of warp threads underlapping in opposition to each other so that the underlaps of each enter and leave from opposite sides of the head of the loop.* For these reasons the simplest warp knitted structures are usually composed of two sets of warp threads and most machines have a minimum of two guide bars.

Fig. 23.8

Further Information

Kettenwirk Praxis – a very informative technical and educational magazine which includes detailed warp knitted samples. Published quarterly by Karl Mayer, together with a full English translation available from branches or agencies, or from Kettenwirk Praxis, 6053 Obertshausen, Postfach 109, Germany.

REISFELD, A., Warp Knit Fabrics and Products, *Knit. Times*, (1969) Part 6, 24 Feb., 35–47; Part 8, 21 July, 75–82.

WEBER, K. P., Warp Knitting Technology, *Knit. Times*, (1970) Part 1, 31 Aug., 32–37; Part 2, (1971) 11 Jan., 62–8; Part 3, 22 Feb., 49–59; Part 4, 29 Mar., 63–5; Part 5, 19 April, 231–9; Part 6, 5 July, 31–41.

WHEATLEY, B., Production of outerwear on Raschel and Tricot machines, *Knit. Times*, Part 1, (1971) 29 Nov., 56–61; Part 2, 27 Dec., 64–70; Part 3, (1972) 28 Feb., 36–41, (Further parts were published throughout 1972 and 1973 with part 15 on 12 Nov. (1973) completing the series.

Textbooks

PALING, D. F., *Warp Knitting Technology*, (1965) Columbine Press.

REISFELD, A., *Warp Knit Engineering*, (1966) Nat. Knit. O'wr. Ass., New York.

THOMAS, D. G. B., *Introduction to Warp Knitting*, (1976) Merrow Technical Library.

24

Classes of Warp Knitting Machinery

24.1 Characteristics of Tricot and Raschel Machines

The two major classes of warp knitting machines are Tricots and Raschels. In the past, *tricot machines mainly employed bearded needles* with a presser bar and *Raschels used latch needles* together with a latch wire or blade. Despite the renewed use of the compound needle (Fig. 23.1), there are still distinctive differences between the two types.

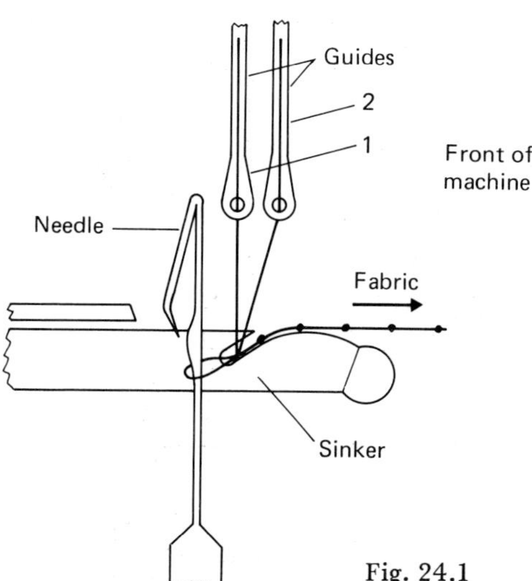

Fig. 24.1

Tricot machines (Figs 24.1, 24.2) have a gauge expressed in needles per inch and chain link numbering 0, 1, 2, 3, 4, etc., generally with three links per course. Their sinkers, which are joined to each other at the front and back, never move clear of the needles as they combine the functions of holding-down, knocking over and supporting the fabric loops.

The fabric is drawn-away towards the batching roller almost at right angles to the needle bar. The warp beams are accommodated in an inclined arc towards the back of the machine with the top beam supplying the front guide bar and the bottom beam supplying the back guide bar. The warp sheets pass over the top of the guide bar rocker-shaft to their tension rails situated at the front of the machine.

Mechanical attention to the knitting elements is carried out at the front of the machine as the beams prevent access to the back. As all the warp sheets are drawn over the rocker-shaft to the front of the machine it is easier to thread up the guide bars commencing with the back bar, otherwise the front warp will obscure this operation. The guide bars are therefore numbered from the back towards the front of the machine because of this threading sequence.

The conventional tricot beam arrangement generally restricts the maximum number of beams and guide bars to four but this is not of major importance as the majority of tricot machines employ only two guide bars.

The small angle of fabric take-away and the type of knitting action provides a gentle and low tension on the structure being knitted which is ideal for the high-speed production of simple fine gauge (28–40 npi)

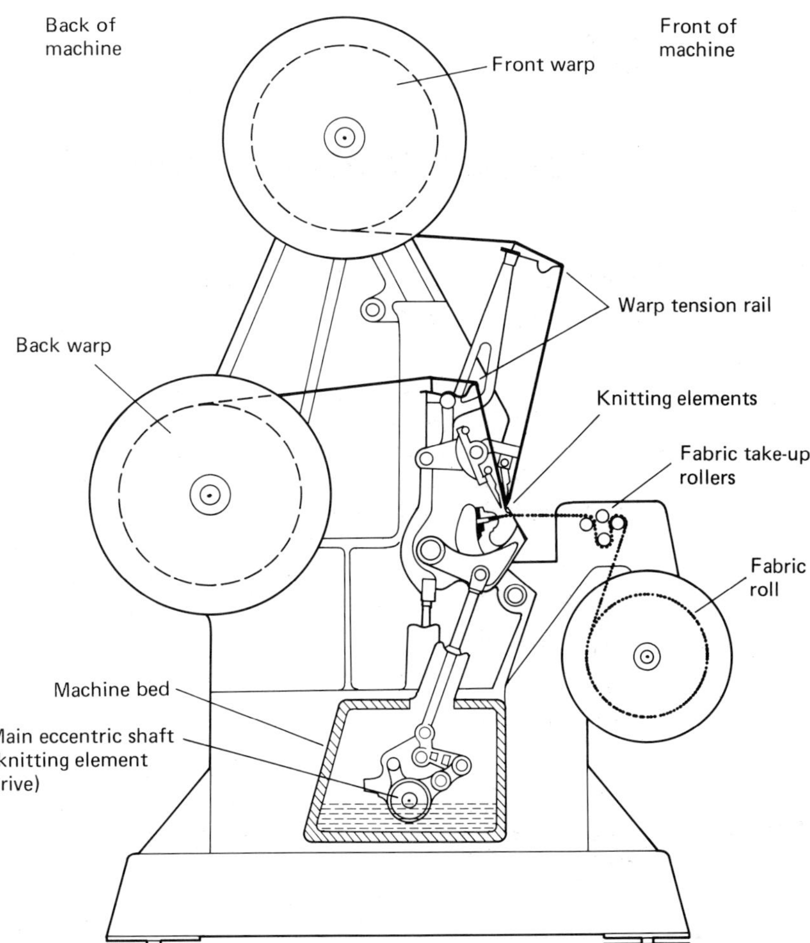

Fig. 24.2

close knitted plain and patterned structures, especially two guide bar structures with both bars overlapping and underlapping.

Raschel machines (Figs 24.3, 24.4) have a gauge expressed in needles per 2 inches (5 cm) so that, for example, a 36-gauge Raschel will have eighteen needles per inch. Their chain links are usually numbered in even numbers 0, 2, 4, 6 etc., generally with two links per course. Raschel sinkers only perform the function of holding down the loops whilst the needles rise. They are not joined together by a lead across their ends nearest to the needle bar so they can move away towards the back of the machine for the rest of the knitting cycle. The needle trick-plate verge acts as a fabric support ledge and knock-over surface.

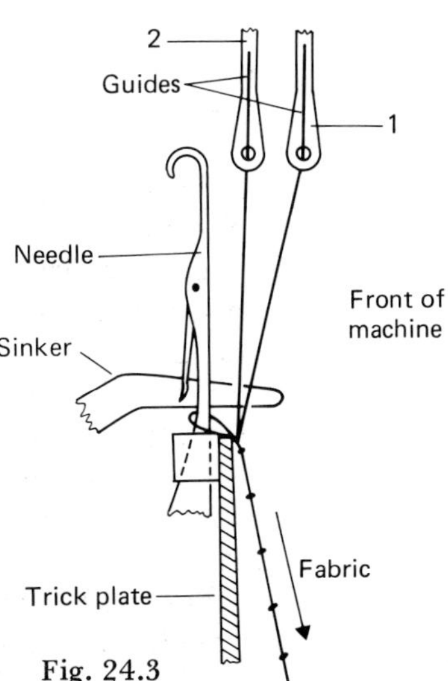

Fig. 24.3

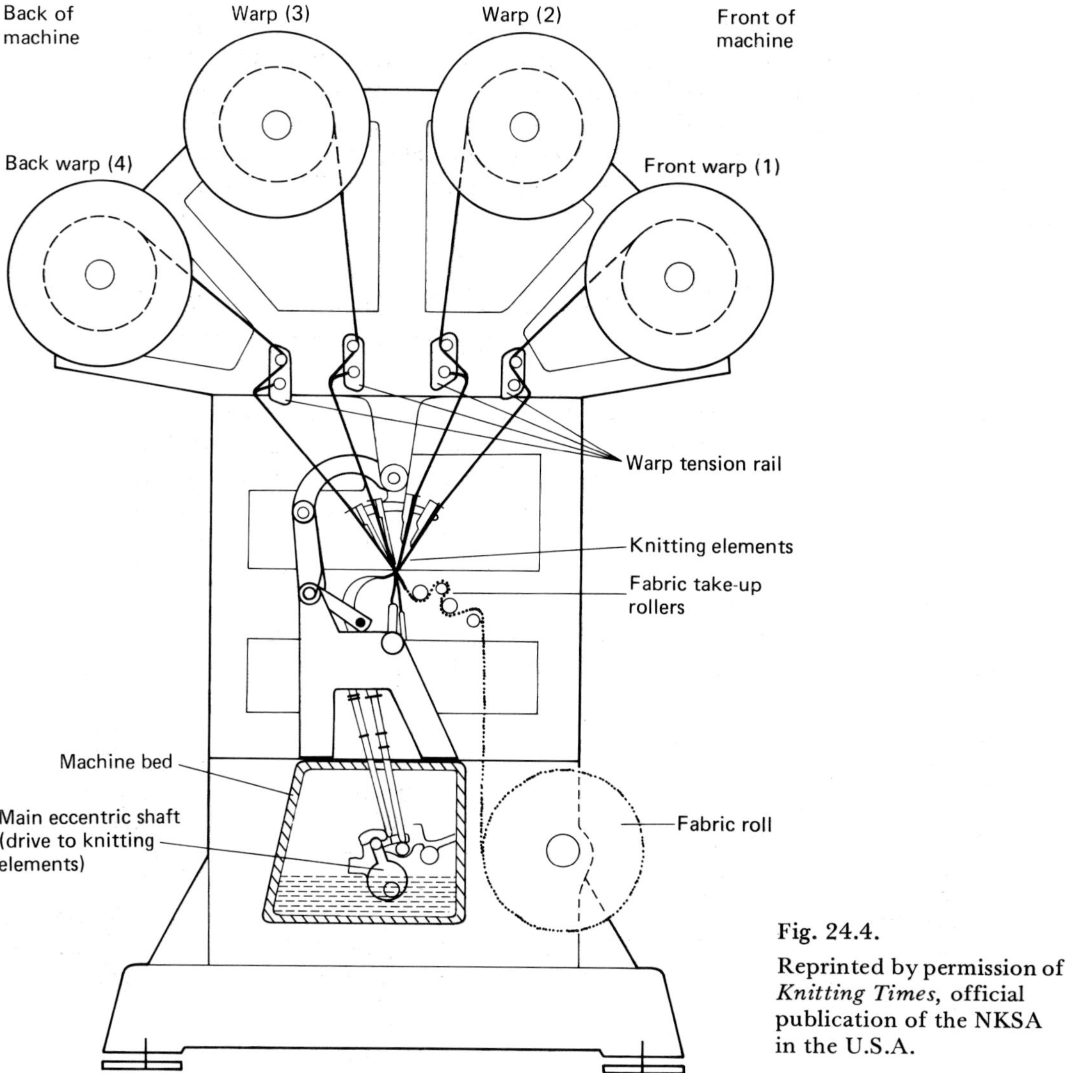

Fig. 24.4.

Reprinted by permission of *Knitting Times*, official publication of the NKSA in the U.S.A.

The fabric is drawn downwards from the needles almost parallel to the needle bar at an angle of 120–160 degrees by a series of take-down rollers. The warp beams are arranged above the needle bar centred over the rocker-shaft so that warp sheets pass down to the guide bars on either side of it.

The beams are placed above the machine so it is accessible at the front for fabric inspection and at the back for mechanical attention to the knitting elements. The guide bars are threaded commencing with the middle bars and working outwards from either side of the rocker-shaft. The guide bars are numbered from the front of the machine.

With the Raschel arrangement there is accommodation for at least four 32-inch diameter beams or large numbers of small diameter pattern beams.

The accessibility of the Raschel machine, its simple knitting action and its strong and efficient take-down tension makes it particularly suitable for the production of coarse-gauge openwork structures employing pillar stitch and inlay lapping variations and partly-threaded guide bars which are difficult to knit and hold down with the tricot arrangement of sinkers. Additional warp threads may be supplied at the selvedges to ensure that these needles knit fabric, otherwise a progressive press-off of loops may occur.

24.2 The Knitting Cycle of the Bearded Needle Tricot Machine

Although in the past, the two guide bar locknit machine has proved most popular in 28- and 32-gauge with knitting widths of 84 and 168 inches (213 and 426 cm) using 40-denier nylon, it is possible to knit yarns from 10 denier nylon up to 1/20's cotton count and machine gauges can range from 10 for coarse staple fibre yarns to 20–24 for textured yarn suitings to 36–40 gauge for fine fabrics in knitting widths up to 260 inches (660 cm) (Fig. 24.5).

The needles, like the sinkers and guides, may be cast in leads or they may be individually cranked to fit into the needle bar.

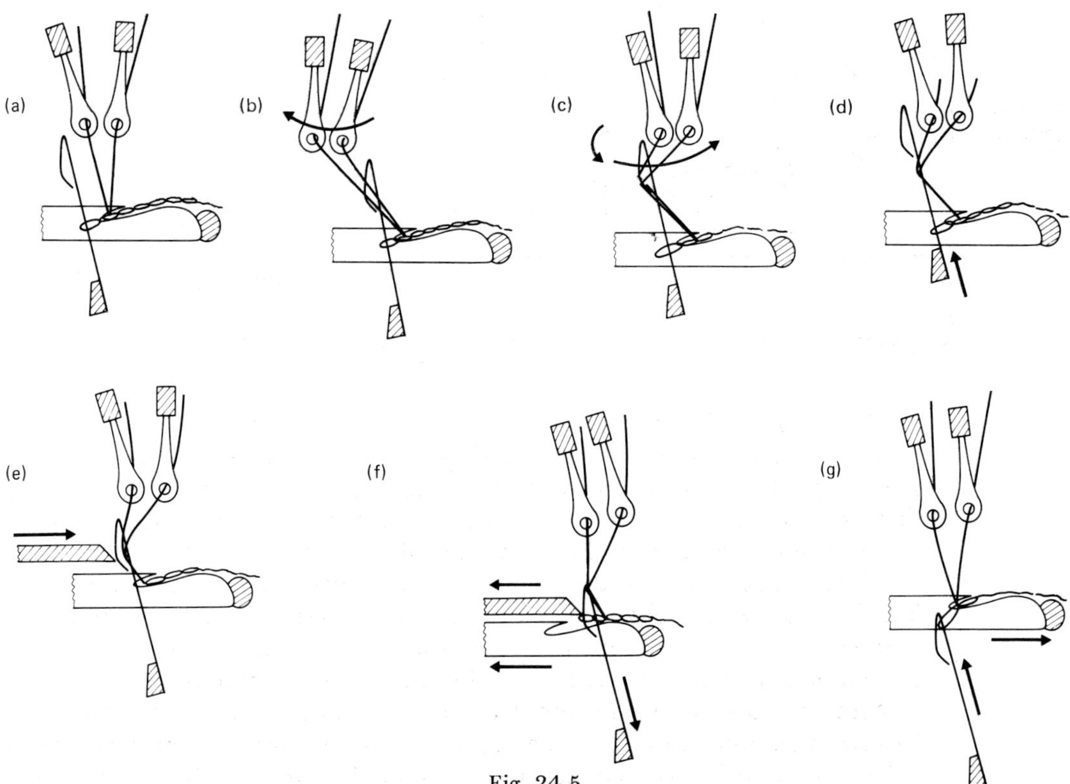

Fig. 24.5

1. *The rest position* (a). The needles have risen to 2/3 of their full height from knock-over and have their beards towards the back of the machine. The presser is withdrawn and the guides are at the front of the machine with the sinkers forward holding the old overlaps in their throats so that they are maintained at the correct height on the needle stems.
2. *Backward swing and overlap shog* (b, c). After swinging through the needles to the beard side, the guides are overlapped across the beards usually by one needle space in opposite directions.
3. *The return swing and second rise* (c, d). As the guides swing to the front, the needles rise to their full height so that the newly-formed overlaps slip off the beards onto the stems above the old overlaps. This arrangement reduces the amount of guide bar swing necessary and therefore the time required.
4. *Pressing* (e). The needle bar descends so that the open beards cover the new overlaps, there is a slight pause whilst the presser advances and closes the beards.
5. *Landing* (f). As the sinkers withdraw, the upward curve of their bellies lands the old overlaps onto the closed beards.
6. *Knock-over and underlap shog* (g). The presser is withdrawn and the continued descent of the needle bar causes the old overlaps to be knocked-over as the heads of the needles descend below the upper surface of the sinker bellies. The underlap shog which can occur at any time between pressing and knock-over usually occurs in opposite directions on the two guide bars.
7. *The sinkers now move forwards* to hold down the fabric loops and push them away from the ascending needles which are rising to the rest position.

24.3 The Raschel Machine

In 1855, German warp knitters in Apolda used warp rib machines made by Redgate of Leicester to knit lace stoles which they sold under the name of Raschel Felix the famous French actress,[1] so that when Wilhelm Barfuss began to build his latch needle rib machines he named them Raschel machines.[2] Originally two vertical needle bars arranged back to back mid-way between each other were employed for producing simulated rib fabrics and in 1914 when the needle bars were placed directly back to back only even-numbered chain links were required.

Until the mid-fifties, the Raschel industry tended to be small employing slow, cumbersome but versatile coarse-gauge universal Raschels. These had two needle bars, one of which could be removed or replaced with plush points, changeable cams and patterning mechanisms which might include fall plate, crepe and fringing motions, chain switching and possibly weft insertion or jacquard.

Modern specific purpose Raschels date from 1956 when a twelve-bar Raschel machine led to the development of the Raschel lace industry.[3] There are now single needle bar Raschels for simple and multi-bar dress and elastic laces and trimmings and curtain nets, high-speed standard Raschels for simple structures such as suitings, versatile multi-purpose Raschels for fancy fabrics, weft insertion and jacquard Raschels and double needle bar Raschels for plush, tubular articles, scarves and string vests.

The Knitting Action of the Single Needle Bar Raschel 24.4

Raschel needles tend to have longer latches than weft knitting machine needles to ensure that the wrapped yarn of the overlap goes onto and not below the latch (Fig. 24.6). There is a trick-plate extending the full width of the machine whose walls preserve the needle spacing and whose verge provides an edge for a clean knock-over. Holding down sinkers, which are thin blades unleaded on their forward edge, move in a horizontal plane over the top of the trick-plate.

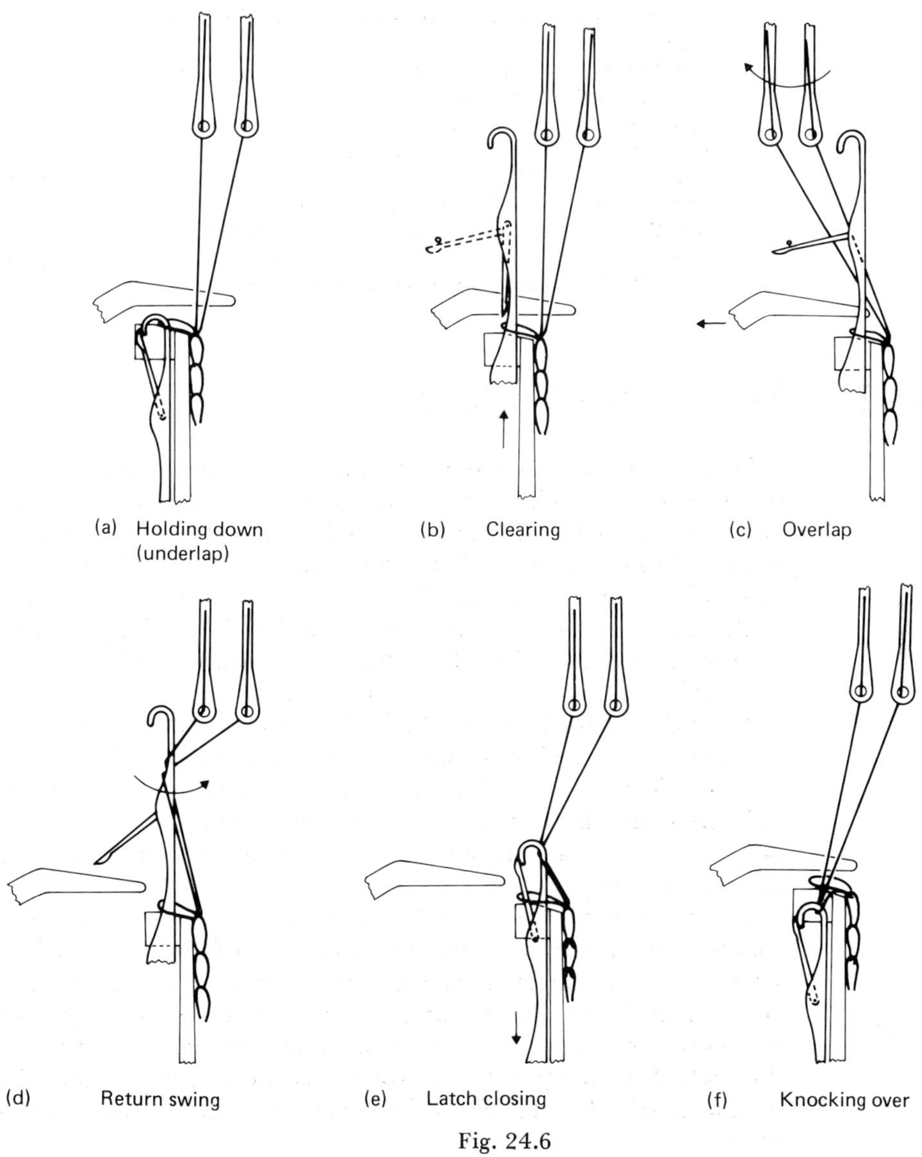

Fig. 24.6

1. *Holding down*. The guide bars are at the front of the machine completing their underlap shog. The sinker bar moves forward to hold the fabric down whilst the needle bar starts to rise from knock-over.
2. *Clearing*. As the needle bar rises to its full height the old overlaps slip down onto the stems after opening the latches which are prevented from flicking closed by latch wires. The sinker bar then starts to withdraw to allow the guide bars to overlap.
3. *Overlap*. The guide bars swing to the back of the machine and then shog for the overlap.
4. *Return swing*. As the guide bars swing to the front the warp threads wrap into the needle hooks.
5. *Latch closing*. The needle bar descends so that the old overlaps contact and close the latches trapping the new overlaps inside. The sinker bar now starts to move forward.
6. *Knocking-over and underlap*. As the needle bar continues to descend, its head passes below the surface of the trick-plate drawing the new overlap through the old overlap which is cast-off and as the sinkers advance over the trick-plate, the underlap shog of the guide bar is commenced.

24.5 Compound Needle Warp Knitting Machines

After its introduction in 1946, the two guide bar British built FNF tricot machine with its tubular compound needles (see section 3.20) became for 10 years the pacemaker of the industry with its speed of 1000 cpm being more than twice that of contemporary bearded needle machines. It also incorporated many new features such as double eccentric element drive, positive warp let-off, light spring warp tension rails and carefully-balanced machine parts. However, it required precise setting-up, its pattern scope was limited and needles and other parts were expensive.

In 1965 the FNF company ceased production, having failed to improve their machine in the face of increasing competition from high-speed bearded needle tricots with single eccentric drives built by the West German companies of Liba and Karl Mayer. The East German Kokett concern, however, continued its production of compound needle tricots.

In 1967 Liba, in a bid to increase production speeds, introduced a new design open-stem compound needle into both Raschel and tricot machinery and by the mid 1970s Karl Mayer was pursuing a similar policy. Now the needle is employed in most high-speed warp knitting machines including double needle bar Raschels. Its short, simple action enables speeds of 2000 cpm to be achieved without the problems of metal fatigue and loop distortion associated with latch and bearded needles.

The open stem needle is simpler, cheaper and more adaptable than the FNF tube needle with individually replaceable hook members and a wider open hook.

The designs of the other elements are similar to those in conventional machines except that the tricot sinkers have flat bellies because the compound needle does not require assistance in landing the old overlap.

The hook members are individually mounted in their bar whilst the tongues are set in leads which are mounted in the tongue bar.

Figure 24.7 illustrates the knitting action of a compound needle warp knitting machine:

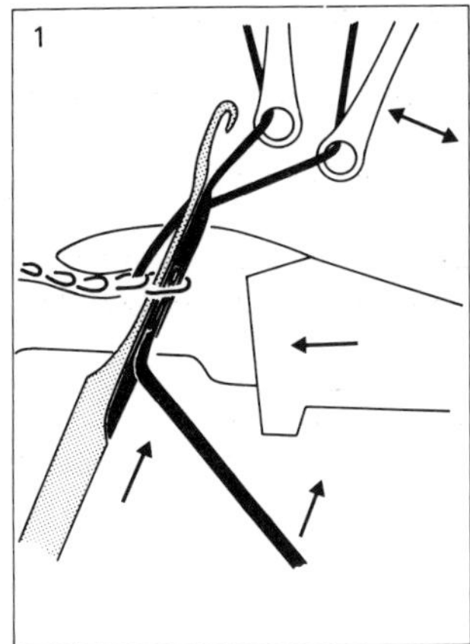

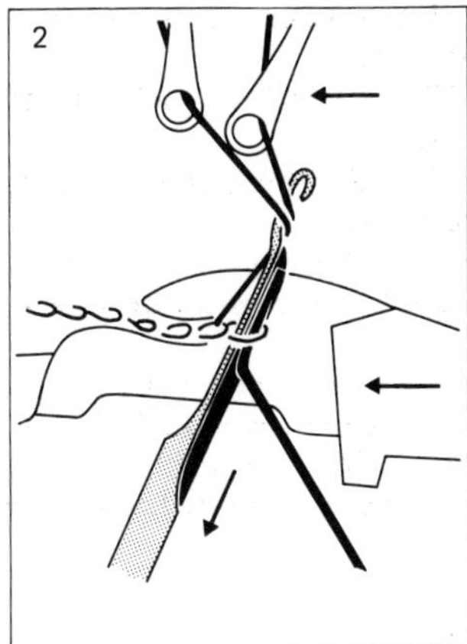

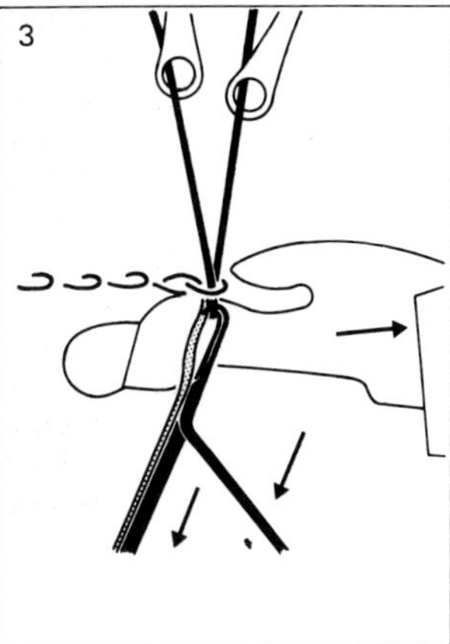

Fig. 24.7

1. *Needle rise and guide bar swing*. With the sinkers forward holding down the fabric the hooks and tongues rise with the hook rising faster until the head of the latter is level with the guide holes and is open. The guides then swing through to the back of the machine.
2. *The overlap and return swing*. The guides shog for the overlap and swing to the front of the machine and immediately the hooks and the tongues start to descend with the tongues descending more slowly thus closing the hooks.
3. *Landing and knock-over*. The sinkers start to withdraw as the needles descend so that the old loop is landed onto the closed hook and then knocked-over as it descends below the sinker belly. At this point the underlap occurs before the needles commence their upward rise and the sinkers move forwards to hold down the fabric.

The Crochet Machine 24.6

In hand crocheting a hook is used to draw a new loop through the old loop with the chains of loops being joined together at intervals. *On crochet machines, the warp chains are separate from the weft inlay and it is the latter threads which join the chaining wales to each other*. The crochet galloon machine, as developed by Sander and Graff and popularized by Kholer, is essentially a highly versatile Raschel with the following unique features (Figs 24.8, 24.9).

1. A single horizontal needle bar whose simple reciprocating action can be used to operate individually tricked latch, carbine or embroidery needles. The patent or carbine needle is used for fine structures and has a sideways crimped beard placed in a permanently-pressed position. Although warp threads can only be fed into the beard from the right

Fig. 24.8. The Crochet Machine. Knitting narrow width elastic trimmings (Jacob Muller).

(necessitating a unidirectional overlap), the old overlaps are automatically cleared and landed by the movement of the needle. Embroidery or lace needles are carbine needles with pointed heads which can penetrate pre-woven structures to produce embroidery effects. The needles can be arranged for coarser gauges or for fancy set-outs when the floating inlay threads may be cut to produce separated fringed edgings.

2. There are no sinkers, instead a fixed hold-back bar is fitted in front of the knock-over verge to prevent the fabric moving out with the needles.

3. The closed lap pillar stitches and inlay threads are controlled and supplied as separate warp and weft respectively. Each needle is lapped from below by its own warp guide which is clipped to a bar whose auto-

matic one-needle overlap and return underlap shog is fixed and is controlled from an eccentric cam whilst its upwards and downwards swing is derived from a rockershaft. The warp yarn is often placed low at the front of the machine.

The weft yarn, which is often placed above and towards the back of the machine, supplies the carrier tubes clipped to the spring-loaded inlay bars fitted above the needle bar and shogged at the rate of one link per course from pattern chains around a drum at one end of the machine. There are usually up to two warp guide bars and up to twelve weft inlay bars.

4. Special attachments are available for producing fancy effects such as cut or uncut fringe edges, pile, braiding (equivalent to fall-plate) and snail shell designs.

Crochet machines with their simple construction, ease of pattern and width changing and use of individual yarn packages or beams provide the opportunity of short runs on coarse or fine gauge fancy and openwork structures and edgings as well as the specialist production of wide fancy fabrics or narrow elastic laces.

Very approximately, the knitting widths of crochet machines may vary between 25 and 75 inches, in gauges expressed in needles per centimetre between 2 and 6 (5–15 npi) and run at speeds between 200 and 350 courses per minute (or more on simple structures).

Figure 24.10 illustrates the knitting action of a crochet machine:

1. *The inlay.* Whilst the needle is withdrawn into its trick, during knock-over of the previous of warp overlaps, the weft inlay tube is lowered so that, as it traverses in an under-lap shog, the weft is laid below the level of the needle and on top of the warp thread which extends from its head to the warp guide.

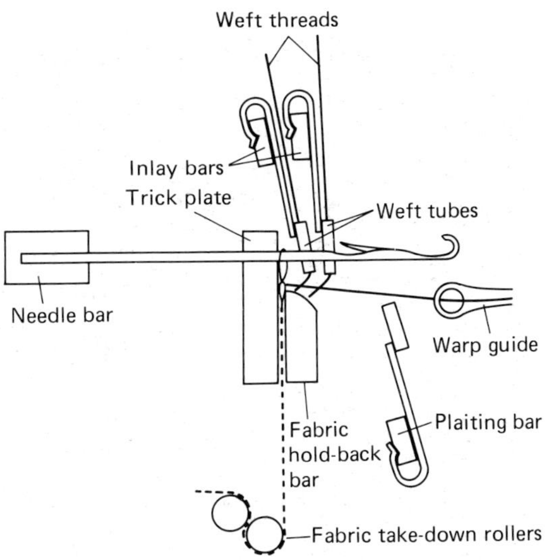

Fig. 24.9. (Knitting International).

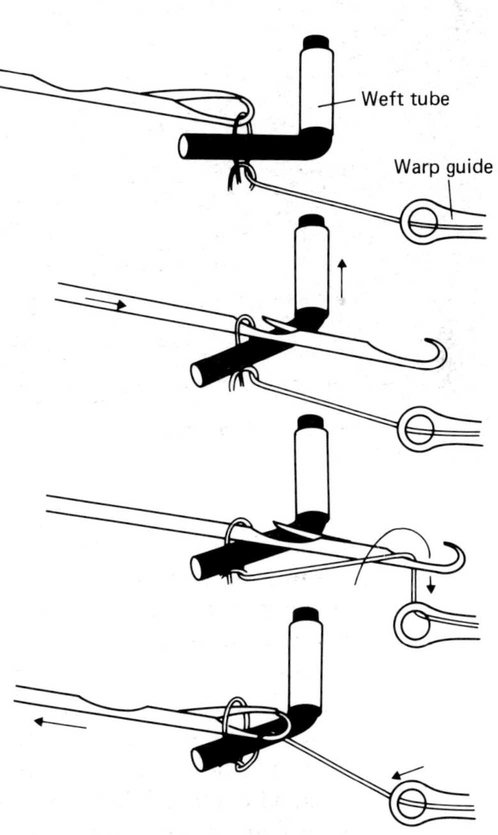

Fig. 24.10. (Knitting International).

2. *Clearing the warp overlap*. The weft tube rises slightly on completion of it traverse movement to allow the needle to move out of its trick to clear its ol warp overlap.
3. *The warp overlap wrap*. The warp guide rises between the needles and auto matically overlaps from the left lowering itself again on the right side of it needle.
4. *Warp knock-over and underlap*. The needle now retires into its trick to knock over the old overlap, whilst the warp guide is cammed under its needle to th start position for its next overlap thus completing the closed lap pillar.

24.7 Warping

Warp is normally prepared as an accumulation of ends wound parallel t each other on a beam. The warp must possess the correct number of ends all of the same length and all wound at the same tension. The ends mus be parallel to one another and evenly distributed throughout the width o the beam. The spacing must be suitable for the gauge and the width of th warp often equals the width of the needle bar in use although it may b composed of a number of sectional beams. Generally warping is carrie out *directly* from the yarn packages placed on a creel to the driven knittin beam because this is the fastest method. For fancy warps and samplin purposes *the indirect* method of building a warp in sections onto a mi and then off beaming the completed warp onto the knitters beam i generally preferred as this involves less yarn packages.

The warping of synthetic yarns involves the need for anti-static elimi nators whilst the warping of staple fibre yarns may require the use of lin removal arrangements and possibly the application of a lubricant to th warp. Special warping machines with reciprocating guides are employed t warp the pattern beams of multi-guide bar machines where only a fev warp ends are required.

Further Information

ANDERSON, D., Growth of warp knitting in the United Kingdom, *Hos. Times*, (1969 32–5, 102–5.

BROWN, F. C., Development and uses of tricot and Raschel fabrics, *Text. Inst. an Ind.*, (1970) **8**, (2), 47–8.

DARLINGTON, K. D., The production of Raschel crochet fabric, *Knit. O'wr Times* (1968) 22 July, 42–5.

DARLINGTON, K. D., Principles of warp knit apparel fabric design (part 14), *Hos Trade Journal*, (1969) Dec., 136–40.

DARLINGTON, K. D., Knitting yarns on Raschel crochet machines, *Knit. Times* (1975) 13 Oct., 22–8.

SMITH, D. C., The future of warp knitting, *Text. Inst. and Ind.*, (1968) **6**, (2), 43–47

SMITH, J. M., The changing face of tricot, *Text. Inst. and Ind.*, (1969) **7**, (7), 182–4

WEBER, K. P., Warp knitting technology (part 8), *Knit. Times*, (1971) 30 Aug. 44–49.

WHEATLEY, B., Historical survey of warp knitting, *Knit. Times Yr. Bk.*, (1974) 104–108, 243.

WHEATLEY, B., Developments in tricot machinery: the compound needle, *Knit. Times Yr. Bk.*, (1976) 130–31, 135.

Modern machines for production of narrow fabrics, *Band- und Flechtindustrie*, (1978) 1, 28–35.

Articles from *Kettenwirk-Praxis* (English Edition)

The compound needle, (1975) 9 (3), 5–7.

Preparation of warp beams for all textile sectors, (1977) 1, 11–12.

Equipment for monitoring the yarns on warping machines, (1977) 2, 8–13.

Tips for processing spun yarns, (1978) 2, 18–20.

Accurate yarn preparation on the HOSM pattern-beam warping machine, (1979) 2, 9–10.

The GDII semi-automatic high production rotating frame creel, (1979) 1, 6–9.

1. Where does the name Raschel Machine come from? *Wirkerie-Und-Strickerie Technik* (1968) Jan., No. 1, p. 11 (translation arranged by C. E. J. Aston).
2. Another possible derivation is from the name Reichel, a German manufacturer, who according to Willkomm (*Technology of Framework Knitting*, 1885) brought the warp loom to Berlin in 1795 (Part One, page 131).
3. WHEATLEY, B., Development of tricot and Raschel machinery over the past 50 years, *Knit. O'wr Times Yr. Bk.*, (1968) 242–257.

25

Plain Tricot Structures Knitted with Two Full Set Guide Bars

These are by far the most popular of all warp knitted structures and are mainly based on a two-course repeat cycle with a change of direction lap at each course. Although the majority has been made on 28-gauge tricot machines using 40 denier Nylon, other gauges, yarn types and counts, as well as Raschel machines, are used.

The two bars make different lapping movements because otherwise, a structure having single needle bar characteristics would be produced. Each guide bar contributes a thread to every overlap, and the two underlaps can be clearly distinguished as they lap to a different angle, extent or direction. Generally, under normal conditions, the threads of the front guide bar tend to dominate the face as well as the back of the fabric (Fig. 25.4).

25.1 Rules Governing Two Guide Bar Structures

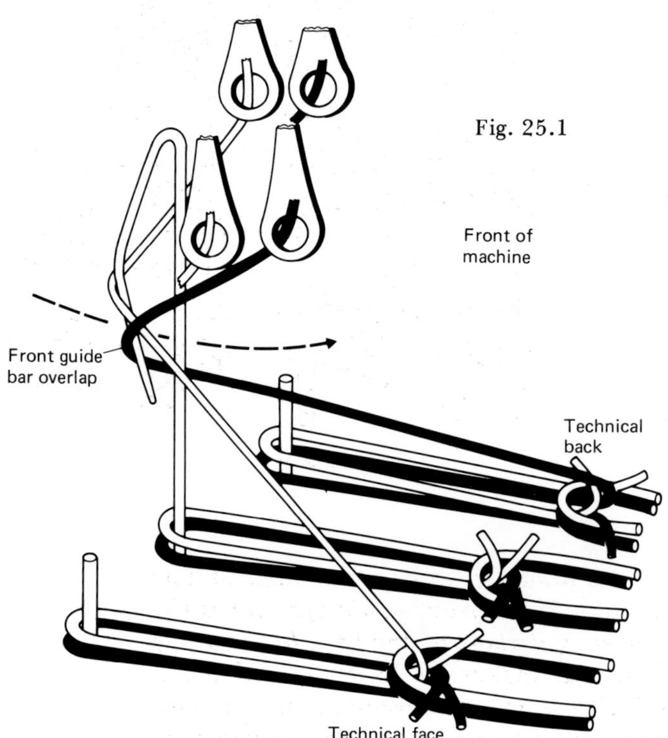

Fig. 25.1

1. As the guides swing through the needles to start their next overlap *the back guide bar is first to lay its underlap on the technical back* (Fig. 25.2) and *the front bar is the last so its underlaps lie on top on the back fabric* (Fig. 25.3).

2. The front bar thread is the first to strike the needle on the return swing after the overlap (Fig. 25.1) and as its bar swings furthest to the front of the machine, it *tends to occupy a lower position on the needle.* If this position is retained it will show more prominently on the under surface, which is the technical face (Fig. 25.2).

3. The following will all tend to cause a warp thread

to occupy a low position on the needle either reinforcing or reversing the normal front guide bar/back plating relationship; a low setting of a guide, a longer run-in, an open instead of a closed lap, and a short underlap movement.

The normal plating dominance of the front guide bar threads on both surfaces of the structure can thus be overcome by carefully-arranged lapping movement. A structure, showing the underlaps of the front guide bar on the surface of the technical back but the overlaps of the back guide bar on the surface of the technical face, is produced if the front bar makes a 2 X 1 closed lap and the back bar makes a 1 X 1 open lap in opposition to it.

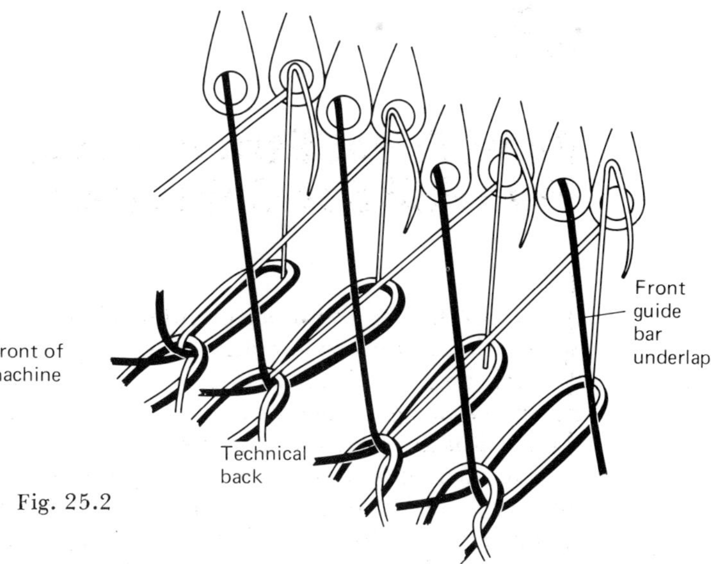

Fig. 25.2

4. If the two bars lap in opposition, the yarns tend to twist over each other in the overlap so that the back bar thread tends to partly show on top of one side limb.

5. *If the two bars underlap in opposition they tend to balance the tension at the needle head producing a more rigid upright overlap stitch. On the technical back the underlaps will cross over each other in the middle between wales and this improves the strength of the structure.*

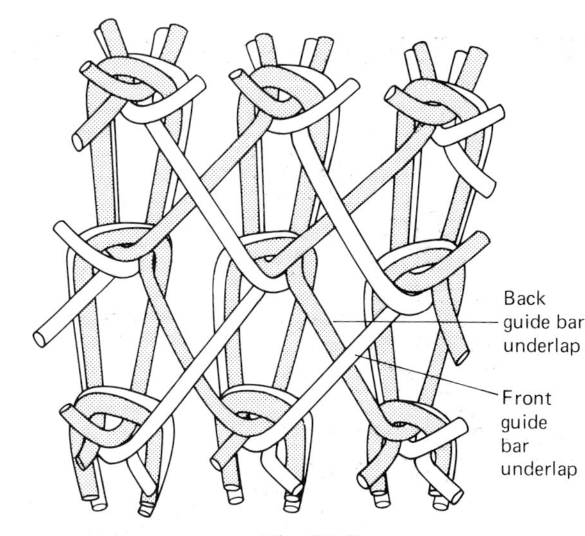

Fig. 25.3

6. A short movement will cause the underlap to lie at an angle and its laps will be under the greatest tension. *If the front guide bar makes the shortest underlap it will tie the longer underlaps of the back bar securely into the rigid structure*, if the front bar makes the longer underlap this floats freely across the back and allows more movement of the yarn within the structure giving it more elasticity and a greater tendency to curl towards the technical face at the top and bottom.

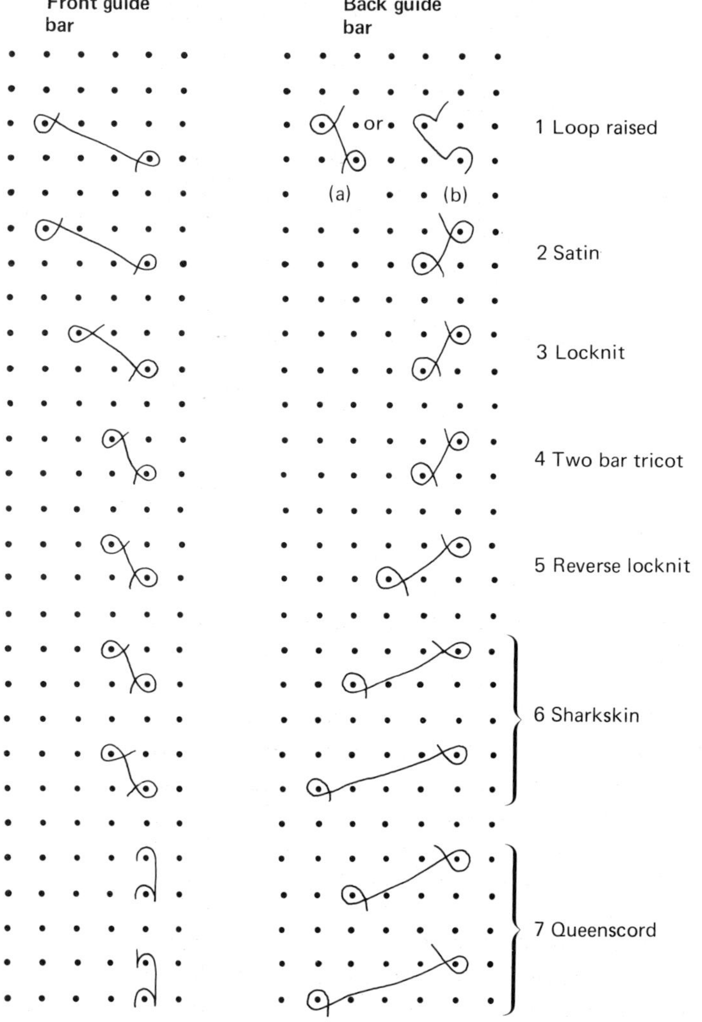

Fig. 25.4

25.2 Two Bar Tricot

Two bar Tricot ('Half Jersey', U.S.A.) is the simplest two-bar structure and uses a minimum amount of yarn (Figs 25.3, 25.5). The two underlaps balance each other exactly as they cross diagonally in between each wale producing upright overlaps. It tends to have poor cover and opacity in fine denier and in continuous filament yarn it tends to split down between the wales either during tentering or button-holing especially if acetate or triacetate yarn is used.

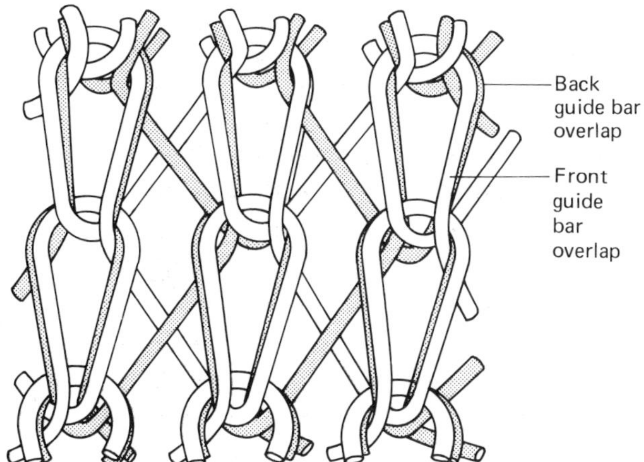

Fig. 25.5

Locknit 25.3

Locknit ('Jersey', U.S.A.) or Charmeuse (France and Germany) is the most popular of all warp knitted structures and accounts for 70–80 per cent of total output. The longer underlaps of the front bar on the back of the fabric improves extensibility, cover, opacity, with a smooth soft handle and good drapability. Its greater cohesion reduces snagging and splitting. Its tendency to curl towards the face at the top and bottom and the back at the sides can be reduced by setting. On a 28-gauge Tricot machine a fabric might be produced from nylon yarn weighing about 30 g/m^2 for 20 den., 82 g/m^2 for 40 den. and 152 g/m^2 for 70 den., in each case the finished wales per inch being more than 37. Shrinkage is generally between 20 and 30 per cent but it can be less. An elasticated fabric for lingerie may be produced on the same gauge using 40 den. Nylon on the front bar and 40 den. spandex on the back with a weight of 158 g/m^2. The elasticity of locknit makes it particularly suitable for lingerie and intimate apparel, a knitting width of 168 inches can be finished between 92 and 100 inches, which is a satisfactory width for handling these structures.

Reverse Locknit 25.4

Reverse Locknit (or 'Reverse Jersey', U.S.A.) has a reduced extensibility and no curling and because of the short front guide bar underlaps it has a lower shrinkage in finished width, being often less than 10 per cent. It is used to a lesser extent than Locknit.

Sharkskin 25.5

Sharkskin is produced by increasing the back guide bar underlap to

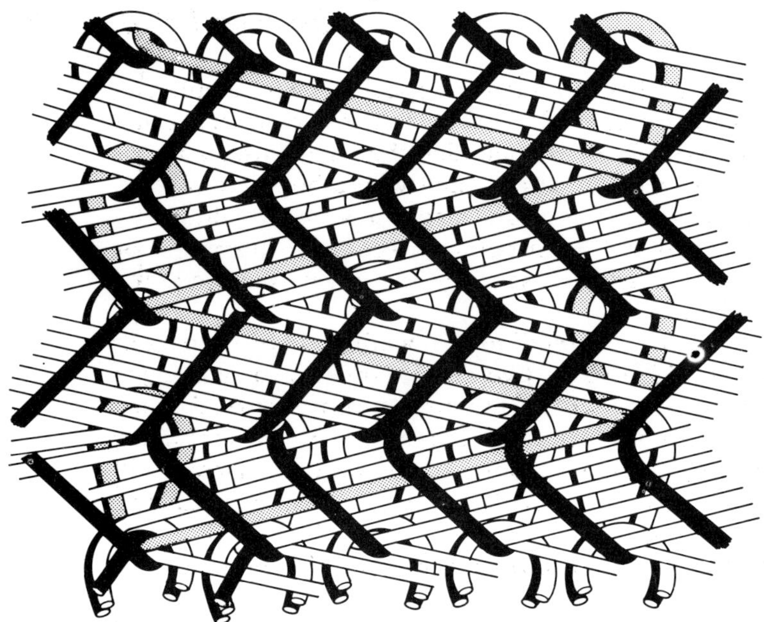

Fig. 25.6

three or four needle spaces making an even more rigid and heavier fabric whose stability makes it useful as a print base (Fig. 25.6).

25.6 Queenscord

This has even greater rigidity than Sharkskin because the front bar makes the shortest possible underlap, the pillar stitch, which tightly ties in the back bar underlaps giving it a shrinkage of only 1–6 per cent. The pillar stitch yarn as it passes up the wale tends to give a slight cord effect and the underlaps of the pillar are unable to balance the underlaps of the back bar so they show inclined overlap stitches (Fig. 25.7).

Fig. 25.7

Double Atlas 25.7

In this structure, two guide bars atlas lap in opposition with identically balanced lapping movements often similarly threaded with colours in order to produce balanced symmetrical designs including checks, plaids, diamonds and circles. Areas of intense colour are obtained where both overlaps on the same needle are of the same colour and paler areas are produced by overlaps having two threads of different colours. Repeats of twenty-four or forty-eight courses can be made but selvedge threads may be required to cover needles at the edges.

In the past, special circular and rectilinear machines have been built termed Milanese machines which cause two sets of threads to make open lap atlas traverses across the needle bed without return traverses. As they reach the selvedge the threads move into the other set (in rectilinear machines). Either single-needle (cotton lap) or two-needle traverse (silk lap) fabrics can be produced. Despite the balanced rounded loops, attractive appearance, multi-colour possibilities, handle, drapability and elastic recovery properties of Milanese fabrics, their slow rate of production has rendered them uncompetitive.

Satin 25.8

This has an increased front guide bar 3 X 1 or 4 X 1 lapping movement compared to locknit giving even greater elasticity but when threaded with continuous filament yarn, the long floats produce a lustrous light reflective surface.

Velour and Velvet Structures 25.9

These are based on producing long underlaps on the front guide bar which are formed into a pile surface on the technical back during finishing.

Brushed velour normally has the same lapping movement as satin with 40–60 denier nylon or polyester yarn in the back guide bar for strength and possibly 55–100 denier viscose or acetate threaded in the front guide bar which is broken into a pile by brushing during finishing. Velvet is produced with a longer underlap on the front guide bar such as a 6 X 1 or even an 8 X 1 lap. These underlaps are cropped or sheared during finishing producing a more regular and prominent pile surface and a width shrinkage of approximately 35 per cent compared with 50 per cent or more for velours. An open tricot lap may be made on the back guide bar to bury the pile yarn on the face and thus produce a more stable structure. On a 28-gauge tricot machine 40 denier nylon might be used for the face yarn and 100 denier rayon for the pile producing a structure with a finished weight of approximately 150 g/m^2.

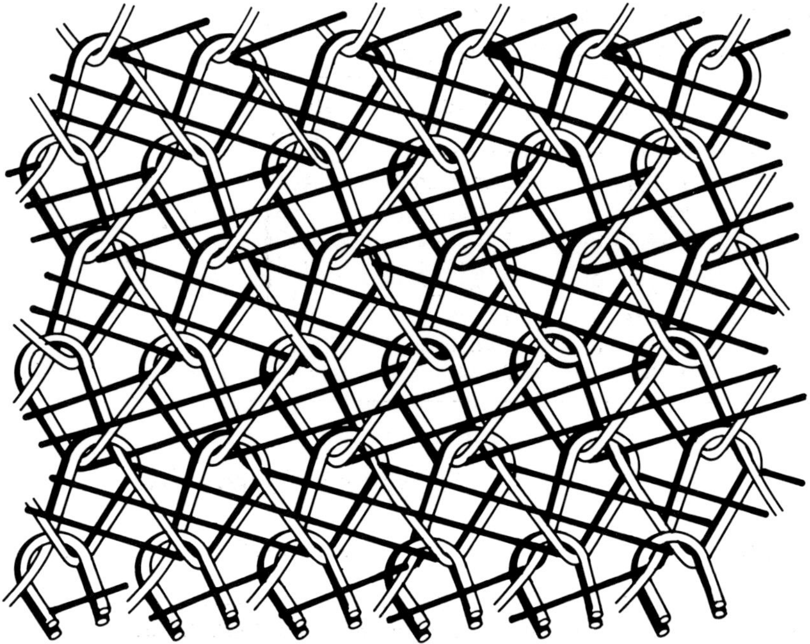

Fig. 25.8

In raised loop velours (Fig. 25.8), both guide bars lap in unison producing an unstable construction with inclined loops similar to those of a single guide bar structure. Stability is achieved later during finishing when double-action pile and counter-pile rollers contact the individual filaments raising them into a mass of fine loops and at the same time consolidating the structure. On 28-gauge tricot machines either nylon or polyester yarn in 40 denier is used for apparel and 90 denier for furnishings.

25.10 Overfed Pile Structures

These are achieved usually by supplying warp at a faster rate to the back guide bar than is required for the conventional structure so that the surplus warp forces its way through to the surface on the technical face as a pile. One example is airloop which is reverse locknit having a front-to-back guide bar run-in ratio of approximately 1.0 to 2.3 instead of 1.0 to 1.24. The structure has a less definite pile and a soft hand. A crepe effect is achieved but the pile height and density tends to vary from centre to edge and the fabric is unstable and stretchy like a single bar structure. Another structure is made with locknit if the run-in of the two bars is the same instead of front-to-back 4:3 ratio. Mechanisms have also been used to produce similar effects, these include a tension bar which dips to feed more yarn for either the overlap or the underlap and patterning by selecting the tension warp threads to reduce the pile yarn then later releasing it to overfeed. Variation in shade is achieved by using two different coloured warps, one in each guide bar.

The table below gives examples of typical run-in ratios.

Run-in ratios for normal flat nylon yarns

Yarn	B–B	F–B	Run-in ratio
Locknit	1–0/1–2	2–3/1–0	3:4
Reverse locknit	2–3/1–0	1–0/1–2	4:3
Sharkskin	3–4/1–0	1–0/1–2	5:3
Queenscord	4–5/1–0	1–0/0–1	9:4
Queenscord	3–4/1–0	1–0/0–1	9:5
Raised loop	1–0/1–2	1–0/3–4	5:9
Tricot	1–2/1–0	1–0/1–2	1:1
Satin	1–0/1–2	3–4/1–0	5:9

Further Information

DARLINGTON, K. D., Analysis of tricot velour fabrics, *Knit. Times*, (1976) 16 Feb., 33–7.

THOMAS, D. G. B., Warp knitted pile fabrics, *Brit. Knit. Ind.*, (1972) Oct., 98–101.

WHEATLEY, B., Production of cut velvet on Karl Mayer tricot machines, *Knit. Times*, (1972) 23 Oct., 78–82.

WILKINS, C., Warp knit terry constructions growing in importance, *Knit. Times Yr. Bk.*, (1980) 106–8.

26

Surface Interest, Relief and Openwork Structures

A warp knitted fabric with a regular surface and uniform appearance is generally produced when all of the following conditions exist:

– each bar is full-threaded with every guide in the same bar carrying a similar yarn;

– each bar makes a regular lapping movement of similar extent at each course;

– when weft is inserted it occurs with a similar yarn at regular intervals;

– warp is supplied to each bar at a constant tension and uniform rate from course to course.

Carefully arranged variation of one or more of the above conditions enables surface interest, relief and openwork structures to be knitted as the guide lines below indicate:

1. Variation in the threading of one or more guide bars (guides threaded with different types of yarn or empty guides without yarn) will alter the appearance of the particular wales lapped by these guides. The effect will run the length of the fabric.
2. Variation in the extent of underlaps produced by a guide bar will affect the appearance of those courses where the variation occurs and if the guide bar is full-threaded the effect will run across the width of the fabric. Similar effects are obtained using weft insertion with different types of yarn or by varying the frequency of insertion.
3. The appearance of the fabric may also be changed at certain courses by varying the rate of warp supply or selectively tensioning the warp threads and thus influencing the length of yarn in the underlaps.

26.1 Miss-Lapping

Miss-lapping occurs when a guide bar (which has usually been knitting) makes neither overlaps nor underlaps for one or more courses so that if it is a front bar, its threads float vertically at the technical back. A simple use of this technique is in two full-threaded 'window pane' effects. The front bar knits a pillar stitch with a striped warp but at the courses where it miss-laps, a single bar semi-openwork effect is produced by the white inclined laps of the back bar which continues its 2 × 1 closed lap movement (Fig. 26.1).

Blind-lapping involves interrupting the warp let-off supply to a miss-lapping guide bar but as the other bars continue to knit, the courses of fabric which they produce will be forced outwards by the yarn tension into a raised pleat on the technical face. Blind-lapping with partly-threaded guide bars will vary the appearance across the fabric width.

The casting-off of overlaps is now being employed in the production of terry fabrics. The ground structure is knitted on alternate needles with the remaining needles being overlapped by the back guide bar at odd courses to form the terry loops. These are cast off at even courses when this bar inlays to ensure that the pile is held in the structure.

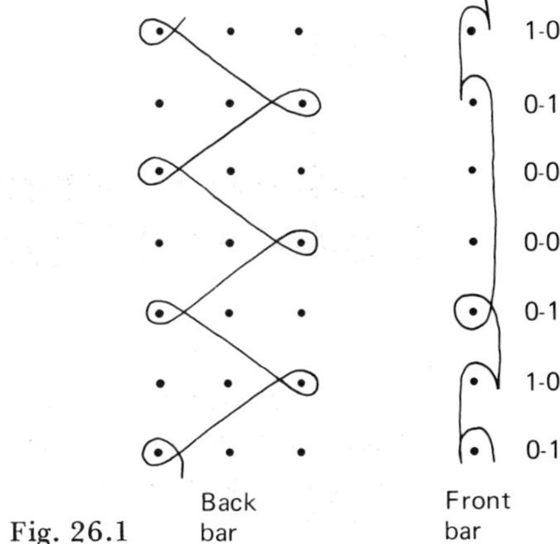

Fig. 26.1

Part-Threaded Guide Bars 26.2

The following are the basic rules when employing part-threaded guide bars for the production of nets, cords and relief designs:

1. During a normal knitting cycle *every needle must receive at least one overlapped thread* but it is not necessary for the same guide bar to supply every needle or for every needle to be overlapped by the same number of threaded guides.

2. The guide bar threading for one width repeat is usually shown in its correct relative position between the needle spaces at the first link of the design with | representing a threaded guide and • representing an empty guide.

3. *Overlaps composed of only a single thread will be inclined whereas loops produced by the overlaps of two bars lapping in opposition will be smaller and upright.*

4. Wales will be drawn together where underlaps pass across between them and will separate at points where no underlaps cross producing net pillars in the former and net openings in the latter (Fig. 26.4, P and O). If a full-threaded guide bar which knits at every course is also used, the effect will still occur in the form of a cord or relief instead of a net.

5. Symmetrical nets are produced when two identically-threaded guide bars overlap in balanced lapping movements in opposition. The threaded guides of a | • | • arrangement in each bar should pass through the same needle space at the first link in order to overlap adjacent needles otherwise both may overlap the same needle and leave the other without a thread.

6. In the production of nets a guide bar should traverse one more needle than the number of threaded guides in a guide bar in order to cross over the threads of the other bar (Figs 26.4, 26.5).

7. In balanced nets the width of the net pillar in wales will be equal to the threading repeat of one bar and half the width will be equal to the number of adjacent threaded guides in one bar.

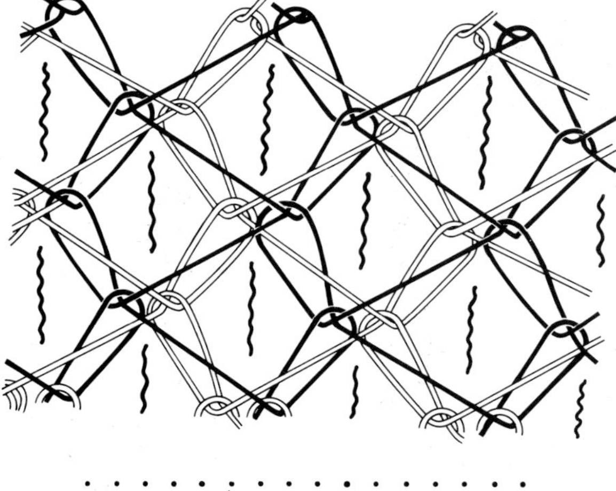

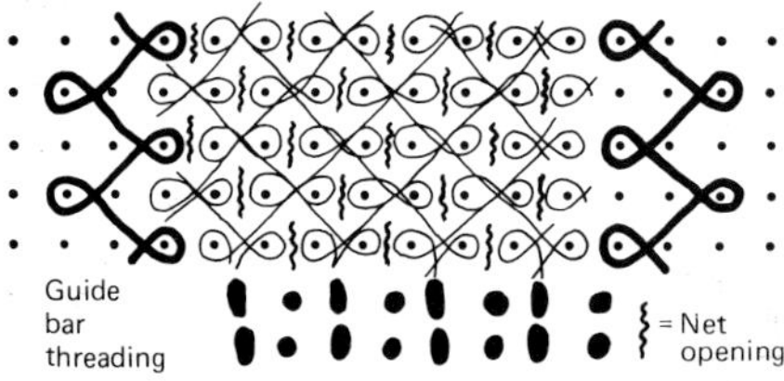

Fig. 26.2

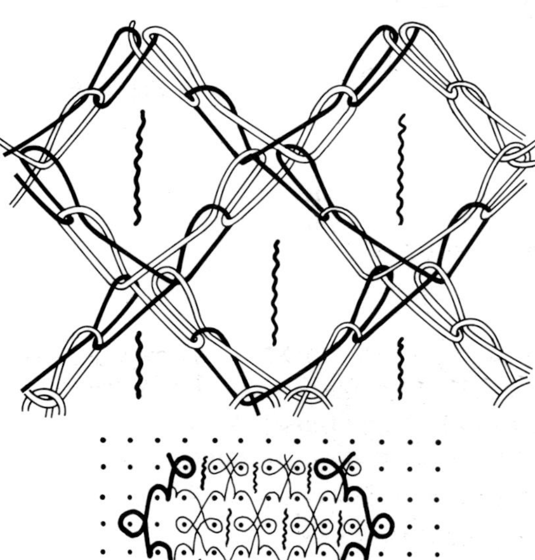

Front bar Back bar

Sandfly net

Front bar 1-0/1-2/2-3/2-1
Back bar 2-3/2-1/1-0/1-2

Fig. 26.3

8. In balanced nets a thread of one guide bar normally laps across the threads of two repeats in the other guide bar during its complete sequence (Fig. 26.4).

9. A vertical net pillar is extended as long as the threading repeat of one bar continuously recrosses the same threading repeat in the other bar. The net opening is terminated as soon as the guides of one bar progress across towards another set of threads in the second bar. An open lap is often used for this progression (Fig. 26.4).

10. In order to traverse across from one pillar to another and return by means of open laps the number of closed laps in a pillar must be an odd number.

Pin net is the simplest net produced with alternately-threaded guide bars. It uses a 2 X 1 closed lap making openings at every other wale and course but its disadvantage is its lack of strength because of the small number of courses and wales involved in the repeat (Fig. 26.2).

Sandfly net is more popular and is diamond-shaped with staggered rows of openings occurring at every other course. The closed laps pull tight and move in the direction of the underlaps to form the opening whilst the open laps help to form the diamond point (Fig. 26.3).

In cord fabrics, the width of the cord will be determined by the number of adjacent threads in the partly-threaded guide bar and the extent of its underlap movement (Fig. 26.6).

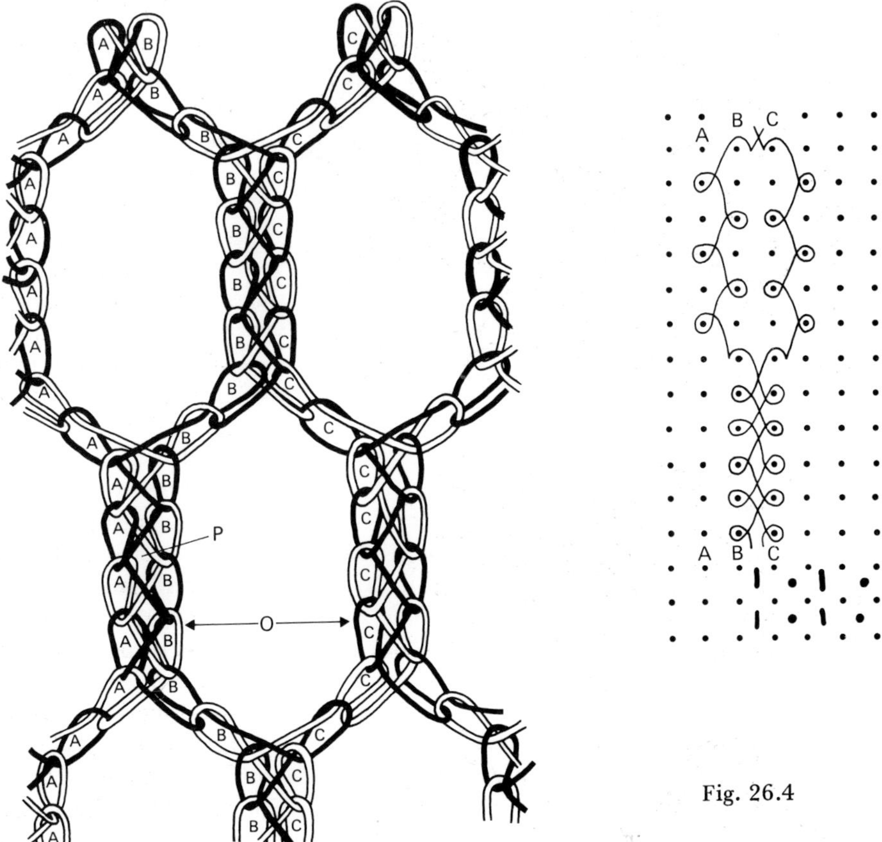

Fig. 26.4

Three wale wide cord

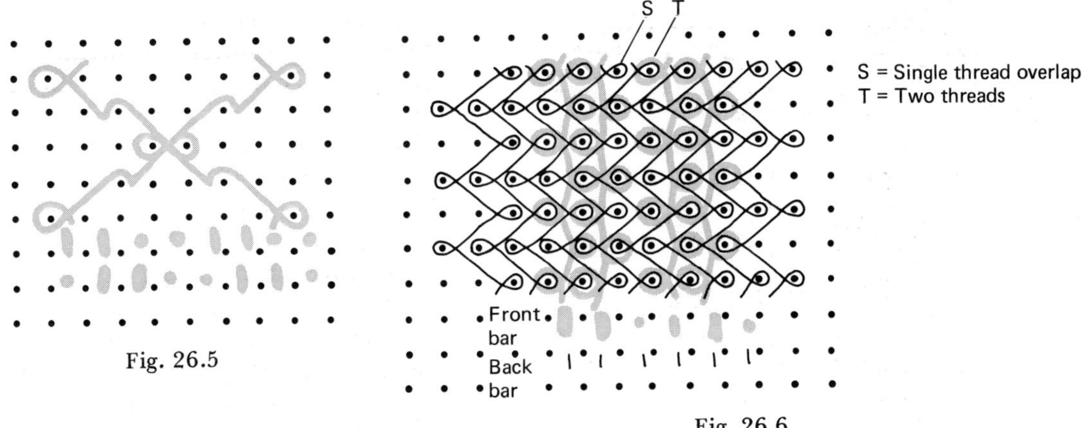

Fig. 26.5

Fig. 26.6

27

Laying-in in Warp Knitting

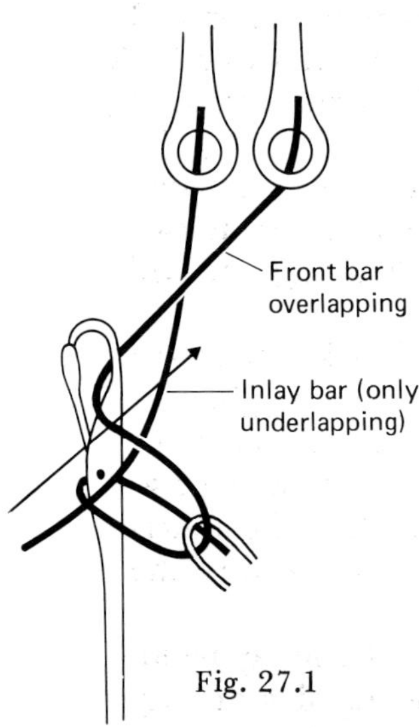

Fig. 27.1

Laying-in is achieved in warp knitting by causing a guide bar to only underlap, its threads will be held in the technical back of the structure only if a guide bar in front of it is overlapping. The yarn will inlay on top of the overlaps during knitting, so that as the guides of the knitting bar swing through the needles for the next overlap their underlaps will be laid on top of the inlay yarn trapping it into the back of the fabric (Fig. 27.1).

An inlaid yarn may pass across part of the knitting width or it may be introduced in a warp direction. Using a weft insertion device a full-width weft may be introduced. The laying-in guide may be specially designed to take coarse or unconventional yarns or to achieve a longer than normal underlap and a pattern mechanism designed only for laying-in may be used as in the case of weft insertion. The Raschel is particularly suitable for laying-in and sometimes the machine is designed to eliminate the swinging movement for the laying-in bars. On the crochet machine, the action of the knitting bar and the inlay bars is separately arranged and derived.

27.1 General Rules Governing Laying-in in Warp Knitting

1. *An inlaid yarn will pass across one less wale than a knitted yarn which has the same extent of underlap.* This is because the latter's overlap will add one further needle space traverse onto the underlap movement, thus a one-needle underlap will cause a yarn to inlay in the same wale and it will take a two-needle space underlap to cross from one wale to another. If a guide bar is full threaded it will put one less thread between a wale than the number of needles it underlaps.

2. To eliminate the overlap movement (in the case of a two-link movement) it is necessary to put two links of the same height at the point where this should take place. Sometimes the pattern mechanism is specially arranged to run at one link per course to cater for the underlap and thus to save links.

3. *The inlaid yarn will be tied in at every wale it crosses* (if the overlapping bar is in front of it) so that if the knitting guide bar is making a

pillar stitch, it will be tied in by the same number of threads as the number of needles it underlaps.

4. If the knitting bar underlaps in opposition to the inlay it will add an extra thread for tying it into the structure so that the inlay will be tied in by one more thread than the number of needles the inlay underlaps.

5. When the laying-in and knitting bars lap in unison there will be one less thread available for tying in the inlay so that the inlay will be tied in by one less thread than the number of needles it underlaps.

6. If the knitting and laying-in bars underlap in the same direction and to the same extent as each other, the inlay will evade the knitting bar underlaps and will slip through onto the technical back of the structure where it will form a straight vertical configuration.

7. If a guide bar makes neither overlaps nor underlaps it will miss-lap and its thread will form a straight vertical configuration between two wales on the technical face, as the underlaps of the knitting bar will prevent it falling through onto the technical back.

8. In order to interweave an inlaid yarn vertically with a knitted yarn it is necessary to cause it to evade for three courses and to miss-lap for one during the repeat, this is because with a normal two-course repeat of the knitting bar the underlaps will only cross that particular wale once so that in a four-course repeat there will only be two courses where the underlaps cross the wales and at one of these there is miss-lapping and at the other there is evasion.

9. If only two guide bars are employed, one knitting and one laying-in, the laying-in bar cannot produce a structure by only miss-lapping or only evading. In the first case, its yarn will fall out between the wales on the technical face and in the second case it will fall out from the back of the structure. Threads making these movements can however, be trapped if other laying-in bars are carefully arranged as to their positions and lapping movements.

10. If two inlay threads cross over each other in a structure, the thread from the bar nearest to the front of the machine will show nearest to the technical back of the fabric.

A fall-plate Raschel termed the Co-we-nit was introduced by Karl Mayer in 1967. It was designed specifically to knit woven-like structure. Despite arousing considerable interest it was commercially unsuccessful for the following reasons:

- its design scope was limited;
- Co-we-nit structures were difficult to mend;
- productivity was low;
- it required better quality yarns than a weaving loom in order to produce an equivalent fabric.

The machine produces two separately timed overlap actions one for knitting the pillar stitch of the front bar and the second for the weft bar behind it which open laps in the same direction but is then pushed from the needle hooks by the fall-plate so that it appears to be an inlay. The two back guide bars gauged twice as fine as the needle bar provide vertical warp threads which interweave with the fall-plate weft yarns by carefully arranged evasion and miss-lapping movements. A half-needle space evasion movement can cause only one of the two threads of the warp bar to cross over the weft on the technical back of the structure which is the effect side.

27.2 Fall-Plate Patterning

The fall-plate is a mechanism (Fig. 27.2) exclusive to latch needle

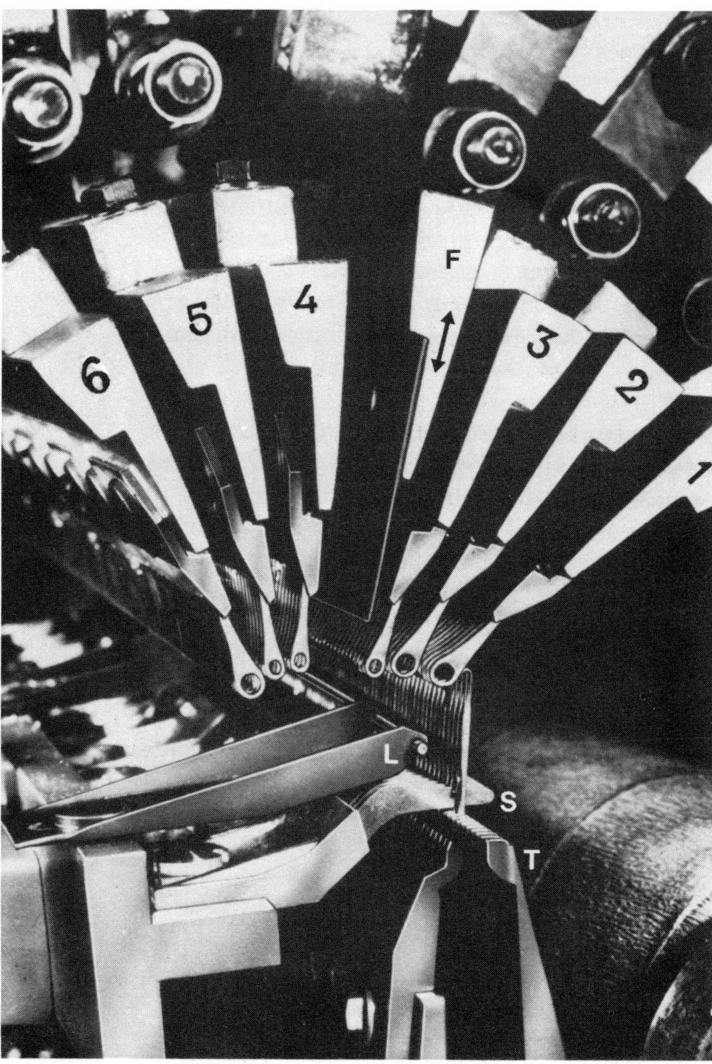

Fig. 27.2. Multi purpose Fall-plate Raschel machine (Karl Mayer). Bars 1, 2, 3- fall-plate guide bars; Bar 4 – Knitting guide bar; Bars 5, 6 – inlay guide bars. L = Latch opening wire; S = Holding-down sinker; T = Trick plate; F = Fall-plate.

Raschel machines although a similar structure termed plaiting can be achieved on crochet machines by wrapping a loop above the chain loop on the latch of the needle as it is moving out to clear. *In both arrangements the fall-plate loop slips from the open lap immediately after formation and joins the technical back of the old loop from the previous course without being pulled through it.*

The fall-plate is a thin metal blade attached to a bar and extending the full width of the machine. It is mounted between the guide bars and is attached to the guide bar brackets so that it makes the same swinging movement but it also achieves a vertical upwards and downwards movement described in the American term 'chopper bar'. The vertical movement of the fall-plate is obtained from a pot cam on the main cam-shaft and is adapted through linkages.

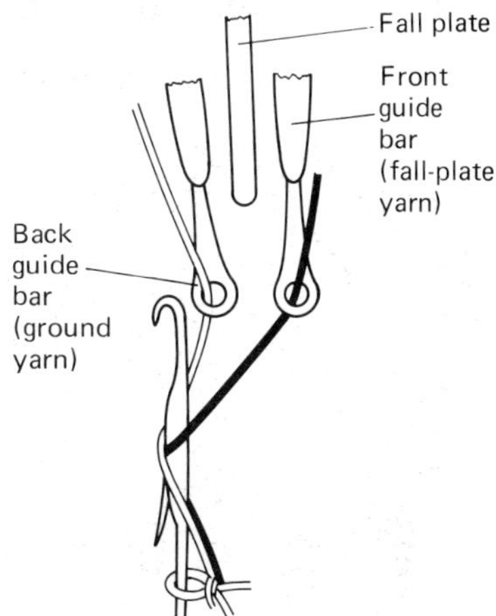

Fig. 27.3

Figures 27.3 and 27.4 illustrate the action of the fall-plate. The Raschel knitting action is normal, the guide bars swing through the needles as they rise, then shog for the overlap and return to the front of the machine. The fall-plate then descends, contacting the threads from guide bars in front of it as they pass onto the latch of the needle. As the fall-plate descends it causes the overlaps formed by those threads to be pushed downwards and off the latches to join the loops of the previous course and to be knocked over with them whilst the overlaps of the guide bars behind the fall-plate remain unaffected in the hooks of the needles ready to form the next course. As the needles rise after knocking-over, the fall-plate is lifted to its high inoperative position where it remains until the next knitting cycle.

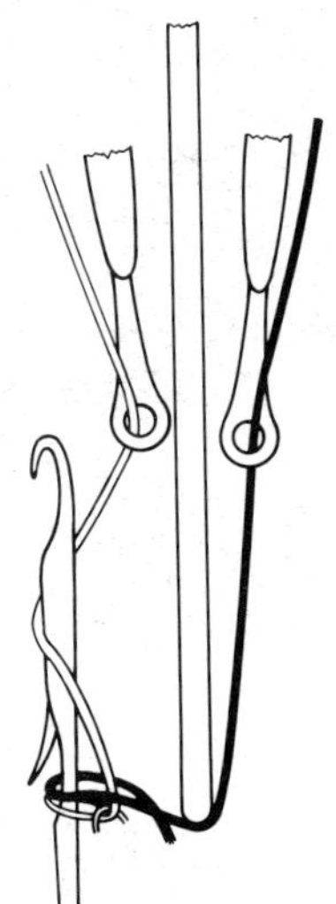

Fig. 27.4

It is necessary to knit the ground structure overlaps on the guide bars behind the fall-plate because these are unaffected by it. Every needle must receive at least one ground structure overlap. It is preferable to overlap the fall-plate yarn in the opposite direction to the ground overlaps as this is less likely to cause the ground overlaps to be lower on the needle stems and thus to be pushed off the latches as the fall-plate threads are pushed down.

As fall-plate yarn is not knitted by the needle hook, fancy or heavy yarns may be used in partly or fully-threaded guide bars. Fall-plate designs use either open or closed lap movements to produce attractive relief designs whose overlaps as well as underlaps show clearly on the technical back often as 'cup handle' shapes (Fig. 27.5). The connection

Fig. 27.5

of the fall-plate pattern yarns to the ground structure is peculiar to its design (Fig. 27.6). *The loop is held down at the technical back of the ground underlap of the course above as well as by the underlap of the course at which it appears.* The fall-plate underlap floats loosely across the fabric up to its next overlap. The overlaps appear at the course previous to that at which they were formed.

Multi-guide bar machines having fall-plate pattern bars controlled by an automatic overlap are used to produce relief designs in lace particularly for curtains. These pattern bars will be positioned at the front of the machine whereas the ground guide bars will be placed behind the fall-plate and any inlay pattern bars will be placed behind these bars.

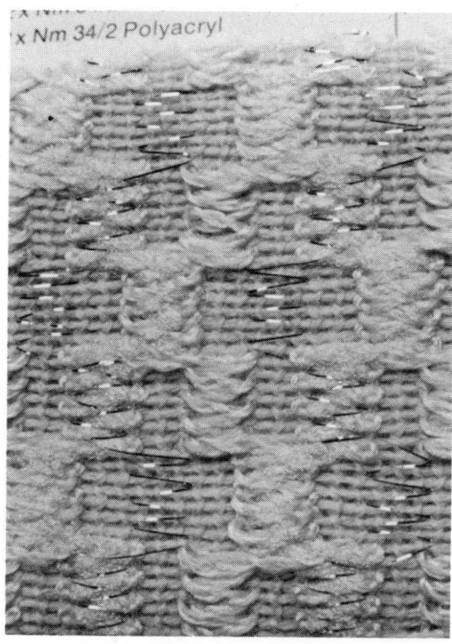

Fig. 27.6. Raschel Fall-plate fabric showing on the technical back of a pillar inlay structure.

27.3 Full Width Weft Insertion

When the needles are in the lowered position during the warp knitting cycle a so-called 'open shed' effect is created at the back of the machine making it possible for a weft yarn laid across the full width of the machine to be carried forward by special weft insertion bits over the needle heads and deposited on top of the overlaps on the needles and against the yarn passing down to them from the guide bars. In this way, the inserted weft will become trapped between the overlaps and underlaps in the same manner as an inlay yarn when the needles rise but unlike the latter, the weft will run horizontally across the complete course of loops. This technique is less restrictive for fancy and irregular yarns than inlay and as a weft covers the full fabric width, yarn can be supplied from individual packages. It has the major advantage that weft can be prepared and laid in advance of the timing of the insertion so that it has less effect on the machine knitting speed.

During the 1930s Sir James Morton's FNF compound needle machine was adapted to achieve weft insertion and by 1938 a prototype model could insert weft whilst knitting at 800 cpm. It was, however, Liba who pioneered the modern principles of single reversing weft insertion for coarse gauge Raschels and magazine weft insertion from a stationary package creel for fine gauge compound needle tricot machines with their Shussomat[1] and Weftloc models introduced in 1967 and 1970 respectively.

The single traversing weft is laid across the back of the machine by a cable-driven carrier which reciprocates on two parallel rods. At the end of the traverse the selvedge return loop passes around a vertical pin which holds the weft in place until required whilst the carrier continues its traverse. The weft pins are attached to the needle bar so the two descend together releasing the full width weft at the moment when the weft bits, one above every alternate sinker, advance over the lowered needle heads to insert the weft (Fig. 27.7). This method of weft insertion produces a selvedged effect with the weft rising at the selvedge from one course of insertion to the next. The knitting width is sometimes divided into a number of knitting widths each having a reciprocating weft carrier. In this way, narrow width fabrics suitable for dish-cloths can be produced. Insertion of the cotton weft may be interrupted between each piece triggering a scanning electronic eye which operates a hot wire to melt the empty nylon pillar stitches across the course. Thus each piece is automatically separated and heat sealed.

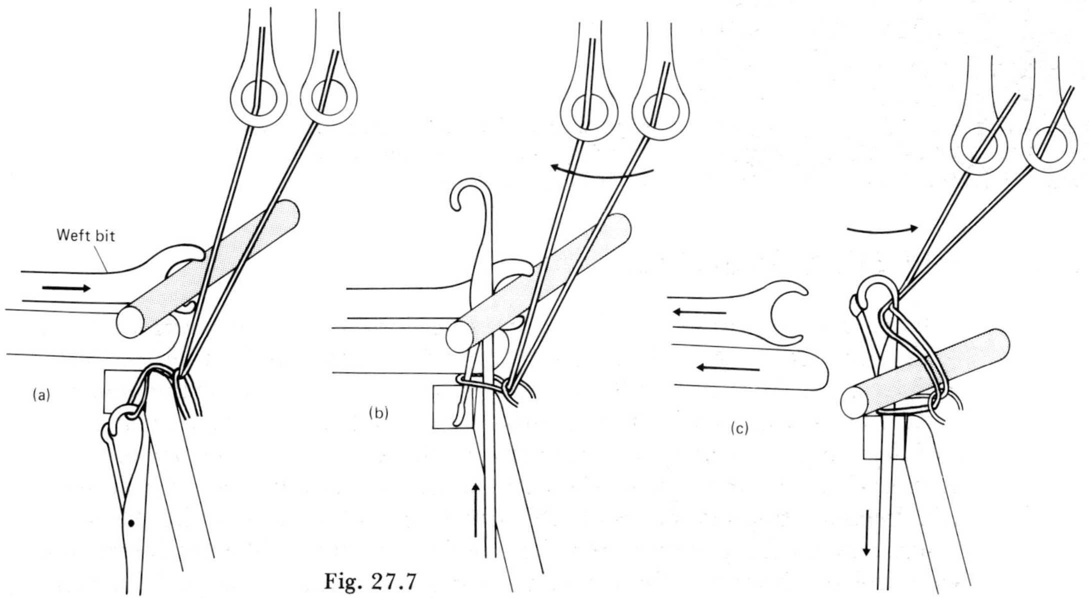

Fig. 27.7

Machines with inlay and knitting bars are used in the production of sun filter curtaining. These employ a pattern chain control of the weft insertion from one end of the machine so that insertion can occur as required from a choice of a number of different wefts. Speeds of about 500 cpm are possible with this type of machine.

The principle of magazine weft insertion is to supply eighteen or twenty-four ends of yarn from a stationary creel to an insertion carriage which traverses across the back of the machine simultaneously laying the ends in parallel form onto the receiving pins of two magazine chains, one at each side of the machine. The chains convey the weft to the weft insertion bits at the rate of one weft per knitting cycle. As the carriage reverses its traverse, each return weft is placed around a receiving pin eighteen or twenty-four positions further along the chain than the pin which first received it in order to accommodate all the parallel weft yarns. Once the weft has been inserted into the fabric, the selvedged edges must be trimmed free of the receiving pins as the chains continue their rotation. It is essential in these cut selvedged fabrics to tightly grip the weft within the structure otherwise wefts may slip or be pulled out, closed rather than open laps tend to be better for this purpose. Patterned effects are achieved by the package arrangement on the creel. Speeds of about 700–800 cpm are obtained.[2]

Other methods such as the use of a propeller or rotating the weft packages on a carousel have been employed but have been found to be too restrictive.

27.4 Cut Presser and Miss-Press Structures

On certain bearded needle tricot machines the possibility exists of pressing only selected needle beards (cut presser work) or only pressing beards at selected knitting cycles (miss-press work). Cut presser machines are generally in tricot gauges from 12–24 and knit either staple spun yarns or textured yarns for blouses, dress-wear, babywear and shawls. The fibre presser blade has sections which are cut away so that needle beards which correspond to these sections are not pressed at that cycle. Although needles can by this means hold their loops for a number of knitting cycles, their beards must be pressed at least once during the pattern repeat. All needle beards in the knitting width are eventually pressed by contact with the solid portions of the presser as a result of the presser being shogged sideways by means of a push-rod and chain links in a similar manner to a guide bar.

For the production of simple shell-stitch fabrics, the presser is cut to the threading of the single guide bar whose total of adjacent threaded guides is the same as the total of adjacent empty guides. For example, a 4 × 4 cut presser (Fig. 27.8) will press the four beards of the needles overlapped by the guide bar and will not press the four beards corresponding to the empty guides so that these needles will hold their loops from a previous course. If overlapped needles are not pressed 'tuck stitches' will be produced whereas drop stitches would occur if non-overlapped needle beards were pressed. It is thus necessary for the presser bar to be shogged sideways in unison with the guide bar.

In order to connect the sections of wales together it is necessary to make an atlas traverse lapping movement across at least two more needle spaces than the number of empty adjacent guides so that in the above example at least six needle spaces must be covered. As held stitches are produced wales will contain different numbers of loops and some wales will contain successive loops which were actually knitted many cycles apart in the sequence. Tension within the fabric produces distortion so that the wales lose their parallel alignment and a three-dimensional surface appearance is created (Fig. 27.9). At the point where the atlas traverse changes direction the absence of connecting underlaps on the far side of the traverse change produces unbalanced fabric tension which draws the two adjacent wales apart.

Guide bar chain	Cut presser chain
5-6	
4-5	4-4
4-3	3-3
5-4	4-4
5-6	5-5
4-5	4-4
3-4	3-3
2-3	2-2
1-2	1-1
1-0	0-0
2-1	1-1
2-3	2-2
1-2	1-1
1-0	0-0
2-1	1-1
3-2	2-2
4-3	3-3
5-4	4-4
5-6	5-5

Held loops

Fig. 27.8. Cut presser blade outline.

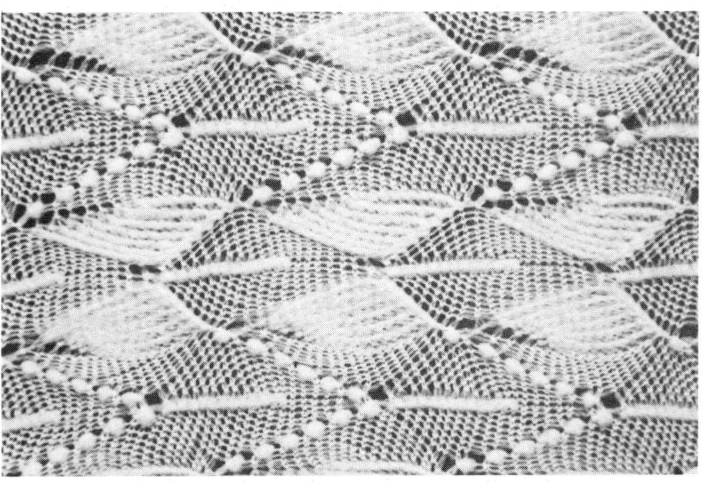

Fig. 27.9. Shell stitch cut presser fabric.

More complex effects may be achieved by employing one or more of the following techniques:

1. A more complex lapping movement;
2. Using more than one partly-threaded guide bar;
3. Accumulation of overlaps without pressing;
4. Double needle overlaps.

Most cut presser machines also have a plain presser bar which, when brought into action by means of a pattern chain, cancels out the effect of the cut presser but necessitates the use of a full-threaded guide bar.

Spot or Knop Effects

These require the use of both a plain presser and a cut presser (Fig. 27.10). The front and back guide bars might be full-threaded and knit a locknit or reverse locknit in cooperation with the plain presser. At various selected points in the production of the fabric, these two bars stop overlapping and the plain presser is withdrawn so that the cut presser operates in conjunction with a partly-threaded middle guide bar to make the knop overlaps.

Adjacent needles hold their ground loops until fabric knitting recommences when the excess knop loops will be thrown upwards in a relief effect on the technical face. When not knitting, the back bar must evade the middle bar and the middle bar must evade the front bar otherwise their vertically-floating miss-laps will protrude between the wales on the technical face.

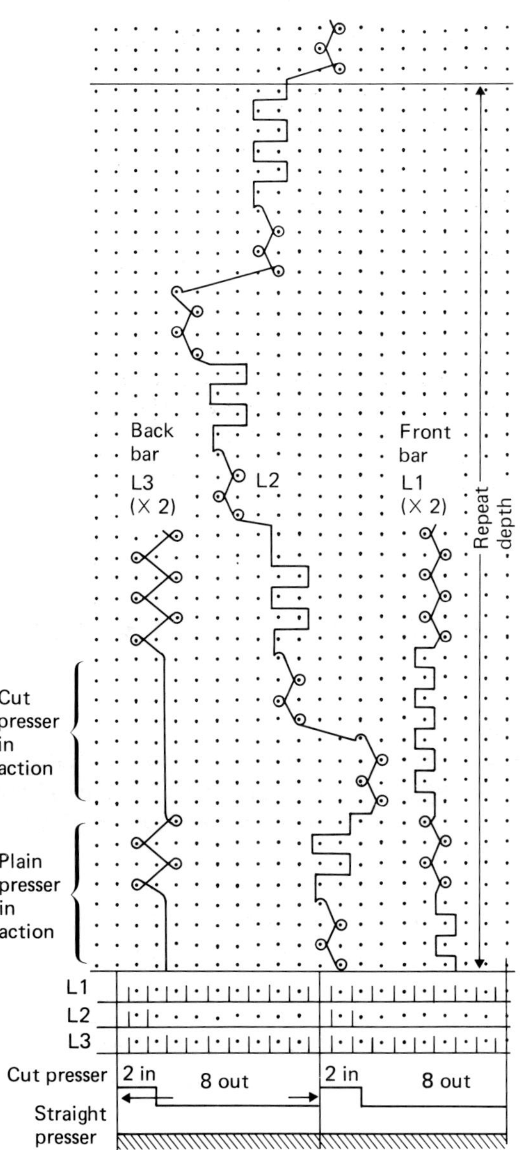

Fig. 27.10

Selective miss-pressing of all needle beards is achieved on modern machines by turning an eccentric disc through 180 degrees inside the circular opening of the presser bar. In one position of the disc the presser advances sufficiently to close the beards, in the other position the presser does not contact the beards.

Selective Miss-pressing

Further Information

DARLINGTON, K. D., New Mayer presser control, *Knit. Times*, (1967) 10 April, 37.

DARLINGTON, K. D., Weftloc: weft insertion knitting, *Knit. Times*, (1973) 27 Aug., 44–8.

NIEDERER, K., Fabric engineering for weft insertion, *Knit. Times*, (1974) 26 Aug., 47–51.

REISFELD, A., Warp knitted fabrics and products, *Knit. Times*, Part 9, (1969) 15 Dec., 28–43; Part 10, (1970) 23 Feb., 42–51; Part 11, (1970) 20 April, 38–42; Part 13, (1970) 17 Aug., 32–43; Part 22, (1972) 10 July, 48–59; Part 23, (1972) 13 Nov., 85–103.

WHEATLEY, B., RM 6–8 VS-W weft insertion machine, *Knit. Times*, (1973) 9 April, 30–8.

WHEATLEY, B., Knitting of outerwear on tricot and Raschel machines (part 15), *Knit. Times*, (1973) 12 Nov., 77–86.

1. DARLINGTON, K. D., Liba Shussomat, *Knit. O'wr Times*, (1968) 22 Jan., 60–1.
2. Liba introduces new version of Weftloc Raschel inlay machine, *Knit. Times*, (1982) 8 Feb., 63–67.

28

Multi-guide Bar Machines and Fabrics

28.1 Lace, Curtain-Net and Elastic Fabrics

Many factors (outlined below) have contributed to the success of warp knitting in the production of lace, curtain-net and elastic fabrics:

1. The inability of the slow traditional lace and net machines to meet rapidly-expanding demands for these types of fabrics;
2. An availability of fine, strong, uniformly regular continuous filament yarns ideally suitable for high-speed warp knitting such as nylon for lace, polyester for curtaining and elastomeric yarns for elastic laces;
3. The Raschel machine was more suitable for utilizing synthetic filament yarn than traditional lace machinery and offered the benefits of low capital costs, reduced requirements for ancillary equipment, less operative supervision and simpler pattern-changing facilities together with higher productivity;
4. Satisfactory imitations of mesh constructions such as tulle and marquisette could be achieved by pillar inlay lapping movements;
5. The introduction of the multi-guide bar lace Raschel in 1955 with its separation of the full sett ground bars from the simple light-weight patterning bars together with the elimination of unnecessary movement and weight has encouraged the development of specific purpose machines with higher speeds and greater patterning capabilities (Fig. 28.1).
6. Improvements in patterning techniques such as jacquard have provided sophisticated design potential for a widening range of end-uses beyond the confines of conventional guide bar lapping facilities.

28.2 Pattern Guide Bars

On conventional multi-guide bar machines, pattern guide bars are only required to supply one thread each for a pattern repeat width, sometimes these are of different counts or types in order to achieve greater effect. To use ordinary guide bars for this purpose would be uneconomical as their weight would lower the machine speed. Also only about eight to thirteen shogging or displacement positions are available so the patterning capabilities would be severely restricted. Instead, light-weight pattern guide bars are used which have drilled holes to which finger guides are screw-attached only at the required spacing for the pattern. These bars are indirectly shogged by a lever arrangement (B) at a rate of one link per course (C) both for inlay and also, when an automatic overlap mechanism is used, for fall-plate or for embroidery patterning[1] (Fig. 28.2).

Fig. 28.1. 42-bar Raschel lace machine (Karl Mayer).

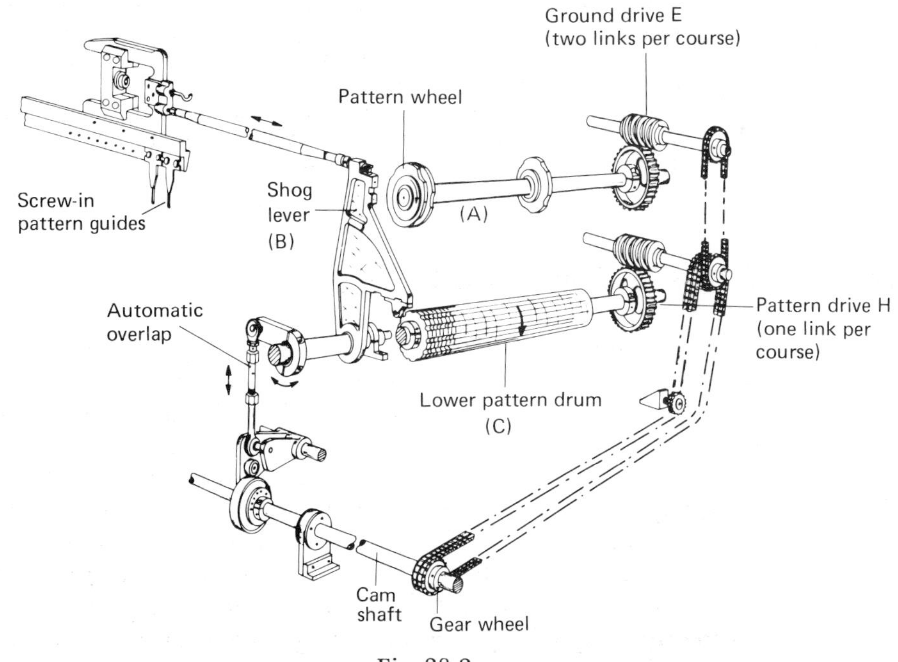

Fig. 28.2

28.3 Nesting

Up to four pattern bars can be 'nested' together so that their guides converge into the same displacement line and they swing as a single guide bar, but they are shogged independently although guides of bars in the same nest cannot cross or approach within two needle spaces of each other (Fig. 28.3). On the 42-bar lace Raschel, thirteen displacement lines are available, the front two are conventional guide bars for knitting the ground, the next may be a conventional bar for drawthreads when knitting trimmings, or it can be one of two nests of two pattern bars, and there are another nine nests each of four bars.

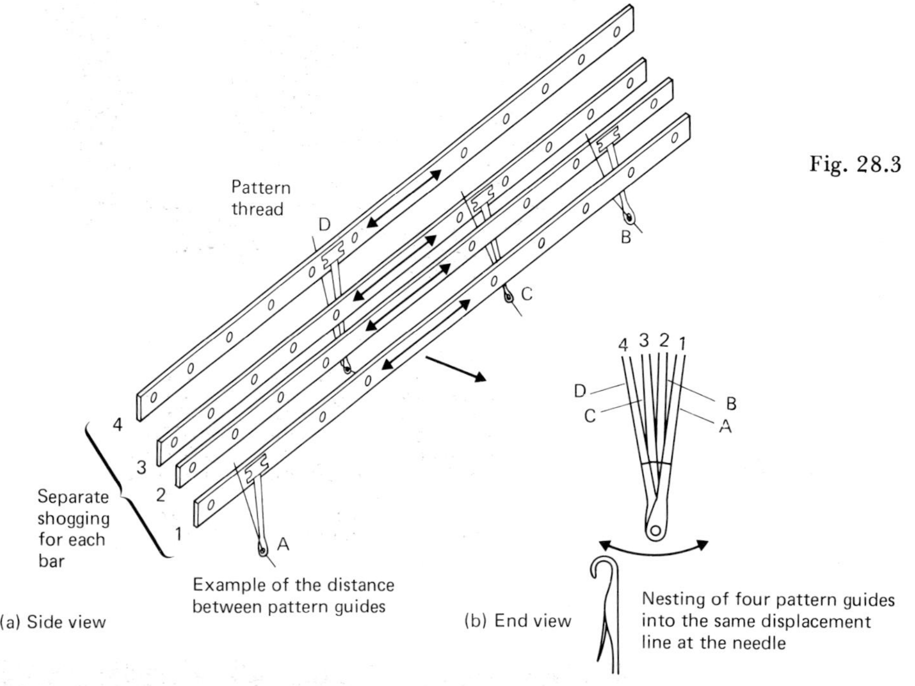

Fig. 28.3

28.4 Multi-Bar Tricot Lace Machines

Multi-guide bar tricot machines with between eight and eighteen guide bars have been built in gauges of 24–28 npi for the production of fine gauge lace.[2] Two full threaded bars are used to knit the ground, such as reverse locknit or queenscord, with fine yarn such as 44 dtex nylon. Pattern bars behind the ground bars are used for inlay effects whilst those in front are employed for embroidery designs in the form of overlaps and underlaps in a textured yarn so that they stand out in relief on the technical back (the knitted overlaps show through from the face and the underlaps float across the back).

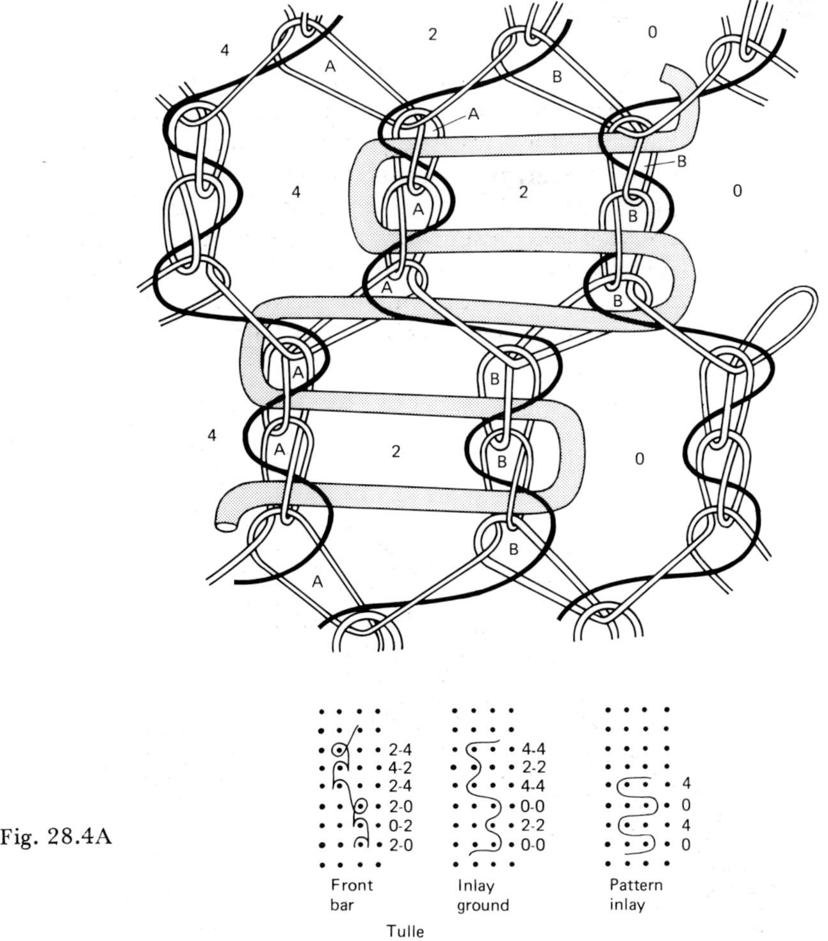

Fig. 28.4A

Fig. 28.4B. Embroidery Patterning.

28.5 Chain Links and Electronic Control of Shogging

The cost of chain links and the labour involved in chain assembly is a major problem with multi-guide bar machines. Ground guide bars are generally controlled directly from links or pattern wheels moving at two links per course (A) whereas the pattern guide bars are controlled indirectly through shogging levers (B) (Fig. 28.2) using only one link per course (either they only inlay or they are caused to automatically overlap in the same direction after the underlap is completed by an eccentric working onto the shogging levers). Leverage in the shogging arrangement can reduce the height and weight of the links and split chain drums which can be stopped during miss-lapping in between motif patterns can further reduce the link requirements. However, lace designs can still involve as many as 15,000 links which can weight over a ton (1000 kilograms).

The Karl Mayer electronically-controlled guide bar shogging arrangement[3] now being introduced for their 42- and 56-bar lace machines is typical of the efforts being made to replace chain links with a simpler and cheaper method of more rapidly-changing patterns. The shogging data is supplied to the bubble memory of a microprocessor by means of a magnetic tape cassette. Pulses are then transmitted which cause magnetic/mechanical switch elements to selectively introduce control elements of which there are six. The control elements can produce shogs of 16, 16, 8, 4, 2 and 1 needle spaces respectively, when introduced together their shogs add up to 47 needle spaces although at a particular course the maximum extent of a shog is 16 needle spaces.

At the 1979 Hanover ITMA exhibition[4] Sulzer demonstrated a Raschel machine whose pattern threads were supplied by computer-shogged steel tapes which could be mounted so closely together that the equivalent of 264 bars were available. A special guide bar and lapping action was necessary for the pillar stitch in order to produce the construction.

28.6 Mesh Structures

Mesh structures may be used alone or as the ground for designs produced by pattern bars. The overlaps and underlaps of the guide bar knitting the mesh will hold the inlay pattern threads from guide bars behind it at each course on the technical back which is the effect side of the fabric. The mesh is usually made by a single full-threaded guide bar knitting an open lap pillar stitch or its variant whose wales are reinforced and joined together by one or more inlay guide bars (often full threaded). The mesh is achieved by wale distortion and knitting tight loops in a fine yarn for the machine gauge.

Tulle This hexagonal mesh is produced by open laps followed by a closed lap which causes the lapping to alternate between two adjacent wales and forms the underlaps and inclined overlaps which close the top and bottom of the staggered mesh holes (Fig. 28.5). The three main Raschel lace gauges are 28-gauge which is coarse gauge (Fig. 28.6) and is mainly used for dresswear with the designs being emphasized by heavy outline threads, 36-gauge which is the standard gauge and 48-gauge which is fine gauge and provides better definition in designs and is also used for lace edgings etc. (Fig. 28.7).

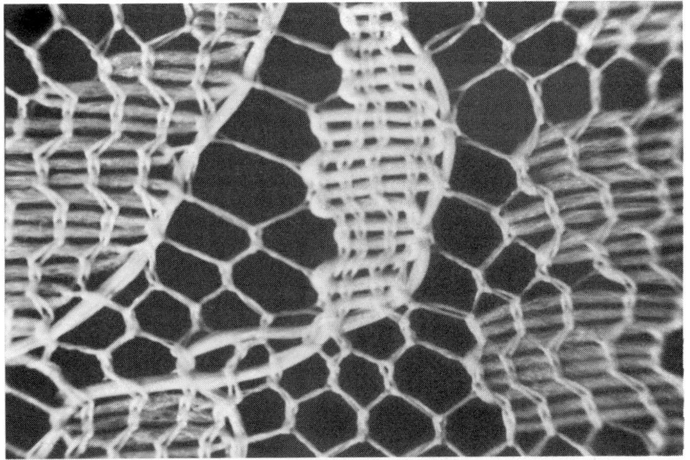

Fig. 28.5. Part of 36-gauge Raschel Tulle lace (Technical face).

Three-course tulle is the standard mesh producing three courses on each wale with the inlay reinforcement lapping in unison. When the pillar and inlay lap in opposition a squarish mesh known as cross tulle or bridal veil net is produced. 3/2 tulle produces alternate rows of smaller mesh and its lapping covers three wales. Five-course tulle produces larger mesh and is more suitable for 28-gauge fabrics.

Hexagonally patterned paper is more useful than point paper when plotting inlay designs for lace. After establishing the staggered vertical column of hexagonals which represent the 0 height link position, each hexagonal in a horizontal row moving away from the 0 link position will represent an increase of chain link height (Fig. 28.4A).

Sometimes more elaborate grounds are produced by varying the inlay movements of partly-threaded bars or a jacquard-controlled guide bar whilst

Fig. 28.6. 28-gauge Raschel lace in a pillar inlay construction, using outline threads (Karl Mayer).

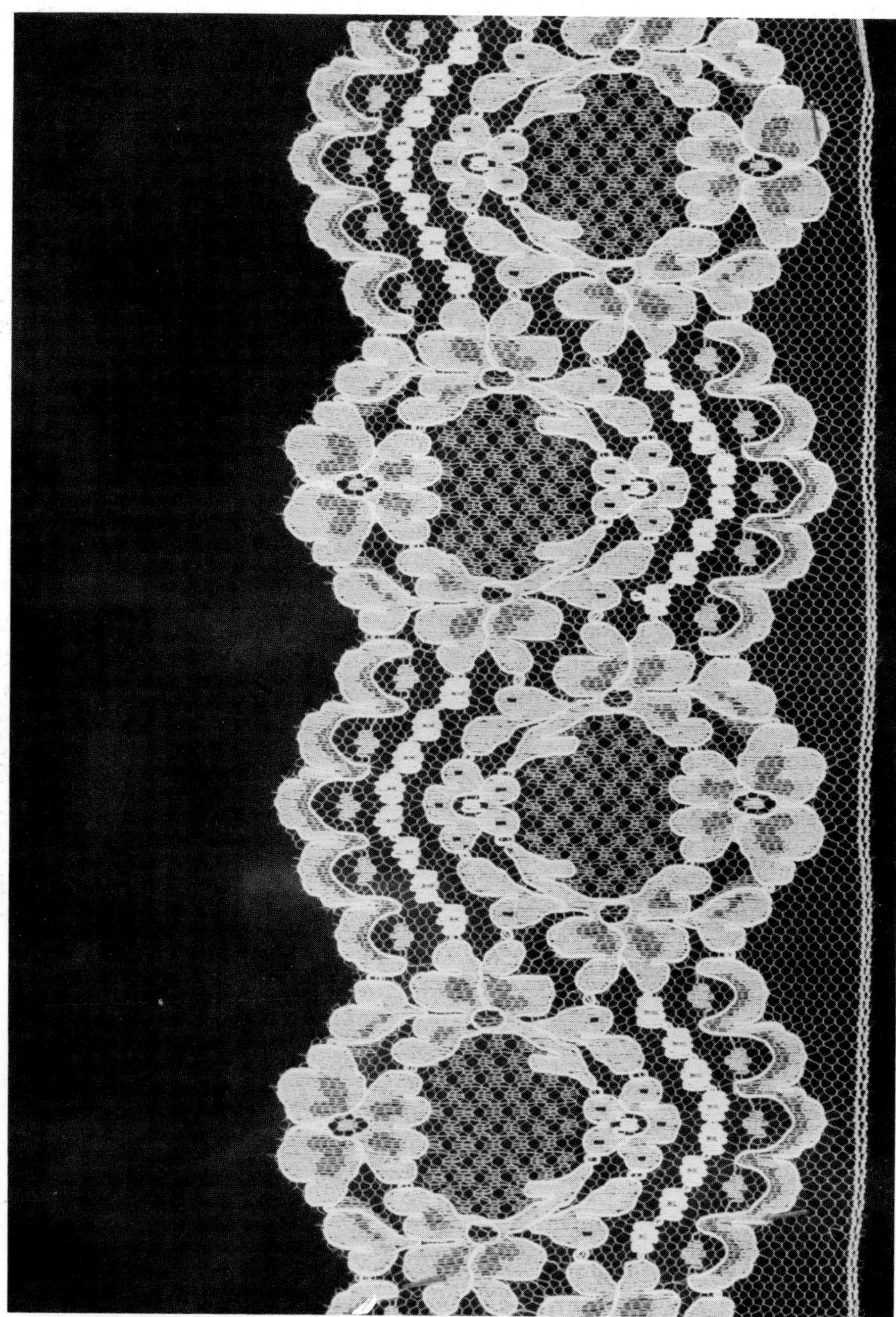

Fig. 28.7. Fine 48-gauge Raschel lace; the edge has been scalloped by cutting (Karl Mayer).

employing a full-threaded guide bar to make a ground pillar stitch.

Marquisette and Voile

These two curtain nets, which are both named after woven constructions, are produced with full-threaded guide bars the front of which makes a pillar stitch (Figs 28.8, 28.9). Heavier, stronger but more expensive meshes are made when two inlay bars lap to different extents in opposition to each other. Marquisette has a square mesh (Fig. 28.8) whereas voile (Fig. 28.9) tends to show diagonal inlays.

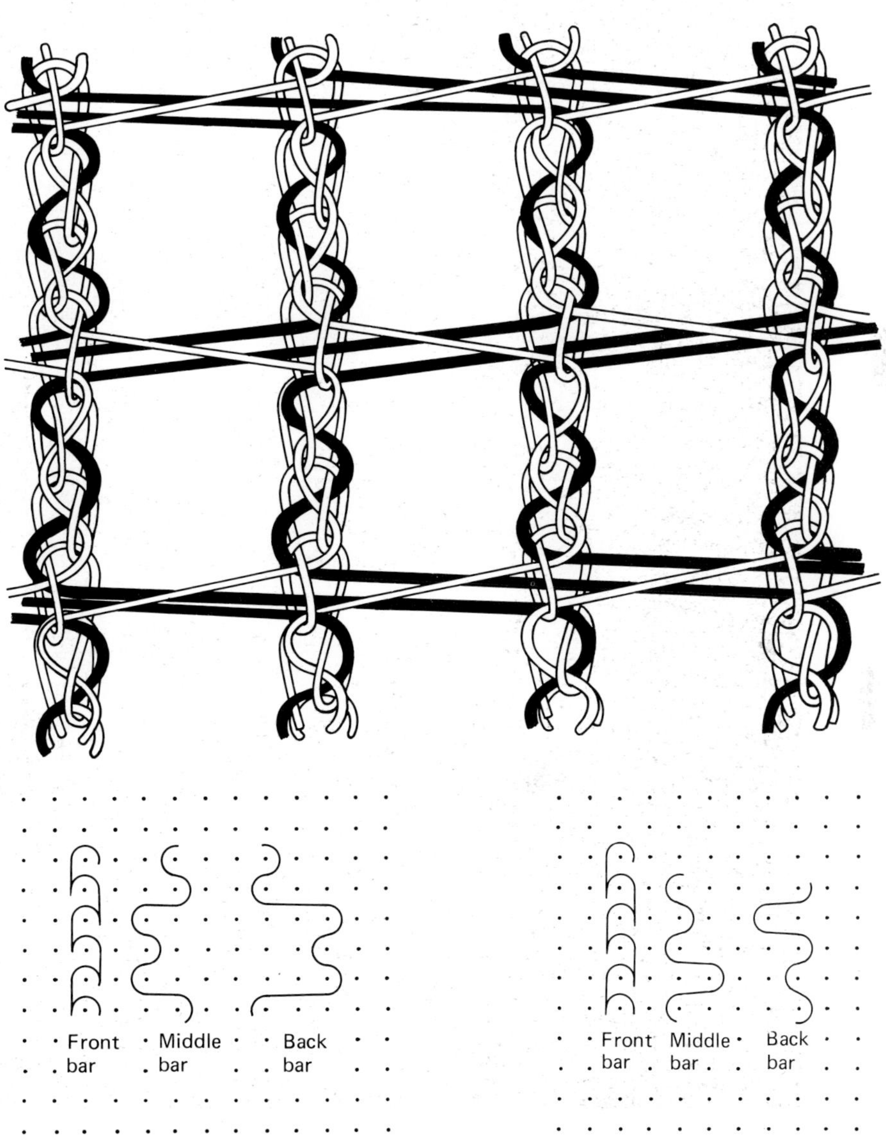

Fig. 28.8. Three bar Marquisette.

Fig. 28.9. Three bar Voile.

28.7 Elasticized Fabrics

Elasticized fabrics have long been used for corsetry, foundation garments and swimwear but the introduction of fine-diameter elastane yarns whose elastic extensibility and recovery can be 'engineered' to particular requirements has extended the use of these structures into lingerie and active sports and leisure wear. Elasticated fabrics are knitted on high-speed Raschel and tricot machines as well as in patterned form on multi-guide bar lace machines. The main prerequisites of these machines is delivery of the elastic yarn under conditions of controlled tension, robust knitting elements which will not deflect under the tension of the elastic yarn and controlled tension for the fabric take-up.

Power net (Fig. 28.10a) is the most widely-known structure for foundation wear. Four half-sett threaded guide bars are used. The two front bars knit the nylon ground and the two back bars inlay the elastic yarn. Only two full-sett beams, one of nylon and the other of elastic yarn may be needed to supply the requirements of the guide bars. This structure may provide a lengthwise extension of 75–85 per cent and a widthwise extension of 65–75 per cent. For fine-gauge fabrics, elastane yarns with counts from 22 to 78 dtex may be knitted into 'stretch tricot' using a locknit construction or special lapping movement shown at Fig. 28.10b. Compound needle high-speed Raschels are favoured for this type of work. In patterned multi-guide bar lace fabrics, the pattern threads are sandwiched in the centre of the structure with the elastane yarn being inlaid by back bars (Fig. 6.13).

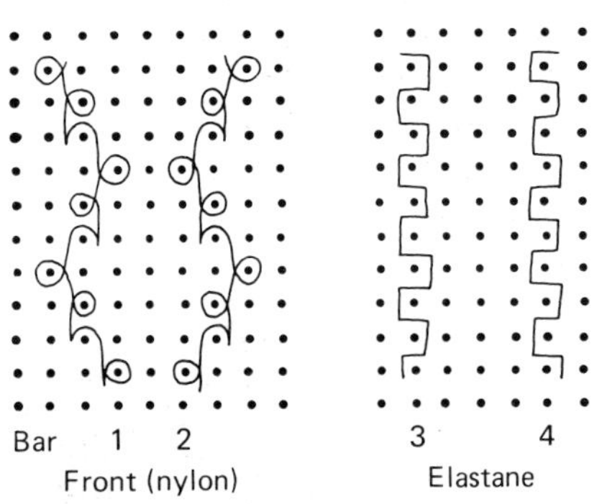

Fig. 28.10

28.8 Jacquard Raschels

Although first employed in the late nineteenth century, the control of individual guide lapping in a guide bar by means of an overhead jacquard has only developed into a sophisticated technique since the late 1960s. On Karl Mayer machines the principle employed is to deflect selected guides in a full-threaded jacquard guide bar by means of dropper pins carried in a separately-shogged displacement pin bar so that those guides have greater or lesser extent of lap than the undeflected guides of the guide bar at that course. The pins are kept in the displacement position or raised out of action by means of a Verdol jacquard apparatus arranged above the machine. By this means, the underlaps of knitting, inlay or fall-plate jacquard bars can be varied in extent or an inlay movement may be converted into a selected overlap thus producing a plated overlap design in colour on the technical face of the fabric.

The jacquard guide bar and the displacement pin bar of these specific-purpose jacquard Raschels are normally both controlled by six-link-per-course pattern wheels to ensure precision timing of the shogging movements. The type of deflection is dependent upon the relative lapping movements of both bars when the pin contacts the guide, so that the guide is either deflected towards or away from its direction of lapping. Figure 28.11 illustrates how a semi-transparent two-needle inlay (A) can

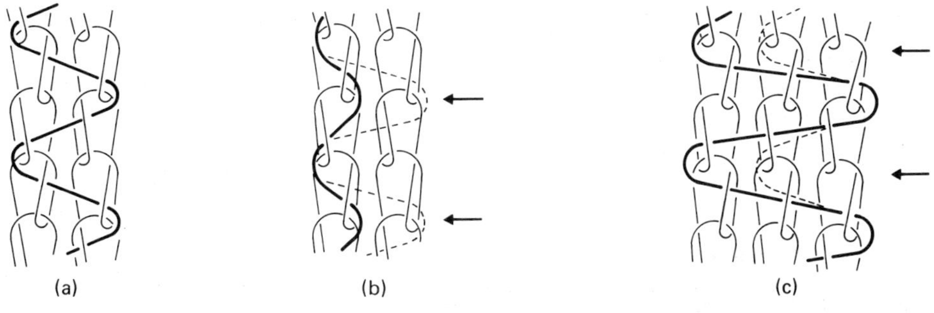

Fig. 28.11

be deflected to the left at odd courses to produce openwork areas of one-needle inlays (B) or at even courses to produce solid areas of three-needle inlays (C).

Usually it is necessary to supply the warp for jacquard bar from individual packages mounted on a creel. There is normally only one, or occasionally two, jacquard guide bars and the rest are conventionally controlled bars. The guides of the jacquard bar may have a gauge twice as fine as the needles so that there are two guides between adjacent needles arranged in two staggered rows (A Fig. 28.12) each capable of having a different yarn type or count if necessary. The jacquard bars are arranged not to swing otherwise the harness strings could become entangled.

The displacement pins are attached by strings to harness cords held by hooks on the bars of a cam operated lifting frame (Fig. 28.12). After each jacquard selection the frame rises lifting any pins whose hooks are attached to it out of action (I). Any spring-loaded pin whose hook is

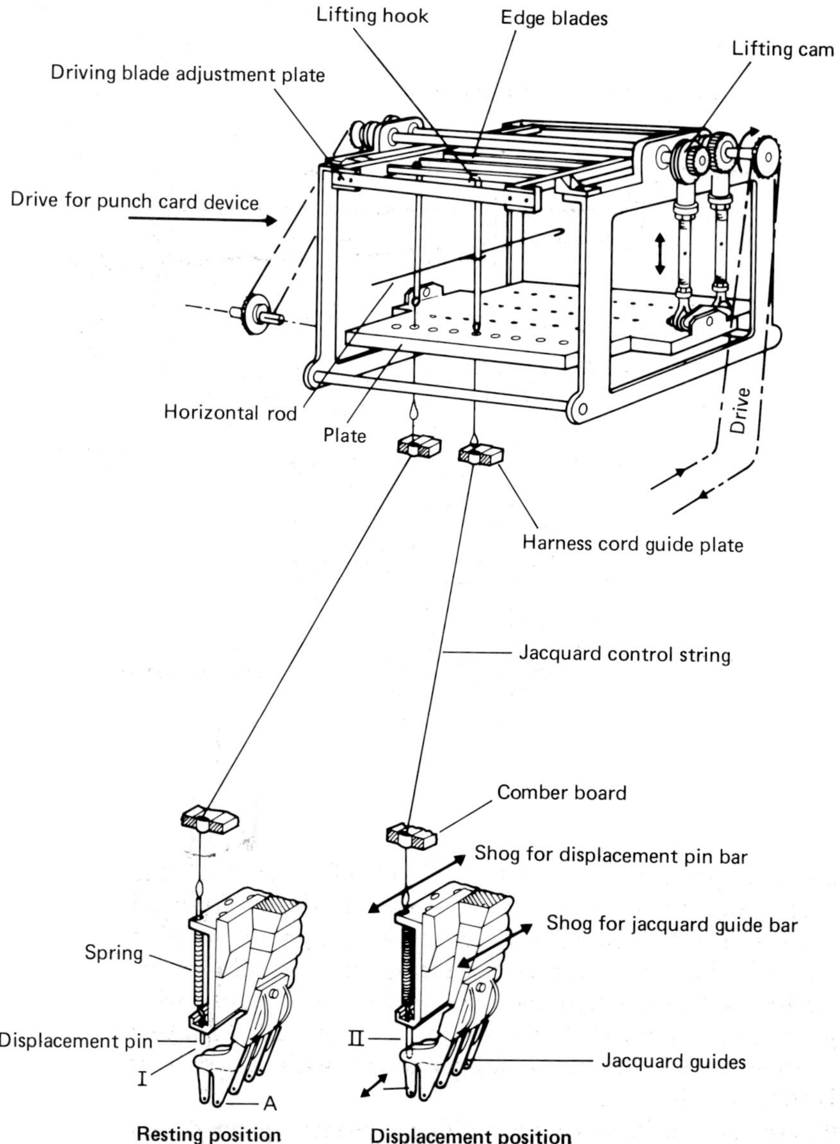

Fig. 28.12

displaced from the bars of the lifting frame by the sideways movement of a horizontal rod attached to it remains in a low active position for displacement (II).

Acting onto the end of each rod is a spring-loaded selection rod which is also attached to a vertical selector pin (Fig. 28.13). The base of each selector pin rests on a punched hole position of the jacquard card. There are twenty-eight staggered columns each of sixteen making a total of

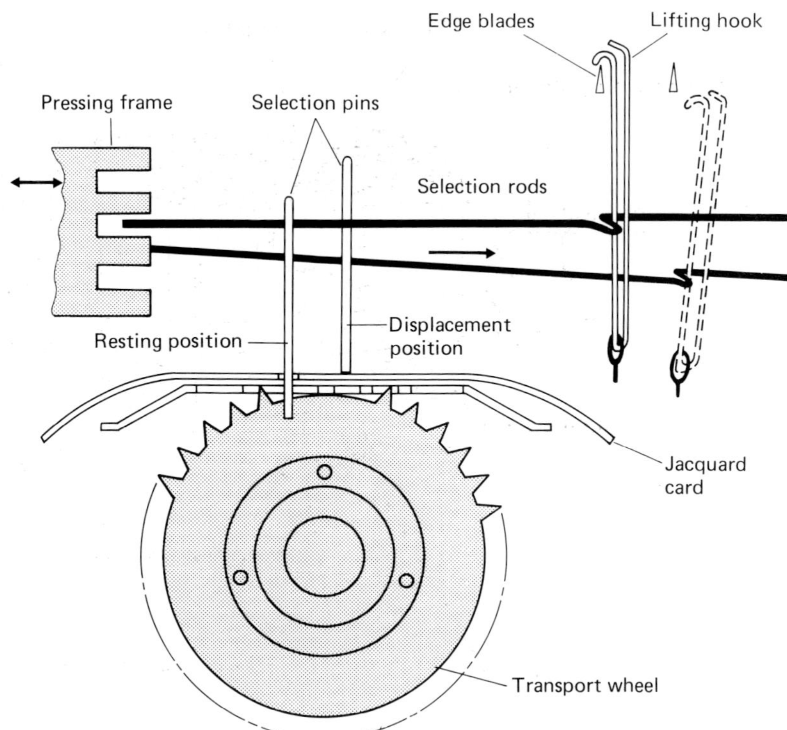

Fig. 28.13

896 individual selection positions on each card. Careful tying of the strings to the harness cords enables very elaborate symmetrically-arranged designs to be produced for the complete area of a bedspread or table cloth. A selection rod is displaced sideways causing its hook to be disconnected from the lifting frame when the end of the rod is aligned with a sideways-moving pressing frame. If, however, its selector pin falls into a punched hole it is lowered so that it no longer aligns with the presser frame bar and it is then not displaced.

Figure 28.4B illustrates the kind of embroidery patterning produced using Multi guide bar Tricot machines.

A microprocessor control has now been developed to replace the mechanical jacquard selection with the data being supplied from a magnetic tape cassette.[5] A displacement pin is only lowered when its associated electromagnet is operated to attract a pawl and release a correcting element allowing the spring to bring the pin down into action. It is estimated that knitting speeds of approximately 30–40 per cent faster than for mechanical jacquard control can be achieved.

On Liba Raschels, the jacquard apparatus selects guides to be lifted to one of two higher levels so that the angle at which the underlap is laid down is changed and this alters its extent.

Further Information

BOHM, C., Highly elastic warp knitted fabrics, *Wirkerie-Und-Strickerie*, (English Issue) (1981) June, 104–8, 113–14.
DARLINGTON, K. D., Methods of patterning for Raschels (part 4), *Knit. Times*, (1977) 18 April, 170–78.
DARLINGTON, K. D., Jacquard design, *Knit. O'wr Times*, (1967) 13 Nov., 44–47.
REISFELD, A., Warp knitted fabrics and products, *Knit. Times*, (1970) Part 14, 15 Sept., 50–9; Part 15, 12 Oct., 48–51.
WHEATLEY, B., *Raschel Lace Production*, (1972) Nat. Knitted Outerwear Assn, New York.
WHEATLEY, B., Raschel drapery and curtain fabrics, *Knit. Times*, (1973) 2 July, 31–9.
WHEATLEY, B., Warp knitting in the eighties (IFKT paper), *Knit. Int.*, (1980) Dec., 55–8.
The jacquard technique has unlimited potential, *Kettenwirk-Praxis*, (Eng. Edn) (1980) 3, 6–8.

DARLINGTON, K. D., *Hos. Trade Journal*, (1968) Oct., 90–94; Dec., 96–98, 103.
DARLINGTON, K. D., *Knit. Times*, (1975) Feb., 33–38.
REISFELD, A., *Knit. O'wr Times*, (1968) 21 July, 75–82; (1970) 20 July, 40–45; (1971) 1 Feb., 63–69.
WHEATLEY, B., *Knit. Times*, (1972) 13 Nov., 78–84; 11 Dec., 52–59.

1. Pattern drives, *Kettenwirk-Praxis*, (Eng. Edn), (1976) 2, 15–18.
2. DARLINGTON, K. D., Multi-bar tricot, *Knit. Times*, (1974) 18 Nov., 45–50.
3. Pattern control without chain links using the new digital mechanism, *Kettenwirk-Praxis*, (Eng. Edn) (1980) **1**, 4–5; (1981) **4**, 1–4.
4. WHEATLEY, B., ITMA review, *Knit. Int.*, (1979) Dec., 65–9.
5. Jacquard tronic R J 4/1, *Kettenwirk-Praxis*, (English Edn) (1981) **1**, 1–3.

29

Double Needle Bar Warp Knitting Machines

Double needle bar Raschels or bearded needle Simplex machines are symmetrically arranged with each needle bed often having identical facilities and knitting once during the 360-degree revolution of the machine's cam-shaft. The vertical needle bars work back-to-back (at an angle of 45 degrees to each other in the case of Simplex machine) with the fabric being drawn downwards in the gap between them. Guides are thus able to pass between needles in both beds as they swing from the front to the back of the machine and vice-versa. As the guide bar lapping sequence involves overlapping and underlapping on each bed in turn, *it is not possible to achieve actions simultaneously on both beds.* Also, compared with single-bed knitting, *an extra or triple swing of the guide bars is necessary after each underlap* in order to swing the guide bars over the bed that has completed knitting so that the other needle bar can rise to commence its knitting cycle.

Double needle bed is thus very much slower than single needle bed warp knitting and basic double-faced fabrics knitted with two full-threaded guide bars are much heavier and more expensive than equivalent weft-knitted double-bed fabrics. *To compete, it is therefore necessary for warp knitted double-bed products to exhibit certain unique properties in order to be worth their production costs.*

Twice as many links will be required per complete cycle as compared with a single-bed machine, with the first half of the links of each complete cycle being used for lapping on the front bed. When drawing a lapping notation, it is useful to indicate that every alternate row of points represents the front bed, either by lettering or by a heavier line of points or both, it may also be useful to space the rows in pairs thus indicating each complete cycle on the two beds.

Two needle bed Basic Lapping Principles 29.1

Using only one full threaded guide bar. Overlapping on one bed only will produce a single-faced structure. Overlapping on both beds will produce a double-faced structure but this will only be cohesive if each guide overlaps at least two different needles in one of the beds during the repeat. To understand the appearance and properties of two-bed structures, it is necessary

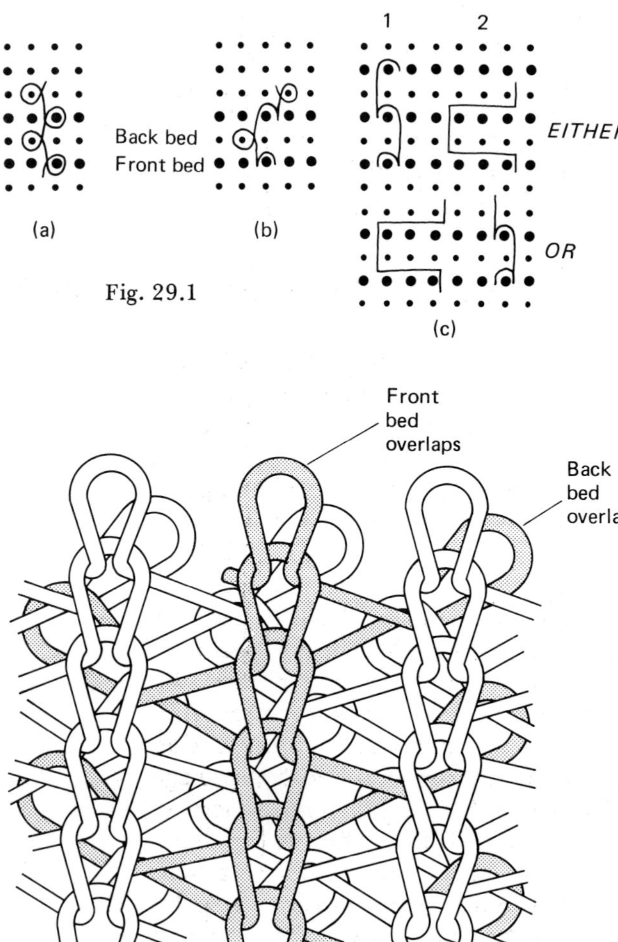

Fig. 29.1

Fig. 29.2

to consider the lapping movements which occur on each needle bed in isolation as if produced by two separate guide bars.

Figure 29.1a illustrates a lapping movement which is unsatisfactory because the warp threads cannot hold the double-faced wales of loops together. Although the Raschel lapping movement is 2-0, 4-6, the overlapping on the front bed is always 4-6 which is equivalent to a closed lap chain on each bed thus the wales cannot be held together in either bed. Figure 29.1b illustrates the simplest lapping movement which can produce a cohesive structure, in this case the lapping movement is 2-4, 4-6/4-2, 2-0. On the front bed, upright loops are produced, as an open lap pillar stitch notation 2-4 4-2 is lapped, whereas on the back bed, the lapping movement is 4-6 2-0 which causes alternate courses to be inclined in opposite directions, but ensures that the wales are held cohesively together (Fig. 29.2).

Using two fully-threaded guide bars

If the front guide bar overlaps only the front needle bed and miss-laps on the back bed and the back bar overlaps only the back bed and miss-laps on the front bed, two separate fabrics will be knitted back-to-back. If, however, the back bar overlaps only the front bed and the front bar overlaps only the back bed, the two separately-knitted fabrics will be connected together by the crossing over of their underlaps. A fabric of double-faced loops each composed of a warp thread from each guide bar is produced if both guide bars overlap both beds.

To understand inlay principles on two beds, it is best to consider each bed as a separate machine with its front (fabric draw-off) on the side remote from the hooks. With inlay, the guide bar nearest to the front knits and holds in place the inlay produced by the back guide bar. Thus for the front bed, the back bar can knit to hold the inlay of the front bar whilst on the back bed, the front bar can knit to hold the inlay of the back bar but not vice-versa (Fig. 29.1c).

A double-faced net structure can be produced with two part-threaded guide bars making a carefully arranged lapping movement so that every needle in both beds receives at least one overlapped thread at every knitting cycle.

The Simplex Machine 29.2

The Simplex machine is used for producing a limited range of fine-gauge high quality specialist double-faced fabrics at rather low rates of production. It was originally designed to knit Simplex fabric in order to replace Duplex glove fabric which was composed of two single-faced fabrics stuck together back-to-back. It has two guide bars and knits plain fabrics and simple mesh designs on standard lapping movements usually controlled from pattern wheels. The gauge range is approximately 28–34 npi with 32 npi being a popular gauge. Cotton glove fabric is still knitted in typical counts of 80/1 to 90/1 cc but yarns as fine and as expensive as 120/1 cc have been knitted. Atlas lapping on a 48-cycle repeat is normally employed to hide count irregularities in the structure and improve the elastic recovery. To obtain the 65–75 per cent width-wise stretch required for glove fabric the fabric is treated in a 30 per cent caustic soda solution during finishing which causes an approximate 50 per cent width shrinkage which is followed by a mild raising process with emery-covered rollers, in order to achieve the suede appearance. Stable print base fabrics for dress-wear are produced with simple repeat movements using 40-denier nylon. A cheaper lighter-weight fabric may be produced from heavier yarns by causing each guide bar to only knit on one bed and inlay on the other so that they hold each other together in the double-faced fabric.

The Knitting Action

Unlike in the tricot machine, the sinkers are not leaded at the front so they can be completely withdrawn from the needles. In order to bring the needle bars closer together, they have no profiled sinker belly and on the newer machines, no throat. Landing is achieved by taking the needle bar downwards whilst still in contact with the presser which, in order to simplify machine movements, may be mounted on top of the sinker bar and move with it. On simple designs knitting high quality yarn, speeds of 300 courses per minute are possible on each needle bar.

Figure 29.3 shows the knitting action on the front needle bar, an identical sequence occurs afterwards on the back needle bar to complete the machine cycle.

(a) *First rise of the needle bar*. The knitting action has been completed on the back needle bar for the previous machine cycle. The front sinker/presser bar has withdrawn leaving the back sinker bar to support the fabric. The guide bars have completed their third swinging movement so

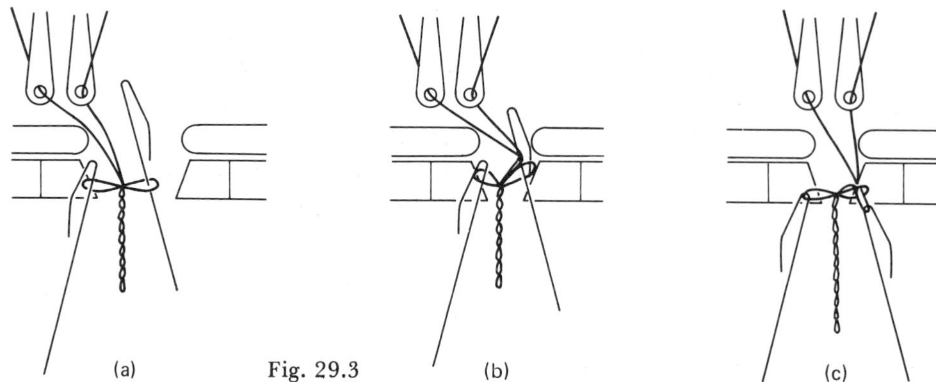

Fig. 29.3

that they are now swinging towards the back of the machine allowing the front needle bar to rise with the back needle bar still near to knock-over and thus helping to hold down the fabric. The front needle bar rises sufficiently to enable the old overlaps under the beards to slide down onto the needle stems.

(b) *Return swing, second rise then lowering and pressing.* As the guides swing to the back of the machine, the warp ends are wrapped over the needle beards. The front needle bar is now lifted to a higher position so that the new overlaps slip from the beards to a high position on the needle stems. As the front needle bar is lowered to cover the new overlaps the front sinker presser bar moves to contact and press the beards so that the old overlaps slide onto the closed beards which descend through them.

(c) *Completion of landing and knock-over, underlap and third guide bar swing.* Whilst the needles descend further to knock-over the old overlaps, the guide bars make their underlap shog behind the front needle bar and then commence their swing towards the front of the machine to allow the back needle bar to rise for second part of the machine sequence.

29.3 The Double Needle Bar Raschel

The double needle bar Raschel as designed by Redgate, later developed into a general purpose machine, mainly knitting shawls and scarves. At first, the needle bars were arranged back to back alternately, as on rib weft knitting machines but they were soon placed exactly behind each other for convenience of guide bar swinging. Between six and eight guide bars might be employed together with various attachments such as a fall-plate, a crepeing motion (which could disengage one needle bar for a pre-selected number of courses), a switching device for moving the guide bar push-rod from one track of the pattern chain to another and simple weft inlay or insertion. The front needle bar could be replaced with a point bar for making plush and pile structures or removed altogether so that the back needle bar could knit single-faced fabrics driven by a new set of cams which doubled its knitting speed.

Improvements in weft knitting and single-bed warp knitting machinery left the double needle bed Raschel isolated as a slow, coarse gauge and very cumbersome type of machine until comparatively recently. However, the arrangement of the elements and knitting action of the Raschel is less complex than that of the Simplex machine, thus offering greater possibilities for adaptation and modification in order to knit special structures at economical speeds, so it is in this direction that developments have occurred.

The conventional knitting action

On the conventional machine, each needle bar in turn is only active for half of the 360 degrees of the knitting cycle, holding-down sinkers are therefore unnecessary as the other needle bar is in the low inactive position and will restrain the fabric loops.

Figure 29.4 shows the knitting action on the front needle bar, a similar action occurs on the back needle bar (for simplicity, only one guide bar is illustrated).

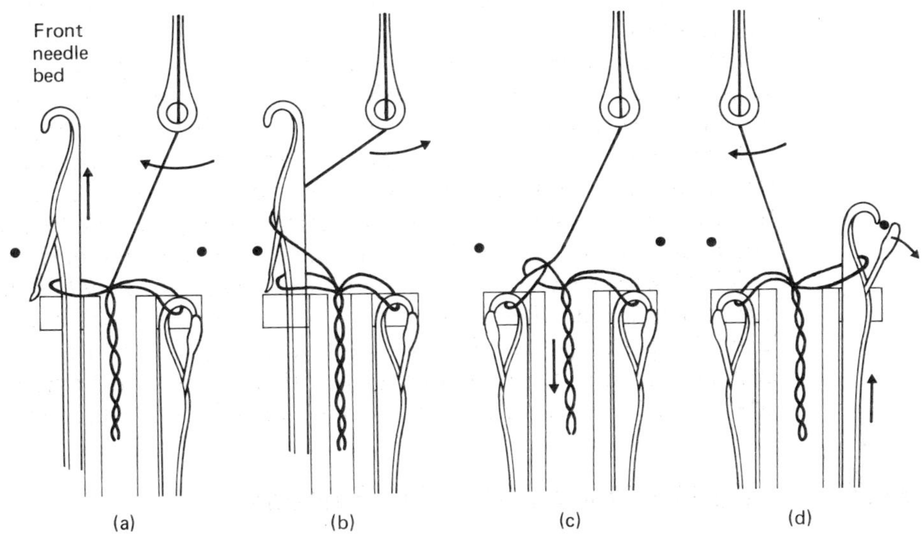

Fig. 29.4

(a) *The Front Needle Bar rise*. The front needle bar is raised to clear the previous course of overlaps from the latches whilst the back needle bar holds down the fabric loops.
(b) *The overlap*. The guide bar swings through between the needles to the front of the machine is shogged for the overlap and swings back.
(c) *Knock-over and underlap*. As the needle bar descends to knock-over the guide bar performs the underlap shog.
(d) *Third swing of the guide bar*. The guide bar now swings over the front needle bar in order to allow the back needle bar to rise and commence its knitting cycle.

In order to increase knitting speeds on modern machines the 180-degree dwell period of each needle bar has either been reduced or eliminated, in the latter case, one needle bar is rising as the other is falling so that the two needle bars are almost continuously moving in opposition, thus effectively doubling the knitting speed. Some machines also have a counter needle bar motion so that the needle bars and trick-plates move towards the guide bars and thus reduce the guide bar swing. As the needle bar in these cases has only a short dwell period and sometimes separate fabric sections are being knitted on each needle bar, holding-down sinkers are necessary.

29.4 Double Needle Bar Raschel Products

In the past, double needle bar Raschels of 24 gauge and coarser were used to knit fancy fabrics in woollen yarn for babywear, nightwear and knitwear. Two such structures were rib and crepe, in the former, certain needles were never overlapped, whereas the latter is actually a knop fabric produced by taking the back needle bar out of action for between two and four courses to hold its loops whilst the front bar continued to knit. Fabrics of this type have faced increasing competition from the improved design possibilities now offered by flat weft knitting machines.

Two other structures which occasionally achieve a limited success in underwear or outerwear are waffle fabric and Brynje string vest, both of which were originally developed in the early 1950s as thermal underwear fabrics for U.S. forces serving in cold climates. Both are produced with two half-threaded guide bars although two other guide bars are often also used to produce the selvedge edges for making up. In 24 gauge, 22/1 combed cotton would be a suitable yarn count. String vest is a double-faced net structure with the underlaps hidden inside, because it is a double needle bed fabric, the net openings are only half as large as the lapping movement representation. Waffle fabric is a solid fabric composed of a series of open pockets alternately placed on both sides of the fabric. Each guide bar makes overlaps over two needles which draws their two adjacent wales together thus leaving a gap between every two wales. Gaps on one side are opposite the two connected wales on the other. This arrangement would give the fabric the appearance of a 2 X 2 rib but after five courses the lapping movement is changed causing the gaps and connected wales to change positions.

Many Raschel double needle bed products are in the form of articles, a number of which can be simultaneously knitted side-by-side across the needle bed. These articles have a length repeat composed of sections of fabric where the lapping cycle of one or more of the guide bars has been altered. The sequence involves a pattern change device for counting the number of repeat lapping cycles in each section and for initiating a change-over of guide bar push-rod control from scanning links in one chain track on to those in another track in order to alter the lapping repeat for a particular guide bar. By this method, a guide bar may be controlled from a choice of two or more chain tracks each having a short, simple repeat of chain links which may be used any number of times, instead of being controlled from one track of an excessively long and expensive chain containing links for every repeat cycle throughout the length of article.

The principle of 'pattern changing' is used in the production of a scarf with knitted-in fringes on each end. Lapping for the scarf section is taken from one set of chain tracks and lapping for the fringe section from another. Each guide bar shogging lever may be controlled from either of two pattern chain drums, the upper drum chain tracks may produce the simple lapping repeat for the scarf section whilst the lapping for the fringe section is achieved by switching the shogging control to the chain tracks of the lower drum.

The scarf fabric is knitted as a continuous strip of double-faced fabric with the fringe sections composed of two wale wide strips each unconnected by underlaps to its neighbour. Each scarf piece is separated from the next by cutting through the centre of the fringe section and seaming the cut ends to secure them. The simple tricot lapping movement produces the width-wise elasticity required for scarves.

Knitting Tubular Articles 29.5

A seamless tube of fabric may be knitted on a rectilinear double needle bed Raschel in a similar manner to on a V-bed flat weft knitting machine. Each bed knits separate single-faced fabrics which are only joined together by underlaps of other partly-threaded guide bars between the beds at the two opposing selvedge needles at each edge. The underlaps may be arranged to be the same as for the needle beds, thus producing a seamless join to the fabric tube.

Figure 29.5 illustrates the basic principles using a base structure of single tricot lapping and four guide bars. *The front bar laps only the front bed, the back bar laps only the back bed and the two middle bars are threaded with only one thread to each complete one selvedge join.* In the first underlap movement towards the RIGHT, the warp threads will rotate anti-clockwise by one needle space in producing the tube on the machine beds. Underlapping in the front bed will be towards the RIGHT, the right-hand selvedge bar will underlap across from the front to the back bed, the back bar will underlap towards the LEFT and

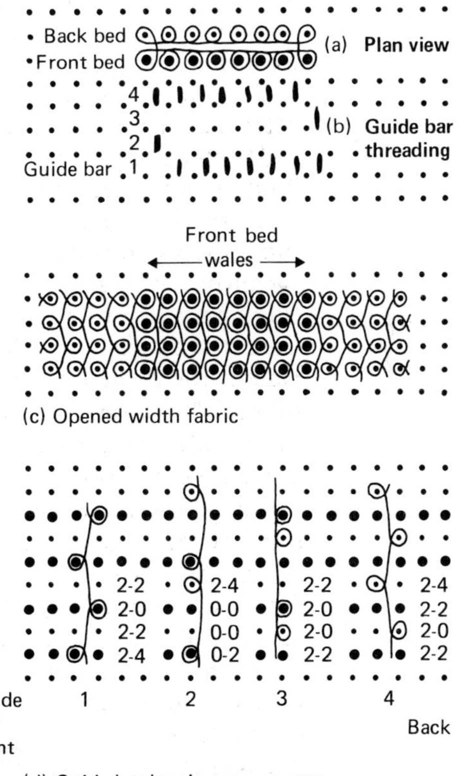

Fig. 29.5

the left-hand selvedge bar will underlap across from the back to the front bed. In the next underlap movement, the direction of lapping will be reversed for each of the guide bars with a clockwise movement.

As one selvedge bar is always overlapping one needle in each bed, the threading of the front and back bars must be one less than the number of needles knitting the fabric in that bed. Two selvedge guide bars are required because when one is overlapping the front bed in a particular cycle, the other is overlapping the back bed. Whilst knitting the tube, no guide bar must overlap on both the front and back beds during the same cycle otherwise a double-faced stitch is produced. If the base movement is a two-needle underlap, two selvedge threads will cross over the beds at each selvedge and each will require a separate guide bar. If the base movement was full tricot, a minimum of eight guide bars would be required, two for each bed and two for each selvedge. Inlay net or part-sett threaded net lapping movements may be used to produce tubes in a similar manner.

Some of the first tubular fabrics were for vests or for fishnet stockings knitting eight to twelve tubes side by side. In 1967, the American Kidde Cocker company introduced the Fashion Master machine for knitting panty-hose and body stockings. By changing the lapping movement of an extra four bars which are lapping in the centre of the fabric, the large tube for the body portion can be divided into two smaller tubes with two of the bars joining two opposing needles across the needle beds for the inner selvedge of one leg and the other two joining the adjacent needles for the other leg, thus knitting a bifurcated article. Graduating stiffening is achieved by infinitely variable control of the fabric take-down and warp let-off, a shifting control moves the guide bar push-rods onto other chain tracks when required and reinforcement is achieved by double-needle overlapping. For approximately two years, hosiery produced on these machines was highly popular.[1,2,3]

The Karl Mayer HDR 16 EEW machine was introduced in 1970 for producing a range of simple garments such as seamless panties, brassieres and pocketings. The technique, which has undergone continuous development, is to form the tube across the knitting width rather than down the wales. Although this causes the article in use to have its courses in a vertical direction, this is of no major disadvantage and the possibilities for achieving simple shaping are considerably improved.

Figure 29.6 illustrates the production of a strip of briefs fabric, it is only necessary to cut through the centre of the connecting joins to separate each article from the next. These joins of short length are in effect knitted side seams, so the briefs are turned inside out after knitting to hide this seam. The first side seam is produced by guides lapping across between the two beds to form a solid double-faced fabric section. Guide bars inlaying on the left selvedge form the knitted-in waist band which is produced on each bed as the guide bars lap on the two needle beds separately in order to produce the waist opening on the left and the first leg opening on the right. Half-way through the courses for the sequence, the right selvedge needles are joined together for a number of courses to complete the first leg opening and close the crotch section of the brief. Single-bed fabric knitting then continues for the second leg after which the bars knit between the beds to form the second side seam and then commence the sequence for the next brief.

On a 75-inch (190 cm) wide machine three brief fabric strips can be knitted side by side giving a production of 360 briefs per hour. It is possible to achieve a cotton terry effect on the inside if necessary. Upper and lower pattern chain drums are employed to control the guide bar shogging levers and these drums may have a split drive and chain stop facilities to further economize on links and provide greater versatility in lapping movements.

The double needle bar Raschel in 12–16 gauge has proved particularly useful for the production of packing sacks for fruit and vegetables from polyolefin in tape, fibrillated or mono-filament form.[4,5] The base structure is usually a pillar stitch inlay which provides a secure non-slip construction (Fig. 29.7). The polyolefin sheets may if necessary be fed directly into the back machine where they are split into separate ends without the need for warping.

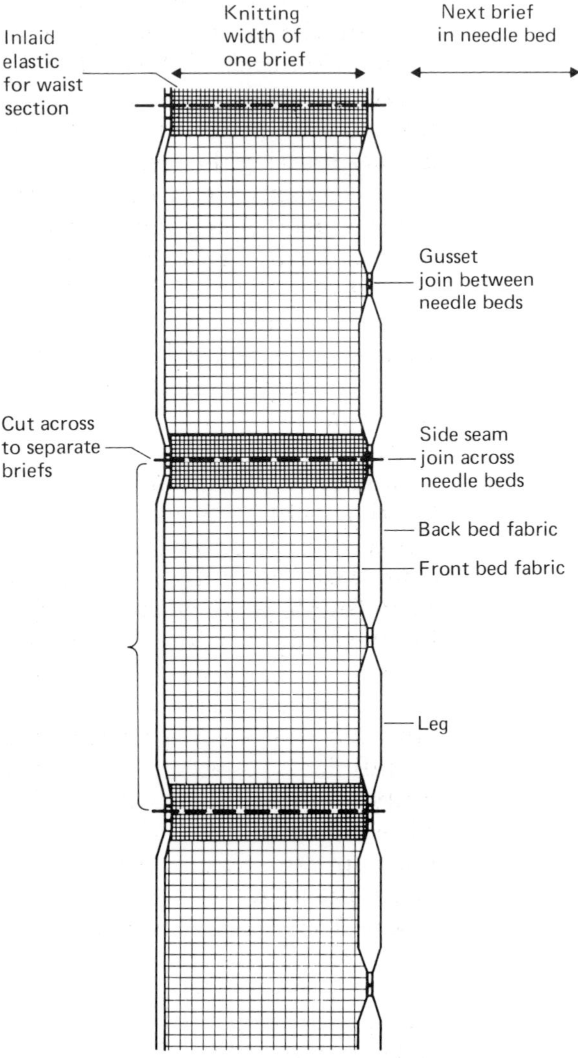

Fig. 29.6

The sacks are knitted sideways at a rate of 250 courses per minute on each bed in a similar manner to the briefs, their depth can thus be varied according to the number of needles knitting in each section. The two fabrics are joined together at the top and bottom to form the side seams and at one selvedge to form the bottom of the sack. At the open end, a draw-thread may be knitted into each side of the fabric and separation of the sacks from the continuous warp knitted strip is achieved afterwards with a hot wire.

Fig. 29.7. Vegetable sacks knitted on Raschel double needle bar machines (Karl Mayer).

29.6 Pile Fabrics

There are two main groups of pile fabrics produced on double-bed Raschels, cut pile and point pile. Cut pile is achieved by knitting a separate base fabric on each needle bed but joining the two together by the lapping movement of the pile which is later slit to produce the two cut pile fabrics. Point or looped pile is produced by replacing the front bar needles by a point or pin bar around which the pile yarns are overlapped, for security the pile yarn may be overlapped in the base fabric on the needle bar or it may be inlaid to economize on yarn and produce a lighter weight fabric.

Cut pile fabrics are employed for a wide range of high pile and end-uses such as simulated fur and skin fabrics, upholstery and coat linings. The Karl Mayer HDR 5PLM is designed specifically for this type of fabric, its Raschel gauges range from 18 to 36, with 32 being most common, in widths from 75–180 inches (190–457 cm) and speeds of approximately 250–300 cpm per needle bar.

Each bed knits alternatively and has a cam-shaft, needle bar, trick-plate, sinker bar and two guide bars with no swinging action. The needle bar and trick-plate swings through these two guide bars to produce the base structure on that particular needle bed. The middle (pile) guide bar has normal swinging facilities for lapping the pile alternatively on each needle bed. As the pile is severed in the centre, its height is half the distance between the two trick-plates, this distance may be altered to give a range of pile height between 2.5 and 30 mm.

Figure 29.8 shows a simple three guide bar construction and Fig. 29.9 a more popular construction using five guide bars, by lapping the pile yarn into two wales any irregularity in the yarn is disguised.

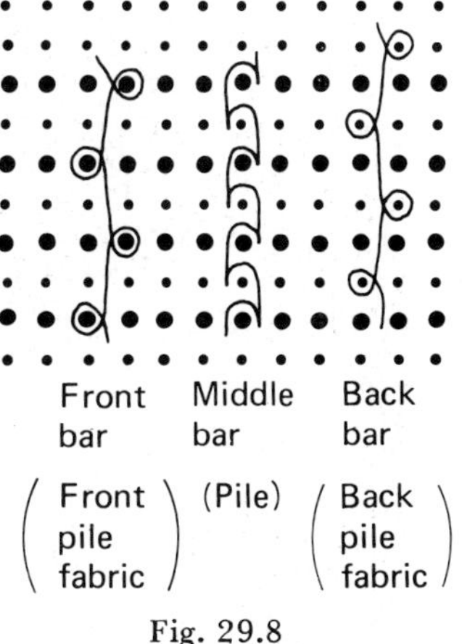

Fig. 29.8

The effect produced is determined by a combination of type of fibre, denier, lapping movement and finishing process sequences whose operations may include one or more of the following: raising, cropping, setting, dyeing or printing and electro-polishing.

In point pile, the loops lie at right angles to the base fabric and on some machines the points are sharpened or contain rotating cutting blades for cutting the pile loops. The structures are particularly suitable for floor coverings and carpeting. On a five guide bar machine in 12 gauge, the front two bars might knit pillar stitches in opposition threaded with 2/30 wc spun polyester with the inlay being supplied by 2/10 wc spun polyester from the back bar whilst the two middle bars supply 5/400 denier textured polyester for the pile overlapping the points and laying-in on the needle bar. Using an eight link per course cycle, the overlap for the points occurs between the first two links and the overlap for the pillar stitches on the needle bar occurs between the second two links, whilst the last four links allows the points and needles to descend for knock-over and for the underlap inlay on the back bar. An unusual use is three guide bar structure for the artificial turf, Astro-turf,[6] whose pile is composed of four, six or eight ends of 500-denier dope-dyed nylon ribbon on a nylon polyester knitted and inlaid base fabric.

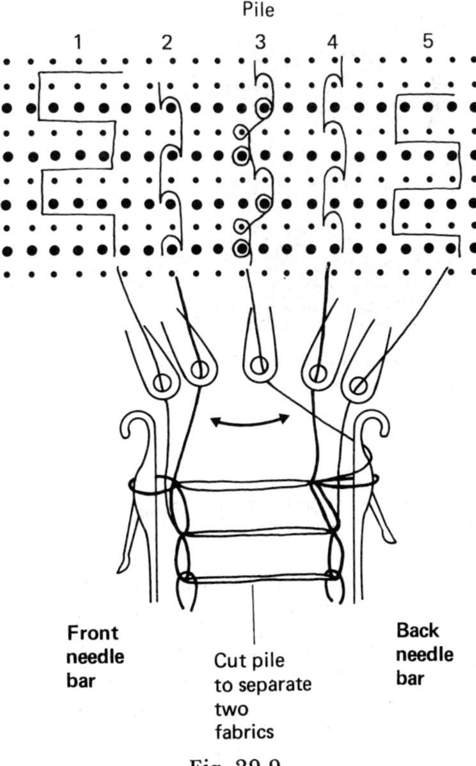

Fig. 29.9

Further Information

BÖHM, C., Warp knitted fabric structures made on machines having two needle bars, English Issue of *Wirkerei- und Strickerei-Technik* (WST), (1980) 2, (3), 44–51.

KIENBAUM, M., Terry towelling production techniques, construction and patterning range (part v), *Int. Text. Bull.*, (1975) 3, 95–106.

REISFELD, A., Warp knitted fabrics and products, *Knit. Times*, (1971) Part 18, 30 Aug., 50–8; Part 19, 6 Sept., 75–89.

REISFELD, A., Warp knit fabrics and products, *Knit. Times*, Part 24 (1972) 20 Nov., 40–7; Part 25 (1973) 9 April, 43–61.

WHEATLEY, B., Production of fur fabrics on Karl Mayer double needle bar Raschel machines, *Knit. Times*, (1972) 16 Oct., 28–37.

WHEATLEY, B., Primer on double needle bar warp knitting, *Knit. Times Yr. Bk.*, (1973) 126–137.

WHEATLEY, B., The production of carpets on Karl Mayer Raschel machines, *Text. Inst. and Ind.*, (1974) 12, (3), 72–5.

WHEATLEY, B., Production of carpeting on Raschel knitting machines, *Knit. Times Yr. Bk.*, (1974) 109–116.

1. MOREHOUSE, J., Seamless tulle hose, *Knit. O'Wear Times*, (1968) 9 Sept., 49–60.
2. HUDSON, J. O., Raschel pantyhose, *Knit. O'Wear Times*, (1970) 25 May, 49–56.
3. ROTBART, J., Manufacture of pantyhose, *Knit. Times*, (1970) 28 Sept., 36–9.
4. WHEATLEY, B., Processing of polyolefin tapes on Raschel knitting, *Knit. Times*, (1973) 16 April, 188–95.
5. DARLINGTON, K. D., Uses of polyolefins in Raschel, *Knit. Times*, (1975) 25 Aug., 12–17.
6. GIBBON, J., In the days of green green grass, *Hos. Trade Journal*, (1969) Sept., 70–2.

Appendix

General Textbooks on Knitting

CHAMBERLAIN, J., *Principles of Machine Knitting*, Vols I, II, III (1950, reprint 1961), Textile Institute.

OFFERMAN und TAUSCH-MARTON, *Grunlagen der Maschenwarentechnologie*, (1978) VEB, Leipzig, (although the text is in German the diagrams are very informative).

REICHMAN, C., *Principles of Knitting Outerwear Fabrics and Garments*, (1961) Nat. Knit. O'wr Assn, New York (now National Knitwear and Sportwear Association, 51 Madison Avenue, New York, NY 10010).

REICHMAN, C., *Guide to the Manufacture of Sweaters, Knit Shirts and Swimwear*, (1963), Nat. Knit. O'wr Assn, New York.

REICHMAN, C., *Advanced Knitting Principles*, (1964) Nat. Knit. O'wr Assn, New York.

REICHMAN, C., *Knitted Stretch Technology*, (1965) Nat. Knit. O'wr Assn, New York.

REICHMAN, C., *Knitting Primer*, (1967) Nat. Knit. O'wr Assn, New York.

REICHMAN, C., *Knitting Encyclopedia*, (1972) Nat. Knit. O'wr Assn, New York.

REICHMAN, C., *Knitting Dictionary*, (1966) Nat. Knit. O'wr Assn, New York.

SMIRFITT, J. A., *Introduction to weft knitting*, (1975) Merrow Technical Library.

WIGNALL, H., *Knitting*, (1964) Pitman.

Textbook Availability

Unfortunately many of the publications referenced throughout this text are now out of print. Your library may possibly obtain them through the British Lending Library System. Both the Kimberlin Library, Leicester Polytechnic and HATRA hold reference stock.

Advice and ordering of any textbook in print is available at Leicester Polytechnic Bookshop, Kimberlin Library Buildings, Mill Lane, Leicester, U.K.

Out of print industrial (including textile and knitting) books are sometimes available and are the speciality of Antiquarian Book Sellers – The Book House, 37 Frederick Street, Loughborough, Leicestershire LE11 3BH (Tel. 0509 61421).

Reference Books

A Guide to Sources of Information in the Textile Industry, (1974) The Textile Institute, – A comprehensive reference publication whose contents include; International Textile Organizations, periodicals, information retrieval services, textile books and directories, organizations for standards and specifications, sources of patent information and sources of textile statistics.

A Brief Guide to Sources of Fibre and Textile Information, H. G. SOMMER, (1973) Information Services Press, Washington DC, U.S.A.

Textile Terms and Definitions, (1978) The Textile Institute.

New Encyclopedia of Textiles. American Fabrics and Fashion Magazine, (1980) Prentice-Hall Inc, NJ, U.S.A.

General Information

Technical Publications for the Knitting Industry

Knitting International (formerly *the Hosiery Trade Journal*) is published monthly by Knitting International, Eastern Boulevard, Leicester, U.K.

Knitting Times (formerly *Knitted Outerwear Times*) is published weekly by the National Knitwear and Sportswear Association, 386 Park Avenue South, New York, NY 10016, U.S.A.

Textile History is published by the Pasold Research Fund Ltd., 23 St. James Square, Bath, U.K.

Wirkerie-und-Strickerie-Technic is published monthly in German and quarterly in English by Meisenbach KG, Postfach 2069 D-8600, Bamberg 1, Germany.

The International Textile Bulletin (Knitting Edn) is published quarterly by Internationaler Textil Service GmbH, Kerslerstrasse 9, CH-8952 Zurich, Switzerland.

Organizations and Institutes

ITMA is the international textile machinery exhibition organized by Cematex, the Association of European Textile Manufacturers. It covers all aspects of textile machinery including knitting and is one of the largest exhibitions of any type in the world. It is held every four years at the beginning of October and recent venues include Hanover in 1979 and Milan in 1983.

KAE is the Knitting Arts Exhibition which is held every four years in the U.S.A. for example at Atlantic City, NJ in 1981.

IFKT is the International Federation of Knitting Technologists (formerly Specialists) with an International Secretariat at Schlossmühle Strasse 11, CH-8500, Frauenfeld, Switzerland. A conference is held in one of the twenty-five member countries each year. The United States branch is known as the American Society of Knitting Technologists (formerly Specialists).

The Textile Institute, 10 Blackfriars Street, Manchester, publishes *Textile Horizons* monthly (this has replaced the *Textile Institute and Industry*), *Textile Progress Quarterly* and other publications. It also organizes conferences.

The Clothing and Footwear Institute, Albert Road, Hendon, London NW4 2JS organizes conferences and publishes *Apparel International.*

The Shirley Institute, Manchester M20 8RV publishes *Textiles* three issues a year.

The International Wool Secretariat publishes *Wool Science Review* containing articles on the knitting properties of wool yarns and fabrics.

HATRA (Hosiery and Allied Trades Research Association), 7 Gregory Boulevard, Nottingham NG7 6LD, U.K., was founded in 1949 as the Research and Technical Centre for the British Knitting Industry. Member firms are involved in the production, dyeing and finishing, and making-up of knitted fabrics and garments. Associate members are mainly suppliers, users or distributors for the industry. Services include information, publications, testing, training and consultancy.

The School of Textile and Knitwear Technology, Leicester Polytechnic, PO Box 143, Leicester LE1 9BH, U.K., founded in 1883, has an international reputation for education in knitting and general textile technology. Full-time, part-time, sandwich and special short courses are arranged covering technical, technological, design and management aspects, and include Certificate, Diploma, Professional and Degree Courses and Post Graduate research.

Index